MW01060504

JOE Black

MORE THAN A DODGER

MARTHA JO BLACK
AND CHUCK SCHOFFNER

Published by Academy Chicago Publishers
An imprint of Chicago Review Press Incorporated
814 North Franklin Street
Chicago, Illinois 60610
ISBN 978-0-89733-753-3

Library of Congress Cataloging-in-Publication Data
Is available from the Library of Congress.

Interior design: Sarah Olson
All photos courtesy of Martha Jo Black

Printed in the United States of America
5 4 3 2 1

Contents

FOREWORD

WHEN I LEARNED THAT THE TITLE OF this book was *Joe Black: More Than a Dodger*, I had to nod in agreement. It definitely sums up the amazing career of a man who was very special to me. Thinking back to my youth, I still visualize going to Ebbets Field with my parents and watching the Dodgers play. In 1952, when I was fourteen years old, right-handed pitcher Joe Black burst onto the Major League scene with such a splash that fans instantly were attracted to him and his imposing six-foot-two frame. Plus, his lively fastball was fun to watch.

Joe won fifteen games and saved fifteen more as a rookie that season, capturing the hearts of Dodger fans everywhere. Few knew of his prior successes with the Negro leagues' Baltimore Elite Giants and with the Cuban Winter League. Joe helped lead the Dodgers to the National League pennant and became the first African American pitcher to win a World Series game in the 1952 postseason. He was named National League Rookie of the Year that season.

This book's remarkable journey guides the reader on and off the playing fields of another era—one that was extremely challenging for a young African American. This was at a time when only six of sixteen Major League Baseball teams had an African American player on their roster. Like Jackie Robinson and other great African American players of his time, Joe endured the ignominy of catcalls, separate living and dining areas on the road, and death threats. He repeatedly withstood insults from those who shunned him because of the color of his skin. As a high school player in Plainfield, New Jersey, coaches told Joe that he couldn't play in the big leagues, strictly because he was black. When he was in college at Morgan State in Baltimore, Joe tried to attend local church services, but was unexpectedly turned away. His mother soothed his wounds with her important credo, "Ain't nobody better than you!" This gave him an inner strength and purpose to bite his lip and learn to keep his fists down, even when the anger was so strong.

Joe was many things: learned, benevolent; an outstanding athlete; a good father to his daughter, Martha Jo, and his son, Chico; and a successful businessman. Joe's education and baseball career equipped him for life after the game. He earned an advanced degree and then worked as a teacher at the elementary, junior high, and high school levels before moving into a high-profile job in the private sector. His years with Greyhound, where he became the first African American vice president of a transportation company, provided him with a post-baseball profession, in which he expertly used his marketing skills and wide-ranging associations. He was fondly known as "Mr. Greyhound."

I'll always remember Joe's keen sense of humor and his big smile. Joe maintained friendships with many of his teammates and opposing players. He was extremely well liked. He truly enjoyed giving back, unselfishly opening doors to help pave the way for many others. Joe always took time to counsel young players. In 1986, he was instrumental in forming the important charity called Baseball Alumni Team (BAT), which later was renamed the Baseball Assistance Team. Still active, BAT raises and directs funds to aid those in need within the game's family. It will always be part of Joe's legacy. He made a difference in people's lives, including mine.

Now, it's time to meet Joe Black.

Peter O'Malley
President, Los Angeles Dodgers, 1970–98

INTRODUCTION

To me, my father was an excellent *example of a hero. This is why I wanted to tell his story. He was an ordinary man who always found the strength to persevere and endure despite formidable obstacles and challenges: he was born into a poor family, the sport he wanted to play was not integrated until 1947, and he took on the responsibility of becoming a single parent after a divorce.*

His family may not have been well off, but they were, and still are, rich in love. The love he received from his family, especially his mother and sisters, made him able to raise a daughter primarily by himself. He undertook both parental roles after winning custody of me in the mid-1970s. He was confident enough in his dual role to give me the sex education talk, attend all of my gymnastics shows, and teach me how to properly dance with a boy before I went to my first dance.

Many people think I adored my father because of the people he introduced me to and the gifts he lavished on me. The gifts were merely tokens of his love, which he expressed in ways that extended far beyond material things. He gave me a good deal of his attention and always lent an ear when I needed advice. When I found out my mother's cancer had returned in the late 1990s, my dad came to Chicago to help me keep my spirits up. I loved my mother very much, even though she and I didn't have the typical mother-daughter relationship. It saddens me that people who said I loved my dad more than my mother ignore the fact that my father spent an enormous part of his time with me.

He was a man who could cry openly when a family member or close friend passed away. He was unafraid to show emotion and knew that it did not make him less of a man.

I pray that my dad knew how much I loved and respected him. I am very blessed to be able to say that Joe Black was my father.

MARTHA JO BLACK

1

Historic Win

October 1, 1952

THE BLEAK, GRAY CLOUDS THAT darkened the Brooklyn sky earlier in the day had broken up and drifted off. With the sun shining freely as it sank in the west, a large shadow crept steadily across the brown dirt of the Ebbets Field diamond.

It was the opening game of the 1952 World Series, and a tall, rangy figure dressed in the gleaming whites of the Brooklyn Dodgers strode confidently to the pitcher's mound. Seven months earlier, Joe Black had been an unheralded minor leaguer trying to make the Dodgers roster, a twenty-eight-year-old rookie who had played only one season of organized ball. But on this first day of October, facing a New York Yankees team seeking its fourth straight world championship, Joe had put himself and his team on the cusp of a historic moment.

The Dodgers, beloved by their loyal fans and pitied by others for their consistent World Series failures, led the favored Yankees 4–2 with the ninth inning coming up. Joe started the game—a move by manager Charlie Dressen that was seen as a huge gamble—and he had gone the distance. If he could get three more outs while holding the Yanks at bay, he would become the first black pitcher to win a World Series game. At a time when one school of thought held that black pitchers couldn't handle the pressure of big games like this, Joe was doing his part to put that notion to rest.

Not that there had been many opportunities like this for black pitchers. Joe was only the third black Major Leaguer to pitch in a World Series. Five years after Jackie Robinson joined the Dodgers and broke the Major Leagues' color barrier, baseball had made progress, but America's national pastime was still a long way from full integration.

Of the eight National League teams in 1952, only the Dodgers, New York Giants, and Boston Braves had integrated. Along with Joe, the Dodgers had Jackie at second base, catcher Roy Campanella, and pitcher Don Newcombe (who was in the army and did not throw one pitch during the season after winning twenty games in 1951).

In the American League, no teams except the Cleveland Indians, Chicago White Sox, and St. Louis Browns had black players. The Yankees remained as white as the cloth in their pinstriped home uniforms. They would not integrate until Elston Howard came up in 1955.

Until Joe fired his first pitch, Newcombe and Satchel Paige had been the only blacks to pitch in a World Series game. Satch, the ageless wonder who somehow won twelve games for the hapless St. Louis Browns in 1952, didn't get much chance at all in October, working two-thirds of an inning of mop-up duty for the Cleveland Indians in game five of the 1948 Series. A midseason pickup by the Indians that year, Paige had sparked the club's pennant drive with a 6-1 record, including two shutouts, and a stingy 2.47 earned run average. Yet he languished on the bench during the series, a forgotten man as the Tribe rode the pitching of Bob Lemon and Gene Bearden past the Boston Red Sox in six games.

Newcombe went 0-2 in the Dodgers' 1949 World Series loss to the Yankees, though he certainly pitched well enough to win the opener. Big Newk gave up only five hits and struck out eleven, but he lost 1–0 to Allie Reynolds, who checked the Dodgers on two hits. Dan Bankhead, the first black to pitch in the big leagues, had gotten into the 1947 World Series with the Dodgers, but only as a pinch runner.

Now, with Joe masterfully shutting down the Yankees' hitters, the Dodgers were poised to achieve something they had never done. In five previous trips, Dem Bums had not only failed to win the World Series but never even managed to win the first game. They always started in a hole. "The Dodgers made all of Brooklyn feel on top of the world," author Michael D'Antonio wrote, "except at World Series time."

But maybe, just maybe, they could hold on and finally start the series on a winning note. Maybe they could show the Yankees and the long-suffering Dodger fans, whose lament of "Wait till next year" had become an all too familiar refrain, that this year would be different.

The fact that Joe Black was the one who had put them in this position was remarkable—even stunning.

>>>>>>>>>>

Joe had reported to spring training in February with only one season of minor league baseball behind him. It was just a so-so season at that—a combined 11-12 record with Montreal of the International League and St. Paul of the American Association, the Dodgers' two Triple-A farm clubs. He was one of the few college graduates in the Major Leagues, having played three sports at Morgan State, though not baseball, because the all-black school in Baltimore did not field a team. Before signing with the Dodgers, he did most of his pitching for the Baltimore Elite (pronounced EEE-light) Giants in the Negro leagues, in the US Army, and in Latin America over the winter.

During spring training in Vero Beach, Florida, Joe had been just one more prospect in a long list of pitchers, hoping fervently for a chance with the big club, because his time to make it was running out. He already had seen many Negro league stars passed over because they were deemed too old to make the jump when the door to the Major Leagues opened. If he hadn't stuck with the Dodgers, Joe might well have suffered the same fate. On the train north after the Dodgers broke camp, Joe tried to explain to journalist Roger Kahn just how badly he wanted to make the team. "If I could express myself as well as Shakespeare," he said, "I still couldn't tell you how much."

Joe had to sweat out the last cuts, and when manager Charlie Dressen named the final three pitchers who would stay with the club, he included Joe, who was ticketed for relief duty. Once the season began, Joe didn't get into a game until May 1. It would be another three weeks before he earned his first victory. He didn't register his first save until May 29.

So how did this rookie reliever end up starting the first game of the World Series, a role traditionally reserved for the team's ace? Was this the result of some twisted logic by Dressen in his attempt to exorcise the Dodgers' demons from World Series past?

As it turned out, Joe Black *was* the staff ace. With Newcombe off serving Uncle Sam, the Dodgers desperately needed someone to step into that role, and Joe was the one who filled it. The veterans of the staff, Preacher Roe, Carl Erskine, and Ralph Branca, all had assorted ailments. That trio completed only twenty of fifty-eight starts in an era when pitchers were expected to finish what they began.

With his starters faltering, Dressen found that in Joe, he had someone who could perk them up. So he kept calling on Joe in relief, and the big right-hander responded—time and time again. Late in the season, perhaps thinking ahead to what he might do in the World Series, Dressen started Joe twice.

"I want to see if you can pitch nine innings," he told Joe.

"OK," Joe replied.

Joe figured it was simply another case of Dressen's tinkering, which was the manager's wont, so he pitched.

He pitched well, too, beating the Boston Braves 8–2 on a three-hitter to give the Dodgers at least a tie for the National League pennant. He got hammered in his second start, an 11–3 loss to the Braves, but the Dodgers had clinched by then and were merely playing out the string.

When the season ended with the Dodgers four and a half games ahead of their bitter rivals, the New York Giants, Joe had pitched in fifty-six games. He was 15-4 with a 2.15 earned run average and fifteen saves. More than any individual game he saved, Joe Black saved the Dodgers' season.

"He put us in the World Series," Carl Erskine said. "He was the main cause to get us there." No wonder that at one point late in the season, Dressen acknowledged that he whispered "a little prayer of thanks for Joe Black every day."

Dressen had said after the final regular season game that either Black or Erskine would start the series opener. The next day, Dressen held court with writers while the Dodgers and Yankees worked out at Yankee Stadium. Ol' Charlie liked to talk, especially when the discussion got around to his favorite subject: himself.

Seeing Joe in the outfield, where he was sweating under his rubber jacket, Dressen whistled for him to come over.

"Throw five pitches," he told Joe.

Joe complied, then looked at his manager to see if he was supposed to do anything else.

"That's my starting pitcher," Dressen declared.

"I thought Erskine," a writer said.

"No," Dressen responded. "Joe Black's starting."

That brought a laugh from Joe.

"I mean it," the little skipper insisted. "I'm serious."

Dressen's announcement was a shocker. Sure, Joe had had a great season. The Dodgers wouldn't have won the pennant without him. He already had been named the National League's Rookie of the Year by the *Sporting News*, known then as the "Baseball Bible." Many assumed he'd be voted the league's Most Valuable Player.

But he was a reliever, a pitcher accustomed to going two or three innings, tops. You don't start someone like that in the first game of the World Series, a rookie no less, against the most successful franchise in all of baseball.

"Dressen did the unthinkable," Erskine said. One writer at the time noted, "Never before in big league history has a champion of either circuit been forced to undertake such a desperate gamble."

But there was a precedent for Charlie's move. Two years earlier, reliever Jim Konstanty had pitched the Philadelphia Phillies to the NL pennant. Konstanty worked seventy-four games that season, all in relief, winning sixteen and saving twenty-two. Later that year, he would be voted the league's MVP.

The Phillies had a solid pitching staff that included future Hall of Famer Robin Roberts, but the starters were worn out by the end of September. Roberts had started three games over the last five days of the season and had gone the distance in the 4–1, ten-inning, pennant-clinching victory over the Dodgers on the final day. Manager Eddie Sawyer didn't feel he could ask any more of Roberts with the dangerous Yankees as the opponent. So he gave the ball to Konstanty for the series opener and the bespectacled right-hander was superb, limiting the American Leaguers to one run and four hits in eight innings. But the Yanks' Vic Raschi was even better, and the New Yorkers won 1–0 on his two-hitter.

Still, most people felt Dressen took a big risk in starting a pitcher with so little big-league experience. Konstanty, at least, was in his fifth Major League season when he started in the series. Joe was in his seventh month. But if Joe could get the job done, the Dodgers would have Carl Erskine going in game two and the crafty Preacher Roe in game three. Joe could come back for the fourth game and maybe the Dodgers would be in control of the series by then. A risk, perhaps, but in Dressen's mind, it was a calculated risk.

Not only that, it was the kind of move Dressen liked to make. He thrived on being unconventional. He liked to surprise people. Some thought Dressen would announce Erskine or Roe as the starter, then trot Joe out to begin the game. *New York Times* columnist Arthur Daley felt Dressen was only doing what he had to do, writing that the Dodgers manager, "a gambler by nature, has to take daring gambles." Daley then added, "In fact, every pitching choice he makes is a daring gamble." The *Times* scribe picked the Yanks in five.

But as Joe pointed out to reporters the day before the game, this Yankee ballclub was different from those that had ruled baseball for the three previous years. "These aren't the same Yankees I saw when they had [Joe] DiMaggio, [Tommy] Henrich, and [Charlie] Keller," Joe said. "They're wearing the same letters on their shirts, but I don't believe they frighten anybody." Before taking that thought too far, Joe noted, "They're a good ballclub. Hope nobody thinks I'm knocking them. But the Dodgers seem to me to be a pretty good ballclub, too."

That's called "bulletin board" material nowadays, remarks an opponent interprets as belittling and uses for motivation. Yet Joe wasn't out of line. Joe DiMaggio, who had gracefully roamed center field for the Yankees since 1936, retired after the 1951 season. Starting infielders Bobby Brown and Jerry Coleman were in the service. Shortstop Phil Rizzuto had turned thirty-six on September 25. Johnny Mize, a key player on the bench, was thirty-nine and just one year from his final season. These Yankees, as Joe had observed, just weren't as formidable as the Bronx Bombers of the past.

But their pitching looked far more reliable than what the Dodgers could offer. They had stalwarts in Yogi Berra, Joe Collins, and Gil McDougald, and they had a twenty-year-old slugger with blond hair and boyishly handsome features to replace DiMaggio in center field: Mickey

Mantle. Then, there was all that history. The Yankees had been in the World Series eighteen times, winning all but four. And they had the "Old Perfessor" himself, wily Casey Stengel, calling the shots as manager. Thus they started off as nine-to-five favorites to win it all—again.

Even with all of that stacked against him, Joe insisted he had not lost any sleep over what he was about to face. "I don't know how it'll be around game time . . . but this is the way I feel right now," he told the writers. "It's just another ballgame, and Charlie has told me to go ahead and pitch the same as I've been doing."

With the Dodgers starting a rookie against them, the Yankees had every reason to feel confident. Besides, they'd have Allie Reynolds on the mound, and no pitcher at the time had enjoyed more success in the World Series than had the solidly built right-hander, known as "Chief" or "Super Chief" because he was part Creek Indian. Reynolds had pitched in eight World Series games, compiling a 4-1 record with one save and a 2.57 earned run average. That mark included the victory over Newcombe in game one back in 1949 and a 10–3 win over the Dodgers in game two of the 1947 series.

Reynolds threw a wicked curve, he could bring his fastball at 100 miles an hour, and he wouldn't hesitate to knock down a hitter to demonstrate who was in charge. Though he was thirty-five years old, Reynolds was at the top of his game in 1952. He went 20-8—the only time in a thirteen-year big-league career that he'd win twenty games—and led the American League in earned run average (2.06), strikeouts (160), and shutouts (six). The year before, he'd pitched not one but two no-hitters. One magazine writer described Reynolds as getting on in years but "bold as any burglar." Clearly, the Yankees appeared to have the best of the pitching matchup.

Dressen, though, was undeterred. Pointing to Joe as he ran sprints in center field the day before the series, the Dodgers skipper told his audience of writers, "If that guy pitches the way he has pitched all season, our chance is as good as theirs."

If Joe faltered, Dressen figured he could call on Preacher Roe, Billy Loes, or Johnny Rutherford in relief. And Dressen apparently reasoned that by starting Joe in game one, he could bring him back not only in game four but also in game seven, if the series ran that long. He must have believed that Joe was the only pitcher on the staff who could handle three starts in seven days. "He needs lots of work," Charlie said. "The only time they hit him good all year was when he had lots of rest."

>>>>>>>>>>

Joe tried to follow his usual routine on game day. He lived on the top floor of a house on Decatur Avenue in Brooklyn with his wife, Doris, their four-month-old son, Chico, and Chico's ten-year-old half-sister, Carolyn Ann Bonds. He ate breakfast and read the newspaper, which, naturally, was filled with stories about his upcoming start on the mound. Before heading for Ebbets Field, Joe wrapped his long fingers around Chico, hoisted him to his shoulder, and walked him around the apartment, enjoying a last few moments of calm.

>>>>>>>>>>

Throughout his life, my father would relish his responsibilities as a parent and cherish his time with Chico and me. He was always involved in Chico's life, from infancy through adulthood. At age forty-five, he became a father again when I was born. Five years later, he fought for and gained custody of me as a single parent after he and my mother divorced.

>>>>>>>>>>

Joe didn't own a car in 1952, so unless he could hitch a ride, he took the subway to the ballpark. That's how it was done then. Most of the Dodger players lived in ordinary Brooklyn neighborhoods next door to ordinary Brooklyn residents. They were part of the borough's fabric and got around just like anyone else, on the subway or trolley. Two of Joe's teammates, Duke Snider and Gil Hodges, once rented a room in a house on Bedford Avenue, the street that ran behind Ebbets Field, just two and a half blocks from the ballpark. They walked to games.

As Joe sat in the subway car crowded with workers, shoppers, and fans heading to the game, not one passenger recognized him. The top pitcher on the National League championship team, a team more tightly bound to its fans and locale than any other in baseball, rode to the game in complete anonymity.

As he dressed at the ballpark, Joe smiled inwardly at the clubhouse banter—the tall tales, the corny jokes, the laughter. Reporters sought some last words from Charlie Dressen and the veteran players: Pee Wee Reese, Jackie Robinson, Duke Snider, Roy Campanella, and Carl Furillo. Joe chatted briefly with the team's trainer, Doc Wendler, then ambled to the dugout and climbed the steps to the field. As he emerged, Gladys Goodding, the renowned Ebbets Field organist, serenaded him with "That Old Black Magic" and Joe tipped his cap in response. "I was nervous," Joe remembered, "but not frightened."

The pennants on the stadium roof flapped in the wind. Bunting hung from railings, decorating the park with splashes of red, white, and blue. The sharp crack from a solidly hit batting practice pitch sliced the air. Gazing out on the green expanse of the carefully tended outfield, Joe couldn't help thinking back ten years, back to when he was a high school senior in Plainfield, New Jersey, and five spoken words shattered a dream.

A scout had seen Joe play and knew he was talented. Joe could fill just about any position. He could run, throw, and hit. But while the scout talked to some of the other Plainfield High players, he walked past Joe as if he were invisible. When Joe asked why, he got an answer that hit him like a punch to the gut. "Sure, you're a good player," the scout said, "but don't you understand? Colored guys don't play baseball." Joe was stunned. He had no idea that in 1942, Major League Baseball was strictly the domain of white players.

But thanks to the skill and courage of Jackie Robinson, Larry Doby, Roy Campanella, and other black players who knocked down the barriers and paved the way, Joe got his chance. And now here he was, pitching in the World Series. "When I was walking out to start the game," Joe recounted years later, "I said, 'I wish that damn scout could see me now.' If I could have remembered his name, I would have sent him a ticket. Colored guys do play."

>>>>>>>>>>

Growing up, Joe knew little of baseball until an October afternoon in 1934 when he first figured out there must be something special about the sport. Just ten years old, he already was doing his part to bring in some money for his financially strapped eight-member family by delivering the local paper, the *Plainfield Courier-News.* Arriving at the *Courier-News* office to pick up his papers, he saw several men crowded around the front window.

He squeezed in among them and learned they were following the World Series—the Detroit Tigers against the St. Louis Cardinals—on an animated scoreboard. Joe looked at all those men and thought: baseball must be a pretty big deal if so many people are that interested in it. So he decided then and there that he was going to play baseball. His family couldn't afford baseball equipment, so Joe practiced pitching by drawing circles on the wall of a building and trying to hit the center of those circles with rocks. He played imaginary games, pretending he was pitching for the Tigers against the Cardinals' "Gas House Gang," baffling the likes of Joe Medwick, Frankie Frisch, and Leo Durocher with his pitches. Other times, he envisioned himself as a shortstop hitting the big World Series home run.

Now that he actually was in the series, it didn't matter what position he was playing. Joe could have been a banjo-hitting utility infielder and felt just as fulfilled. He had realized his dream. "Winning and losing didn't make any difference after that," he once said. "It's not often that you can have your boyhood dream come true."

Dream or not, there was now a reality that he couldn't ignore. He had to face those damn Yankees and get them out. He would need sharp control, guile, and, probably, a little luck. Some timely hitting by his teammates would help, too. All that had worked in his favor during his sensational rookie season. But this was different. This was the World Series against the ultraconfident Yankees, the bad boys of baseball. Just another game? Who was he kidding? As much as Joe wanted to look at it that way, he knew better.

Joe was an imposing figure on the mound, six foot two inches tall, weighing 220 pounds, long-armed and strong. You couldn't say much about his pitching repertoire, because he didn't have one. He got by on just two pitches: a hopping fastball that could hit 95 miles an hour and a little nickel curve that broke like a slider. He succeeded because of his control. He could hit catcher Roy Campanella's glove no matter where Campy held it. If the situation demanded that he come in tight on a hitter, he wasn't afraid to brush him back.

"He couldn't do anything wrong that year," reserve infielder Rocky Bridges remembered. "He put his pitches where he wanted them, it seemed like. He had that slider, he could pinpoint that thing."

Standing at attention with his teammates during the national anthem, Joe looked around one more time, still thinking about all he had gone through to reach this point: the cutting words of the scout, pitching eight seasons in the Negro leagues, traipsing around Latin America in the winter, and showing up at spring training without a Major League contract, hoping it would be the year he finally made it.

"I looked at third base and there's Casey Stengel and Frank Crosetti and Bill Dickey, Yogi Berra, Mickey Mantle, Hank Bauer, Phil Rizzuto, Gil McDougald, Vic Raschi, Allie Reynolds, Billy Martin, but not a dark face," Joe recalled years later. "Then you look at first base—Charlie Dressen, Cookie Lavagetto, Jake Pitler and Jackie Robinson, Pee Wee Reese, Duke Snider, Gil Hodges, Roy Campanella, Carl Furillo, Preacher Roe, and I found myself saying, 'Thank God for the United States where you have a chance to make your dream come true. Here I am, man. I'm in the W-o-o-o-rld Series and nobody can do anything 'til I throw this baseball.'"

Wearing a red number 49 beneath the underlined blue "Dodgers" script on his jersey, Joe wiped his right hand on the side of his flannel pants as he walked out to warm up for the first inning. If he was wiping away nervous perspiration, who could blame him? John Debringer would write in his *New York Times* game story that Joe "found himself cast in as difficult a role as ever was assigned to a rookie."

At the same time, Joe knew he could rely on the team around him. In baseball, it's important to be strong up the middle, and the Dodgers certainly were that, with a future Hall of Famer at each of those four positions: Campanella, second baseman Jackie Robinson, shortstop Pee Wee Reese, and center fielder Duke Snider. At first base, the Dodgers had Gil Hodges, a powerful hitter, nifty with the glove, and one of baseball's good guys, who, unfortunately, would struggle through the series without a hit. To his right, at third base, Joe had slick-fielding Billy Cox, who used a ratty, beat-up glove but gobbled up everything that was hit in his direction.

The outfield had the best arms in baseball with Carl Furillo in right field and Andy Pafko in left, flanking Snider. For Joe, though, the most reassuring sight was Campy squatting behind the plate. They had known each other since their days with the Baltimore Elite Giants. Campy was smart, always in control, and a dangerous hitter. A pitcher peering in for the sign got an extra dose of confidence just seeing Roy Campanella back there. "Everybody talks about the Dodgers' hitting," Joe said at the time, "but this is the best fielding team I ever saw." The numbers bore that out. The Dodgers led the league in fielding percentage that season and set a National League record by committing only 106 errors. It was a solid team, one of the best the Dodgers ever fielded, and the Yankees were wary. "You didn't know whether to feel sorry for the Dodgers or view them as you would a dangerous, wounded animal," Mickey Mantle said.

>>>>>>>>>>

Joe had a compact windup with only a small leg kick. He'd lean forward and hold the ball behind him on his hip as he looked in for the catcher's signal, almost like a discus thrower before he starts spinning. Then he'd explode into his delivery, finishing with a long stride toward the plate.

Once Joe completed his warm-up pitches, Campy fired the ball down to Jackie, who began the ritual that marks the start of every inning—whipping the ball around the infield. First to Pee Wee, then to Hodges, then to Cox, who encouraged his pitcher with a "Go get 'em" as he placed the ball in Joe's glove. "Do your stuff, big man," Pee Wee added. Jackie reminded him to relax and just pitch his game. Hodges offered a friendly smile and said, "Hold 'em, Joe. We're going to get some runs."

They trotted back to their positions, and then it was just Joe and the Yankees' leadoff hitter, Hank Bauer. Time to go to work.

Bauer, playing right field, wasn't your typical contact-hitting leadoff man. If Joe was Dressen's surprise, putting Bauer at the top of the order was Stengel's. Bauer was a powerfully built six-foot, two-hundred-pounder, a former pipe fitter and highly decorated Marine veteran who twice was wounded in the Pacific Campaign in World War II, taking shrapnel in the back on Guam and in the thigh on Okinawa. He was as tough as they come. Years later, when Bauer was managing the Baltimore Orioles, *Time* magazine would call Bauer the "brightest and ugliest face in baseball." Another writer said Bauer played baseball "with a fullback's ferocity."

Most fans had thought Irv Noren would lead off, but Stengel had tinkered with his batting order all season—he used ninety-nine different lineups—so it was no big deal for him to try one more. Besides, he felt there were advantages to Bauer hitting first. Having slugged seventeen home runs and batted .293 during the season, Bauer could lead off the game with an extra base hit or even a home run. He was fast enough to score from first on an extra base hit. He could break up a double play. Simply put, he was a difficult out.

Joe wound up and came in with a fastball, letter high, that Bauer took for a strike. Up in the press box, Roger Kahn took notice. "You could see right away he had a good fastball this October day," Kahn would write. Bauer eventually flew out to Pafko in left. Number two hitter Phil Rizzuto did the same and the dangerous Mantle popped up to Pee Wee. Joe was out of the inning, one-two-three.

Brooklyn pitchers would breathe a sigh of relief every time they got Mantle out in this series, because he'd become a royal pain in the rear to the Dodgers. In the opener, however, Mantle was just hoping to fare better than he had in the 1951 Fall Classic against the New York Giants. Playing right field in game two of that series, Mantle raced toward a ball that Willie Mays blooped into short right center. As he closed in on the ball, Mantle heard center fielder Joe DiMaggio yell, "I got it," and slammed on the brakes. His spikes caught on the rubber cover of a drain hole buried in the outfield grass, his right knee twisted, and the ligaments popped. "The pain squeezed like a vise around my right knee," he recalled. Mantle would play no more in that series and had surgery a few days later.

Reynolds retired the Dodgers in order in the bottom of the first and Joe pitched a perfect second inning. Then his close friend and spring-training roommate, Jackie Robinson, gave him a lift by driving a 3-2 pitch from Reynolds into the left-field seats in the bottom of the second. Dodgers 1, Yankees 0.

The lead didn't hold up. Joe misfired on a pitch to Gil McDougald leading off the third, and the Yankees' third baseman sent the ball into the left-field seats, just above the leaping Pafko's glove. Campy had wanted the pitch low and outside, but it came in high and inside. "That," the veteran catcher would say after the game, "was quite a variation." Kahn thought Joe looked "fidgety" after McDougald connected. But he quickly settled down, striking out Martin, Reynolds, and Bauer to escape further damage.

The score remained 1–1 through five and a half innings, though Joe twice had to work out of trouble, with help from Furillo and Pafko. In the fourth, Rizzuto opened with a single and Mantle beat out a bunt as Joe slipped to the ground in his haste to field the ball. The Yankees had a rally brewing, but Joe—with a timely assist from Furillo's strong right arm—snuffed it out.

Berra forced Mantle at second with a grounder to Hodges, but Mick slid hard into Pee Wee Reese to break up the potential double play. Rizzuto went to third, putting runners at the corners with one out and Collins coming up. When Collins lined out to Furillo, Rizzuto tagged up at third and started toward the plate. He wouldn't get far. Furillo, born in eastern Pennsylvania, was known as the "Reading Rifle" because of his powerful right arm. Fans would arrive at the ballpark early just to watch him throw in warm-ups. After gloving the ball Collins hit, Furillo gunned it to home so quickly that Rizzuto had to scurry back to third.

Recalling that play years later, Rizzuto said Furillo's throw "took our breath away."

"I love defensive baseball," the man called Scooter added, "and a throw like Furillo's was worth the price of admission. I was just sorry it happened when we were the other team." When Irv Noren grounded out to Jackie, Joe was out of the inning.

Pafko bailed Joe out the next inning. McDougald walked leading off and thought he could make it to third when Martin singled sharply to left. Bad idea. Pafko scooped the ball up and fired a perfect strike to Cox, who slapped on the tag.

"Out!" third base umpire Bill McKinley shouted.

"No!" McDougald screamed.

McDougald had committed one of baseball's cardinal sins: he had made the first out at third base. He later protested—and quite loudly—that he touched the bag before Cox even swung to make the tag. "He hasn't tagged me yet," McDougald stormed to writers in the clubhouse afterward. McDougald would insist it was the biggest call in the game. Martin had taken second on the throw, and if there had been runners on second and third with one out, McDougald said the infield would have played in. When Reynolds followed Martin with a sharply hit grounder, McDougald felt certain the ball would have gone through for a hit. Instead, with the infield at normal depth, Pee Wee fielded the ball easily and threw Reynolds out at first.

Bauer then hit a sinking liner to left that might have fallen in with a lesser fielder out there. Pafko, though, was too quick. He charged in and made a diving, sliding, knee-high catch that retired the side. Pafko chuckled when he recalled that catch. "I spent a lot of time on my stomach," he said. "I caught more line drives laying down than standing up. I dove for everything."

Collins gave Joe a scare in the sixth inning with Berra on first and two outs. The left-handed hitting first baseman lined a shot to right field and Dodger Nation held its collective breath, letting it out only when the ball curved foul. Collins then grounded to Hodges for the third out.

Finally, in the bottom of the sixth, the Dodger hitters gave Joe some breathing room. Pee Wee singled with two outs and that brought up Duke Snider, who had struck out eight times in five games while going a paltry 3-for-21 during the 1949 World Series. Reynolds had fanned him three times in the first game alone, and Snider had burned for a chance at redemption ever since. "By the time [that] Series was over, I wanted to pack my .143 batting average and get out of town as fast as I could," Duke wrote in his autobiography.

Well, redemption was at hand. Pee Wee took second when Reynolds bounced a curve ball past Berra. Then, with the count 2-1, the Yankee right-hander tried to sneak a fastball past the left-handed hitting Snider. Duke crushed it, driving the ball over the scoreboard in right field and onto Bedford Avenue for a 3–1 Brooklyn lead.

It was up to Joe to hold it.

He pitched a scoreless seventh, thanks mainly to a couple of slick plays from Cox. After Noren walked leading off, Cox zipped in front of Reese to grab McDougald's grounder and start a double play. When Martin, the next batter, ripped a shot down the third base line, Cox roamed behind the bag, knocked the ball down, then picked it up and fired to first in time to nip the hustling Yankee second baseman and end the inning.

Things got tense again in the eighth when Gene Woodling, hitting for Reynolds, drove a ball off the screen in right center. The ball caromed past Snider and rolled toward left field, giving Woodling, who couldn't run at full speed because of a groin injury, time to hobble all the way to third. He scored easily when Bauer flew out to Snider, and it was a one-run game again at 3–2.

Joe had relieved in situations like this many times during the season, getting the call to protect a narrow lead. But he had always come in fresh from the bullpen on those occasions. Could he remain effective with seven and one-third innings already on his arm? He had pitched nine innings only once—when Dressen started him late in the season—though he did have a relief stint of eight innings and another of seven and two-thirds innings. Still, some of the Dodger faithful in the crowd of 34,861—the largest ever for a World Series game in Brooklyn—had to be squirming in their seats, wondering if Joe was wearing down and about to get into more trouble with Rizzuto and Mantle due up next.

Joe used to tell Chico and Martha Jo, his children, to "stay strong" when difficulties arose. Stay strong and you can work your way through anything, he'd advise them. Joe did just that with the Yankees, quashing any worries that he was fading by retiring Rizzuto on a fly ball to Snider and fanning Mantle for his fifth strikeout.

>>>>>>>>>>

My father never bragged about his baseball career. He didn't sit me down and start in on something like, "Did I ever tell you about striking out Mickey Mantle in the World Series?" But I saw his mementos and photos, and he had the glove he wore in 1952 bronzed. When I was little, I'd sometimes get that big glove down as I played with my Barbie dolls and had Barbie sit in it. I still have that glove.

A lot of former players came by—Don Newcombe, Lou Johnson, Earl Wilson. I met Dusty Baker when he was still a player. I have photos of players holding me when I was little. And everybody was an "uncle" to me. My father would introduce us: This is Mr. Newcombe, who would say, "Don't call me Mr. Newcombe. Call me Uncle Don." Lou Johnson would also say, "Call me Uncle Lou."

Since my father's death in 2002, so many of his friends, both in and out of baseball, continue to call me or e-mail me to make sure I'm OK.

>>>>>>>>>>

The Yankees turned to Ray Scarborough in the eighth to try to keep them within a run, and he disposed of both Joe and Billy Cox. That brought up Pee Wee, who had taken a spill in the fourth inning when Mantle slid into him. His thigh was injured in the collision and he had to go down under the stands to run while the Dodgers batted to keep the leg loose. Reese had hit only six home runs in 149 regular season games, but he showed off some power when he connected with a pitch from Scarborough and deposited the ball in the left-field seats. The Dodgers had a two-run lead again, and Pee Wee, who also homered in the 1949 series, became the first Brooklyn player to hit two out of the park in the Fall Classic. Snider hit a comebacker to Scarborough for the third out and there was just one inning to go. Three more outs and the Dodgers would have their first-ever 1–0 lead in a World Series.

>>>>>>>>>>

Yogi Berra, the cleanup hitter, was up first for the Yankees in the ninth. He led the team in home runs (thirty) and RBIs (ninety-eight) during the season, and Joe would say after the game that he concentrated harder on the chunky catcher than other hitters, because Yogi had the potential to hit one out at any time. He got decent wood on a pitch and smacked it to right center, but Snider ran it down, leaving Berra 0-for-4 on the day. One away and Collins up next. Joe dispatched him with a ground ball to Jackie, and now he was just one out from carving his own niche in baseball history.

Irv Noren stepped in, the Yankees' last hope to get something going. Noren, a left-handed contact hitter obtained by the Yankees from the Washington Senators early in the season, was 0-for-2 in the game with a walk. An excellent athlete, Noren was good enough on the hardwood to play for the Chicago franchise in the National Basketball League, the forerunner to the NBA. He'd spent time in the Dodgers' farm system and would end up finishing his career with them in Los Angeles in 1960.

Joe still had plenty of pop on his pitches and, with two strikes, delivered a fastball letter high. Noren tensed and dropped his left shoulder as if he was going to swing. But he held up and let the ball go by. Umpire Babe Pinelli lifted his right foot, pivoted on his left, brought his right arm up, and punched Noren out.

Game over.

Joe had a six-hitter and Dressen looked like a genius. (Four years later, in his final game behind the plate as a Major League ump, Pinelli would punctuate another historic World Series moment, calling the Dodgers' Dale Mitchell out on strikes to end Don Larsen's perfect game.)

With the final out recorded, Campy brought the ball out of his glove, pumped his right arm and headed for the mound as Noren kicked the dirt with his right foot, lowered his bat, turned to look back at the stands, then shuffled off toward the dugout. Joe showed no emotion at all as he calmly walked off the field while accepting the handshakes and back-slaps of teammates converging on him.

Up in the stands, where Joe's sisters Phyllis, Ruby, and Leola were sitting, it was an entirely different scene. Giddiness reigned. The excitement was too much for Ruby, who fainted. "It was thrilling," Phyllis said. "I was jumping up and down. But I wasn't a nut like my sister. I didn't faint."

It's a wonder Joe didn't faint, too, having gone through so much that year. The uncertainty of spring training, when he was never sure he'd make the team. Waiting impatiently in the bullpen the first couple of weeks of the season before Dressen finally called on him to pitch. The racially tinged insults from narrow-minded fans and opponents. A letter in September that threatened him with being shot if he dared show his face at the Polo Grounds in a key series against the Giants.

After all that, Joe had done much more than live out a lifelong dream. He had left his mark on the game, a mark that no one could erase. While more and more black players would break into the big leagues, it would be twelve years before a second black pitcher won a World Series game. In game five of the 1964 Series, Bob Gibson of the St. Louis Cardinals beat the Yankees 5–2 and, like Joe, gave up a mere six hits.

Gibson handcuffing the Yankees came as no surprise. With his fierce, take-no-prisoners demeanor, Gibson was one of baseball's most dominant pitchers of the 1960s. But a rookie reliever starting for only the third time as a Major Leaguer? Few could have imagined anything other than the Yankees chasing him all the way back to the bullpen.

Joe would never have another season like 1952. He would lose his confidence and control, get shipped back to the minors, traded to the

Cincinnati Reds, win only fifteen more games, and be out of baseball by 1958.

But on that fall afternoon at Ebbets Field, five years after Jackie Robinson had opened white baseball's doors, Joe Black, who had arrived so unexpectedly seven months earlier, strode through and proved he had the courage, tenacity, and yes, the right stuff, to succeed on the grandest stage in American sports.

2

A Shattered Dream

WHAT TURNED OUT TO BE ONE OF the most important episodes in Joe Black's life happened on an ordinary fall afternoon in his hometown of Plainfield, New Jersey. It was early October in 1934, school had let out for the day, and ten-year-old Joe made his way to the office of the local newspaper, the *Plainfield Courier-News,* to pick up the papers he delivered to his ten daily customers. The few pennies he made on each paper were important to his family; they needed every cent Joe, his siblings, and his parents could muster. The Depression gripping the nation exacerbated that challenge, and it was only with the help of government relief that they managed to get by.

Joe saw a group of men gathered in front of the newspaper building as he approached and wedged his way in among them to see what had drawn their attention. What was going on, he wondered. Had someone been killed? Not at all, one of them said. They were following the World Series on an animated scoreboard set up in the front window.

"The world what?" Joe asked.

"The World Series," the man explained. "The Detroit Tigers are playing the St. Louis Cardinals."

Newspaper offices across the country once set up such scoreboards so fans could follow the series. Workers receiving telegraph messages of plays from the game reproduced them with lights and graphics, an early form of the online sites and apps now used by millions of fans on their computers or phones.

The man went on to explain that the series winner would be the world champion. Huh, Joe thought. He had never heard of the World Series. But if it commanded that much attention, it must be a big deal, and if it was a big deal, he wanted to be part of it. Joe watched for a while and saw that somebody named Hank Greenberg hit a home run off a guy named Dizzy Dean. That must have been important, too, he figured. When he finished his paper route, he'd have to tell his mother.

"So we were sitting around and my mother said, 'Why are you smiling?'" Joe related. "I said, 'I know what I want to do when I get big, Momma. I want to be a baseball player.'"

His mother laughed, but Joe Black had found his calling.

>>>>>>>>>>

Joe was born February 8, 1924, the third of six children in the family of Joseph Black and Martha Watkins Black. His parents called him Sonny. They had moved to Plainfield a few years earlier, part of the Great Migration of blacks to Northern cities to seek better jobs and escape the onerous segregation and Jim Crow laws of the South. Joseph came from Georgia, Martha from Virginia. Neither had any education beyond grade school. They settled in an industrial-residential city with a diverse population in northern New Jersey—eighteen miles from Newark, twenty-four miles from New York City.

Joseph was a mechanic, but he had a hard time finding work in that field. When a garage did take him on, it was only to sweep the floor or pump gas, a waste of his talent. "A lot of people said my dad could take a car apart and put it back together, he was that good," Joe's sister Phyllis Greer said. Phyllis, three years younger than Joe, was the fifth child and was followed by Allean. Ruby was the oldest, born two years before Joe. Another daughter, Leola, was born a year after Ruby. Alvin came along two years after Joe. That was a lot of mouths to feed on little money.

Joe's father sometimes fixed cars on the street in front of their house. If it had not been for the Works Progress Administration, the New Deal program that put the unemployed in public works jobs, the family might not have made it. Joe also remembered his father driving cabs and delivery vans before finally finding work in a factory. He was a quiet, easygoing man who did what he could to meet his responsibilities as a father and husband. "He was a good father," Phyllis said. But Martha Black was the one who kept things going. She was the rock everyone could cling to, the matriarch who ruled the household.

Martha was tall, stout, and "overflowed with love and concern for her family," Joe said. At five foot eight and 180 pounds, she had a presence more commanding than her husband, who was a couple of inches shorter and several pounds lighter. Martha hugged her children frequently, cooked their meals, washed their clothes, and encouraged them in all their pursuits. She could also be a tough disciplinarian. There were consequences for the child who did something wrong if Martha found out about it, often a whipping. The wayward child usually had to go out to the hedges and cut the switch Martha would use to administer her "lesson."

"If you didn't bring the right size, you had to go back and get another one," Phyllis said. When Joe faced a whipping for fighting a friend who tormented him by singing "Old Black Joe," he made sure to get a thick switch, because he knew his mother would be even madder if it broke.

Another time, Joe's mother caught him lying about an incident at school. Joe was upset that the teacher had not called on him when he knew the answer to some questions, so he told his mother that the teacher had been picking on him. When his mother looked into it, the teacher said Joe had not been working up to his potential and spent too much time joking around with a friend. Martha sided with the teacher, and her departing words left Joe with a feeling of dread: "I'll see you when I get home tonight." He knew he'd get a whipping and he did, along with admonishments from his mother about lying and falsely accusing others. Then came something almost as bad: Ruby and Leola teased him unmercifully as he tried to do his homework, mimicking his whimpering and pleading, "Momma, I won't do it anymore."

Joe once joked that all the whippings he received helped him in football, because his backside was so hardened that when defenders jumped on him, they felt like small children. Yet Joe never thought his mother was abusive. She constantly reminded her children of how much she loved them, and her pride when one of them accomplished something was evident. Still, she wasn't about to let any of them go astray. She lacked the education to help them with their schoolwork, but she had the moral strength to teach them right from wrong. Joe never hated his mother for punishing him. Quite the opposite, in fact. He loved and respected her so much that, well, there was no other term for it: he was a "momma's boy."

"She was the best mother in the world," Phyllis said. "We wanted things and we knew we couldn't get them, but she tried very hard to do what she could. To Joe, there was nobody like his mother."

Martha took in laundry, scrubbing the clothes in a suds-filled tub against a washboard, wringing them out, and then pressing them with an iron heated on the stove. She also worked as a domestic, cleaning the houses of well-to-do whites. Though she often came home exhausted, she still summoned the energy to cook filling meals with whatever ingredients she could scrounge up. "My mother was one of those types of women who could make something out of nothing when it came to feeding us," Phyllis said. "We never went to bed hungry. We always had food on the table. It may not have been steak, but we survived."

On weekends, Joe's mother outdid herself. She usually prepared some kind of meat—baked ham, roast pork, southern fried chicken, meat loaf, even duck on occasion—along with sweet potatoes, home fries, or rice with country gravy. Martha baked cornbread and homemade rolls. And afterward, Joe's favorite part: dessert. He'd salivate at the thought of chocolate or coconut cake, sweet potato pie, and homemade ice cream. Joe had a sweet tooth, and it would stay with him the rest of his life.

>>>>>>>>>>

When my father wasn't traveling, we always had dinner together. He enjoyed cooking, though clearly his favorite part of dinner was dessert. If he grilled steaks and potatoes for a main course, he had to finish with a rich dessert. Even if he did not eat all of the steak and potatoes, he would always eat the whole dessert.

My father also made special omelets and great spaghetti. He made chitlins at Christmas. Chico to this day would pay for our father to come down from heaven to make him spaghetti. Dad would pull out all the ingredients for his special spaghetti sauce the night before and then make it from scratch.

My mother's youngest son from her first marriage, Jerome, said he didn't like eggs. One day my dad said, "Try mine." He put cheese, bacon bits, scallions, and peppers in the pan with the eggs and Jerome said it was the only way he would ever eat eggs again. When I think about my father cooking, it reminds me of the television show Throwdown! with Bobby Flay, *because he could do the same thing in the kitchen.*

>>>>>>>>>>

Joe and his family lived on East Fourth Street in a mixed neighborhood on Plainfield's east side. The Jersey Central Railroad ran in front of their house, but there was no wrong side of the tracks. Folks on one side were just as hard-pressed economically as the folks on the other side. It got so they could tell time by the trains that rolled past. Children from black families in the neighborhood went to school and played with kids from Irish, Italian, Polish, and Jewish families. They got along because they were bound by a common thread: they were all poor. They'd fight on occasion, but hard feelings didn't linger. The combatants usually were back playing together the next day. Because of that, Joe grew up without prejudice and unaware that any existed, even if Plainfield did have pockets of segregation. Phyllis recalled that in one of the town's theaters, blacks had to sit on a particular side. In the others, they had to sit in the balcony. The city's roller-skating rink was off-limits to blacks until the 1940s, and Phyllis said when she applied for a job at the local five-and-dime after she graduated from high school, she was told the store didn't hire coloreds.

New clothes were too much of a luxury for the Black household, so Joe and his siblings wore hand-me-downs. When journalist Roger Kahn interviewed Joe for his best-selling book *The Boys of Summer*, he noticed a photo of Joe at age six with no shoes, wearing a shirt and tattered shorts. "That," Joe told Kahn, "was my Sunday best." Joe's son, Chico, still shakes his head in disbelief when he thinks of that photo. "Oh my God, that was his best," Chico said. "I can't imagine what his other clothes looked like."

Some of his clothes came from the white families who employed Joe's mother, discarded because they had been outgrown or were too worn. Joe's pants often were patched and his shirt collars were frayed. In junior high school, Joe felt ashamed when boys mocked him for wearing clothes they used to own. But Joe's mother tried her best to see that her children were presentable, no matter the condition of their clothes. "My mother could do laundry, so when she got finished, we looked as good as new," Phyllis said. "We didn't go to school dirty."

The sneakers Joe and his siblings wore were cheap and poorly made. But Joseph Black wanted his children to think they had good shoes, so he ran forty-yard races against them and let them win. Then he'd tell them the lightweight sneakers helped them win or point out that the lack of a design on the bottom gave them speed.

>>>>>>>>>>

In their early days in Plainfield, the Blacks lived in a second-floor flat heated by a potbellied stove that burned coal and wood. The stove warmed only the living and dining rooms. Kerosene lamps lit the house and portable kerosene-burning stoves heated the bedrooms. An ice box kept their food and milk cold. A large bowl or pan sat under the ice box to collect the water as the block of ice melted, and it had to be emptied from time to time. That task initially fell to Ruby, being the oldest and presumably the strongest. Like most youngsters, Ruby was impatient, so instead of scooping out some of the water first, she'd lift the pan—filled to the edge with water—and try to carry it to the sink. Joe figured she batted around .333 in that task, a fine mark in baseball but not so good when you're spilling water on the floor and on yourself two out of every three times.

Responsibility was impressed upon on the Black children early: they were given numerous chores around the house. When old enough, they found work to contribute financially. Joe and Leola carried the baskets of freshly laundered clothes to Martha's customers. Ruby washed windows and walls. Alvin did odd jobs for local merchants. One chore no one wanted was crawling out from under a pile of warm covers and stoking the fire in that potbellied stove on a cold winter morning. You never wanted to be the first one up, Joe recalled, because you'd have to get that fire going. He and his siblings even risked being late for school just to avoid being the first one out of bed. Despite the grumbling, Joe thought the chores made the kids feel they were contributing to the family. It was the least they could do for their parents, who struggled so hard to put food on the table and keep a roof over their heads. When Joe was ten, the family moved two doors down to a house heated throughout by a furnace—pure luxury after relying on a stove and portable heaters.

Along with his paper route, Joe and a friend, Jimmy Troiano, hustled for money. They searched the streets and alleys for discarded pop bottles, cigarette packs, and newspapers. They could redeem the bottles for a nickel apiece. They removed the tin foil from the cigarette packs, rolled it into one-pound balls, and sold them to junk dealers for five cents each. Joe and Jimmy could get twenty cents for every hundred pounds of bundled newspapers. When he got older, Joe earned a dollar each Saturday night for scrubbing the floors in a dry cleaning store and a dentist's office. He got down on his hands and knees with a brush and a bucket and worked his way across the floor, which took some time. It seemed to Joe that the dentist's floor was two hundred feet long. It was a tough, menial job, but the money made it worthwhile.

Joe and Jimmy also made money in less honest ways. They begged for nickels outside the local theaters, saying they needed the money to buy a ticket for a show. On a good Saturday night, they could make five to six dollars between them. Sometimes, they resorted to outright thievery, swiping the coins people left at an unmanned newsstand when they bought a paper.

Joe and his friends expended a lot of energy taking advantage of delivery trucks left open while the drivers went inside the store. First, Joe would check out the area to make sure he didn't see anyone who knew his mother, because if she learned what he was doing, oh man, he didn't even want to think about the consequences. When he was certain no one was looking, Joe would lift a bottle of Pepsi-Cola from a crate in the truck and stuff it into his pocket, then trot over to an unattended pie truck, grab the pie of his choice, and take off. He'd run down an alley, climb the concrete fence surrounding the Public Service Company yard, sprint across the yard, and hide behind one of the two large gas storage tanks, where he'd catch his breath. From there, he'd saunter to the train station and eat his ill-gotten goodies in the waiting room, while keeping an eye out for the police. Call it petty crime or simply youthful hijinks, but Joe didn't think he was doing anything wrong. "Instead," he said, "I considered it fun because of the challenge of outwitting the nosey people who were walking the streets."

>>>>>>>>>>

With her third-grade education, Martha Black could barely read and write. She was determined that her children not suffer the same fate. They had to do chores and they had to work, but school came first. Woe to the child who replied "Nothing" when asked what he or she learned in school that day. For the next several minutes, they stammered away while trying to explain to their mother how they could sit in class all day and not learn a thing. Joe's mother often went to the teachers and insisted that her children get the same homework assignments as the more well-to-do students. When Joe and his siblings brought work home to show their mother what they had done, she told them she was pleased even though she couldn't read what she had just seen. "She made us feel she cared what we did," Joe said.

>>>>>>>>>>

When my dad became a parent, he was huge *on education. He always read to me when I was a child. His mother never had much formal education, but she knew how important it was and never accepted anything less than her children's best effort in school.*

Anytime I wrote a report in high school, I had to show it to my father. When he opened my report cards, we discussed my grades and talked about any that had changed from the previous term. When he worked on his speeches in the dining room, I had to do my homework next to him at the table as well.

My father traveled often in his job, and yet I never lacked his attention. When he was on the road, he called every day. If he had a speech in the evening, he always called before he left the hotel. During our conversations, he would ask me what I had learned in school and if anything had been particularly difficult. My dad went to all the PTA meetings at my school. He introduced himself to all my teachers and principals so they would understand they were dealing with someone keenly interested in his child's education.

If my father had to go out of town during one of those times we didn't have a housekeeper, he took me with him—but only after calling the principal to explain that I would be out of school for the next few days and to get my homework for that period so I could keep up with my class. We took those assignments with us and he made sure I finished them. If you were Joe Black's daughter, school was something you did not avoid.

>>>>>>>>>>>

The *Courier-News* printed the school honor rolls, and some of the women Martha worked for let her know when they saw her children's names. When Martha finished her work, they gave her the paper so she could take it home and tell the kids what she had learned. Though she had signed their report cards, she didn't know exactly what they meant. But her pride was obvious. "We'd see the sparkle in her eyes," Joe said.

On Joe's first day at Plainfield High School, he came home disconsolate. The school system then usually put black students in trade or "practical" courses—the boys in industrial arts, the girls in home economics. Joe chafed at that. He wanted to study math and English and history. His mother was furious when he told her about his classes and said they'd go see the principal the next day. Joe was embarrassed to be seen walking to school with his mother. He could hear other students snickering, because if your mother was along, that usually meant you were in trouble. On that day, though, it was the principal who was in trouble. Martha stormed into the office and demanded an explanation. The principal said shop classes would better prepare Joe for a job, because he probably wouldn't go to college. Whereupon Martha Black lifted her considerable bulk out of the chair, looked the principal in the eyes, and pointed a finger at him.

"Don't you tell me how poor we are or what's gonna happen to my children," she said in that stern tone mothers the world over have mastered. "You just put Sonny back in those classes with those rich kids or it's going to be me and you!"

The principal said he would see what he could do. As it turned out, he could do quite a bit. The next day, Joe was out of the technical track and in college prep courses. Martha Black had spoken. That evening, she reminded her children that she'd always be there for them if they had a problem, and told them they never had to feel inferior to anyone. She left them with a saying that stuck with Joe for the rest of his life: "You ain't no better than anybody else and ain't nobody better than you." When Joe wrote his self-published autobiography in the early 1980s, he titled it *Ain't Nobody Better Than You*.

>>>>>>>>>>>

I'm sorry that I never met my father's mother, who was certainly a remarkable woman. She died in 1964, five years before I was born. But my father talked about her. She was the rock in my dad's life. That's why he made sure he was the rock in mine. Just as my grandmother protected my dad, he always protected me. His mother, more than anyone, influenced his life.

If my grandmother had not been such a strong presence in my father's life, I don't know what direction he would have gone. If she had not been the type of woman she was—loving, encouraging, a mother who did everything she could to boost her children's self-esteem—I don't know if my dad could have gone through those times when African Americans had to sit in the back of the bus and baseball kept them out. My father treated people with kindness and respect. He was always looking to help somebody.

I know and understand this now: it's sad that most people don't realize how blessed they are until their parents are no longer with them.

>>>>>>>>>>

After Joe saw those men following the World Series in the *Courier-News* window that day in 1934, baseball took hold of his life. He started listening to games on the radio and reading about Major League stars in the paper. He didn't have a glove or a bat or even a ball—there was no money for anything as expensive as sports equipment—but he made do. Joe drew circles on the wall of the Public Service Company building and tried to throw rocks inside the lines, all the while pretending to himself that he was striking out Joe Medwick or Charlie Gehringer. His idol became Hank Greenberg, the Detroit Tigers' slugging first baseman, though he once acknowledged he didn't know why. Perhaps, he thought, he had heard Greenberg described as strong and talented and smart, qualities Joe admired. Plus, Greenberg had hit that home run off Cardinals ace Dizzy Dean in the first game of the '34 series. To do that, he must have been good, Joe figured. So he tried to copy everything Greenberg did, including his batting stance—bat straight up, elbows out, standing tall.

Joe had no way of knowing it then, but years later, he and his hero would be bound by a common tie: bigotry dogged them both. Joe endured taunting and jeering because of his race. Greenberg, from the time he joined the big leagues, was stigmatized because he was Jewish.

In game one of the 1935 World Series, the anti-Semitic remarks from the Chicago Cubs dugout were so blatant that umpire George Moriarty stopped the game, walked over, and scolded the Chicagoans for comments that he said "went beyond the realms of common decency and sportsmanship."

Eventually, Joe's uncle, Frank Watkins, gave him a tennis ball and an old glove. Joe sometimes hit with half a bat or a broomstick. When he heard that Major Leaguers wore spikes, Joe stuck his feet in tin cans so he could get the feel of running and walking on metal. One day, Nathan Selzer, who owned a body shop just down the street from Joe's family, saw Joe throwing rocks against the front stoop of his house. Joe waved, as he always did when Mr. Selzer drove by. But on that occasion, Mr. Selzer did not wave back. Instead, he tossed something to Joe and drove off. It was a baseball. Joe had never even held a baseball before that moment, let alone owned one. He slept with that ball for a year.

Joe and his friends at first played ball on the playground at school or in empty lots. They cleaned up one of those lots themselves, with some "encouragement" from the police.

A police officer approached one day while Joe and his friends swapped tall tales and outright lies in front of the Public Service Company. The officer said he wanted to play a game and when they agreed, he told them to line up in single file. Then he asked, "What month comes after February?"

"March," they responded in unison.

"That's right," the officer said. "March right down to the police station." It seems the police had caught on to their Pepsi-pie truck raids and coin thefts from the newsstands. The future Dodger and his friends weren't quite as artful as they had imagined. So how should they be punished? First, they were given a tour of the jail, and if that was meant to frighten Joe and his friends, it worked. After seeing the hard bench that served as a bed and the thick bars, they wanted no part of that. Then a sergeant talked about reform school, sending another shudder through Joe's gang. Believing a lesson had been taught, he told Joe and his buddies to report to the vacant lot next to Handy Andy's at four o'clock the next afternoon. "Now get out of here!" the sergeant added.

They kept that appointment and were surprised to see several police cars drive up. They were even more surprised when the officers pulled out bats, sponge-rubber balls, rakes, and shovels. The officers would teach Joe and his friends how to play baseball, but first the boys had to clean up the field. Maybe, the sergeant figured, if the youngsters got interested in sports, they'd lose interest in stealing.

It certainly turned out that way for Joe. He and his friends eventually organized a team, the East Fourth Street Cardinals, and when they started to think they were pretty good, they moved up to the city's Junior League Baseball program. They quickly discovered they were in over their heads. Their first batter in their first game, Ulysses Phillips, got conked in the head with a pitch and collapsed in a heap as his teammates gasped. After seeing Phillips go down, "nobody wanted to bat," Joe said. Phillips was OK and managed to trot to first base, but the awe-stricken Cardinals had few baserunners and lost 32–0. The Cardinals won just one game that year, and that was by forfeit. But they were a determined bunch who kept showing up and by the next season, they were much more competitive.

When Joe tried out for the baseball team at Plainfield High School as a freshman, he heard the school supplied the mitt and all the equipment for the catcher. For someone who had been excited just to be given a baseball, that was a big deal, so Joe told the coach, Jack Liddy, that he was a catcher. Except he wasn't. Joe did fine with pitches that were across the plate or to his left. But when the pitch tailed off to his right, he stabbed it with his bare hand. Liddy stopped the proceedings after a few minutes, looked at Joe's hand, which was swollen and red, and explained that a catcher has to move his feet and shift his body so he can grab every pitch with his mitt. Then he sent Joe home to soak his hand, marveling that it wasn't broken.

Listening to his coach, Joe learned enough about catching to play the position for the junior varsity team. He also played first base, third base, and left field during his high school years, but never pitched. Plainfield had two strong pitchers when Joe was a senior, and he had to catch because no one else could handle their fastballs. Joe was a free swinger at the plate and ran the bases aggressively. One baserunning jaunt was especially memorable.

Early in high school, Joe couldn't afford spikes, so he borrowed a pair from a friend, Dougie Taylor. The problem was, Dougie wore size eights and Joe had to curl his toes up to squeeze his size nine feet into the shoes. When Joe lashed a pitch into the gap, he smelled triple, and as he rounded second base, he heard a pop. A couple of steps later, he heard another pop. The shoes had split, the soles had fallen off, and only the tops of the shoes remained on his feet. "So when I got to third base, I said, 'Look! I have on spats,'" Joe said. He eventually bought his own spikes, using the money he earned from his weekend floor-scrubbing jobs.

Joe developed quickly as a ballplayer. By age sixteen, he was playing with his father and uncle on a men's team. They made him an infielder, putting him at second base or shortstop. During his senior year of high school, Joe and his friends formed their own team, the Plainfield Black Yankees. The accommodating owner of a local sporting goods store sold them uniforms at cost; it was the first time Joe and his buddies had real uniforms for their sandlot team. They wore them proudly.

"We couldn't get home from church fast enough on Sundays to put on those uniforms," Joe said. They didn't play until three o'clock in the afternoon, but they got dressed by 11:30 and then paraded up and down the street until it was time to head for the ballpark. Playing with the Black Yankees put Joe against some good competition. Monte Irvin, who later would star for the New York Giants, played for the Orange Triangles. Scotch Plains had a seventeen-year-old left-handed power hitter named Don Newcombe, who would later become the right-handed power pitcher for the Brooklyn Dodgers.

Joe also played football at Plainfield High, growing from a scrawny five-foot-six, 140-pound freshman to a six-foot-one, 205-pound senior. He had designs of starring as a single-wing tailback. What he became instead was a tackle and an end. He played the latter position so skillfully that it changed his life: without football, Joe could never have gone to college.

In basketball, Joe would say he had more desire than talent. He enjoyed the physicality of battling for rebounds under the basket, and when he scored, it usually was with a hook shot. Occasionally, he'd notch a few points from the perimeter with a two-hand set shot.

Mostly, though, basketball was just a way for Joe to bide his time until the spring brought baseball, the sport that fueled his dreams. His mother couldn't understand his fascination with baseball and feared it would get in the way of his education. She wanted Joe to have a better life than hers, and education was the only way she could see that happening. But Joe was positive that one day, he'd become a big-league player and play in the World Series, just like Hank Greenberg.

"The game was an enthusiastic thing for me," he said. "It made me feel when I was on the field that I was somebody. Because nobody looked at whether you were rich or poor once you were on that ballfield."

But they did look at a player's skin color, and in 1942, that made all the difference.

Joe's high school and semipro teams had enough good players to attract the attention of professional scouts. One day, Joe saw a scout talking to some of his teammates, but the guy ignored him. It was like he was invisible. Joe was a good hitter and he could run. He had a strong arm. So why wasn't he getting any attention? Finally, Joe confronted him.

"Hey, you've seen me play," Joe told him.

"Yeah. You're a good ballplayer," the scout said.

"So how come you're not talking to me?" Joe asked.

"You're colored," the man replied.

"I know that," Joe said.

"Then why are you asking me that?" the scout said.

"Because," Joe replied, "I led the team in hitting three years. You're not talking to me."

"You're colored," the guy said. "Colored guys don't play baseball."

"What do you mean?" Joe asked incredulously. "I play every day."

"Yeah," the scout said, "but they don't play in the big leagues."

Joe was stunned. He couldn't play Major League baseball because he was black? Wasn't he an American, living in a country where everyone was supposed to have the same opportunities? Whatever happened to all men being created equal? All his life he had run with a mixed crowd. He assumed the rest of America did as well and then, *pow*, he learned it wasn't so. "A left hook to my jaw by Joe Louis or a bullet into my body would not have pained me more than those words," Joe later wrote.

Tears welled in his eyes and he ran home crying. Through the years, Joe had carefully cut out pictures of Major League players and pasted them in three scrapbooks. He flipped those books open and, for the first time, noticed that every single player was white. Not a black face among them. He had never before given their skin color a second thought. To him, they were just players, representatives of what he wanted to attain.

Then anger took over and he ripped up all the pictures—except for one of Hank Greenberg. Joe still needed a hero. He couldn't give up on Hank.

"I never thought my skin pigmentation would make a difference," he said. "All through high school I played football and basketball and baseball. The other teams had them, black and white. We had them, black and white. And suddenly, my dream is shattered."

His anger quickly gave way to hate. Whites became his enemies because they were keeping him out of baseball. He hated them for it, and he stopped hanging out with his friends. He spoke to his white classmates only when they spoke to him first. He moped, and his mother noticed. She knew her son too well. He wasn't himself and she had to find out why.

"I don't like white people," he told her.

"What are you talking about?" she asked.

"They won't let me play because I'm colored," he answered.

"Sonny, your friends didn't do anything," she said. "That's the way this country is. That's why we moved up here."

Martha explained about segregated schools and neighborhoods in the South, about the signs designating water fountains and restrooms for blacks and whites. She cautioned Joe against painting all whites with the broad stroke of racism and prejudice, reminding him that his white friends had nothing to do with preventing him from playing baseball. She urged him to remember all the good times he had enjoyed with his friends, and eventually, Joe's anger dissipated. Martha Black may not have been book smart, but she was wise in the ways of the world—and of her children.

Joe still harbored a baseball dream, but pushed it to the back of his mind and decided he needed to find a job. He landed one at the factory in Elizabeth, New Jersey, where his father and sister Leola worked. Joe was given the task of stacking four one-hundred-pound rolls of copper on a hand truck and delivering them to different parts of the plant. He didn't stay there long. Once his mother learned what he was doing, she jumped all over her husband for allowing her son to take a job like that. To preserve household harmony, Joe said he was going to quit anyway, because the factory was too far away. But he wanted to work, so he took a job cleaning presses at a printing company on the graveyard shift, eleven o'clock at night until seven o'clock in the morning. Ten years later, those same presses would print his picture as a pitcher for the Brooklyn Dodgers.

For many blacks, factory work was the best they could hope for. But Joe had another opportunity, and he could thank three whites for getting it: Jack Liddy, his high school football and baseball coach; William Sette, his English teacher; and Henry Banta, his guidance counselor. They told him about college scholarships—Joe had never heard of such a thing—and helped him apply. He received several offers, including one from Morgan State in Baltimore. His father hoped Joe would go to Morris Brown in Atlanta, because he had grown up in Georgia. But Joe had read about segregation in the South after that talk with his mother and he wanted no part of Georgia. His mother favored Morgan State, because a sister, Emily, lived in Baltimore. Joe never knew how his teachers came upon Morgan as a place he should consider. In the end, he would be thankful they did.

In later years, as Joe thought back on the stinging words of the baseball scout, he recalled that Jesse Owens was given a ticker-tape parade in New York after winning his four gold medals in the 1936 Olympics. The parade was followed by a hotel banquet in his honor, but Owens wasn't allowed to ride the main elevators at the hotel. "I wondered if at that moment he felt empty and without pride," Joe said. Joe certainly remembered feeling that way when he was told blacks couldn't play in the Major Leagues. And that reminded him of words once spoken by the Reverend Martin Luther King Jr.: "Being a Negro in America means trying to smile when you want to cry."

Joe did indeed cry that day his dream was shattered. But even broken dreams can be patched back together. It would just take a while for Joe to make that happen.

3

A Second Newcombe?

Spring Training 1952

THE TRAIN SLOWED AS IT APPROACHED the station in Vero Beach, Florida, and Joe rose from his seat to gather up his gear. It was mid-February in 1952 and while Joe's long trip from Norfolk, Virginia, was over, a new journey was about to begin. At the urging of his father-in-law, Frank Byrd, he had signed the minor league contract the Brooklyn Dodgers had sent him, even though he felt insulted at not being offered a deal from the Major League club. Joe had split the 1951 season between the Dodgers' Triple-A teams in Montreal and St. Paul, then won the pitching title in the Cuban Winter League. He thought he deserved a big-league contract—and the higher salary that went with it. Maybe so, his father-in-law had said, but he reminded Joe of all the time and effort he had put forth just for a chance to play big-league ball—he was already twenty-eight years old—and how it would be a shame to waste it. So go to Florida, he advised, and show them you deserve to be on the big club. Within two days, Joe was packed and on the train.

Joe's resentment began to fade as the train made its way south. Yes, he was on a minor league contract, but he was trying out for the Dodgers, not one of the farm clubs. And he felt fortunate to be part of an organization that had a spring training complex, Dodgertown, where all players—black and white—could live, eat, practice, play ball, and relax without being subjected to the Jim Crow attitudes that still prevailed in Florida at the time. Dodgertown had a swimming pool, a basketball court, a shuffleboard court, pool tables, and ping-pong tables. Occasionally, movies were shown for the players.

But say Joe wanted to go to church. Unless he attended the Catholic church, he'd have to catch a ride to Gifford, the black community next to Vero Beach, to find a church that would let him in. Blacks couldn't get a haircut in Vero Beach and weren't allowed to eat in most restaurants. They were banned from beaches, golf courses, and theaters. Cleaners wouldn't accept their laundry. If blacks wanted a night out, they had to go to Gifford. When the team traveled for exhibition games and had to spend the night, Joe and the other black players stayed in a hotel for "their kind" while the rest of the team slept at a "whites only" hotel. Joe resented that treatment, but he understood he had to deal with it. And they had Dodgertown, a former naval air station the Dodgers had converted into a complex to house and train everyone in the team's system. In the midst of a segregated city, Dodgertown was, in the words of author Jules Tygiel, "a haven of tolerance."

Including his time in the Negro leagues, Joe had spent six full seasons and parts of three others as a professional baseball player. Yet he was as nervous as the rawest rookie. On his first morning in camp, he was supposed to be in uniform at nine o'clock. He got to the clubhouse half an hour early, started to open the door, then backed off. He reached for the handle again, then backed away. Suppose he didn't see Jackie Robinson or Roy Campanella inside. Who was he going to talk to? And who was going to talk to him? It must have been like James Earl Jones's character in *Field of Dreams* when he's invited to join Shoeless Joe Jackson and the other "ghost players" in the cornfield. He hesitates, sticks his hand in the corn, pulls it out, and looks back toward home plate with an expression that says, "Do I really want to do this?" Eventually, he plunges into the tall corn and disappears.

Joe felt the same uncertainty when he arrived in Dodgertown and was told he'd be rooming with Jackie Robinson. He had met Jackie when both were playing Negro league ball, but that was a long time ago. Jackie was an icon among blacks, the one who paved the way, the one who had endured the slurs and insults and made it possible for Joe to get his chance with the Dodgers.

"Hey, nigger, why don't you go back to the cotton field where you belong?"

"They're waiting for you in the jungles, black boy."

"Hey snowflake, which of the white boys' wives are you dating tonight?"

"We don't want you here, nigger."

Jackie had hit the dirt untold times to avoid knockdown pitches. He had been spit on and spiked. Many of his own teammates wouldn't talk to him or warm up with him. In those early days, Jackie had been the loneliest man in baseball. He told Joe that at times he got so frustrated he'd go home to his wife, Rachel, and cry on her shoulder. Jackie absorbed it all without retaliating. Because if he had, it would have been over. Branch Rickey's great experiment would have failed and Joe wouldn't have gotten his chance. Jackie "was a warrior who swallowed his ego so that his people could be a part of America's No. 1 pastime, baseball," Joe wrote years later.

That's why Joe admired and respected Jackie more than anyone except perhaps his mother. He and other Negro league players had rooted for Jackie when he played for the Montreal Royals in 1946 and then when he broke in with the Dodgers the following year. "What'd Jackie do last night?" someone invariably would ask as they scanned the newspaper for the latest box score. Black fans across the country did the same thing. Former Major League infielder Ed Charles remembered pulling for Jackie as a twelve-year-old growing up in Florida. "I'm praying that Jackie Robinson never makes an error, that every time he comes to bat he gets a base hit," Charles said.

Joe knew Jackie Robinson wasn't the best black baseball player of his time. If skill had been the only factor, players such as Josh Gibson, Buck Leonard, Leon Day, Cool Papa Bell, Ray Dandridge, and Pee Wee Butts would have been taken ahead of Jackie. But Joe doubted any of them could have handled the abuse. Dodgers general manager Branch Rickey chose Jackie because he believed Jackie could take it. Joe knew he certainly couldn't have been the first. "I might have taken it for a couple of days or maybe a week," Joe said in a 1973 interview, "but then I'd have grabbed one of them in the dugout runway or outside the ballpark and popped him . . . and right there Mr. Rickey's whole black program would have gone down the drain."

As they became better acquainted, Jackie talked to Joe about the difficulty and frustration of remaining silent in the face of the abuse that rained down on him. "Joe," he once said, "sometimes I thought the burden was a little too heavy, and I almost gave in. But I talked to my God and I talked to Rachel, and I knew that 'I' was not more important than 'we.' I knew guys like you were depending on me. But it wasn't easy."

Joe and Willie Mays used to try to think of another player who could have done what Jackie did. They couldn't come up with anyone.

>>>>>>>>>>

The Dodgers hoped that by rooming Joe with Jackie, some of the second baseman's competitiveness might rub off on him. Club executives thought Joe was great for seven innings, but felt he lost his competitive edge after that. Hanging with Jackie might help him maintain that edge, they reasoned. And Jackie Robinson was nothing if not competitive. Leo Durocher, a rather feisty fellow himself, once said of Jackie, "This guy didn't just come to play. He came to beat ya. He came to stuff the goddamn bat right up your ass."

When Joe found his room in Dodgertown, he saw two beds and stopped. He didn't know which one to take. Jackie was the star, the man. Who was Joe Black to decide which bed was his? What if he took the one Jackie wanted? He was sitting in a chair by the window, wondering what the next few weeks held for him, when Jackie walked in. Jackie had already been a big name when Joe first met him back in 1946 at the York Hotel in Baltimore, but Joe remembered him as quiet and polite, not at all standoffish as he had expected. Jackie was the same on that February day in 1952. They shook hands and then Jackie eyed his new roommate, checking him out from head to toe.

"You're twice as big as I thought," Jackie said.

"Yeah, I'm big," Joe said.

"Can you fight?" Jackie asked.

"Yeah, I can fight," Joe replied.

"Well," Jackie said, "we're not going to fight."

Joe was puzzled. Why should they have to worry about fighting? Because it was still going on, Jackie said. It wasn't as bad as before, but five years after he came up, the name calling and insults hadn't stopped. Mostly it was fans and not players, Jackie said, but many still felt there was no place in America's pastime for blacks. Joe just shook his head in resignation. Why, after all this time, couldn't players be judged on their performance, not on their skin color? At least he was with a team on which he thought he'd get a fair shake.

That didn't make him any less apprehensive when he walked up to the clubhouse door the next morning. The large block letters that spelled out DODGERS CLUBHOUSE seemed intimidating. They reminded Joe of just how close he was to achieving his dream. At the same time, he realized there also was a chance he'd fail. Joe said he must have reached for that door and backed off five times before finally stepping inside. And, just as he feared, Jackie and Roy Campanella, his former teammate with the Baltimore Elite Giants in Negro league ball, were nowhere in sight. Uh-oh. Now what? He stood there frozen in place, like a kindergartner just left off by his mother on the first day of school, too nervous to move.

Thank goodness, he'd say later, for Preacher Roe. Elwin Charles Roe emerged from the Ozark Mountains in Arkansas to become one of the Dodgers' top pitchers in the late 1940s and early '50s. The skinny left-hander succeeded on guile and control and, as he confessed to *Sports Illustrated* after he retired, a spitball that broke sharply downward. He'd entertain teammates and writers with homespun stories of life in the South and was easily taken as a country bumpkin. But Roe, like Joe, had gone to college and taught high school math in the off-season. He had been known as Preacher since he was three, when an uncle who had just returned from World War I asked young Elwin his name. Out of the blue he answered, "Preacher," apparently because he liked the minister at the family's church. So it was that Preacher Roe, a white man from the South who was coming off the best season of his career—a 22-3 record with a 3.04 earned run average—became the first person in the Dodgers clubhouse to greet Joe.

Ol' Preach extended his hand, introduced himself, and called out to clubhouse attendant John Griffin that Joe Black was present and needed to be shown to his locker. Joe never forgot the warmth of Roe's welcome;

three years later, he'd do the same for a young, nervous rookie named Sandy Koufax. Joe tried to stay cool as he dressed, but he couldn't help looking around. Here he was in the same clubhouse with Duke Snider, Pee Wee Reese, and Gil Hodges. Even then, long before Roger Kahn immortalized them as "The Boys of Summer," they were bigger-than-life figures to anyone who knew anything about the Dodgers—or baseball, for that matter. Finally, Joe heard a familiar voice.

"Hey Joe, welcome to Dodgertown."

It was Campy.

"Man, where've you been?" Joe asked, relieved to see his former batterymate.

Campy said he'd been in the whirlpool and told Joe to quit gaping and finish dressing. Then in walked manager Charlie Dressen, a short, stocky man who was rarely at a loss for words. Dressen was serious, and he got right to the point. This was a new season, he told them. The 1951 season, which had ended in such heartbreak for the Dodgers, was over. It happened. It hurt. But it's time to forget about it and move on.

Hurt? It was devastating. That spring training session was the first time the Dodgers had been together since suffering the most crushing loss in the franchise's sometimes star-crossed history. In the last inning of the last game of a best-of-three playoff series, Bobby Thomson's three-run homer off Ralph Branca—the now famous (or infamous, depending on your allegiance) "Shot Heard 'Round the World"—lifted the New York Giants to a 5–4 victory over the Dodgers, sending the Giants to the World Series and the Dodgers to an off-season haunted by memories of what they'd let slip away.

After beating the Boston Braves in the first game of a doubleheader on August 11, 1951, the Dodgers had led the National League pennant race by thirteen and a half games over the second-place Giants. Dressen had been so giddy about his club's success and his archrival's struggles that he declared, "The Giants is dead." He couldn't have been more wrong. The Dodgers dropped the second game of that doubleheader and the Giants caught fire, winning sixteen straight games and thirty-seven of their last forty-four. The Dodgers weren't horrible during that stretch, going 26-22. They just couldn't match the Giants' torrid pace.

On the last day of the season, the Dodgers had to go fourteen innings to beat the Philadelphia Phillies just to stay tied for first. In retrospect, it might have been easier on the Dodgers and their legions of loyal fans if they had lost that game. Then there would have been no playoff, Bobby Thomson would have remained just another solid player, and Ralph Branca would have been spared the ignominy of giving up the most notorious gopher ball in baseball history. But no, the Dodgers seemed destined to make it as painful as possible. As writer Hy Turkin once put it: "Though it doesn't cost a cent to become a Dodger fan, the strain on heart and soul is extremely costly. That's because win, lose or draw, the Dodgers never do things the easy way."

The rivals split the first two games of their playoff, setting up the decisive contest at the Giants' home park, the Polo Grounds, on October 3. When the Dodgers took a 4–1 lead into the bottom of the ninth inning with Don Newcombe on the mound, it appeared the Giants finally were dead. But they rose up one more time. With one run in, two runners on, and Newcombe out of the game, Thomson belted Branca's second pitch into the left-field seats. It was so stunning that even the Giants' fans stood in silence for a moment until what had just happened sank in, touching off a delirious celebration. As broadcaster Russ Hodges screamed, "The Giants win the pennant! The Giants win the pennant!" over and over, sports writers tapped every bit of their vocabulary to describe what they had seen.

"The art of fiction is dead," Red Smith wrote in the *New York Herald Tribune*. "Reality has strangled invention. Only the utterly impossible, the inexpressibly fantastic, can ever be plausible again." Arthur Daley wrote in the *New York Times*: "It was incredible. It couldn't happen and yet it did happen." Bill Bryson Sr. wrote in the *Des Moines Register* that as the crowd noise swelled, "the double-decked stands of the Polo Grounds rocked in their forty-year-old foundation."

Before trudging glumly to the clubhouse from his spot in left field, the Dodgers' Andy Pafko could do nothing but watch helplessly, his neck craned, his right shoulder against the wall, as the ball sailed over his head. "I had the best look at it of all the people in the world," he said. Brooklyn fans had thought it couldn't get any worse than 1950, when the Phillies' Dick Sisler hit a three-run homer in the tenth inning of the last game of the season to eliminate the Dodgers, but they found to their collective dismay that, indeed, it could.

"That was as bad as it gets," said Jerry Reinsdorf, who grew up in Brooklyn and became the chairman of the Chicago White Sox and

Chicago Bulls. "I don't think any of us have ever recovered from that. I saw Bobby Thomson in 2003 and I told him I still hated him."

Talk show host Larry King also celebrated and suffered with the Dodgers back then and wrote that Thomson's home run left him "as sad as I had felt since my father died." Author Donald Honig, another who endured the highs and lows that went with being a Brooklyn Dodgers fan, wrote that to him, Thomson's home run "sails on as a yet unindicted crime."

In recounting that '51 season, writer Kevin Baker suggested the Dodgers might have spared themselves and their fans all that agony if they had called Joe up late in the season, his theory being that Joe might have saved a game or two, which is all the Dodgers would have needed to stave off the Giants. So why didn't they bring him up, especially when rosters expanded in September?

"Was it another case of one black player too many?" he wrote in a collection of baseball writing titled *It Ain't Over 'Til It's Over.* "Would it have been too much for white America—or, more likely, baseball's all-white management—to have one big, smart, black fireballer relieving another and blowing away white batters to clinch the pennant?"

Maybe Joe could have helped. But it's also possible he might not have been ready at that point. It would be several weeks into the 1952 season before Joe earned Dressen's trust. Who's to say Dressen would have had the faith to call on him at a critical time in the heat of a pennant race? Things happened as they did and everyone in Brooklyn had to learn to accept it over that long, torturous winter. But spring training always brings with it a renewal of hope, and so it was with the Dodgers.

Duke Snider saw "nothing but a positive attitude" when the Dodgers assembled in Vero Beach. "Rather than feeling down and out, we felt we were better than any other team in the National League," he wrote in his autobiography.

"Sure we discussed it," Andy Pafko said. "It cost us the World Series. But that was a year ago. Every year was a different year." Jackie Robinson doubted the Giants could do the same thing again. "They deserve all the credit in the world," he said, "but those things just don't happen every year."

So Joe found himself with a team ready to look ahead and forget the past, and he was eager to make a good impression. Maybe too eager.

While the pitchers were running that first day, Billy Loes pulled Joe aside.

"Are you a racehorse or something?" he asked.

"What are you talking about?" Joe said.

"You don't have to run that fast," Loes told him.

"I'm not running that fast," Joe said.

"You're not?" Loes countered. "Look at the rest of us."

Joe was just running the way he always had, but he agreed to pull back a little so he wouldn't look like a showoff. The next day, he couldn't help himself and went overboard again, at least in the eyes of the Dodgers' staff and some players. Dressen was looking for somebody to throw batting practice and Joe volunteered. It had been ten days or so since he last pitched in Cuba, so he was ready to test his arm again. After he threw a couple of pitches to Pee Wee Reese, Jackie yelled, "Joe! This is batting practice. You're throwing too hard." Too hard? Joe didn't think so. If they wanted to see hard, he'd show them. He warned the catcher and then let go with a fastball.

"Now that's hard," he said.

"I get the meaning," Gil Hodges said.

Joe thought he was throwing only half-speed and was surprised the others thought he was throwing hard. Carl Furillo was up next and warned Joe that he was working on his batting stroke so be ready. What Furillo meant was that he was likely to hit one back up the middle, and on about his third cut, he did just that, sending a screaming liner right back to the mound. Joe got his glove up just in time and later would say he learned a valuable lesson that day. He was in the big leagues and a pitcher had to be on his toes. As fast as the ball gets to the plate, it often comes back even faster. He later learned that his batting practice episode had sparked a debate among the veterans over who was faster: Joe or Newcombe.

That night, Jackie sat down with Joe to have a talk. He understood that Joe was throwing half-speed, but that still was too fast for guys who hadn't swung a bat since that devastating loss to the Giants in October. Today, players find places to hit and work out all winter. When Joe played, most of the guys had off-season jobs and didn't pick up a bat or a ball until spring training. That's what camp was for—to get in shape, loosen up the arm, and sharpen the batting eye. Because of that, Jackie said Joe needed to take even more off his pitches.

Jackie also noticed that Joe was doing more running than the other pitchers. He said some of the white players were grumbling about his intensity and wondered if he was just trying to impress Dressen. Joe was surprised that Jackie would even ask that question. He'd always been taught that the legs were important to a pitcher's durability and control, and running was the best way to keep the legs in shape. He explained to Jackie that through his conditioning, he was able to run and look like a 190-pounder when he actually weighed 220. He also pointed out that because he really had only two pitches, he had to rely even more on his conditioning and control. Jackie said he understood, but Joe still felt a little sheepish about being viewed as a showoff.

>>>>>>>>>>

Though Joe had gone just 11-12 in his two Triple-A stints the previous year, his velocity generated some early buzz in camp, and it intensified after the *New York Times* proclaimed in a headline, HURLER IS TERMED FAST AS NEWCOMBE. That wasn't the first time Joe had seen himself likened to Big Newk. While he was pitching for Montreal the previous year, some newspaper reports suggested that in Joe, the Dodgers had found another Newcombe. Under the *Times* headline, reporter Roscoe McGowen wrote that Joe had been hailed as "the second Don Newcombe," partly because he was almost as big as Newk, both were right-handers, and both came from New Jersey. But after Joe showed off his fastball to half a dozen reporters, McGowen noted that maybe it wasn't such a facetious designation after all. Joe figured Dressen staged the pitching demonstration just to generate some headlines. Well, it worked. After he threw a curve, Joe heard Dressen tell the reporters, "See, it's one of those dinky curves like Newcombe throws." Dressen was quoted in the next day's papers as saying Joe had a good chance to make the team. But the very next day, Dressen said he wasn't any surer about Joe than he was of the other new pitchers.

Joe was flattered by the comparisons, but he had to face reality: he was no Don Newcombe. Anyone who knew anything about baseball would understand that his fifteen-minute pitching demonstration paled beside what Newcombe had accomplished with the Dodgers. Dressen just wanted to steal that day's newspaper thunder from the Giants and Yankees, and he had succeeded. Joe had to deliver in the exhibition games if he was going to make the club. Forget becoming the second Don Newcombe. He just wanted to become the first Joe Black.

The Dodgers certainly could have used a "second Newcombe," though, because the real one was sworn into the US Army on February 26 and wouldn't pitch for Brooklyn again until 1954. Newcombe was the first successful black pitcher in the Major Leagues and had won fifty-six games in the three seasons before Uncle Sam called. This included a 20-9 mark in 1951, when he tied for the National League lead in strikeouts. If Joe—or anyone else for that matter—could come anywhere close to matching those numbers, the Dodgers would be delighted.

Some, however, thought Joe was just another face and arm in the line of black pitchers the Dodgers had signed in hopes of finding an ace. While Newcombe became a star, Dan Bankhead had only one modestly successful year, John Wright never made it to the majors, and Roy Partlow didn't either. Now along came Joe Black, twenty-eight years old, college educated, with a big fastball, that nickel curve, and . . . what? No other effective pitches, really. But he could be tough to hit when he had his control, and after everything he had gone through in his life so far, he wouldn't back down from a challenge. Still, "the Dodger brass was not optimistic that Black would pitch well for the Dodgers," Peter Golenbock wrote in *Bums*, his history of the Dodgers.

That pessimism was borne out in the team's first exhibition game. Joe pitched one inning in a 5–2 loss to the Boston Braves in Miami, and it wasn't a very good inning. He gave up three hits, two runs, and a walk, and uncorked a wild pitch, prompting McGowen to write in the *Times*, "Joe Black, who said yesterday that he was 'no Don Newcombe' more or less confirmed his estimate." Joe told reporters he tried to steer his pitches and as a result, "threw up a lot of nothing." He vowed that the next time he pitched, no one would score on him.

Dressen gave Joe a chance to back up those words, starting him against the Philadelphia Phillies in Miami on March 13. Scheduled to go the distance, he shut out the Phillies on two hits through the first five innings. But he gave up two unearned runs in the sixth, then fell apart in the seventh, walking three batters, hitting another, and surrendering a grand slam to Willie "Puddin' Head" Jones. His line for the game: seven runs, five hits, three strikeouts, and three walks. The Dodgers' hitters saved him from a loss and they won 8–7.

While he had been solid in those first five innings, Joe started to worry, because Dressen wasn't talking to him. Was it just a prelude to being sent back to St. Paul? Joe was among several new pitchers the Dodgers had tried out that spring, a group that included Mal Mallette, Johnny Rutherford, Johnny Podres, Ben Wade, and Bob Alexander. He knew he had to be as good as or better than those guys to make the team. Earlier, he had read his name frequently in the newspaper columns. Lately, the newspaper chatter focused on the other pitchers and Joe never got mentioned. He knew it would sting if he had to spend another year in the minors.

>>>>>>>>>>

Joe was commiserating with Jackie one day, fretting over whether Dressen would give him enough chances to show what he could do, when his roommate smiled and said, "What are you worried about? You got it made." Jackie then asked Joe if he had noticed two white women watching him and following him around when they were at Dodgertown. Joe said he'd seen them, but didn't think anything of it. Well, Jackie said, he should think something of it, because one was Kay O'Malley, wife of team owner Walter O'Malley. "She thinks you're cute," Jackie said.

Fine, Joe thought, but she wasn't the manager. He felt he had to go to Dressen and confront him.

"Why is it when I get hit, you don't talk to me?" Joe asked when he finally cornered the little manager.

"Maybe you're not as good as I thought you were," Dressen replied.

Joe then noted that most of the other pitchers were working only a couple of innings at that point. He had pitched seven innings and was unscored on in the first five. Why wasn't he judged on those innings? Dressen agreed that Joe had a point and he'd take it into consideration.

The next time Charlie used him, Joe pitched the final two innings of a 4–1 victory over the Dodgers' Fort Worth minor league team, allowing two hits and no runs and striking out three. That was more like it. "I guess that's when they made up their mind I was going to be a relief pitcher," Joe said years later. "Back in those days, nobody wanted to be a relief pitcher because you were the humpty. If you're not good enough to be a starter, put him down in the bullpen. I'd never thought about being a relief pitcher."

>>>>>>>>>>

Though the Dodgers trained at Vero Beach, they played thirteen exhibition games that year in Miami, 140 miles down the coast. Miami's hotels were segregated, so Joe and the other black players couldn't stay with their white teammates. They were housed at the Sir John Hotel in a historically black neighborhood known as Overtown, and while Joe still cringed at the Jim Crow laws of the South, he felt the blacks got the better end of the deal in lodging. The rooms were clean and comfortable, the hotel had a swimming pool, the restaurant served soul food and West Indian food, and all the top black celebrities of the day stayed there. The Dodger players had a chance to rub shoulders with the likes of Sammy Davis Jr., Nat King Cole, Dinah Washington, Joe Louis, and Sugar Ray Robinson.

One day, Duke Snider and Pee Wee Reese tagged along with Dodgers vice president Buzzie Bavasi when he went to the Sir John to give the players their meal money. Joe said Pee Wee and Duke took one look at the women around the pool and suggested to Bavasi that maybe the blacks and whites could trade hotels. The white players mingled with what Joe described as a more mature clientele. Duke and Pee Wee were blunter. "You've never seen so many old women in bathing suits," they said. They didn't get their wish.

Pee Wee and Duke were fixtures in an everyday lineup that was as solid as any in baseball. At first base, Gil Hodges had smacked forty home runs in 1951 and was entering the prime of his career. In the middle of the infield, Jackie at second and Pee Wee at shortstop remained productive hitters and threats on the basepaths even though both were thirty-three years old. They had combined for 29 home runs and 45 steals in the year before, when Jackie hit .338. Pee Wee would lead the league in steals in 1952, while Jackie would hit .308 and score 104 runs. They still had it. Slick-fielding Billy Cox, performing wonders at third base with an old glove that looked about to fall apart, was coming off a year in which he hit .279. With Campy behind the plate, the Dodgers had the National League's reigning MVP, the first of three such awards he'd win. Outfielders Carl Furillo in right, Duke Snider in center, and Andy Pafko in left could all hit; they had some power—especially Snider—and played their positions skillfully. Each had strong arms, especially Furillo. Only the most daring or foolhardy baserunners challenged the man known as the "Reading Rifle," who had mastered the fine art of playing the odd ricochets and caroms off the tricky right-field wall at Ebbets Field. No need for Dressen to tinker with that group.

The pitching was a different matter. Newcombe's absence created considerable consternation among the Dodger brass. Where were they going to find the twenty victories the big right-hander represented? Plus, could they really expect another twenty-two-win season from Preacher Roe, who was thirty-seven years old? Clyde King had won fourteen games coming out of the bullpen in 1951. That was more than he had won in his previous four seasons combined. Was another year like that possible?

Dressen had said at the start of camp that maybe he could find favorable matchups for certain pitchers and two of them could go 10-5 or 10-6, thus accounting for Newcombe's twenty wins. At one point, the Dodgers looked at swinging a deal for Ewell Blackwell, who had won sixteen games for the sixth-place Cincinnati Reds in 1951 and would have been a frontline pitcher for the Dodgers. But in late March, Reds manager Luke Sewell said he couldn't afford to give up Blackwell or one of the other starters in which the Dodgers had shown interest, Ken Raffensberger and Herm Wehmeier. Thus, the Dodgers had to find the pitching they needed from their own ranks.

Despite the talk about Joe being another Newcombe, he was pretty much an unknown to the other players. Carl Erskine, one of the mainstays of the pitching staff, said that's how it was with most newcomers. He said he once was told the Dodgers had two hundred pitchers in their farm system just waiting for someone on the big club to falter so they'd get a chance to move up. "I hadn't heard about Joe Black. I didn't have any preknowledge about what he did," Erskine said. "I don't think anybody said, 'What did this guy do in the minors? What was his record?' Part of the reason was we were all focused on our own fate. We couldn't focus on much else because the competition was pretty fierce. It was all aboveboard stuff. We never had any bitter feelings about each other. It was management's move and you hoped you got moved the right way. But sometimes you got moved the other way."

That would be Joe's fate if he didn't perform. He got his fourth chance to pitch when the Dodgers played the Boston Red Sox in Miami on March 22, and he started. It was his first time facing Ted Williams, the "Splendid Splinter," the player many regarded as the greatest hitter of all time. Joe admitted to being awestruck when Williams settled into the batter's box. Hmmm, Joe thought, he really did squeeze his hands around the bat, just like everybody said. Joe wound up and fired a fastball low and away, which Williams took for a strike, looking the ball into Campy's mitt all the way. Campy called for another fastball and Williams took that for strike two. Joe started to get cocky. He figured Williams didn't want to swing the bat that day, so instead of wasting a pitch, which would have been expected in that situation, Joe uncorked another fastball. In the blink of an eye, Williams drove the ball on a line 350 feet to left field for a two-run double. Standing on second, Williams called out to Joe, who was rubbing the ball before pitching to the next batter.

"You're going to be a great player," Williams said.

"Why?" Joe asked.

"You've got a hell of a fastball," Williams replied.

Joe said, "Yeah, you just showed me." And Williams called back, "But everybody's not Ted Williams."

Joe went six innings that day, giving up seven hits and three runs, all unearned. He walked one and struck out three. It would be twelve days before he would pitch again, but he had learned another lesson. Warming up before the game, Joe heard some fans talking. "That's Joe Black, their new Newcombe," one said. "Oh yeah," another chimed in. "I gotta see if he can throw as hard as Newk." The more Joe heard the word Newk, the more he started thinking he should pitch like him. Subconsciously, he was changing his motion to resemble Newcombe's. When fans oohed and aahed over the sound of his fastball popping into the catcher's mitt, it only reinforced Joe's notion that he should throw like Newk. But all he did was wear himself out before throwing his first pitch in the game, something Campy pointed out afterward. "You aren't Don," the veteran catcher said as they sat on the Sir John Hotel patio. "I watched you warming up and I thought to myself that you were throwing your best pitches before the game."

Much of the talk that spring centered on Johnny Podres, a nineteen-year-old left-hander who had gone 21-3 with a 1.67 earned run average in Class D ball in 1951 and seemed ticketed at least for Triple-A in 1952—and maybe the big club. After the first three weeks of camp, Dressen had hailed Podres and another rookie, twenty-nine-year-old Ben Wade, as the standouts among the new pitchers. Wade, who had toiled in the minors for eleven years, also caught Jackie's eye. Jackie thought Wade, with a "fine fastball, good curve, and a lot of experience," had the best chance to replace Newcombe in the rotation. As camp progressed, Johnny Rutherford started raising eyebrows. The twenty-six-year-old right-hander strung together sixteen straight scoreless innings during one stretch and seemed to have a good chance of making the team.

After his March 22 game against Ted Williams and company, Joe had to wait until the Dodgers began making their way north before pitching again. Just before the Dodgers broke camp, Dressen said Joe would have to "show me something more" before he could be assured of making the team. Joe did just that, working six scoreless innings and giving up only two hits against the Boston Braves in Mobile, Alabama. Joe felt that performance clinched his spot on the Dodgers roster, though it was several days before he knew for sure.

It was common for teams to barnstorm their way home after spring training, and the Dodgers-Braves games often attracted a large contingent of black fans who wanted to see Jackie, Campy, and Boston's fine outfielder Sam Jethroe. An overflow crowd of 9,000 saw their game in Chattanooga, Tennessee, a landmark event because it was the first game at the city's Engel Stadium that featured both black and white players. The night before, a crowd of 6,506 in Nashville's renowned Sulphur Dell ballpark saw the two clubs whack five home runs. The game at Mobile drew a crowd of 10,503, a throng so large that the city's policy of separating the races by forcing black fans to sit in the right-field bleachers couldn't be enforced. The seats filled so quickly that fans were allowed to stand in the outfield. There were so many in right field that Carl Furillo ended up playing about fifty feet behind Jackie at second base. The teams agreed that any ball hit into the right-field crowd would be a ground-rule double, and the Braves ended up winning 5–4 on two balls hit into that mass of fans in the thirteenth inning.

Joe made his final appearance of the spring when he pitched the last seven innings of a 4–1 loss to the Baltimore Orioles, at that time a Triple-A team in the International League. Relieving Preacher Roe, Joe scattered seven hits and allowed only one run. The Dodgers finished the exhibition season with three games against the Yankees in New York and Brooklyn. Dressen didn't use Joe in any of those games. For the spring, Joe appeared in six games, worked twenty-six innings, and gave up thirteen runs and twenty-six hits. He had to hope that was good enough to get him a spot on the team, because there was nothing more he could do. It was all well and good that the owner's wife thought he was nice-looking, but that wasn't going to cut it with Charlie Dressen. Everyone knew that Preacher Roe, Carl Erskine, Ralph Branca, Clem Labine, and Chris Van Cuyk would lead the rotation. Any questions that remained, as always, involved the rookie pitchers. Some would make the team, but which ones? Bob Alexander had been sent to Montreal on March 28, so that left Joe, Johnny Rutherford, Ben Wade, Johnny Podres, and Mal Mallette in contention for the three remaining spots.

Finally, with the season opener just forty-eight hours away, Dressen called Joe into his Ebbets Field office and delivered the news: The Dodgers had bought his St. Paul contract. They also kept Rutherford and Wade and sent Podres and Mallette to Montreal. Joe was one of the last players added to the Dodgers roster, but at that point, he didn't care. He was a Major Leaguer at last.

4

Joe College

ITS SUMMER SLUMBER OVER, THE Morgan State campus in Baltimore, Maryland, buzzed with activity in early September 1942. Returning students at the historically black college renewed acquaintances and made new friends. Nervous freshmen walked hesitantly between buildings, wondering if they were going to the right place for their next class. One of those freshmen, Joe Black, recently arrived from New Jersey, took it all in and, for the most part, liked what he saw. Especially when he lingered in an area of campus known as "the circle" and watched the female students as they "sashayed about the grounds and buildings." Not long after that, Joe's eyes were opened in another way.

The school required all freshmen to attend the first college assembly, and once the session was called to order, everyone was told to stand and sing the national anthem. So Joe rose and began belting out the words he knew so well, "O say can you see . . ." and then stopped. Everyone else was singing something else: "Lift every voice and sing, till earth and heaven ring . . . " So he just stood and listened, puzzling over this song he'd never heard before.

When the singing stopped, he turned to the female student next to him and asked, "What song was that?"

"The Negro National Anthem," she replied, giving Joe a quizzical look.

"There ain't no such song," Joe shot back.

"There is. And when the assembly is over, I'll prove it," she said.

An hour later, she led him to the library, opened a book, pointed to a page, and said, "There!" And Joe saw for himself the words an entire segment of the population had adopted as its anthem.

Lift every voice and sing, till earth and heaven ring,
Ring with the harmonies of liberty;
Let our rejoicing rise, high as the listening skies,
Let it resound loud as the rolling sea.

It was all new to Joe, even though the lyrics had existed for nearly half a century. They were written in 1900 by James Weldon Johnson, who was the principal at the Stanton School in Jacksonville, Florida. Johnson wanted to do something special to welcome Booker T. Washington to the segregated school, so he had five hundred students recite his poem. Johnson's brother, John, later set the words to music.

Joe studied the words and tried to figure out how they might apply to him and to blacks in general. He was quickly finding out that growing up in his mixed neighborhood in Plainfield, while ideal in learning to get along with all races, had not prepared him mentally for Morgan's all-black environment. Nor had he learned anything about his own heritage. His experience at Morgan would fill in those blanks.

>>>>>>>>>>

The excitement had built in the Black household as summer waned and the day of Joe's departure for Baltimore approached. Joe would be the first in his family to attend college. For his mother, Martha, who had hammered home the importance of education while Joe was growing up, this was a joyous occasion. Who could have imagined one of her children going to college? "We were very proud of him," said Joe's sister Phyllis.

It wouldn't be easy, though, because Joe's scholarship didn't quite cover everything. He wasn't sure what would happen when he told his parents he still had to come up with twenty dollars a month, a big chunk for the family in those days. "They just sat, looked at me, looked at the floor, looked at each other and then finally I heard, 'I think we'll be able to raise the money each month,'" Joe recalled. Those words came from his mother, and she smiled as she said them. His oldest sister, Ruby, took a job at Bamberger's Department Store in Newark to help with Joe's expenses. Martha Black added what she could to the college fund and by the time Joe got ready to leave, they had enough to cover his expenses. Ruby helped out additionally by using her employee discount when Joe bought clothes. He picked out a new pair of pants, two shirts, some underwear, and a raincoat. They couldn't afford a suit or an overcoat. With so few belongings, Joe didn't need a footlocker. What he had barely filled two cardboard suitcases.

When the big day arrived, Joe's family accompanied him to the Plainfield train station, where he would catch a B&O southbound for Baltimore. As Joe got ready to board the train, his mother tried to cram a year's worth of instructions into five minutes. "Sonny," she said, "we wish we coulda given you lots of clothes to take with you, but you know we don't have a lot of money. Besides, you're not going down there to be pretty, you're going to college to study and learn something." Listen to the teachers, she admonished, get good grades, be careful, and don't act like a smart aleck. "And write sometimes," she added. After hugs all around, Joe hopped up the steps onto the train and it chugged out of the station, taking him to a new and horizon-broadening phase of his life.

As the train steamed through the New Jersey countryside, Joe thought about the words in the Declaration of Independence:

> We hold these truths to be self-evident, that all men are created equal, that they are endowed by their Creator with certain unalienable Rights, that among these are Life, Liberty and the pursuit of Happiness.

That prompted him to consider his own confused feelings about race. He had been denied a chance to play professional baseball because the game was run by whites who didn't want blacks to be a part of it. Yet three white men, Jack Liddy, William Sette, and Henry Banta, had helped him get his scholarship to Morgan State. "The racial jumble had me in a topsy-turvy world," he said. It would only intensify once he got to Baltimore.

Joe had never considered Baltimore to be a southern city. After all, it was less than two hundred miles from Plainfield. But in racial matters, Baltimore reflected the Jim Crow attitudes common in cities much farther south. Joe knew he was in a different environment when he stepped off the train at Baltimore's Mount Royal Station and saw a sign that read Colored Waiting Room. What, he asked himself, was he getting into? Jackie Robinson's wife, Rachel, wondered the same thing after Jackie played there with the Montreal Royals in 1946. She said the abuse that Baltimore fans hurled at Jackie was the worst she had ever heard, and for the first time, she feared for his safety. Rachel cried in their hotel room that night, so upset that she told Jackie she wanted him to quit.

Architecturally, Mount Royal Station was striking, notable for its tall arched windows and clock tower rising from the center of the building. It must have been an impressive sight to Joe. His first glimpse of the Morgan campus, however, left him feeling empty. Because he was going to play football, Joe had arrived two weeks before the rest of the student body, so the place looked deserted. He had expected to see a campus that resembled Princeton or Rutgers, which he had seen while playing high school baseball. What he saw instead was a complex that reminded him of a plantation with buildings sprouting here and there. It was not an encouraging sight.

Located on the city's northeast side, Morgan State was founded in 1867 as the Centenary Biblical Institute by the Baltimore Conference of the Methodist Episcopal Church. It was charged originally with training young men for the ministry, then broadened its scope to educate both men and women as teachers. The school was renamed Morgan College in 1890 to honor the Reverend Lyttleton Morgan, who was the first chairman of its board of trustees and donated land to the college. The college moved to its present site in 1917, two years after receiving a $50,000 grant from Andrew Carnegie, and remained a private school until the state of Maryland bought it in 1939. Carnegie Hall, built in 1919, remains the oldest original building on the present campus, and that's where the taxi from the train station dropped Joe.

Joe wasted little time settling in, though he had to haul his suitcases down one hill and up another on the opposite side of a road to find the men's dormitory, a trip that did nothing to endear him to the place. "The trek only reinforced my belief that I was not going to like it here and I would soon be returning to Plainfield," he wrote. Joe was given a room on the third floor, where freshmen lived, and was told he could find one of the football coaches, Eddie Hurt or Talmadge Hill, in a building that resembled a barn. Neither coach was there, but Joe checked out his gear from the equipment man and suited up. Looking in a mirror, he thought he looked pretty sharp. He smiled and said to himself, "Big Joe." He trotted over to the stadium and saw thirty-five to forty players working on blocking drills. They paused to check out the new arrival and then a small man came over and introduced himself. "Hello, I'm Coach Eddie Hurt."

Again, Joe was disappointed. All his coaches in high school had been at least five foot ten and 175 pounds. Hurt, whom Joe had heard so much about, looked to be about five foot six and 145. He was slim and soft-spoken, hardly an imposing figure. But Hurt's stature among coaches far exceeded his physical size. By the time Joe arrived at Morgan, Edward Paulette Hurt already was an iconic figure. Hired in June 1929 after coaching at Virginia Seminary & College in Lynchburg, and just twenty-nine years old, Hurt took charge of Morgan's entire athletic program—football, basketball, and track. He remained as basketball coach until 1947, coached the football team until 1959, and kept his track duties until 1970.

In 1942, Morgan was coming off its eighth Colored Intercollegiate Athletic Association (CIAA) championship in Hurt's thirteen years as coach. So dominant were Hurt's teams in the 1930s that, starting with a 38–0 victory over Cheyney State in the 1932 season opener, the Bears went fifty-four straight games without a loss. They didn't lose until falling to Virginia State 15–0 in Petersburg on Thanksgiving Day, 1938. Morgan's record during that stretch was an eye-popping 47-0-7, including three unbeaten, untied seasons. In 1934, the Bears played eight games and did not allow a single point. When Hurt finally hung up his football whistle after the 1959 season, he had won fourteen conference championships and compiled a 173-51-19 record. Two of his football players, Roosevelt Brown and Len Ford, are in the National Football League Hall of Fame.

Hurt's basketball teams weren't bad, either, winning four CIAA titles. In track, his teams won thirteen CIAA championships, while his athletes captured eight individual NCAA titles and twelve AAU championships. The best of Hurt's runners was George Rhoden, who once held the world record in the 400 meters and won the Olympic gold medal in that race in Helsinki in 1952, running for Jamaica. Rhoden also anchored the Jamaican team to victory in the 4x400 relay, setting a world record. Another Hurt-coached athlete, Josh Culbreath, won the bronze medal in the 400-meter hurdles at the 1956 Melbourne Olympics and broke the world record in the 440-yard hurdles in 1957. Also a two-time winner at the Pan Am Games, Culbreath was the first great black intermediate hurdler, the predecessor to Edwin Moses, Danny Harris, Angelo Taylor, Derrick Adkins, and André Phillips.

Hurt introduced Joe to Talmadge "Marse" Hill, another revered figure in Morgan athletics and Hurt's right-hand man in all three sports. Hill, a former Morgan State athlete, was so respected that when the university opened a new field house in 1974, it was named for him. Morgan State now plays in the Mid-Eastern Athletic Conference and that league's all-sports award for men also carries Hill's name. Hill helped the conference get established while serving as its first president.

But on this late summer day in 1942, Hill was interested only in what the new kid from Jersey could do. He told Joe he was running the players through one-on-one blocking drills and asked if he was ready to jump in or would he rather wait until the next day. The other players stared at Joe, waiting for an answer. He knew he had only one choice. "I'm ready," he declared.

Joe was solidly built at six foot two and 210 pounds. He had been taller than most of his teammates and opponents in high school, so he figured he could hold his own in the drill. Then Hill yelled, "Come on over, House." Joe gulped as one of the biggest human beings he had ever seen trotted over to line up against him. "He can't play," Joe stammered. "He's a giant." Clarence "Big House" Gaines indeed was a large man. Gaines would later make his name as a Hall of Fame basketball coach at Winston-Salem State, where he won 828 games in forty-seven years. At Morgan State, he was a six-foot-five, 238-pound lineman who towered over his teammates. Gaines had weighed 265 as a freshman the year before, picking up his nickname the day he set foot on campus. The athletic department's business manager, James "Stump" Carter, happened to be walking by and stopped when he saw Gaines. He looked the big man up and down, whistled, and declared, "Man! The only thing I've ever seen bigger than you is a house." Back home in Paducah, Kentucky,

Gaines had been called "Sully," after a large boxer in the comics named Sullivan. He liked "Big House" much better. "I *was* bigger than a house," he said.

After getting roughed up by House, who was more agile than he appeared, Joe realized he had reached a different level of competition. "It was a strange and new experience for me to see an athlete who made me look and feel small," he said. "A mental adjustment was needed." College sports was going to require smarts as well as size and strength.

But he was glad that House was on *his* team—and he wasn't the only one who felt that way. Halfback Cal Irvin, whose brother, Monte, played baseball in the Negro leagues and later would star for the New York Giants, knew a hole would open wherever Gaines blocked. So great was his trust that he once told Gaines, "Clarence, if you start running down the middle of the field, I will be right behind you. If you run down the sidelines, I will be behind you. If you run up into the stands, I will be behind you."

Joe had been recruited as a running back in Morgan's potent single-wing offense. But he knew he'd never beat out Oscar Givens, the team's star at the position, so he became intrigued when he saw Talmadge Hill working with the ends and noticed there were only five players. Joe Eggleston was the only one in the group who weighed more than two hundred pounds. Mel Hurtt and Mike Hawthorne were agile and fast, but both weighed about 170. Joe had a decision to make: Did he want to remain at a "glory" position and get in a few plays while spelling the ultratalented Givens? Or did he want to gamble that his size would enable him to earn a starting spot at end?

Joe told Eddie Hurt he also had played end in high school and asked if he could try out at that position. Hurt gave his OK, but kept Joe with the backs. About a week later, though, Hurt pulled Joe aside and said he'd like him to work with the ends. As preseason practice continued, Joe saw during blocking and tackling drills that his size gave him an edge over Hurtt and Hawthorne and he would probably earn the starting job. He did—at right end, next to "Big House" Gaines at tackle. Joe also earned a nickname after teammates noticed his atrophied index fingers, the result of a lifelong defect. Teammates started calling him "Digits" because he had to extend those fingers awkwardly to catch passes. Years later, the bent finger on his right hand would have a lasting impact on his baseball career.

>>>>>>>>>>

His first Sunday on campus, Joe got up early and dressed for church. He was from a church-going family and he knew his mother would expect him to continue attending services. He walked to a Presbyterian church about three blocks from campus and as he entered the building, an usher approached.

"May I help you?" the man asked.

"Yeah," Joe said. "I'm coming to church."

"You can't come in here," the man said.

"Why not?" Joe asked.

"You're colored," the man responded.

"I know I'm colored," Joe said. "But I'm a Presbyterian. Isn't this a house of God?"

"Yes," the usher said, "but you can't come in here."

Joe was dumbfounded. The usher's words stung with the same intensity as those he had heard from that scout back in Plainfield. He wasn't allowed in a church? How could that be? "Lord," Joe thought, "why don't you come down and tell this man that I'm a child of God and I'm entitled to come into your house?" Politely, the man steered Joe to the door, directed him to a bus stop a couple of blocks away, and told him how, with a change of buses, he could get to Pennsylvania Avenue. There he would find several churches he could attend. Hurt and discouraged, Joe shuffled back to campus and didn't go to church that day. "In less than four months," he wrote, "I had been hurt deeply, because of my skin color, by the two entities that were close to my heart—Major League Baseball and America, the land that I love." That sting would only deepen.

Theaters in Baltimore were segregated. Blacks were barred from many movie houses. Joe was watching a movie in one of the black theaters on Pennsylvania Avenue, the heart of the city's black entertainment district, when he spotted a white man in the audience. He jumped out of his seat, grabbed an usher, and said, "There's a white guy in there. Why don't you put him out?" The usher then explained about whites being able to go anywhere they wanted even though blacks were restricted to their own establishments.

"What are you talking about?" Joe said. "If we can't sit in theirs, how come they can sit in ours?"

"Because that's how it is," the usher replied.

"Man, I don't understand," Joe muttered as he headed back to his seat.

When the weather turned cooler, Joe went to a department store to buy an overcoat, because he knew the raincoat he had brought with him wouldn't get him through the winter. A pleasant female clerk helped him choose one and as Joe put one arm in a sleeve, he heard a man yelling at the clerk. Then she hurried over and said, "Sir, I'm sorry, you can't try it on."

"What do you mean I can't try it on?" Joe said.

"If you want it," she said, "you have to buy it. You take it home."

"Suppose it doesn't fit," Joe said.

"You can't bring it back," she stipulated.

Joe returned the coat to the rack and left the store shaking his head. There seemed to be no end to racism's pettiness. How can you buy clothes if you can't try anything on? "I told my mother," he said. "They just sent me a coat from Jersey. That was a difficult thing for me to adjust to. I just didn't understand it."

>>>>>>>>>>

The contrast between what Joe experienced in the city and the environment he found on campus could not have been more stark. In town, he was regarded as a second-class citizen. At Morgan, he was shown that as a black person, he could take pride in his race. His self-esteem grew as a result.

At the library, his friend from the assembly guessed that Joe did not know about noted black figures like Crispus Attucks, Phillis Wheatley, Harriet Tubman, Booker T. Washington, George Washington Carver, Garrett Morgan, or Dr. Daniel Hale Williams. She was right. Joe had read about Booker T. Washington and George Washington Carver, but had not heard of the others. He would learn that Crispus Attucks was one of the first casualties in the American Revolution, shot to death in 1770 in what became known as the Boston Massacre. Phillis Wheatley, a poet in the 1700s, was the first black woman to have her work published in this country. Harriet Tubman was an escaped slave who helped escort other slaves to freedom and later spied for the Union army in the Civil War. Garrett Morgan was an inventor who developed a safety hood and smoke protector similar to the modern gas mask, and Daniel Hale Williams was a cardiologist credited with performing the first successful open-heart surgery, in 1893.

Remarkable, Joe thought. Why didn't he read about those accomplishments in US history class? Because, his friend explained, schools in the North were white-oriented and never bothered to teach that blacks did more than pick cotton. "Blacks truly had made contributions to science, medicine and literature," Joe would write many years later. "Was this why some whites tried so hard to portray blacks as uneducated monkeys? Was it out of fear? Were they being threatened?"

At the same time, Joe's Morgan education gave him a foundation to believe that "I was somebody." He no longer wished he was white. God had given him a mind for thinking and working, Joe reasoned. It was up to him to use it. He recalled a passage from Isaiah 40:30–31:

> Even youths grow tired and weary, and young men stumble and fall, but those who hope in the Lord will renew their strength. They will soar on wings like eagles; they will run and not grow weary, they will walk and not be faint.

Joe got mixed results from his classroom work. He flunked history, complaining that he found the class boring because the professor lectured in a monotone voice. He couldn't follow the lecture or find what the professor was talking about in the textbook. Later, Joe retook the class and passed. On the other hand, he soaked up everything in his health education class, taught by Talmadge Hill. Hill lectured with a flair that kept his students rapt. Few cut his class. Hill's students called him "Gov"—short for Governor—because they appreciated his elegant attire in the classroom. Joe thought Hill had such an extensive wardrobe that he could change suits twice a day. "I'd sit in classes, stare at him and silently wish that one day I could stand before an audience and articulate like Gov," Joe said.

Joe had a ways to go at that point. He was getting a "C" in speech, because he froze when he had to stand in front of the class and talk. Traits from his New Jersey upbringing still slipped through when he'd say "Youse guys" or "Whatcha gonna do?" Somewhere along the line, though, the inspiration sparked by Hill's classroom lectures took hold.

When the university dedicated the Talmadge L. Hill Field House in 1974, the keynote speaker was Joe Black. Hill thanked Joe for his remarks that day in a letter, which Joe framed and hung in his home. "On Dedication Day, October 25, you provided for me the greatest thrill of my life," Hill wrote. "I was completely overwhelmed by your articulate and soul-stirring dedicatory address."

>>>>>>>>>>

Because of World War II and its manpower demands, fielding a football team was challenging for schools like Morgan State and others in the CIAA. They were already operating on tight budgets. With the war going on, they often had to make do with trimmed-down rosters. When Hurt sat down to plan out the 1942 season, he had two open dates on his schedule and no idea how many players he'd have. Some who had been eligible to return were in the service or working in civilian defense-related jobs. Other key players had graduated. His concerns intensified when only six veterans reported for the first practice in early September. Fortunately for the Bears, one of those returning players was Oscar Givens, a legitimate triple-threat back. He was the team's best passer; he had ripped off several long gainers the previous season on his plunges into the line, and he could kick. He was only nineteen years old, too young to be drafted at that point, though with the demand for soldiers increasing, the minimum age was lowered from twenty-one to eighteen in November of that year.

End Joe Eggleston and guard Preston Grimsley, who would both become starters, also returned, as did back Carstell Stewart. "Big House" Gaines showed up a few days after practice started, much to Hurt's relief, and Joe came in as part of a freshman class that included promising players like Carl Chavis and Frederick Burgess. By mid-September, Hurt had twenty-eight players in camp. More arrived when school opened September 21. The Bears would be competitive after all, and the school said it was determined to complete its full eight-game schedule.

Elsewhere in the CIAA, North Carolina A&T had forty-two players for its first practice, but most were freshmen. Lincoln University in Oxford, Pennsylvania, had just ten lettermen at early practices. With only seven returning lettermen, Bluefield in West Virginia would have to rely heavily on newcomers. Shaw University in Raleigh, North Carolina, at first canceled three games, then terminated its season in October after four of its nineteen players were drafted into the armed forces. St. Paul Polytechnic Institute in Lawrenceville, Virginia, called off its entire season, as did St. Augustine in Raleigh, North Carolina, and Cheyney in Pennsylvania. Lincoln ended up canceling five games. In contrast, Howard University in Washington, DC, seemed well stocked with thirty-three players in camp, including sixteen returnees.

Adding to the complications were wartime travel restrictions. Teams were not allowed to charter buses or trains and they were told they wouldn't receive any extra gasoline for private cars. With that in mind, administrators from CIAA schools agreed that a school could cancel a game on one day's notice if it couldn't arrange transportation to the game site.

Hurt never did find an opponent for his team's September 26 opening game, and he wasn't alone in failing to fill open dates. By late September, CIAA teams already had canceled twelve games during a two-week period. Hurt did find an opponent for October 3, however. The Bears opened their season that day against the Aberdeen Commandos, a team from the Quartermaster Detachment at the Aberdeen Proving Grounds northeast of Baltimore. Such military teams, often made up of former college players, would fill the schedules of many colleges and universities during the war years.

While scrimmaging had been held to a minimum during preseason drills because the Bears were low on numbers, Joe and his teammates had grown tired of practice and were eager for the opener. They could have been scheduled to play a high-school team or the Washington Redskins and it wouldn't have mattered. They just wanted to hit someone from another team. As Joe warmed up on that Saturday afternoon, he looked up at the stands and remarked, "Everybody here is colored."

"Well," a teammate noted, "what did you expect?" The teammate didn't realize that this was the first time Joe was playing in an all-black setting.

It wasn't much of a game. While Aberdeen had its share of ex-collegians, they were no match for the quick, well-schooled Morgan eleven. The Bears piled up 499 yards of offense, all on the ground, and romped to a score of 94–0. Givens scored five touchdowns and Stewart added three, including a 59-yard scamper. Morgan scored 28 points in the first quarter and piled it on with 40 in the final period.

Joe, however, was unhappy with his play. He didn't think he was as aggressive as the college game required. Of the few yards the military team managed to gain, most came around Joe's end. Talmadge Hill also saw that Joe needed to play with more fire, so he came up with a ploy in practice the following week to bring that out. During a scrimmage, with Joe on defense, Hill told the offense in the huddle that the "Bear" from Plainfield was bragging that no one was going to run around his end. Naturally, they ran the next few plays right at Joe. After a pulling guard knocked him on his keister a few times, Joe got riled, figured out how to play off the blocks, and started tackling the ball carrier. Hill grinned, clapping his hands and exclaiming, "Big Joe has arrived. He wants some bear meat."

Eddie Hurt expected a tougher game the next Saturday at Virginia Union, traditionally a difficult foe for Morgan State. The Panthers did put up a better fight than the military team, but Morgan still won handily, 33–7, on a pleasant afternoon in Richmond, Virginia. Five different players scored touchdowns for the Bears and Joe had a hand in one, catching a pass from Givens and then lateraling to Mitch Whittingham, who scampered the remaining sixteen yards to the end zone.

The first two games set the tone for another big season at Morgan State. With Joe starting every game, the Bears went 6-1-1, the only blemishes being a 6–6 tie with Bluefield and a 6–0 loss to Johnson C. Smith. The Bears had made the trip to Bluefield by train, leaving at 6:25 AM on Thursday, two days before the game, and arriving late that night after a fifteen-hour trip. Hurt was able to obtain only twenty-eight train tickets, so the Bears were a bit shorthanded. They also might have been overconfident. They were the highest-scoring team in the country and had outscored their first three opponents 169–7. But they managed only 166 yards against the fired-up Big Blues, who earned the tie with a touchdown pass in the final seconds. The Bears avoided a loss only because Bluefield missed the extra point kick.

Hurt also had to improvise when the team traveled to Oxford, Pennsylvania, to play Lincoln in mid-October. He bought tickets on the regularly scheduled bus that ran through Oxford, which was about halfway between Baltimore and Philadelphia on US Highway 1. That was the main highway running along the Eastern Seaboard, from the northern tip of Maine to Key West. The thirty-five players on the trip had to scramble for seats, but the journey must not have been too taxing. Morgan blocked two punts before the game was five minutes old and routed the Lions 42–0. Joe fell on the second blocked punt at the Lincoln ten-yard line, setting up Givens's pass to Whittingham for the Bears' first touchdown.

Even with a loss and a tie on its record, Morgan State remained in contention for another CIAA championship, keeping its title hopes alive with a 24–3 victory over Hampton on November 14, a game that drew four thousand fans to Morgan Stadium in near-zero-degree weather. Joe stormed through the Hampton line to block a punt and fell on the ball to set up his team's second touchdown. Virginia State beat North Carolina A&T that same day, meaning Morgan's annual Thanksgiving Day game with Virginia State in Petersburg, Virginia, would decide the championship.

There was concern on the Morgan side, because Givens, the key to the Bears' offense, had missed two games with a shoulder injury. They got along without him in those games, but they would need him in Petersburg. The time out must have been just what he needed, because Art Carter wrote in the *Afro-American*, Baltimore's black newspaper, that Givens's passes "hit the mark with the accuracy of a circus knife-thrower" and Morgan State won 30–0. Despite gas rationing, overcrowded trains, and war work, seventy-five hundred fans made their way to the game and saw Givens complete nine of twelve passes for 169 yards and three touchdowns. Joe joined the scoring parade when he caught a ten-yard TD pass from Whittingham, who had returned a punt seventy-five yards for a touchdown just ninety seconds into the game. The Bears were CIAA champs again, and Joe could bask in the satisfaction of knowing that he had played a role in making it happen.

The big victory made for a pleasant train ride back to Baltimore, but Joe and some of his teammates soon began thinking about another sport. Just as they had done in high school, several Morgan football players moved smoothly from the gridiron to the hardwood. The basketball season opened with the same uncertainty that Eddie Hurt had felt back in September as football practice got underway. The wartime ban on pleasure driving complicated the task of getting to road games. There was a chance one or more of his players would get drafted. Even home games presented a challenge, because the team played off campus at the New Albert Auditorium. Students couldn't drive to the games and the school wasn't allowed to charter buses to take them, so they had to use public transportation. Coaches could drive players to the arena in their cars because that was considered occupational use, but players could not drive their own cars to games—if they even had a car—because they were amateurs. Another concern: three-fourths of the players were in the Enlisted Reserve Corps, subjecting them to almost immediate call to the military. Four of the previous season's top players already were in the army, another had graduated, and two others did not return to school. "We will try to do what we can," Hurt said in mid-January. "If things get too bad, we may have to call a halt, but we will carry on as long as we can."

The Bears could put plenty of talent on the floor. Givens was nearly as accomplished on the court as he was on the gridiron and was named the team's captain. Givens and Cal Irvin started at forward. Joe Eggleston, a second-team all-CIAA selection in football, played center, with Bob Smith and Aubrey Woods at guard. Joe and "Big House" were subs, brought in to give the starters a blow and to bang around under the basket for rebounds. Basketball wasn't Joe's best sport and he knew it. He thought the coaches were kind just to include him on the team.

North Carolina College dominated CIAA basketball in the 1940s under Coach John B. McLendon. The NCC coach had learned the game from its inventor, Dr. James Naismith, while an undergraduate at Kansas University in the 1930s, though he was not allowed to play for the Jayhawks because the team was segregated. McLendon is credited with helping to speed up the game by playing an up-tempo style, and in 1979 he followed his mentor into the Basketball Hall of Fame. During the early 1940s, NCC had a burly inside player named John Brown, but the team relied mainly on its quickness. "We used to refer to them as Big John Brown and the four track stars," Joe said. "They executed fast breaks like Jesse Owens running the 100-yard dash."

Even with McLendon's juggernaut to contend with, Morgan led the CIAA standings as the calendar turned to March. Then Hurt's worst fears were realized. Seven players were summoned for active army duty on March 2, including Oscar Givens, Joe Eggleston, and Aubrey Woods.

Of the thirty Morgan students called up that day, twenty-one were football players, meaning Hurt would have to scramble to field a team in the fall. The call-ups left the basketball team with only six original players—Joe, Cal Irvin, "Big House," Boo Brown, Hayes Allen, and Bob Smith, who was to report after the Bears played their final game. Morgan State's pared-down squad lost that game 41–33 to Johnson C. Smith.

>>>>>>>>>>

With basketball season over and Morgan State having no baseball team, Joe looked forward to a leisurely spring of hanging out on campus and watching the women stroll by. Eddie Hurt thought otherwise. One day, as Joe put on his Mr. Cool act to try to impress a female student, Hurt pulled him aside and told him to report to the track at three o'clock. Puzzled why Hurt would want him on the track team, Joe nevertheless showed up at the appointed time. Hurt explained that because so many Morgan men had gone off to war, he needed bodies and Joe's was as good as any. Joe remained reluctant, because he saw no point in training to run. "It was always my belief," he said, "that only fools and mules would run around a quarter-of-a-mile track ten or fifteen times a day and then run a race of 100 or 200 yards." So Joe tried to talk his way out of joining the team, telling Hurt he had never run in a formal track meet. No matter, Hurt responded. He'd watch Joe for a couple of days and then decide which events would suit him.

Hurt thought that because of Joe's size, he could be competitive in the weights. But he was a bust. His best effort in the shot put covered a mere thirty-five feet, more than nine feet short of the CIAA record at the time. He could hold his own in the javelin and discus, but he was afraid of hurting his arm so he asked to try other events. In April 1943, Joe wrote his mother to tell her he was doing fine and oh, by the way, he was a high jumper and hurdler on the track team.

Joe jumped using the western roll, in which the jumper planted his foot, kicked the other leg up and—hopefully—rolled over the bar. Some form of this approach was the preferred method of jumping until Dick Fosbury revolutionized the event with his backward Fosbury Flop in the late 1960s. Joe could clear six foot four inches, which he thought was a pretty good jump, just a half-inch shy of the CIAA record at the time. He was competitive in intramural and some varsity meets and was feeling OK about himself—until Morgan State faced the team from Camp Lee, Virginia. Camp Lee had two jumpers, Josh Williamson and Don Barksdale, who "quickly made me realize I was in the wrong sport," Joe said.

While Joe strained to clear six feet, Williamson and Barksdale were passing. When the bar got to six foot four, both took their first jumps and they cleared the height easily. "Their clearing the bar didn't intimidate me," Joe reflected years later, "but the fact that they were still wearing their sweat suits while making the jump really humbled me." Joe needn't have felt that way. All Williamson did in his athletic career was win five US high jump championships. Barksdale twice placed among the top six in the high jump nationals, won the "hop, skip, and jump" (now called the triple jump) at the 1944 national championships, and was the first black to play on the US Olympic basketball team, winning a gold medal in the 1948 London Games. He's in the UCLA Hall of Fame along with such luminaries as Jackie Robinson, Kareem Abdul-Jabbar, Bill Walton, Walt Hazzard, John Wooden, Gary Beban, Arthur Ashe, and Evelyn Ashford.

Joe was a decent hurdler, though he never won a race. His main hang-up in the high hurdles was that he was afraid of tripping over a hurdle and falling on his face, so he jumped rather than stretched over the hurdles. In the lows, he'd clip along at a fast pace until the last hurdle. Then, for some reason, he'd jump instead of stepping over it and invariably, another runner would pass him. Joe wasn't disappointed when track season ended and, as it turned out, he never would have to worry about being asked to join the track team again. The US Army called in the summer of 1943 and Joe joined the ranks of the other Morgan State athletes serving their country. By the time he returned to school in 1946, all the other ex-GIs were back and Eddie Hurt had plenty of able-bodied veterans to fill his track squad. Joe did rejoin the football team, however, and it became a season to remember.

The world was at peace, the nation was on the verge of a postwar boom, and Jackie Robinson was completing his groundbreaking season with the Montreal Royals when the Morgan State Bears assembled to begin practicing for the 1946 season. And they were loaded. Joe, who had spent the summer pitching for the Baltimore Elite Giants, was among twenty players from previous years who had returned to Morgan after their college careers were interrupted by military duty. Eight had earned all-CIAA honors between 1940 and 1943, including stalwarts like Oscar Givens, Unk Campbell, Mitch Whittingham, Flan Couch, and Joe Eggleston. Because of their time in the military, these men were older than your average college student. Joe, for example, was a twenty-two-year-old sophomore.

Eddie Hurt rarely allowed himself to get too excited about an upcoming season, because he knew there was always a chance to be disappointed. But even he had to be thrilled over the talent on his first postwar team.

Morgan State had managed to continue its winning ways during the war years, going 5-0 in 1943, 6-1 in 1944, and 5-2 in 1945. The Bears won the CIAA championship in both 1943 and '44. With many players also back from the 1945 team, Hurt had a dilemma: should he play the younger guys who had helped fashion a winning record the year before or go with the veterans who had done so well before going off to war? He decided to resolve the question with a scrimmage, old guys versus the younger ones. Givens, Campbell, Whittingham, and Big Jim Turpin carried the ball for the veterans. Terry Day, Art Berry, J. C. Nelson, and Don Johnson led the 1945 lettermen. The two teams mostly slugged it out between the twenty-five-yard lines, the thud of leather against leather accompanied by grunts, groans, and teammates yelling encouragement. Joe felt that after sixty minutes, each side had earned new respect from the other. Some of the older guys became starters and so did some of the younger players.

All the military veterans rejoining the team created another problem for Hurt. Eighty-four players in all came out for football, but the school had uniforms for only fifty. Often during practice, a player had to undress on the field and give his equipment to a teammate so that player would have a chance to scrimmage. Others never even got a chance to scrimmage. After dealing with personnel shortages throughout the war years, Morgan suddenly had too much of a good thing.

The only newcomer who cracked the lineup was Al Gilbert, who played right tackle next to end Joe Black. While playing defense, Joe developed a special fondness for his teammates on the right side: Gilbert, Flan Couch or Tom Kelson at linebacker, and Mitch Whittingham at safety. He said they functioned as a unit and gave the offense different looks by changing positions. Joe remembered opponents scoring only one rushing touchdown against the right side of the defense during his two-plus years on the team.

Morgan State's entire defense rarely gave up a touchdown in 1946, running or passing. The Bears rolled to an 8-0 record that included four shutouts. Only once, in a 13–12 victory over West Virginia State, did an opponent score more than one touchdown, and the *Afro-American* insisted one of those scores was tainted. According to the newspaper, the game film showed Virginia State quarterback Linwood Greene put his knee on the ground while picking the ball up before throwing a touchdown pass and thus should have been ruled down at that point. That same film, the newspaper said, also showed Joe should have been credited with a touchdown reception on a pass the officials ruled incomplete after declaring he was out of the end zone. It was a bitterly contested game and two players from each side were ejected. Though the two schools had met only once before, in 1945, hard feelings were festering and three days after the game, West Virginia State severed football relations with Morgan State.

One of Morgan's victories was a 35–0 rout of Grambling a week after the West Virginia State game. Joe and his teammates had kidded Hurt about scheduling that game, because at the time Grambling was nothing more than a small, little-known school from Louisiana. That eventually would change, of course. In 1946, Eddie Robinson was still in the early stages of a fifty-seven-year coaching career during which he'd win 408 games and send more than two hundred players to the National Football League. Robinson's star then was Paul Younger, a powerful running back who was known to Joe as "Mr. Big" but later became better known as "Tank." Younger had scored twenty-three touchdowns as a seventeen-year-old freshman in 1945, and while he broke loose for an eighty-six-yard run against Morgan, the Bears managed to drag the six-foot-two 209-pounder down before he reached the end zone. Younger would become the first athlete from a historically black college to play in the NFL and was good enough to earn selection to the Pro Bowl four times.

Morgan kept winning despite a slew of injuries. Halfback Terry Day, a two-time all-CIAA selection, got hurt in the opener and missed most of the season. Bert Coppock went out with an injury in the West Virginia State game. Mitch Whittingham broke his leg against North Carolina A&T on November 2 and George Watkins suffered a chest injury in that game. Art Fauntleroy, Jim Turpin, and Mel Hurtt also missed time because of injuries. The Bears survived because of their depth, and they closed the season with a 6–0 victory at Virginia State on Thanksgiving Day to secure another CIAA championship. The *Pittsburgh Courier* later declared Morgan State and Tennessee State, which went 10-0, conational champions of black college football.

>>>>>>>>>>

My father's experience at Morgan State was a major factor in deciding where I would go to college. When we started to talk about which colleges might interest me, he said, "Here," and then put a piece of paper on the table. "Here are all the black colleges," he said. "Pick one." He thought I needed the experience of living in a predominantly African American environment. He felt there was no better way to learn about our history and culture, just as he had done at Morgan State.

We lived in Phoenix, Arizona, which was like a big suburb then. Our neighborhood was all Caucasian. I didn't have an African American friend until I met Charisse in the fourth grade, when I switched from private to public school. I didn't know about the black national anthem, "Lift Every Voice and Sing." There was no gospel music at our Presbyterian church. My father believed I needed to be around more African Americans so I could embrace my culture, more than what I would get just going to New Jersey every summer and spending time with my family.

My dad mentioned that Ennis Cosby, Bill Cosby's son, was going to Morehouse in Atlanta. My father and Bill Cosby had been friends for years and I knew Ennis, so I said I would attend a college in Atlanta. Morehouse was a men's college; I attended Spelman, the women's college across the street. I was amazed to see so many African Americans at the same time. It was all new for me, because it was unlike what I had experienced growing up.

>>>>>>>>>>

That was Joe's last full season as a college athlete. He reported for Morgan State's 1947 football season, again after pitching for the Elite Giants during the spring and summer, and reclaimed his starting job at right end. Whittingham, Fauntleroy, and Turpin also were back, but Eddie

Hurt faced the challenge of replacing many of his previous stars, including Oscar Givens, Joe Eggleston, Unk Campbell, Terry Day, and Flan Couch. Joe continued to pitch for the Elites during the Bears' preseason camp, twice pitching the Negro league club to victories over an all-star team that included several members of the Baltimore Orioles.

Morgan State opened the season with a 31–0 thrashing of Delaware State, Joe setting up the first touchdown with a thirteen-yard reception. The next day, he pitched the Elite Giants to an 8–7 victory over the International League all-stars. The Bears went to New York City the following weekend to play North Carolina College at the Polo Grounds, the site of dozens of college football games through its history. Morgan State won 19–6 and the *Afro-American* singled Joe out for his stellar play on defense. But Joe got kicked in the head during the game, and afterward he began questioning whether he wanted to keep playing college football. He was establishing himself as a solid pitcher with the Elite Giants. If he was to have a future in sports, it would be on the diamond, not the gridiron. To Joe, the ringing in his head was a warning that he "had no business getting his brains kicked out just for the fun of it." He left school not long after that and accepted an offer of $800 a month plus round-trip transportation to pitch in Venezuela.

Joe was still a long way from graduating, and he knew his mother would be devastated if he didn't finish. So Joe kept returning to Morgan on breaks from baseball until he earned his degree in 1950, nearly eight full years after enrolling. But Joe was enriched with a lifetime of experiences during those years. He had been steeled by the rigors of playing in the Negro leagues. He learned to adapt to foreign cultures while pitching in Latin America. His teachers and fellow students at Morgan State had taught him that as a black man, he had reason to be proud. And the degree he earned would, in the end, become as useful as his strong right arm.

Maybe even more so.

5

A Dodger at Last

April–May 1952

JOE WAS SO EXHILARATED WITH THE news that he had been added to the Brooklyn Dodgers roster that he never heard manager Charlie Dressen discuss his pay. Dressen explained that while the Major League minimum salary was $5,000, the team always paid more than that. Joe just smiled and signed his first Major League contract—for $6,000. "I thought I was rich," he said. "It made me feel good." He and his wife, Doris, who was seven months pregnant, then took a bus to Plainfield, though Joe probably could have walked there on air. Even with that contract, Joe felt there was a chance he could be sent down at any time, so he and Doris put off looking for a place in Brooklyn and decided to stay with Joe's parents until he was sure he'd stick.

Joe felt he had not pitched up to his ability in the spring, in part because he'd had a sore arm for several days. He thought it could have been that his arm was simply worn out. He had pitched 170 innings in Triple-A ball the previous summer, then gone right to Cuba, where he had thrown another 163 innings during the winter season. Joe never told anyone about the soreness until after it had cleared up. He particularly wanted to keep quiet about his arm trouble in front of Dressen and the other coaches. If Dressen had known, Joe thought, "he wouldn't pitch me, and I wanted to pitch."

Once in Plainfield, Joe was eager to tell his parents that he had made the team. The news had already been published in the paper, but that didn't diminish the moment for Joe. Seeing Martha Black's joy was even better than knowing how much money he was making. He had always been "Sonny" to her and still was. Joe was just as excited to tell his father, but Joseph Black had not yet returned home from his job as a taxi driver. By the time he did, Joe and Doris, exhausted by the day's events, were asleep.

His father left again early the next morning, before Joe could share his news. He wanted to deliver the good word personally, so he walked to a nearby pool hall to wait until his father returned from a run. As he waited, he overheard some men talking. One was saying he doubted Joe would stick with the Dodgers and figured he'd be shipped to Montreal. Then Joe heard something that really stung. "Y'all know Sonny Black ain't good enough to play for the Dodgers," a man said. "Heck, he had trouble winning games at Cedar Brook Park."

Joe couldn't believe it. Those same guys had patted him on the back and encouraged him years before when he pitched for the Plainfield Black Yankees. To hear them put him down like that, it was all he could do to keep from storming into the room and berating them for their hypocrisy. Yet Joe himself wasn't sure he'd stick, and that's why he was in Plainfield, after all. He fought back his urge and stepped outside to wait for his father, who was elated when Joe delivered the news. He also had some advice. "Sonny," his father said, "you got to fool those big hitters like Willie Mays and Stan Musial. They can hit those fastballs. Fool them with an in-shot or drop." Joe didn't have the heart to tell his father those pitches wouldn't work. Instead, he promised he would use them when he finally got a chance to pitch. His father smiled and was happy, which is all Joe had wanted to see.

Jim Gilliam, Joe's good friend, did not make the big club in 1952. The Dodgers were set with Jackie at second base and Billy Cox at third, and they had depth with utility infielders Bobby Morgan and Rocky Bridges. Gilliam returned to Montreal, where he would have another big year, batting .301, driving in 112 runs, scoring 111 runs, lashing 39 doubles, and drawing 100 walks. Those numbers would result in a promotion to Brooklyn in 1953, reuniting Gilliam with his friend.

>>>>>>>>>>

The Dodgers opened the 1952 season against the Braves in Boston, and they put a formidable everyday lineup on the field. Campanella, Hodges, Robinson, Reese, Cox, Pafko, Snider, and Furillo were as good a combination as any in baseball, a fine mix of power, speed, ability to get on base, defense, and strong arms. The question at that point was a pitching staff minus one Don Newcombe. But if it held up, the Dodgers certainly had a chance to win the National League pennant that had barely eluded them the year before. Journalist Joseph M. Sheehan for one was confident in the mound corps, writing in the *New York Times* that the Dodgers had "almost an embarrassment of pitching talent." Others, like *Times* columnist Arthur Daley, weren't so sure. Daley picked the Philadelphia Phillies to win the NL crown, on the strength of twenty-one-game winner Robin Roberts anchoring the pitching staff and pitcher Curt Simmons returning from military duty. "If this be treason," he wrote, "make the most of it." The New York Giants, a Dodger fan's favorite team to hate, were strong again, though the Polo Grounders suffered one grievous loss before the season started and soon would incur another.

As the Dodgers made their way north with the Boston Braves, the Giants were playing the Cleveland Indians in Denver on April 2 when star outfielder Monte Irvin broke his right ankle sliding into third base. Irvin had gone from first to third on a single by Willie Mays and, in the end, he didn't even need to slide, because shortstop Ray Boone cut off the throw from the outfield. Angry Giants fans felt third baseman Al Rosen had tricked Irvin into sliding by pretending he was taking a throw. "When my ankle popped, you could hear it all over the stands," Irvin recalled. "Everybody said it made a terrible noise. I can't remember it popping, but I know it sure hurt." Irvin's injury was a serious setback for the Giants, losing a player who had batted .312 the year before, led the league with 121 RBIs, and hit .458 in the World Series against the New York Yankees. Looking back on the play, Joe King of the *New York World-Telegram* noted that "no scene throughout the season was as grim and costly to the Giants as the slide Irvin didn't have to make in a game he didn't have to win." It would only get worse for the Giants. Mays, the team's fleet center fielder and NL Rookie of the Year in 1951, would be called to active duty in the army in May. That one-two punch to the Giants would be a huge boost for the Dodgers in their pennant hopes.

Joe knew he'd be pitching out of the bullpen, so he'd have to wait for a starter to falter or tire before he'd get his chance. He had confidently told Dressen after signing his contract that he would win for the Dodgers. In fact, he thought he could win twelve games. Dodgers vice president Fresco Thompson certainly didn't share Joe's confidence. He didn't think Joe could win more than half a dozen games. "His curve doesn't break more than three, four inches and 20 men in the league are faster," Thompson said. "We have three ourselves—Loes, Wade and [Ray] Moore."

For the longest time, Joe had to wonder if he'd win even one game. The Dodgers got off to a sizzling start, winning eight of their first nine games, and Joe languished on the bullpen bench. Preacher Roe went the distance three times in that stretch, beating the Braves twice and the St. Louis Cardinals once. When Roe was on like that, he frustrated batters by incessantly nibbling at the corners of the plate. Upon hearing Roe was pitching, Campy would say, "Well, they can cut the middle out of the plate and throw it away. Ol' Preach ain't gonna use it."

Left-hander Johnny Schmitz also beat the Braves in a complete game, Ralph Branca did the same against the Giants, and Chris Van Cuyk tossed a seven-hitter in a 2–1 win over the Braves. Clyde King and Ben Wade relieved Van Cuyk in another win over Boston, while Carl Erskine and Billy Loes finished after Clem Labine failed to retire anyone in a comeback victory over the Giants in twelve innings. In a 6–0 loss to the Giants, Loes relieved Wade. When the Cardinals pounded the Dodgers 14–2, Dressen called on Erskine, Bud Podbielan, and Johnny Rutherford to try to stem the tide after he lifted Van Cuyk in the first inning. Two weeks in and Joe still had not thrown a pitch in a game. He began to wonder if he'd be looking for a place to live in Montreal instead of Brooklyn. "I didn't feel I was part of the team," he said. "I referred to the other players as 'you fellows,' never as 'us.' I didn't even autograph baseballs the club gives away to hospitals and sick kids because I didn't think my name belonged on them."

Joe's only contribution had been shagging flies in warmups, playing pepper, and pitching batting practice to stay loose. And he eventually got fired as batting practice pitcher, which he couldn't understand.

"I throw the ball over the plate," he told Jake Pitler, one of the team's coaches.

"That's the trouble," Pitler shot back. "We're losing too many damn balls in the stands."

It seemed Joe's pitches were just a little too fat. When payday came around, Joe felt embarrassed to take his check.

>>>>>>>>>>

April 1952 may have been a washout for Joe Black, but May brought opportunity. A Ladies Day crowd of 25,588 turned out at Chicago's Wrigley Field on Thursday, May 1, to watch the hometown Cubs play the Dodgers. They liked what they saw. The Cubs roughed up Dodgers starter Ralph Branca for eight hits and five runs in three and two-thirds innings. Johnny Schmitz relieved in the fourth inning and gave up two more runs while pitching through the sixth. The Dodgers trailed 7–0 and were doing nothing against Cubs pitcher Johnny Klippstein. At that point, Dressen had used eleven different pitchers. To start the seventh inning, he summoned his twelfth arm. He called on Joe.

Joe's appearance probably didn't create much buzz. There might have been a handful of fans who remembered seeing something about Joe being compared to Newcombe, and some might have been intrigued when they saw a strapping black player striding to the mound. That would have been understandable, because the Dodgers, Giants, and Braves were the only teams in the National League that had black players then. The Cubs wouldn't have a black player until Ernie Banks and Gene Baker joined the team in September 1953. Most fans, though, probably weren't paying much attention. Why should they? The game was all but over and folks started thinking about what they wanted to do after the game. Joe was just another guy coming in from the bullpen to mop up a lost cause for the Dodgers.

Was it fate or just an incredible coincidence that Dressen tapped Joe at that moment? Because the very first batter Joe faced in his first real Major League game was Hank Sauer, the slugging outfielder who that fall would edge Joe in a controversial vote for the National League's Most Valuable Player Award. Sauer had come up with the bases loaded in the first inning and cleared them with a double. But he did no damage against Joe, who struck him out looking. Joe then retired Randy Jackson on a called third strike and got Toby Atwell on a grounder to Jackie at second. Joe had set the Cubs down one-two-three and that was his day. With the pitcher's spot due up in the top of the eighth, Dressen lifted Joe for pinch hitter George Shuba. Joe would complete many more innings like that in 1952, but no one—not Dressen, not Joe, not the writers, not the fans—could have foreseen it on May 1. Joe simply had done his job and that was that.

It did not, however, earn him a regular spot in Dressen's thinking. Over the next six games, five of them victories, Dressen went to his bullpen only four times, summoning Loes and Rutherford twice each. At that point, the pitching had held up better than anyone could have hoped. Good thing, too, because while the Dodgers got off to a great start at 13-4, the Giants stood only a half game behind at 13-5. Joe still didn't feel he was earning his keep, but at least he had signed on with a winner. On May 10, however, the Dodgers dropped a doubleheader to the Philadelphia Phillies and fell into second place, one and a half games behind the Giants. Joe relieved in the seventh inning of the opener and finished the game, giving up three hits but no runs. He did his part by giving his team a chance, but Phillies pitcher Karl Drews had quieted the Brooklyn bats all day and he finished with a two-hitter in a 4–0 victory.

For Joe, that game was significant for a couple of reasons. He had shown he could hold up in a moderately long relief stint and it was his first big-league appearance at Ebbets Field, the quirky, intimate ballpark the Dodgers called home. Opened in 1913 on what essentially had been a garbage dump and tucked into a city block in Brooklyn's Flatbush section, it was a cozy place that put fans near enough to the field that they felt they were part of the action. "You were so close to the field, sitting anywhere in that old park, that you could hear the players talking to each other," said Red Patterson, a former Dodgers vice president. That intimacy created a closeness between ballclub and fans unmatched in any other Major League city. "They loved us and we loved them," Duke Snider once said. "It was very special."

Some of the ballpark's denizens became as well known as the players. Hilda Chester rang her cowbell from the bleachers. The often musically challenged Dodger Sym-Phony—a band that had a trumpet, trombone, cymbals, bass drum, and snare drum—roamed the stands. The ballpark's organist, Gladys Goodding, became so renowned that she was inducted into the Brooklyn Dodgers Hall of Fame in 1995, the same year Joe went in. It was a decidedly hitter-friendly park, measuring 343 feet from home plate to the left-field wall, 384 to center, and only 297 to right, though the right-field wall was nineteen feet tall and was topped by a nineteen-foot-high fence, which kept numerous balls in play. Then there was the massive scoreboard, which jutted out five feet from the wall at a forty-five-degree angle. A neon SCHAEFER BEER sign rose from the top of the scoreboard and told fans how a play was scored—the "h" lighting up for a hit and an "e" lighting up for an error.

"Ebbets Field was a difficult park to pitch in, and I'm sure any pitcher who pitched there had earned run average problems that he might not have had in another park," said Carl Erskine, who won 122 games in twelve seasons with the Dodgers in Brooklyn and Los Angeles. But in his case, Erskine said, the team on the field behind him offset any handicap from pitching in the bandbox park, because "we had a team that could take better advantage of Ebbets Field than anybody who came in." Long after his career had ended, Johnny Rutherford said the Hall of Fame should have a special wing for pitchers who fared well at Ebbets Field, because even the weakest hitters could knock the ball out of the park.

There was little parking in the area, so most fans walked, took the bus, or rode the subway to games. Jerry Reinsdorf didn't have much money when he was growing up in Brooklyn, but the future chairman of the Chicago Bulls and Chicago White Sox could see a Brooklyn Dodgers game on the cheap. He spent a nickel taking the subway to the ballpark, bought a general admission ticket for $1.25, then walked the mile and a half home after the game. Reinsdorf loved the Dodgers, but didn't recall any sentimentality over Ebbets Field at the time. "I don't think anyone thought Ebbets Field was a great ballpark," he said. "It was tiny. It was a bandbox. We didn't think of it as a shrine when they were playing there. It became a shrine after they left." It certainly was shrine-like for Rutherford. "There was, and is, no baseball stadium like it," he said. "The best place in the world for a ballgame."

>>>>>>>>>>

The Dodgers rebounded from the doubleheader loss to the Phillies to win three of four before Joe pitched again. That came May 16, 1952, against the Pittsburgh Pirates at Ebbets Field, and it was his first chance to pitch in a tight situation. The Bucs scored three times off Erskine in the second inning and had a runner on first when Dressen brought Joe in to try to calm the storm. He succeeded, but only after giving up a double and a sacrifice fly that produced another run, leaving the Dodgers trailing 4–0. Dressen lifted Joe for a pinch hitter in the bottom of the second and the Dodgers rallied to win 6–4. That was the Dodgers' twenty-fourth game and Joe had appeared in only three. His totals: four and two-thirds innings, four hits, no runs, three strikeouts, and a walk—not bad, but hardly the kind of numbers that would draw much attention. And he certainly didn't have to worry about being overworked. All he could do was deliver when called on and hope that would spur Dressen to call on him some more.

His next chance came six days later, against the visiting Cincinnati Reds. The Dodgers went in with a five-game winning streak, including a 19–1 blowout of the Reds the night before, but they led the Giants by only half a game. They had to keep winning to keep those pesky New Yorkers at bay, but the streak looked to be in danger when the Reds scored three times off Rutherford and Erskine in the seventh inning to take a 7–3 lead. The Dodgers got a run back in the bottom of the seventh, and when Erskine was lifted for a pinch hitter that inning, Dressen needed another pitcher. He sent Joe out in the top of the eighth and, looking like the pitcher who would in time become a dominant force out of the bullpen, he shut the visitors down. Joe set the Reds down in order in the eighth, striking out Roy McMillan, retiring pitcher Frank Hiller on a grounder to Pee Wee Reese, and fanning Grady Hatton.

His quick work in dispatching the Reds must have ignited a spark in the Dodgers dugout, because their bats came alive. Pee Wee and Jackie singled and Campy, who had missed the previous three games because of a bruised thumb, belted a home run to tie it and chase Hiller. Andy Pafko greeted reliever Frank Smith with a double, took third on Duke Snider's sacrifice bunt (even future Hall of Fame sluggers had to know how to bunt in 1952), and scored on a fly ball to left by Gil Hodges, putting the Dodgers up 8–7. Joe struck out to end the inning, then went to the mound in the ninth to try to protect the lead his teammates had handed him.

He did just that. He fanned Bobby Adams and got the dangerous Ted Kluszewski on a fly ball to Snider in center. Johnny Wyrostek then nicked Joe for a single, bringing Bob Borkowski to the plate as the potential winning run. Borkowski was a good enough hitter that a pitcher had to bear down to get him out and Joe did, retiring him on a grounder to Gil Hodges at first base. The Dodgers won and Joe had his first Major League victory. (In 1955, the Dodgers would trade Joe to the Reds—for cash and Bob Borkowski.)

The win was a big moment for Joe, but something even more important in his life happened four days later. Finally feeling secure of his place with the Dodgers, Joe and Doris had rented an apartment on the top floor of a house on Decatur Street in Brooklyn, a couple of miles northeast of Ebbets Field. Around six o'clock in the morning on May 26, Joe hopped out of bed and yelled, "Doris, you're urinating on me!" Doris tried to calm him down and told him she had no control over the water seeping from her body, so Joe grabbed some towels and stuffed them between her legs. Then he called the doctor and breathlessly told him that Doris couldn't stop urinating. The doctor couldn't keep himself from laughing. "Joe," he said, "your wife isn't urinating. The water has broken. Get her ready and take her to the hospital."

Joe didn't have a car, but their landlady, Vivienne Williams, lent them hers to take Doris to the hospital. The maternity ward staffers at Jewish Hospital of Brooklyn were waiting when Joe and Doris arrived, and they whisked her into the delivery room. Joe hardly had time to pace and fret, because he was paged to the receptionist's desk a few minutes later and handed a phone. It was the doctor, who told Joe, "You're the father of a little shortstop." Joe was so excited, so overcome with emotion he could barely speak. "It's a boy," he mumbled to the doctor. "How's my wife? Can I see her? When can I see my baby?" A few minutes later, Joe was escorted into Doris's room and saw her cuddling a newborn with shiny black hair. Joe grinned as he looked on the scene and felt flattered when Doris said they should name their child after him. Joe wanted to honor their fathers, so their son became Joseph Frank Black. But he always would be known as Chico, the nickname Joe picked up in Cuba, the place where little Chico had been conceived.

For Joe, it turned out to be fortunate that Chico was born early in the day, because the Dodgers played the Giants that night at the Polo

Grounds. Joe spent the day hustling from store to store buying diapers, bottles, blankets, and a bassinette. Chico had come two weeks early, so he and Doris had yet to stock up on those items. He finished in time to get to the Giants' park before the game and pass out cigars in the clubhouse. By the seventh inning, the Dodgers needed him on the mound. The Dodgers and Giants had a bitter rivalry that was only exacerbated by Bobby Thomson's home run in that 1951 playoff game. "I didn't like any of the Dodgers except Gil Hodges," Thomson said. "We never talked to them. We were like a bunch of kids that way."

Having Leo Durocher and Charlie Dressen as the managers added to the intensity. Durocher had managed the Dodgers in the 1940s, then left midway through the 1948 season to take over the Giants. This made him a reviled figure in Brooklyn. Dressen had been a coach under Durocher with the Dodgers, then became Leo's rival when he took the Brooklyn job after the 1950 season. It was as though they were playing for the pennant every time they met and, in a sense, they were, because both clubs were often contenders. Each manager tried to outfox the other with pitching and lineup changes. Durocher often tried to intimidate the Dodgers by having his pitchers, Sal Maglie in particular, brush back hitters, prompting Dressen and the Dodgers to retaliate.

So it was on May 26 at the Polo Grounds, the massive U-shaped edifice with a ridiculously deep center field—483 feet from the plate—that Dressen began maneuvering early. He pinch hit for his starting pitcher, Preacher Roe, with the bases loaded in the second inning, and George Shuba delivered a two-run single to tie the score at 2–2, the Giants having taken an early lead on Thomson's two-run homer. Charlie promptly pulled another surprise, sending Roy Campanella, who didn't catch that day because of his thumb injury, onto the field to run for Shuba. Leo then yanked his starting pitcher, Jim Hearn, and brought in George Spencer, who got Bobby Morgan to hit a comebacker that the reliever turned into a double play to end the inning.

The Giants broke the tie in the third when Whitey Lockman tripled off Carl Erskine and scored on Thomson's fly ball, and Lockman homered off Erskine in the fifth for an insurance run. Joe relieved in the seventh and did his part, retiring all six batters he faced. Roscoe McGowen called it "flawless hurling" in his *New York Times* story the next day. But the Dodgers couldn't touch Spencer, who gave up only three hits over the final seven and two-thirds innings to finish the 4–2 victory. This started a three-game Dodgers losing streak that dropped them two and a half games behind the Giants when play ended on May 28.

But that was a day Giants fans had been dreading, because it was the last they'd see of Willie Mays until 1954. Mays went 0-for-4 in a 6–2 victory over Brooklyn at Ebbets Field, then reported for army duty the next day. "I suppose it sounds heartless, but as a Dodger, I have to say that I'm glad he's going," Carl Furillo said. "No one shed any tears when I went into the service." First it was Monte Irvin's broken ankle, then it was Willie Mays going into the service. The Giants were in first place, but the Dodgers had to like their chances of overtaking them.

A second significant event occurred for the Dodgers on May 29: Joe Black recorded his first save. Relieving Chris Van Cuyk at the start of the sixth inning with the Dodgers leading the Braves 5–3 at Ebbets Field, Joe finished the game and was almost perfect. He allowed only one baserunner—on a single by Walker Cooper—and the Brooks won 7–3 to break their losing streak. Two days later, the Dodgers were back in first place.

For Joe, the Dodgers-Giants rivalry wasn't so bitter that he couldn't hook up with friends after a game. He had gotten to know Monte Irvin and Hank Thompson, a Giants outfielder, in the Negro leagues, and they met for a late snack the night Joe had pitched at the Polo Grounds. Fans greeted Irvin and Thompson as they walked through the restaurant, offering encouragement and telling them they were sure to repeat as National League champions. Then Joe heard someone say, "The colored relief pitcher for the Dodgers looks good, but he's going to burn himself out. Can't nobody throw that hard all year." Whereupon Irvin introduced Joe as the Dodger pitcher they had just mentioned. The fan later approached Joe and said he meant no disrespect. He just felt the Dodgers would ruin him by using him so much. Joe smiled and let it slide.

Besides, Joe was hardly being overworked. Through thirty-six games, he had pitched only six times, working twelve and two-thirds innings without allowing a run. He had given up eight hits while striking out eight and walking only one batter. Joe was giving Dressen every reason to keep using him and eventually, the little skipper would depend on Joe to save the season. He needed a little prompting, though, and in June 1952 it would come from one of the great pitchers of the past, that ol' country boy hisself, Dizzy Dean.

6

A Dream Reawakened

Nine months at Morgan State had turned into an eye-opening experience for Joe Black, exposing him to both the ugly and the uplifting sides of life outside his New Jersey hometown of Plainfield. The segregation and discriminatory practices he found in Baltimore at once hurt, frustrated, and perplexed him. He was a human being and an American, so why couldn't he attend whatever church he wanted or shop for clothes like anyone else or wait for a train in the same room as white passengers? But his professors and fellow students at Morgan State had helped Joe overcome any Jim Crow–imposed feelings of inferiority by showing him what black scientists, writers, thinkers, and doctors had accomplished, instilling within him a sense of pride in who he was and what he could become.

So when the spring term ended, Joe stayed in Baltimore and got a summer job working on the campus grounds with fellow athletes Cal Irvin and Fred "Biscuit" Burgess. Occasionally, Joe took the train back to Plainfield to spend the weekend with his family. A couple of times, Cal invited him to play for the Triangles, a semipro baseball team out of Orange, New Jersey, about fifteen miles from Plainfield. One day in mid-June, Cal suggested they go to a Negro National League game between the Baltimore Elite Giants and the Newark Eagles. Baltimore and Newark who? Joe had no idea what Cal was talking about, so his friend explained how blacks had formed their own baseball leagues because they were barred from Major League Baseball and they had many star players, including Cal's brother Monte, who played for the Eagles. All of that was news to Joe.

"You mean that there is a Negro National League?" he asked.

Not only that, Cal said, there also was a Negro American League, a Negro all-star game, and a Negro World Series. Whatever events the white major leagues had, the black leagues had as well. That was enough to convince Joe. He had to see these guys play.

Actually, Joe already had been to a Negro league game. He just didn't understand what he saw at the time. His father took him to a game at Yankee Stadium and pointed out many of the players, including George "Mule" Suttles, the most powerful hitter in Negro baseball after Josh Gibson. Suttles was a huge man, six foot six and weighing as much as 270 pounds. As befitting a man that size, he swung a big bat, reportedly as heavy as fifty ounces. Reporter William G. Nunn wrote that Suttles swung that bat "as if it were a toothpick" when he belted the first home run in a Negro leagues all-star game at Chicago's Comiskey Park in 1933, a two-run shot that carried into the upper deck in left center. The home fans would yell "Kick, Mule, kick" when he came to bat, then wait in gleeful anticipation of where he would hit the ball next. Outfielder Charlie Biot remembered the big fella hitting a spitball so hard "you could actually see the saliva fly off of it when it went over the center field fence."

Joe's father told him to pay attention when Suttles came to bat, and sure enough, Mule hit one out. Still, the significance of the game never registered with Joe—that blacks were out there playing in their own league. "They were just names to me," he said. But his conversation with Cal Irvin had given Joe a better understanding of Negro league baseball, and his excitement grew as the bus he and Cal were riding neared Bugle Field, home of the Elite Giants. All this time he thought his dream of playing big-league ball had been buried, only to learn there was a major league for black players.

The Elite Giants evolved from a semipro club called the Standard Giants in Nashville, Tennessee, where owner Tom T. Wilson ran a numbers operation (which was illegal), and a nightclub, the Paradise Ballroom. Wilson was affable, a sharp dresser, and a major force in Nashville's black community. He organized the Standard Giants in 1918, then changed the name to Elite Giants three years later, after the team developed a reputation as a solid ballclub.

The Elites joined the Negro National League for the 1930 season, moved to the Negro Southern League in 1932 following the collapse of the NNL, then joined a new NNL in 1933. With the Nashville economy souring, Wilson moved his team to Detroit in 1935, but stayed there for only a few weeks before shifting to Columbus, Ohio, to finish the season. The Elites then moved again, this time to Washington, DC, for the 1936 and 1937 seasons, before finally settling in Baltimore in May 1938. Once there, Wilson's club became one of Negro baseball's most successful franchises. Fans cheered players such as Biz Mackey, Roy Campanella, Pee Wee Butts, Henry Kimbro, Jonas Gaines, Bill Byrd, and, eventually, Joe Black.

Bugle Field was a quaint six-thousand-seat ballpark built in 1912 in a black community in East Baltimore, at the corner of Federal Street and Edison Highway. With its wooden fences and bleachers, it certainly was no showplace. *Serviceable* might be the best term to describe it. The ballpark hosted amateur and professional soccer games, high school and professional football games, boxing matches, rodeos, and lacrosse matches as well as baseball. Fans complained that the bleachers were rough and uncomfortable, and that they were exposed to the elements. "If it rained, you just got wet, that's all," said Frederick Lonesome, who often traveled to Bugle Field from his home in the Old West area of Baltimore, where most of the city's blacks lived.

The ballpark sat less than three miles south of the Morgan State campus, an easy bus ride for Joe and Cal. As they settled into their seats, Joe was eager to see how the two clubs played. He noticed that not only were all the players black, so was 99 percent of the crowd. Both teams had standout players. The Eagles, managed by Mule Suttles, had first baseman Lennie Pearson, catcher Leon Ruffin, pitchers Max Manning, Len Hooker, and Leon Day, and a nineteen-year-old second baseman named Larry Doby, who was destined for a groundbreaking career with the Cleveland Indians. A year earlier, Day had racked up eighteen strikeouts in beating the Elites 1–0. Managed by George Scales, the Elites featured second baseman Felton Snow, first baseman-pitcher Bud Barbee, third baseman Frank Russell, outfielder Henry Kimbro, and Bill Byrd, Andy Porter, and Bill Harvey on the mound.

As the game progressed, Joe and Cal didn't see much that impressed them and they ridiculed some of the play.

"Man, we can play better than that," Joe said.

They jeered a batter who swung and missed at a pitch right over the plate and mocked a fielder who misplayed a ball. They went on like that for a while until Joe felt a tap on his shoulder. He turned and saw a well-dressed gentleman he would later describe as "some fat man."

"You guys pretty good, huh?" the man said.

"Yeah, we can play," Joe responded.

"How good?" the man asked.

"We play better than those guys," Joe insisted.

The man introduced himself as Vernon Green, the Elite Giants' secretary and business manager; he would later become the team's owner. Perhaps amused by the two young braggarts, Green challenged them to show up at the team's next practice. "Why don't you come out and show me how good you are?" Joe's eyes lit up. "Ooooh, yeah!" he thought, and they eagerly agreed to return.

Turning back to the game, Joe noticed that the teams played with more flair and speed than he had seen in his semipro games back home. The fastballs suddenly looked much faster, the hitters much sharper. Negro league players relied more on speed than their Major League counterparts. While blackball had its share of bashers such as Josh Gibson, Mule Suttles, and Luke Easter, the players were far more adept at smallball: hit and run plays, stealing, taking the extra base at every opportunity, and bunting, which Negro leaguers turned into a work of art. "How many Major League ballplayers can bunt?" former Kansas City Monarchs outfielder Alfred "Slick" Surratt asked during a 2001 appearance with Larry Doby and Joe. Surratt asserted, "I could put a ball in a teacup." Shortstop Paul "Jake" Stephens was said to be so adept at bunting that he "could pick it out of the catcher's glove after it went by."

Few who ever played the game, black or white, were faster than James "Cool Papa" Bell, who in a game against Major League all-stars scored from first base on a bunt. Wild Bill Wright stood six foot four and weighed 220 pounds, but could run like a thoroughbred. He was timed circling the bases in 13.2 seconds. Sam Jethroe, who would become the first black player for the Boston Braves, was so fast he was nicknamed "the Jet." One player said Jethroe could "outrun the word of God." What Joe saw was, indeed, a fast game.

Joe jabbered about the upcoming tryout all the way back to campus. Cal, though, had second thoughts, fearing he'd lose his college eligibility if he hooked up with a professional team. Joe was too gung-ho to care. Besides, he soon learned that because Morgan State and other CIAA schools didn't have baseball, he wouldn't violate any rules playing for the Elites. Cal nevertheless conferred with his brother Monte.

Ballplayers sometimes competed under assumed names in those days so they wouldn't jeopardize their amateur status. "I did when I was younger," Monte Irvin said. "But six years later, when Cal was there, communications were a little bit better. So I told him I wouldn't advise him to do it. Go ahead and take your scholarship and be careful not to lose it. He took my advice" and decided against attending the tryout.

Joe couldn't get to Bugle Field fast enough on the appointed day. But as he approached the ballpark, doubt began to creep in. Was he good enough to play in the Negro major leagues? He was only nineteen years old and these guys were pros. As he looked around the cramped clubhouse, his thoughts were interrupted when a player walked over and asked if he was the college boy Vernon Green invited to try out. It was player-manager George Scales, who inquired what position Joe played.

"Shortstop," Joe blurted.

Scales looked askance, thinking Joe was awfully big for a shortstop at six foot two and 210 pounds—but the veteran Negro leaguer agreed to give the enthusiastic college kid a chance. He sent Joe out to shortstop and hit him some grounders. Joe liked it when Scales hit the ball to his right so he'd have to backhand the ball and show off his arm by making a throw from deep in the hole. He felt his arm was on an ego trip. After about ten minutes, Scales called Joe in to hit. The pitcher threw at half-speed, giving Joe a chance to make contact and show some power. When he was finished, Joe looked anxiously at Scales. OK, the manager said, the next game is against the Homestead Grays. Show up and you'll play.

Could it be this easy? One brief tryout and he was on the team? Joe was ecstatic, but he needed to know more about what he was getting into, so he sat down with players Wesley "Doc" Dennis and Frank Russell and picked their brains about playing Negro ball. He learned about the East-West All-Star Game, year in and year out the biggest event in black baseball. They told him players were paid from $200 to $900 a month, which seemed a fortune to someone from a family that had to scrounge for every dollar. He learned that three of the team's biggest stars were gone. Catcher Roy Campanella, shortstop Pee Wee Butts, and outfielder Wild Bill Wright had jumped to the Mexican League, where Wright would win the triple crown that season. Andy Porter, a hard-throwing right-hander, had just returned from Mexico to give the pitching staff a boost. Now Joe was getting a chance to show what he could add to the club.

Game day came and Joe's heart pounded with excitement as he slipped on his Elite Giants uniform. Years later, he'd recall that he felt that same rush the first time he walked into the Brooklyn Dodgers' spring training clubhouse. Bugle Field was a long way from Dodgertown, though. Negro league facilities were spartan compared to those used by white Major Leaguers, but Joe nevertheless felt he was in the big time. Fans were filling the seats as Joe walked from the clubhouse. By game time, the ballpark was close to full, and Joe noticed that some of the fans—about five hundred of them, he estimated—were white. Joe tried to look nonchalant as he strolled past the Grays warming up, but he couldn't help noticing the difference between the Negro leaguers and the college guys he was used to. These fellows were *big*, he thought.

As Joe waited in the dugout for his team's turn to warm up, a large man in a Grays uniform approached and asked who was pitching. This was Josh Gibson, perhaps the most feared hitter in the history of black baseball.

"Porter," he was told.

The big man smiled, looked at Andy Porter, and spoke with the confidence of knowing he could do just what he said. "Porter," Gibson said, "ol' Josh feeling pretty good tonight, so I think I'm going to hit you over that fence [pointing to left field] and then over that one [pointing out to center field], and maybe I'll take you over that one [indicating right field]." Josh then laughed and walked away.

At the time, Joe didn't know the other players. "Who was that guy?" he asked Porter.

Porter flashed a big smile and replied, "That's ol' Josh Gibson trying to mess with my mind."

Joe didn't think Gibson was all that big physically, but he figured anyone who talked like that must be a good hitter. In the game that followed, Joe saw that yes, Josh could indeed hit a baseball. And hit it a long way. Gibson smacked one of Porter's pitches for a home run over the left-field fence and clobbered another over the center-field fence. His blast to right field hit the top of the fence, Joe recalled, just missing a home run. Porter was no hack, either. The big righty had been a mainstay of the Elite Giants staff in the 1930s before jumping to Mexico for five seasons. His fastball had plenty of pop, he could throw a nasty slider, and he had good control. The Elites were glad to have him back.

Joe's plate appearances were far less impressive than Gibson's: no hits and three strikeouts in four times up against Edsall Walker, a powerfully built left-hander. If a manager could pick a pitcher for a rookie to face in his debut, it wouldn't have been Walker. He could throw 100 miles an hour and was called the "Catskill Wild Man," a reflection of his control—or lack thereof. He was known to warn batters that he might throw at them. "It took a pretty strong heart to dig in too deeply when Edsall Walker was on the mound," author Brent Kelley wrote in his book, *Voices from the Negro Leagues*. "I could throw hard," Walker said, "but I couldn't throw straight."

The veterans tried to help Joe slough off his sorry effort at bat, telling him it was nothing more than first-game jitters and he'd do better the next time. Somewhat consoled, Joe nevertheless sneaked back into the dormitory at Morgan so no one could ask him how he'd done.

But the next time wasn't better; it was even worse: four times at bat, four strikeouts. Joe already felt embarrassed and distraught. What he heard next only added to his distress. "You should turn in your uniform," George Scales roared, "because you couldn't hit a bull in the ass if it ran across home plate!"

Joe quickly saw that Negro league pitching was unlike anything he had faced before. Catchers everywhere often chat up batters, but these catchers rattled Joe and got into his head. "When you're playing ball back in Jersey, everybody's throwing strikes," Joe said many years later. "I never heard anybody say, 'Now, you've got to watch out for this guy. He's a little wild.' Then he'd stand up behind me, 'Don't hit this man in the head. He's a nice-looking young boy.'"

Joe recalled turning to the catcher and asking, "What did you say?"

"I told you he's a little wild," the catcher replied. "I wanted to let him know, don't throw that ball up there." By "up there," he meant Joe's head.

After Scales exploded, Joe felt like saying the heck with it and walking out on his dream of playing professional baseball. Then he looked at the manager and mumbled, "I know I looked bad at bat, but I deserve another chance because I'm really a pitcher." Scales started to walk away, then turned, looked at Joe, and decided to give the kid one more chance. He could come back to practice and try to prove he could pitch.

Joe knew himself well enough to understand that telling Scales he was a pitcher wasn't quite accurate. He threw more than he pitched. "Satchel [Paige] was a pitcher, Jonas Gaines was a pitcher, Bill Byrd was a pitcher, except Bill Byrd could throw some spitballs. Most of us, though, we were throwers," Joe said, recalling those years. "We let it go at 95 miles an hour. If you hit it, OK. If you don't, we got you."

Ten years later, during his second season with the Dodgers, Joe threw some pitches into an instrument placed across home plate to measure his speed, which was clocked at 93.6 miles an hour. The technician told him he probably threw 98 to 99 miles an hour, with his fastest pitches missing the slot in the measuring device. In 1943, at age nineteen, Joe felt he was even faster.

At his pitching tryout, Joe first threw to a catcher, then was asked to try to strike out Doc Dennis, a reserve infielder and average hitter, and Bill Hoskins, a rangy outfielder who hit .412 in 1941. Joe could see both batters were nervous. They noticed he could throw hard. They just weren't sure he knew where his pitches were going. Hoskins and Dennis hit a few and missed a few. Satisfied with what he saw, Scales told Joe he would start against the New York Black Yankees.

As he dressed the night of his pitching debut, Joe tried to calm his nerves by imagining he was back in Jersey pitching in the Twilight League, an amateur baseball league in central New Jersey that had been in existence since 1923. Joe thought the Black Yankees didn't look as physically imposing as the Grays, but they had some good players. Manager Hack Barker, who played center field, was an all-star in 1940. Johnny Hayes was a solid catcher. Pitcher Bob Griffith was known for his control. First baseman Bricktop Wright and outfielder Zack Clayton were excellent athletes who doubled as basketball players for the Washington Bears, the reigning world-professional champions. Clayton also had played for the New York Renaissance, another all-black basketball team, when they won the world pro championship in 1939. He later would appear with the Harlem Globetrotters and eventually would become a boxing referee who'd work many championship fights, including Muhammad Ali's "rope-a-dope" knockout of George Foreman in Zaire in 1974.

Joe's first game as a Negro league pitcher was a duel between a hard thrower and hard hitters. The hard thrower prevailed early. Through five innings, Joe nursed a 2–0 lead with seven strikeouts and two walks. "Then someone moved the fences in closer and I became overconfident because my pitches were no longer missing their bats," he said, poking fun at himself. "Balls were going against or over the walls." Scales finally pulled his shaken pitcher in the sixth inning. As debuts go, it didn't merit many stars. But his teammates apparently had seen something in the young hurler and offered words of encouragement. They told him he showed potential and would become a winner once he learned how to pitch. It seemed he was being accepted as part of the team.

Those good feelings lasted just three days. They ended when Joe received a letter that began, "Greetings from the President of the United States." It was his draft notice, ordering him to report for induction on July 27. The need for able-bodied young men was growing by the week as the United States waged war on two fronts. It was Joe's turn to join that effort. Joe Black was about to become GI Joe.

The Elite Giants management also must have been encouraged by what Joe showed as a pitcher, because they told him he could rejoin the team when he received weekend passes and furloughs. Joe would have preferred to stay with the club and resume his schooling in the winter, but at least he'd have a few chances to continue his baseball career.

>>>>>>>>>>

The war years turned out to be years of prosperity for Negro league baseball. Black Americans looked for entertainment and war industries provided jobs, so they had money to spend. Unemployment dropped sharply and incomes for urban blacks rose. Negro league owners reaped the benefits of that combination.

Like their Major League counterparts, many Negro league players traded their baseball uniforms for military gear. But some of the best players ever to grace the diamonds of black baseball weren't called into the service, so fans still got to see top-flight competition. Stars like Josh Gibson, Cool Papa Bell, Satchel Paige, Willie Wells, Lennie Pearson, Leon Day, Double Duty Radcliffe, and Buck Leonard were still going strong. Back after a stint in the Mexican League, catcher Roy Campanella flashed the skills that would make him a three-time Most Valuable Player for the Brooklyn Dodgers. During the final year of the war, 1945, the Kansas City Monarchs showcased a flashy shortstop named Jackie Robinson.

Fans flocked to games to delight in the abilities of these superstars, some of whom would be enshrined at Cooperstown, and the East-West All-Star Games drew their biggest crowds ever at Chicago's Comiskey Park—from 45,179 in 1942 to a whopping 51,723 in 1943. In 1942, '43, and '44, the East-West Game outdrew the Major League All-Star Game.

Regular season games also drew well in places like Briggs Stadium in Detroit, Shibe Park in Philadelphia, and Chicago's Wrigley Field, where 19,000 turned out one day for a four-team doubleheader to honor Paige. "Even the white folks was coming out big," Satch said. "They'd heard about me and Josh Gibson and about guys like us, and they knew there'd be a good show whenever we were out there."

In the early summer of 1944, an estimated 12,000 fans at Yankee Stadium saw the Birmingham Black Barons sweep the Black Yankees in a doubleheader. Dan Bankhead, on leave from the army, struck out fourteen for the Black Barons in the nightcap, a 13–0 victory. Three years later, on August 26, 1947, Bankhead entered a game in relief for the Brooklyn Dodgers to become the first black pitcher in Major League history.

Though little more than tip money by today's standards, player salaries reflected the good times of the war years. An average player could make $400 to $500 a month, with a star getting as much as $1,000 monthly. That was substantially higher pay than that of the early years of Negro league baseball, when players had to get by on $150 to $200 a month. At a time when the average American worker made around $2,400 a year and a new car could be bought for $1,000 or less, black baseball stars in the 1940s fared well. And they could supplement their income through postseason barnstorming and winter league play in Latin America. The door to the Major Leagues was still closed—though it would be opening soon—but in their own realm, the top black baseball players made enough to live comfortably.

That would soon change, of course, because the popularity of Negro league baseball waned sharply once Jackie Robinson and other black players moved to the Major Leagues. But Joe Black was lucky enough to have experienced Negro league ball at the height of its popularity, because the Elite Giants, just as they had promised, brought him on board to pitch when he was on leave. Because he spent the first eighteen months of his army stint on the East Coast, Joe got enough work on the mound to compile a 3-1 record in 1944 and a 2-2 mark in 1945. The *Baltimore Afro-American* referred to Joe in August 1945 as the "sensational Camp Crowder flinger," drawing the description from the Missouri army base where Joe was stationed at the time. He was with the Elites during their push for the second half title in the Negro National League in 1945, but the Homestead Grays closed fast and finished two games ahead of Joe's club to win the championship.

The experience Joe gained during those two years made him feel that, at last, he was a professional baseball player. It wasn't the big leagues to which he had aspired as a teenager, but at the time, it was close enough. He no longer felt that sting of rejection. "It was healing and a satisfaction," he said years later. "OK, they don't want us in, we have our own league. We're just as good as those guys are." To Joe, pitching to the likes of Josh Gibson, Buck Leonard, Larry Doby, Monte Irvin, Piper Davis, and Luke Easter in Negro ball was just as challenging and exciting as facing Mickey Mantle, Yogi Berra, Stan Musial, Ted Kluszewski, and other Major Leaguers who batted against him in later years. "They were not myths," Joe said of the Negro league stars. "They were reality."

With his first weekend pass in 1944, Joe joined the Elites in Philadelphia and met a teammate who would wield great influence in his career: catcher Roy Campanella. "Campy," as he was so often called, had joined the Elite Giants six years earlier at the age of sixteen and soon became a full-fledged star, a savvy handler of pitchers who swung a big bat. He had just rejoined the Elites after playing the previous summer in Mexico when manager Felton Snow introduced him to Joe. "Soldier boy, just listen to ol' Campy," Campanella said. "He'll take care of you."

Joe would learn with the Elite Giants and later with the Brooklyn Dodgers that he was, indeed, in good hands when Campy was behind the plate. He also discovered that Campy had his back even if he wasn't catching. In a game against the Memphis Red Sox at Yankee Stadium, Joe pitched and Campanella played left field. Though short and squat at five foot nine and 195 pounds, Campy could move when the occasion demanded, and this was one of those times. He ran down two long fly balls, reaching into the left-field stands to save Joe from giving up home runs. After the second catch, Campy trotted into the dugout and with mock seriousness told Joe, "Junior, you'd better get something on the ball because you're running me to death." Campy also homered in that game.

Joe learned from other players as well. Jonas Gaines, a skinny left-handed pitcher who had been in the Negro leagues since 1937, hammered home for Joe the importance of staying in shape, keeping his poise, and controlling his pitches. Bill Byrd, one of the top spitball artists in black baseball, talked to Joe about the importance of controlling something else: his libido. "You're young and you throw hard," Byrd noted, "and you have a chance to be a good pitcher. But don't let your fastball leave through the head of your pecker."

>>>>>>>>>>

Joe was still in the army when he heard news of an event that would not only reshape baseball but help trigger changes in the social fabric of America: Jackie Robinson had signed with the Brooklyn Dodgers' Montreal farm team. The date was October 23, 1945. Jackie would become the first black player in whites-only organized baseball in modern times, and his influence would extend well beyond the diamonds on which he tormented pitchers with his prolific hitting and daring baserunning. "Jackie's breakthrough foreshadowed the greatest civil rights movement in this country this century," then–National League president Len Coleman said in 1997. By crashing through barriers in what had been a segregated enterprise, Jackie "knocked down hurdles and created opportunities for people in all walks of life," Coleman said.

Because of Dodgers general manager Branch Rickey's bold move in signing Jackie, and the succession of black players who soon followed him into the Major Leagues, Joe always felt baseball ran ahead of other institutions in breaking down racial barriers. He realized that baseball before Jackie had clung to its segregated ways as stubbornly as any other entity, and even after Jackie, it was 1959 before the last all-white team in the majors, the Boston Red Sox, finally integrated. But Jackie's first game in the majors on April 15, 1947, came seven years before *Brown v. Board of Education*, the U.S. Supreme Court decision that set the stage for school desegregation, and eight years before Rosa Parks sparked the Montgomery bus boycott by refusing to surrender her seat to a white passenger. The Civil Rights Act wasn't enacted until 1964, a full seventeen years after Jackie donned his Dodgers uniform for the first time.

When Tom Payne became the University of Kentucky's first black basketball player, he endured the same type of harassment, taunts, and jeers that had rained down on Jackie—and that was in 1971. That same year, baseball was so thoroughly integrated that the Pittsburgh Pirates, who would win the World Series, fielded an all non-white lineup in one game: six blacks and three Hispanics.

But someone had to be first, and it was Jackie.

Joe and many other black players celebrated Jackie's signing, believing that if Jackie succeeded, others in the Negro leagues would get the same chance. "We all thought: Great! Great! The door is open," Buck O'Neil said. Joe said when he heard the news, "I was 18 all over again. I started dreaming. And that's what happened to most of the guys in the Negro leagues." Jackie's signing also caught the attention of a teenage athlete living just outside Birmingham, Alabama. "We all rooted for the Dodgers," Willie Mays said, recalling that time. "From the day he signed, I knew I had a chance to play Major League ball. When I got married, my wife was a Dodger fan."

At the same time, the newly inspired Negro leaguers kept their fingers crossed, hoping and praying that Jackie could stand up to the abuse without lashing back. Because if he did strike back and was run out of baseball, who knew how long it would be before another black player got a chance. Joe understood that in joining the Dodgers, Jackie "was carrying the burden of creating job opportunity for thousands of young men."

Some, however, couldn't understand why Jackie was picked when better, more experienced players were available. There was no doubting his athletic talent. Jackie had lettered in football, basketball, baseball, and track at UCLA. In football, he twice led the nation in punt return average and he averaged 5.9 yards rushing for his career. He led the Pacific Coast Conference's Southern Division twice in scoring in basketball; in track, he won the NCAA broad jump title in 1940. He even played professional basketball, scoring in double figures four times during a brief stint with the Los Angeles Red Devils in the winter of 1946–47.

But Jackie had played only one season in the Negro leagues, with the Kansas City Monarchs in 1945. While hundreds of Negro leaguers spent years scuffling around the country without getting a sniff from white baseball, Jackie was one-and-done. Pitcher Verdell Mathis said years later, "There were 100 better players in the Negro Leagues than Jackie." But he hastened to add that "we were as glad as hell because if Jackie made it, then we could make it."

Satchel Paige, black baseball's premier pitcher, had always figured that when the Major Leagues integrated, he'd be the first to get the call. When it turned out to be Jackie, it "hurt me deep down," Satch said. "I'd been the guy who'd started all the big talk about letting us in the big time," he wrote in his autobiography. "I'd been the one who'd opened up the Major League parks to the colored teams. I'd been the one who the white boys wanted to barnstorm against. I'd been the one who everybody said should be in the majors." Satch did get his chance, though not until 1948, when he helped the Cleveland Indians win the American League pennant.

One who would never get that chance was Josh Gibson, regarded as the best player ever in Negro league baseball. A catcher with a strong arm, Gibson was a powerfully built man who hit prodigious home runs that became the stuff of legend. Some stories hold that games were stopped after a particularly long Gibson home run so it could be measured. The mayor of Monessen, Pennsylvania, stepped off one at 512 feet. At Comiskey Park, loudspeakers sat on the center-field wall, about eight feet off the ground and 435 feet from home plate. Gibson lashed one screaming liner that smashed into a loudspeaker dead center and stuck in it. The umpires stopped the game so a groundskeeper could pry the ball out. "He hit it so hard it would bend," former pitcher Wilmer Fields told author John B. Holway.

That folks across the land vividly remembered Gibson's home runs only added to his legend. "Everywhere you'd go, you'd hear, 'Josh hit one out of there,'" Joe recalled. "'See that stack over there? Josh hit one just to the left of it.' You go down South, 'See those cornfields out there? Josh's ball was rising when it went over there.'"

Gibson was thirty-three years old and already in declining health when Jackie signed his Montreal contract. He was drinking heavily. His power had dropped off sharply. During the winter of 1945–46, while playing in Puerto Rico, Gibson was found, in the nude, wandering the streets of San Juan, and was committed to a sanitarium. He was released in the spring, returned to the United States, and played what would be his final season in 1946. A few months later, on January 20, 1947, Josh Gibson died at the age of thirty-five.

Joe was among those who believed the disappointment of never getting a chance to play in the Major Leagues contributed to Gibson's death. In his final season, "You could see he didn't have the same zest," Joe said. Another top black star, Buck Leonard, was nearly four years older than Gibson, but continued to produce even after being passed over by white baseball. Nearing the age of thirty-seven, Leonard was still good enough to win his third Negro National League batting title in 1948 and tie for the lead in home runs. "Buck still had it because of his pride," Joe said. "He wanted to win. Josh wanted to win, but the drive of being number one wasn't there anymore. Because he felt he had been cheated."

Others, including Gibson biographer William Brashler and Gibson's son, Josh Jr., frowned on the death-from-a-broken-heart theory. But hardly anyone doubted that Gibson, in his prime, could have succeeded in Major League Baseball. He just happened to suffer the same fate as so many others: the opportunity came too late. It did, however, come in time for Joe Black. He just had to pay his dues first.

>>>>>>>>>>

While Negro league players made more money than the average black worker, their lives were anything but cushy. Their official "league" contests accounted for only a fraction of the games they played. Most games between Negro league teams were played on weekends. Then the players climbed aboard a bus and headed for the hinterlands to play exhibition games anywhere the owners felt they could make money from ticket sales. They'd play semipro outfits, Negro minor league teams, local "all-star" teams, and anyone else willing to face them. Often, they rode all night to reach the next destination. Sometimes, they'd play a day game in one town and a night game in another. Many restaurants still clung to

Jim Crow traditions and wouldn't serve them, or would force them to go to the back door to pick up a bag of sandwiches. They led a grab-and-go, eat-on-the run existence, playing in the shadows and on the fringes, far from the glamour of Major League Baseball. "It was just a continuous scuffle," said Johnny Davis, who played in the outfield for the Newark Eagles. "Play here this afternoon, another game tonight, ride 600 miles, play somewhere else."

League games often were played in Major League parks like Yankee Stadium and the Polo Grounds in New York, Griffith Stadium in Washington, DC, and Shibe Park in Philadelphia, giving black ball players a taste of the high life. But exhibitions often took place in far scruffier surroundings, like sandlot diamonds or run-down municipal fields. "Sometimes out in western Kansas they'd make the ballpark the day we got in town—some pasture," said George Giles, who started his Negro league career with the Kansas City Monarchs in 1927.

Larger cities had Negro hotels. When teams ventured into smaller towns, the team would usually arrange for players to stay with black families. If such homes weren't available, players had to get creative. Buck O'Neil said he and his teammates sometimes slept in funeral homes. If restaurants wouldn't serve them, the black community might fix a meal in one of its churches. Finding a restaurant or grocery store that catered to blacks was a bonus. "We had to eat in those restaurants because we were restricted to that part of town," Joe said. "Anytime we got into a city and we didn't know where to go, we just asked where the railroad tracks were, go on the other side and that was the black community."

Sometimes there was no place to stay, so the players rode all night and slept on the bus. "A lot of times we couldn't take a bath after the ballgame," Giles recalled. "I remember once in Colby, Kansas, we set tubs of water out in the sun to get them warm so we could take a bath." Max Manning, who pitched for the Newark Eagles in the 1940s, recalled getting on the bus after a doubleheader in Omaha, Nebraska, on a Friday night and heading for Baltimore, where they had a game on Sunday. "We rode and we rode and we rode," he said. "We got to Baltimore in time. We had to dress in the bus. We pulled into the park, Bugle Field. After all that riding, guess who had to pitch? Me. What amazes me is how present day ballplayers will squawk about a flight to Los Angeles and complain about jet lag. They really don't know what hardship is: no trainers, no hot water and still get out and play."

When Joe traveled with the Elite Giants, the players got two dollars a day in meal money. Food was relatively cheap then, but it still took some ingenuity to stretch that stipend. "You had to have a good friend. Otherwise, you'd starve a little bit," Joe said. The two players would pool their money, and when the team stopped at a store, they'd buy a loaf of bread, a pound of bologna, some mayonnaise, and two big bottles of Pepsi, which cost a nickel each. "That was your breakfast and lunch," he said. "They'd pull the bus aside, you'd make your sandwich, eat it and you'd keep going."

For Joe, it was hardly the best life, but definitely not the worst. "Under the conditions," he said, "we fared OK. We had segregated hotels. To save money, they'd take a bath towel and cut it in half. Now it was a hand towel and a bath towel." There were no washcloths. Joe got accustomed to washing his face with his hands or using his hand towel. The rooms varied from tolerable to bug infested. In some hotels, he'd be jolted awake in the dark and think his roommate had been pinching him. They'd fuss about that until turning the lights on and finding bedbugs all over them. "So, the next day you report it," Joe said. "Now you come in from the ballpark, you smell—they sprayed gasoline on them and set the springs on fire to burn them up. Then they'd spray the mattress. Now you're sleeping." Many times it proved easier to just sleep with the lights on.

Appearances were important to Negro league players. They wanted to be regarded as professionals, so they dressed the part. On Sundays, Joe and his teammates wore suit and tie, no matter how hot or humid it might be. The fans looked sharp, too, because many came directly from church, the men in suits, the women in their finest and most colorful hats and dresses. "You'd like to go out on the town and stay overnight so you could meet some of them," Joe said. "But most of the time you got right back on that bus and hit the highway."

Even during the week, Joe and his teammates had to wear nice slacks and neat casual shirts. Overalls and plaid shirts were taboo. Those were the dress of poor folk and farmers, an image Negro league owners wanted to avoid. "You usually had a white shirt, rolled up the sleeves and sat on the bus," Joe said. "You learned how to sleep sitting up. That bus would be bouncing down the road and you'd drop your head. Next thing you know, six hours later, where are we?" Then they'd get off the bus, change into their uniforms—if they weren't already wearing them—and play. At times, they couldn't even avoid travel on game days. The Elites and Philadelphia Stars sometimes played an afternoon game in Baltimore and then both teams, still in uniform, climbed aboard their respective buses, drove to Philadelphia, and played a night game. "Now, you better have some sandwiches on that bus," Joe said, "or you don't eat until like eleven o'clock at night."

The players looked forward to games in league cities, because they brought relief from the rigors of exhibitions in the boondocks. They stayed in more upscale hotels, often played in Major League stadiums, and certainly ate better food. In Philadelphia, Joe remembered going to a restaurant run by a black spiritual leader who called himself Father Devine, saying "Peace, Father," and getting a meal for ten cents. In New York, Negro leaguers often stayed at the Woodside Hotel in Harlem, where they crossed paths with Count Basie, Ella Fitzgerald, Louis Armstrong, and other black entertainers. Just down the street from the Woodside, Joe and his teammates could get a meal of red beans, rice, greens, and chitlins for fifteen cents. "You were in hog heaven then," he said. "We used to say, 'This is it!'"

>>>>>>>>>>

When Joe reported for spring training with the Elite Giants in Nashville in April 1946, a month after his army discharge, the club assigned a seventeen-year-old infielder named Jim Gilliam to be his roommate. From that pairing, a lifelong friendship blossomed. They later would become teammates on the Brooklyn Dodgers, and Joe so valued their relationship that Gilliam became the godfather to Joe's son, Chico. "If he had a dollar, I had a dollar and vice versa," Joe said. "We bared our souls to one another." They were polar opposites in personality. Where Joe was outgoing and talkative, a storyteller who loved to laugh, Gilliam was shy and quiet, someone who kept things to himself. Those differences only seemed to cement their friendship, and Joe always believed he got his chance with the Brooklyn Dodgers in part because of Jim "Junior" Gilliam's reserved nature.

Gilliam grew up in Nashville and spent the 1945 season with the minor league Nashville Black Vols, playing so well that the Elites, the club's parent team, invited him to try out in spring training. He soon picked up a nickname that stuck for the rest of his career. Noticing that Gilliam, a right-handed batter, had trouble with right-handed pitchers, manager George Scales yelled, "Hey, Junior, get over on the other side of the plate." Along with gaining his nickname, Gilliam became a switch hitter and, eventually, an all-star. He didn't have a strong enough arm to play third base, which had been his position, so Scales made him a second baseman, another move that led to his success.

Joe felt his friend was always self-conscious about his lack of formal education. Because he left high school to become a professional ballplayer, Gilliam never earned his diploma. But Joe encouraged Junior to expand his reading beyond the sports pages in the newspapers and, as he did, Joe saw him become more confident and talkative. In baseball, Gilliam was as studious as they came. He watched other players closely and always looked for ways to improve himself. Whenever they could get away, Jim persuaded Joe to spend his meal money and accompany him to games at Yankee Stadium or Ebbets Field so Junior could study Major League second basemen. Sometimes he borrowed Joe's meal money and went by himself. "He would watch every move the infielders made and he'd study the hitters by the hour," Joe said.

Gilliam played the 1946 season with the Elites as a reserve behind veteran second baseman Sammy T. Hughes, giving the youngster yet another chance to learn the nuances of the position by observation. Hughes retired after that season and Junior succeeded him, teaming with slick shortstop Pee Wee Butts to form one of the Negro leagues' best double-play combinations.

Joe, meanwhile, still was trying to evolve from being a mere thrower to someone who truly could be called a pitcher. He listened intently when the team's veteran pitchers offered advice. Once Jackie Robinson signed with the Dodgers, Joe found that older players in general were eager to help promising youngsters. Most understood that they were too old to get a look from white baseball, so they did what they could to prepare the younger players, like Joe, who might have a chance. "I accepted and appreciated their assistance," Joe said, "because as the other players, I, too, was hoping that some scout would say, 'Bingo, you are our candidate for the Major Leagues.'" The old-timers also urged the younger guys to behave, because the Major Leagues would not sign black players who hotdogged or drank or caroused. "Watch yourself," Willie Wells used to say. "You never know who's looking at you to sign you."

The Elite Giants called on Joe to pitch regularly in 1946. As for how many games he won that season, it depends on the source. Negro league statistics never were kept as extensively as those in the Major Leagues. Stats for most players were sketchy, incomplete, and at times in dispute. And the figures for "official" Negro league games didn't include what the Negro leaguers did in all those exhibition games they played while crisscrossing the country. Thus, Joe's 1946 record is listed as 4-8, 4-9, or, as Joe kept himself, 6-4. Nevertheless, Joe knew there remained a lot to learn. "I was still throwing and not locating," he wrote years later.

But even then, Joe could be formidable when he was on his game. He handcuffed the Philadelphia Stars 5–1 on a five-hitter in late June, pitching "over, under and around" the visitors' bats, the *Afro-American* declared. Joe also dominated the Stars at the plate, going 3-for-3, scoring twice, and driving in two runs.

In September, he helped the Elites sweep a doubleheader from a white all-star team composed mostly of players from the International League's Baltimore Orioles. As Joe matured, he began pitching as much with his head as with his arm. He learned he didn't have to use all of his pitches in one inning, though with only a fastball and what Campy and others called a nickel curve, Joe didn't have much room to tinker with variety. But he found that if he could control and locate his fastball, which in those days he could throw in the high 90s, his little curve would be that much more effective in later innings.

Against some hitters, though, even a well-placed, blazing fastball wasn't enough. Buck Leonard, who played in a record thirteen Negro league all-star games, could stand in against Joe and drive his fastest pitches right back at him. "It got to the point that Gilliam used to say, 'You know what? With Buck Leonard, you throw it up there 200 miles an hour, he's going to knock it back 600 miles an hour. So why don't you just lob them up there?'" Joe was far from the only pitcher Leonard knocked around. The left-handed batting first baseman was known as "the black Lou Gehrig," a player who could hit for both average and power and was tough to strike out. "You could put a fastball in a .30-30 rifle and you couldn't shoot it across the plate by him," pitcher Dave Barnhill once said.

>>>>>>>>>>

The most coveted honor in Negro league baseball was selection to the East-West All-Star Game, and Joe wanted that as much as anyone. "I was consumed with the desire" to play in that game, he wrote in the foreword to Larry Lester's extensively researched book on the all-star classic, *Black Baseball's National Showcase.* It finally happened for him in 1947. Pitching for the East in front of 38,402 fans at New York's Polo Grounds, Joe worked the sixth, seventh, and eighth innings of an 8–2 loss to the West in the second of the two all-star games that year. He gave up two runs and five hits while striking out two and walking one. His performance was less than sparkling and he did not figure in the decision. But just getting into the game told Joe he might have what it takes to become a first-rate pitcher. And Jackie Robinson was in the process of opening an opportunity for Joe to become that kind of pitcher in the Major Leagues.

Negro league players had closely followed Jackie's progress with Montreal during the 1946 season, when the former Kansas City Monarch proved his mettle in white baseball by leading the International League in hitting (.349) and runs (113). The black newspapers dutifully reported on every move Jackie made and crowed over his accomplishments. Black fans and players would grab the paper and immediately open it to the sports pages to see what Jackie had done. Even more important to those who dreamed of following him into white baseball, Jackie kept his cool amid all the racial taunts hurled his way.

Jackie was aggressive and quick-tempered. If he lashed back, it might be years before organized baseball would take a chance on another black player. "You just kept pulling for him," Joe said. And praying. "We silently asked God to continue providing Jackie with the strength to turn the other cheek," Joe recalled. There was a selfish aspect to that hope for someone like Joe, because if Jackie could take it, maybe he'd get a chance, too. The scrutiny and abuse intensified when Jackie joined the Brooklyn Dodgers in 1947, and though he may have seethed inside, his composure held. And the door cracked open a little wider.

Newark Eagles star Larry Doby crossed the line in July when he joined the Cleveland Indians. Joe said he helped send Doby off on a positive note by serving up his last hit as a Negro league player. "After the game, Larry told me he was going to Cleveland," Joe said. "It was thrilling." Not long after that, the St. Louis Browns signed Hank Thompson and Willard Brown. Roy Campanella was catching in Montreal, while pitcher Don Newcombe was spending his second season with the Dodgers' farm club in Nashua, New Hampshire. Dan Bankhead became the Major Leagues' first black pitcher when the Dodgers brought him up in late August. His pitching was nondescript—a 7.20 earned run average in four appearances—but he did hit a home run in his first plate appearance. It couldn't be called a wave of integration, but it at least was a trickle. Scouts openly attended Negro league games, so it only stood to reason that more and more black players would be signed. As Joe saw it, "Players in their thirties started looking in mirrors to see if they could pass for 25 or less."

The turning point in Joe's Negro league career came in 1948. He had spent the winter getting his first taste of Latin American baseball while pitching for Magallanes in the Venezuelan league, and as the Elite Giants got ready for a new season, Joe was hailed as the potential staff ace. "Black gained considerable experience pitching against the diamond stars in the Latin country," the *Afro-American* declared, "and has taken full advantage of the new points he learned." With Gilliam taking over full time at second base and teaming with shortstop Pee Wee Butts, the paper said Elite Giants fans could expect to see plenty of double plays. Joe, fellow right-hander Bill Byrd, and lefties Jonas Gaines and Rob Romby made up a formidable pitching rotation, while the outfield of Lester Lockett, Frank Russell, and Henry Kimbro contributed to the belief that the Elites could make a run at the Negro National League title. They came close, winning the first-half championship before losing to the second-half champion Homestead Grays in three straight games in a playoff for the pennant.

Joe went 10-5 in the 1948 season (he gave himself credit for only nine victories) and again pitched in the second East-West Game. And this time, he stood out. Joe allowed only two hits while blanking the West stars over the final three innings to earn a save in the East's 6–1 victory before 17,928 at Yankee Stadium. His teammates included Gilliam, Minnie Minoso, Luke Easter, and George Crowe, all of whom would go on to play in the Major Leagues.

April 1949 found Joe back at Morgan State pursuing his degree, so he missed spring training. Also missing was one of black baseball's major leagues. The Negro National League folded in the fall of 1948 after owner Effa Manley, who would become the first woman inducted into the Baseball Hall of Fame, sold the Newark Eagles and the franchise moved to Houston. The Homestead Grays and New York Black Yankees pulled out of the league, so the remaining National League teams, including the Elites, were merged into the Negro American League to form a ten-team circuit. The Eastern Division had the Elites, New York Cubans, Philadelphia Stars, Indianapolis Clowns, and Louisville Buckeyes. The Western Division teams were the Kansas City Monarchs, Chicago American Giants, Birmingham Black Barons, Houston Eagles, and Memphis Red Sox.

Interest in Negro league baseball was now fading as the Major Leagues continued to sign black players. Attendance dropped and owners struggled to make a profit. Josh Gibson, who had been a major draw, was dead. The biggest drawing card among current black players, Satchel Paige, had gone to the big leagues with the Cleveland Indians. Black baseball's long-standing problems, such as sketchy record keeping and inconsistent scheduling, became even more detrimental.

Black newspapers increasingly covered Major League Baseball, sensing that fans were more interested in reading about blacks in organized ball than those in the Negro leagues, a trend that upset Joe. He was disappointed upon picking up a black newspaper to find a "whole page on the Brooklyn Dodgers and scarcely a mention of what the Negro Leagues are doing." The *Baltimore Afro-American* began running the Major League schedule and listing the black players on each team. It also ran a weekly summary of how Jackie Robinson, Larry Doby, Roy Campanella, and the other black players fared each day. At the same time, Elites owner Vernon Green complained in mid-May 1949 that he couldn't figure out his team's place in the standings.

The Negro American League persevered, however, and Joe matured into one of its top pitchers. His personal records show him with fifteen victories in 1949 and fourteen in 1950. Other sources credit him with eleven wins and eight wins. Regardless, opponents knew that when Big

Joe Black was on the mound, they were probably in for a frustrating time. He would come at them and come at them hard. And with a clean ball.

Negro league pitchers were notorious for using knives, nail files, razors, screwdrivers, whatever they could find, to scuff baseballs so they'd spin and move in unnatural ways. "They danced so wickedly on their way to the plate that even a blind man would know the balls had been doctored," former umpire Bob Motley asserted. But Motley said Joe didn't need any tricks. He just stood out there, reached back, and fired what the ump called an "insane fastball." Off the field, Motley found Joe to be a gentleman, sharp and dignified. On the mound, though, he took on a different persona. He turned deadly serious, Motley said, and "with an almost Marine-like bearing, he bullied batters into submission."

Motley recalled a time he was working the plate and Joe faced Lester Lockett, a former Elite Giants teammate who had moved on to the Chicago American Giants. "Lester Lockett once fouled off so many of Black's fastballs in an at-bat that the crowd grew restless, as did I," the former ump related. "After having over a dozen of his fastballs foul-tipped by the right-handed-hitting Lockett, Black fired off the nastiest slider I've ever seen. The ball looked like it was going to pelt Lockett in his ribs, but at the last second it shot back across the heart of the plate, belt high. It shocked the heck out of me. Excited by the beautiful pitch, my instincts sent me flying into the air as I belted out, 'S-T-T-R-R-R-I-I-I-I-K-E T-H-R-R-E-E-E! YOU'RE OUT!' Frozen and stunned, all Lockett could do was stand there looking like road kill after rigor mortis had set in." When Motley said he flew into the air on his strike three call, he meant that literally. Motley was a showman who frequently exaggerated his calls by leaping or doing the splits. If Joe's pitch was as breathtaking as Motley insisted, he certainly would have been demonstrative on his call.

Joe helped the Elite Giants win the 1949 NAL Eastern Division championship, which they followed with a four-game sweep of the Western Division champs, the Chicago American Giants, to claim the league championship. The Elites opened the championship series at Bugle Field with a 9–1 victory behind Bill Byrd, who scattered seven hits. Joe got cuffed around for sixteen hits in game two, but received enough support to win 5–4. The two teams moved to Norfolk, Virginia, the next night and the Elites prevailed 8–4. Then it was on to Comiskey Park in

Chicago, where the Baltimore club scored three times in the sixth inning en route to a 4–2 victory. The Elites were league champs and they celebrated in the clubhouse, but not by dousing each other with beer. Beer was too good to waste. "We drank the beer," outfielder Butch McCord told author Bob Luke, adding, "I drank OJ."

The *Afro-American* summed up the entire championship series with a seven-paragraph story on page twenty-eight. That same edition, September 24, ran a headline across the top of page 1: JACKIE REGAINS BATTING LEADS AS BUMS BLAST CARDS. The story accompanying that headline carried sports editor Sam Lacy's byline and jumped to the second page. Inside were three other stories about the Brooklyn Dodgers and their black stars—Jackie, Campy, and Don Newcombe—and two about former Negro leaguer Sam Jethroe, then with the Montreal Royals. The Elites had become a mere afterthought in their own city.

The Elite Giants slipped to second place in the East in 1950, though Joe certainly bore no blame for that. He won seven of his first eight decisions and was selected to start the East-West Game for his division. On a chilly August day at Chicago's Comiskey Park, Joe had a rough outing despite early support from his friend Jim Gilliam, who drove a pitch from Vibert Clarke into the left-field stands for a 1–0 lead. The West erased that cushion by scoring twice off Joe in the third, though only one of those runs was earned. He allowed four hits in his three-inning stint, but got off the hook for the loss when the East tied it with a run in the fourth.

Earlier that season, in May, Joe had just joined the team after completing the work for his college degree when he made his first start against the Birmingham Black Barons. An old friend, Bill Greason, was the opposing pitcher. Both relied on heat, so when they faced each other, they didn't waste any pitches throwing curves. That meant when they batted, they could take hefty cuts because they knew what was coming. His first time up, Joe connected with a fastball and sent it deep to center field. He saw the center fielder racing back for the ball and laughed to himself, figuring he at least had a double, maybe a triple. But as he steamed toward second, Joe's smile turned to shock. The outfielder had run down his drive, had caught it for an out, and was already throwing the ball back to the infield.

Mumbling under his breath, Joe stomped back to the dugout, sat down next to Gilliam and asked, "Who the heck is that guy?"

"That's Willie Mays," Gilliam replied.

As he would see through the ensuing years, Joe was just one of many batters whose hopes for an extra base hit died in Willie's glove.

>>>>>>>>>>

The 1950 season was Joe's last in Negro league baseball, because the door that Jackie Robinson had cracked open finally swung out wide enough to let Joe in too. He had yearned for so long to hear the news that a Major League club wanted him, yet he could never just assume it would happen. And then, there it was, a telegram informing him that his and Jim Gilliam's contracts had been purchased by the Montreal Royals, the Brooklyn Dodgers' top farm club, and they were to report to spring training at Vero Beach, Florida, in February. He read the wire over and over, just to make sure of what it really said. Looking back on that day years later, Joe thought of the lyrics soul master James Brown sang:

I don't want nobody to give me nothing.
Open up the door, I'll get it myself.

Having become such good friends, it seemed fitting that Joe and Jim Gilliam would get their chance in organized baseball together. Joe held the belief that he got his chance *because* of Gilliam.

Back in February, the Elites had sold Gilliam and pitcher Leroy Ferrell, a promising right-hander, to the Chicago Cubs farm club at Springfield, Massachusetts. They went to spring training at Haines City, Florida, but three weeks later, both were released. The president of the Cubs minor league system, John T. Sheehan, told the Elites it didn't look as though Gilliam would be able to hit well enough at that level to stick. Joe didn't think that was the case. They had been teammates for four years, and he had watched Gilliam enough to know he could hit. He blamed his friend's troubles on his insecurity. Gilliam had grown up in a segregated environment and had played baseball only with other blacks. His stint with the Cubs organization was his first exposure to integrated sports and, according to Joe, he withdrew. On the bench, Gilliam sat off in the corner by himself. He rode in the back of the bus. He didn't talk to the other players. "I couldn't integrate," Joe recalled Gilliam saying. When the Dodgers started looking at Gilliam, Joe believed they were convinced that all he would need in order to get comfortable was a roommate he knew. Joe Black was the perfect choice.

Joe always felt he was a throw-in, and one account bears that out. A former Dodgers official, Mickey McConnell, wrote in 1979 that the organization bought Joe and Gilliam for a total of $5,500. Based on McConnell's recommendation, Dodgers president Branch Rickey wanted to buy Gilliam for $4,000. But the Elites asked for $5,000 and said they would throw Joe into the deal. McConnell had not seen Joe pitch, so the Dodgers countered with $4,000 for Gilliam and $500 to look at Joe, agreeing that if they kept Joe, the Elites would get an additional $1,000.

In the end, the sale price amounted to $10,000. A picture of a check that ran in the *Sporting News* showed Montreal paid that sum for Joe and Junior, with an option on Ferrell. Pitcher Ferrell also went to spring training with the Dodgers organization in 1951, but he was drafted into the army, hurt his shoulder playing in a military football game, and never played in the Major Leagues.

The check for Joe and Gilliam arrived in April 1951. Not long after that, Nashville nightclub owner William "Sou" Bridgeforth bought the Elite Giants for $10,000 and moved the team back to the Tennessee capital. However, the Elites ended up playing most of their 1951 games on the road, in places such as Buffalo, New York, Chicago, and Memphis. During one stretch, they hooked up with the New Orleans Eagles, who had moved to the Crescent City from Houston, for a series of games in Louisiana. It was clear the franchise was in its final throes. The team folded after the season, and the Elite Giants name was lost to history.

>>>>>>>>>>

It could be argued that Joe's greatest success in black baseball came in a diluted league bereft of its former glory. That doesn't mean he didn't benefit from those years. His confidence grew as he got better at locating his two pitches. He learned to channel the fierce disposition he brought to the mound while remaining easygoing and likable off the diamond. And all he endured in the Negro leagues—the long bus rides, the second-rate hotels, the crummy fields, the meals on the run—shaped him into someone who would forever appreciate what it takes to achieve a dream.

Joe also benefited from another experience during those years: winter ball in Latin America. He took that first opportunity in Venezuela in 1947 after getting hurt early in Morgan State's football season. Rather than risking another injury on the gridiron, he jumped at an offer of $800 a month plus round-trip transportation and achieved a respectable 7-5 record. Jackie Robinson had played in Venezuela on an all-star team in 1946, and when Joe showed up, the local media inferred, much to his amusement, that he and Jackie looked like twin brothers. Joe considered that one of the high points of his stint there. The Magallanes team was poor defensively and so lacking in punch that Joe pinch hit nine times.

Winter ball south of the border long had been an attractive option for Negro league players, who could make extra money and live for a while in a place free of the prejudice they so often encountered in the United States. Joe liked the money, too, along with the opportunity to continue honing his pitching skills, and he played in the Dominican Republic, Nicaragua, and Mexico before landing in a winter league that would help him take the final steps to the Major Leagues. Cuba sizzled in those days, a hot spot for vacationers and fun-seekers as well as for baseball players. It would turn out to be perfect for Joe Black.

7

Dizzy Dean Speaks Up

June 1952

JUNE BEGAN WITH THE DODGERS trailing the New York Giants by half a game and starting a two-game set against the Chicago Cubs at Wrigley Field. Wrigley had no lights then, so everything was played in the natural light of day. The Cubs were destined for a second-division finish in 1952, but they had been playing well early in the season, so they were not a team the Dodgers could overlook, especially in the friendly confines—well, friendly for the Cubs, anyway—of Wrigley and its ivy-covered outfield walls.

The Dodgers showed up to play, jumping to a 3–0 lead in the second inning to give starter Ben Wade a nice cushion. Wade kept the Cubs in check until the eighth, when he gave up a two-run, two-out triple to player-manager Phil Cavarretta. That was enough for Charlie Dressen, who summoned Joe from the bullpen. With Cavarretta representing the tying run on third, Joe fanned Eddie Miksis on a 3-2 pitch to end the inning. Dressen must have liked what he saw from Joe, because he sent him out for the bottom of the ninth after the Dodgers went down in order. Joe would face the number two, three, and four batters in the Cubs lineup as he tried to protect his team's one-run lead.

He got into immediate trouble. Bob Ramazzotti singled sharply to left on the first pitch and Joe threw the ball into the dirt at second on Gene Hermanski's bunt, putting runners on first and second with no outs. If there ever was a time Joe had to bear down, this was it, because power-hitting Hank Sauer came up next. He quickly got two strikes on the big swinger, who drilled the next pitch into the hole at shortstop. But Pee Wee Reese gloved the ball and tossed to second to force Hermanski. Getting Sauer was a relief, but Joe still wasn't out of the woods. The tying run was on third, Sauer stood as the potential winning run on first, and there was only one out. With the crowd of 40,389, the second-largest of the season to date in the National League, pleading for a hit or even a sacrifice fly, Joe silenced the throng by striking out Toby Atwell on four pitches and pumping three straight strikes past Dee Fondy.

The Dodger players rushed from their positions and charged out of the dugout to swarm Joe and congratulate him. Joe and his teammates had even more reason to celebrate a couple hours later, when the St. Louis Cardinals completed a doubleheader sweep of the Giants. The Dodgers were back in first place—by a full game. And they would stay in first the rest of the season.

Joe felt the relief stint at Wrigley Field was the turning point of his season, all the more so because of what happened the next day. Joe saw Dressen talking to a guy in the dugout, and Dressen called him over. Charlie then introduced Joe to Dizzy Dean, the former Cardinals pitching great who had become a broadcaster. "Charlie, this guy fires that ball just like ol' Diz used to do it," Dean said. "And you're not a smart man if you don't pitch that man, 'cause just like Diz, he just blows that ball past those hitters." From then on, Joe believed that Dean's comment persuaded Dressen to make him the club's top reliever. "If Dizzy Dean hadn't said anything, I'd just be humptying around," Joe said.

Over the next thirteen days, Dressen called on Joe five times. And his workload would only get heavier. In his classic best-seller *The Boys of Summer*, Roger Kahn wrote that he could still see Joe walking to the mound from the bullpen in the right-field corner of Ebbets Field. "He wore Number 49 and he approached with all deliberate speed," Kahn wrote, "holding a jacket in one hand, reaching the mound, exchanging a sentence with Dressen, who was half his size, taking a ritual pat on the flank from the pitcher he replaced and, with evident confidence and a certain impatience, going to work."

During that early June stretch, Joe saved a victory for Preacher Roe against the Reds at Cincinnati's Crosley Field, got his second victory of the season with three innings of shutout ball against the Cardinals in St. Louis, and preserved a 4–3 victory for Carl Erskine with three and two-thirds shutout innings against the Reds at Ebbets Field. He relieved Erskine in the fifth with runners on first and second and one out and got a big assist from Jackie Robinson, who leaped to spear a line drive by Hank Edwards and doubled Ted Kluszewski off first.

In the game at Cincinnati, Joe took over for Roe in the ninth inning with one out, a runner on third, three runs in, and the Dodgers leading 6–3. He retired Grady Hatton on a fly ball to center, which drove in Bobby Adams with the fourth run, then got the muscular Kluszewski on a popup to end it. Roe went to 5-0 with that victory, and Joe was only too happy to save it for the lanky left-hander who had greeted him on that first day of spring training and helped settle his nerves. After that first meeting, Preacher often chatted with Joe while they shagged flies in the outfield during batting practice, and he was generous in sharing advice. "Preacher was always coming over to me and talking like we had known each other for a long time," Joe said. "He says, 'You know, I feel like I can say things to you I can't say to Jackie.' He said, 'You seem more understanding. Jackie has a little chip. I don't blame him, the way they treated him, but you don't have that.' So he would give me pointers."

Another white teammate, Carl Furillo, the strong-armed right fielder, also befriended Joe. A solidly built six-foot-tall 190-pounder, Furillo once told him that if abuse from fans got too rough, "I'll go up to the stands and get them." Furillo and Joe often did calisthenics together and occasionally, they'd go fishing during spring training. One of those forays took them deep into the Florida woods in an episode that later had Joe shaking his head and wondering, "What was I thinking?"

Furillo's wife, Fern, accompanied them on that outing and they had fished for about twenty minutes when Carl said it was time to go pick up their two boys. He said he'd get them and told Fern to stay and keep fishing with Joe. So it was Joe and Fern, an attractive white woman in shorts, alone at the pond. Joe didn't think anything about it until a couple of days later when he read a newspaper story about a black man being savagely beaten because he had traveled through a southern town with a white female companion. That made Joe shudder to think what might have happened if a couple of white racists had come upon Joe and Fern at the pond. "You can bet that once they saw pretty Fern, wearing shorts, they would not believe that the colored man had pure thoughts," Joe wrote.

Furillo helped Joe get his victory over the Cardinals at Sportsman's Park in St. Louis with a two-run homer in the eighth inning. Joe had relieved Carl Erskine in the bottom of the seventh with the score tied at 2–2 and blanked the Cardinals the rest of the way, allowing only a pair of harmless singles.

Joe faced Stan Musial for the first time in that game, and as the great left-handed hitter settled into his peek-a-boo stance, Joe heard a voice booming from the St. Louis dugout. "Hey Stan," the guy yelled, "with that big black background, you shouldn't have trouble hitting that white ball." Joe stepped off the rubber, glared into the dugout and saw nothing but blank faces. Jackie rushed in from his position to ask Joe if he had seen who yelled. Joe said he hadn't and Jackie told him guys like that were gutless and always hid. "Forget it right now and work on Musial," he told Joe. Joe did just that, and retired the left-hander on a fly to center. When Joe bumped into Musial the next night, the future Hall of Famer apologized. "I'm sorry that happened, but don't let things like that bother you," Musial said. "You're a good pitcher." Joe told that story many times through the years, always remembering the dignity shown him by one of the game's great players.

For Joe, it was never the good players who bothered him. He felt most of the insults came from the benchwarmers, because they saw black players as a threat to their job security. Joe said those types of players had been comfortable for so long and then all of a sudden, blacks came into the big leagues and they could play. As integration continued, more and more white players would be losing their jobs. "Rather than respond as an athlete and become more competitive," Joe wrote, "too many of them chose to hide in the dugouts and shout profanity and racial slurs at the black ballplayers. Those cowardly acts angered us, but the dastardly actions made us more determined and more competitive rather than intimidated."

St. Louis, where racial attitudes were more reflective of the Deep South, was not a welcoming place for the early black players. While white players ate and slept in luxury at the Chase Hotel, blacks had to stay at the Adams Hotel, which was generally clean but lacked amenities their white counterparts enjoyed—including air conditioning, which made a big difference in steamy St. Louis. In 1953, the Chase management agreed to allow the Dodgers' black players to stay there. But when Joe, Campy, Jackie, and Jim Gilliam met with the manager, they were told they couldn't sit in the lobby, use the swimming pool, or eat or drink in the rooftop restaurant. In other words, they could stay, but they had to stay out of sight. Joe said he, Campy, and Gilliam went back to the Adams, but Jackie insisted on remaining at the Chase. "I'm not gonna let them chase me out of here, that's what they want," Jackie said. "I'm staying right here." By 1954, visiting teams could house all of their players at the Chase, though blacks didn't feel welcome even then. Joe said he and his black teammates once waited an hour to be served at the Chase's restaurant and it wasn't that busy. Home run king Hank Aaron recalled that black players "always had rooms facing a brick wall or the alley where they threw the garbage."

Cincinnati, just across the Ohio River from Kentucky, also could be a troublesome place for blacks. Joe remembered being seated next to the service doors or behind a pillar in hotel restaurants. Aaron said it was difficult to find any restaurant in Cincinnati that would serve black players. He and Billy Bruton once tried to eat at a place called the Cat and the Fiddle, where they sat and sat until realizing the place was about to close and no waiter was coming to their table. "We walked around town for a while and never did find a place that would let us buy a meal."

Joe had thought he would encounter the most abusive fans in St. Louis, but in his memory, Philadelphia—the City of Brotherly Love—had the worst. One fan in particular grated on him. "They had a fat guy and they'd send him to spring training to get into shape," Joe said. "I remember I saw him in Clearwater, Florida, against the Phillies. I came out of the dugout and I heard him: 'Robinson, you're a baboon!' I thought, what the heck? I was about three steps behind [Jackie and heard], 'There's a monkey behind you!' I looked up, there's the big fat guy. I'd be in the bullpen and I heard that voice, 'They're going to bring black Joe in there in a little bit.' I thought, oh man. But they found out they couldn't irritate Jackie. I guess they figured, we'll try the new guy."

It was because of the abuse Jackie took that Joe had so much respect for Pee Wee Reese, the little shortstop from Kentucky who stood beside his black teammate in an open display of solidarity despite the taunts from fans and opponents. Accounts differ on exactly when and where the episode occurred. Some have it happening in Cincinnati, some in Boston, others said Philadelphia. It might have happened in Jackie's first season, 1947, when he played first base, or later when he was at second base. It probably even happened more than once. But the gist of the story was the same: on a day the abuse was particularly blatant, Pee Wee walked over to Jackie, stood next to him, and put an arm on his shoulder as if to say, "We're with this guy so lay off." There are no known photographs of the moment, but the story circulated widely, including through the Negro leagues when Joe pitched for the Baltimore Elite Giants. That a white Southerner had made such a clear picture of friendship to Jackie resonated through the black community. Joe made sure Pee Wee knew that.

"Colored people in this country, they love you," Joe told the Dodgers captain. "Because you were the first outward sign that we saw that a white player had accepted Jackie."

"Joe," Pee Wee said, "we'd been some places they had been getting on him, but this day they were getting on him and he was standing at second waiting for the throw down and I looked and I could see his jaw just tightening and tightening. And I said, 'Oh my God, he's ready to explode.' I didn't know what to do, so I just walked over to him and was going to talk to him and I just put my arm up there and said, 'The hell with those guys.'"

At Reese's funeral in Louisville in 1999, Joe reminded the mourners of the shortstop's gesture, telling them, "Pee Wee helped make my boyhood dream come true to play in the majors, the World Series." He said he told Pee Wee, "When you touched Jackie, you touched all of us." The episode also made an impression with Pee Wee's white teammates. "Think of the guts that took," Carl Erskine said. "Pee Wee had to go home and answer to his friends. I told Jackie later that [Reese's action] helped my race more than his." A statue memorializing Pee Wee's gesture now stands outside MCU Park, home of the Class A Brooklyn Cyclones.

Just as Pee Wee had helped keep Jackie calm, Jackie did the same for Joe. He told Joe what to expect in each city throughout the league and what he might hear from fans and opposing players. If the abuse got particularly vicious while Joe was pitching, Jackie would walk to the mound and settle Joe down so his anger wouldn't consume him. "They called me coon and nigger and Old Black Joe and all that garbage," Joe recalled, "And every time I felt like fighting when it came from the stands, Jackie would just put his hand on my shoulder and say, 'You can't fight. Maybe some day, but not now. You can't fight.' It was hard to take." Other times his message was simpler. "Forget it," he'd say. "Just pitch."

>>>>>>>>>>

Joe wasn't perfect in his June outings, though he never cost the club a game. He relieved Ralph Branca in the ninth inning against the Pittsburgh Pirates at Forbes Field on June 3 and was touched for an RBI single by Joe Garagiola and a run-scoring double by Jack Merson. The first run was charged to Branca and both were unearned, because Pee Wee had dropped a throw on a force play for an error. Johnny Rutherford was sent in to replace Joe for the final out and preserved the team's 6–4 victory.

Garagiola's hit was an omen, because for some reason the modest-hitting Pirates catcher would torment Joe at the plate. Garagiola hit .273 in 1952, but he went 4-for-5 against Joe with a double, three RBIs, and three walks, two of them intentional. Joe later was quoted in the *Sporting News* as saying Garagiola and Bob Addis of the Chicago Cubs were the two toughest batters for him, a remark that Garagiola wore as a badge of honor. Still, he was puzzled why Joe would say that, so he asked him about it the next time they crossed paths. As Garagiola remembered it, Joe said, "You do hit me hard. I said to Campy, [do] you tell him what's coming? Nobody hits me that hard." Garagiola laughed at the memory. "I carried the clipping around," he said. "Hey, I've got a thing that says I'm the toughest hitter in the National League." In his *Sporting News* column, Oscar Ruhl originally said Garagiola went 8-for-9 against Joe. After famed Dodgers statistician Allan Roth pointed out it actually was 4-for-5 with three walks, Ruhl noted: "When all is said and done, a walk is as good as a single against a toughie like Black."

In a June 8 game against the Cincinnati Reds at Crosley Field, Joe gave up three hits and two runs in just two-thirds of an inning, but the Dodgers had a big day at the plate and won 11–7. He had another rough outing in St. Louis three days later after relieving Preacher Roe in the first inning with two runners on, two runs in, and one out. He yielded a two-run single to Dick Sisler that tied the score at 4-all before getting out of the inning, then was replaced by Clem Labine after the Cardinals loaded the bases against him. Still, Joe's numbers through thirteen games were impressive enough to get Dressen's attention: Joe had given up only four runs, just three earned, in twenty-four innings while striking out sixteen and walking six. He was 2-0 with four saves and starting to show the consistency that would make him one of the season's biggest surprises.

When Joe was called out of the bullpen in the fourth inning against the Chicago Cubs at Ebbets Field on June 18, he put in his longest stint of the season, working five and one-third innings. The Dodgers trailed 2–1 when he came in and he held the Cubs in check until that pesky Bob Addis belted a three-run home run, only the second round-tripper of his career, in the ninth inning. Prior to that, Joe had not allowed a run in eighteen innings at home. He left with his club trailing 5–4, but got off the hook when the Dodgers rallied to win 6–5 in ten innings.

Carl Erskine no-hit the Cubs the next day in a 5–0 victory, missing a perfect game only because he walked opposing pitcher Willie Ramsdell on four pitches in the third inning. "I was pitching too fast then," Carl said. "It looked like rain and I wanted to get the inning over quickly." Rain eventually interrupted the game for forty-four minutes, but it didn't bother Erskine, who dispatched the Cubs in one hour, forty-eight minutes of playing time.

Ramsdell stayed in the game until being lifted for a pinch hitter with one out in the ninth inning, at which point he headed for the clubhouse. As Bill Roeder of the *New York World-Telegram & Sun* related the story, Ramsdell was asked if he wanted to appear on a postgame television show as the other team's star, because he had been the only Chicago player to get on base. He would get fifty dollars for the appearance, but there was a catch. Eddie Miksis was coming to bat with two outs in the ninth and if he got a hit, *he'd* be on the show and collect the fifty dollars. Ramsdell then was escorted to a room under the stands to watch Miksis bat on a TV monitor. As Erskine got ready to pitch, Ramsdell cupped his hands around his mouth and, according to Roeder, yelled, "Come on, Carl, strike the bum out!" Miksis worked the count to 3-2 before grounding to shortstop Pee Wee Reese, who tossed to Gil Hodges at first for the final out, ensuring Ramsdell of his fifty bucks. A month later, the Cubs shipped Ramsdell, a thirty-six-year-old kunckleballer, to the Los Angeles Angels of the Pacific Coast League and he never appeared in the majors again.

Erskine's gem, coupled with Pittsburgh's defeat of the Giants, boosted the Dodgers to a five-game lead over the New Yorkers. The Brooks then finished the month strong, winning seven of ten to stay in control. Joe pitched four times in the last ten days of June as Dressen started to call on him regularly, and he allowed only one run in four and two-thirds innings while picking up a victory to go to 3-0 for the month.

He got the victory in finishing a 4–2 win over the Boston Braves at Ebbets Field on June 28, taking over in the eighth inning and blanking the Braves on one hit the rest of the way. Gil Hodges made him a winner by belting a two-run walk-off homer in the bottom of the ninth off talented leftie Warren Spahn. It was the fifteenth round-tripper of the season for the moon-faced first sacker. Hodges was a quiet man and one of the strongest in baseball, powerfully built at six foot two inches tall and two hundred pounds. He was in the prime of his career at the age of twenty-eight and would finish the season with thirty-two home runs before suffering through a disastrous World Series.

On this day, however, Joe was grateful for Gil's home run, and also for the way his usually stoic teammate tried to relax him in a tight spot with Stan Musial coming to bat. Hodges trotted over from first base and asked Joe if he knew how to pitch to Musial.

"Yep," Joe answered. "Keep fastballs down and away and jam him with the breaking pitch."

Hodges smiled, held the ball up, and said, "That sounds right, but if I was pitching, I'd call time out, ask for a bucket of water and swallow this pill."

Joe pitched the ninth inning in a 4–0 loss to the Philadelphia Phillies on June 30, giving up a home run to Willie "Puddin' Head" Jones on his first pitch before getting the next three batters out. The Giants swept a doubleheader from the Boston Braves that day, so the Dodgers went into July with a three-and-a-half-game lead and Joe Black establishing himself as the team's go-to guy in the bullpen.

8

GI Joe

BY THE SUMMER OF 1943, JOE HAD studied and played sports in an all-black environment at Morgan State and had played baseball in a segregated league, one black team against another, with mostly black fans in the stands. On July 27, he joined a United States Army that was likewise segregated. Blacks were shuttled into their own units, usually commanded by white officers. They had their own barracks, recreational facilities, and post exchanges, in most cases inferior to those used by white soldiers. While white enlisted men trained for combat, black draftees generally did the grunt work or served in support roles. They loaded and unloaded equipment, drove trucks, built roads and bridges, worked in mess halls, or served as hospital orderlies. In the Navy, they often worked as messboys or shipboard stewards, though many blacks drove the DUKW, the Navy's ship-to-shore landing craft. The general feeling among military commanders at the time was that blacks lacked discipline, intelligence, and the courage to fight. Black soldiers felt they were fighting one war overseas against fascism and imperialism and another at home against racism.

More than one million black men and women joined the armed forces during World War II. Many from the ranks of the Negro leagues served: Leon Day, Larry Doby, Monte Irvin, Max Manning, Jackie Robinson, Hank Thompson, Buck O'Neil, Leon Ruffin, Willard "Home Run"

Brown, Jimmie Crutchfield, Sammy T. Hughes, Jonas Gaines, and Dan Bankhead.

Some spent time in combat zones. Leon Day landed at Utah Beach on D-Day. Doby was stationed on the Pacific atoll of Ulithi as the US Marines island-hopped toward Japan. Irvin landed in Normandy with a unit of combat engineers two months after D-Day, then helped build roads and bridges across France. Before leaving for France, Irvin's unit guarded a supply depot near Plymouth in southern England. German planes bombed and strafed the depot only hours after his unit moved out. "If we hadn't moved," Monte recalled, "all of us might have been killed." Later, while Irvin's outfit guarded a gasoline depot in France during the Battle of the Bulge, he and his fellow GIs started itching for combat. Irvin thought the army didn't know what to do with black soldiers who, because they weren't fighting, felt they weren't making a contribution. Then they heard stories from some of the 101st Airborne paratroopers who saw action.

"You don't want to be up there at the front," the paratroopers said. "Those German eighty-eights are really mean and you've got the cold and hardships up there, too."

"After that," Monte said, "I didn't hear too much complaining anymore."

But thousands of black soldiers and airmen did fill combat roles. Among the most famous were the Tuskegee-trained pilots who escorted bombers on their runs over North Africa and Europe and shot down more than 100 enemy planes. The all-black 761st Tank Battalion fought its way across France and Germany in the final push that ended the fighting in Europe. Though not in actual combat roles, blacks made a major contribution driving trucks in the famous "Red Ball Express" that delivered needed supplies, often through hostile territory, to the troops slogging toward Germany.

>>>>>>>>>>

As Joe's military induction date approached, his emotions ran from eagerness to fear to acceptance of a duty to his country. Joe at first looked at his draft notice as an invitation to a party. Thousands of men were going into the service. How bad could it be? That changed when he began reading about the war with more than just cursory interest. The battlefields of Europe and the Far East suddenly seemed much closer to home. Casualty figures took on a new relevance. He read about the families who placed a gold star in a window of their home after losing a child to the war. At times, he recalled, "I would grimace as I thought of a bullet going through my body or that I might be killed. I was certain of one thing: I didn't want to die and I tried to think of ways by which I could fail my induction physical."

Joe's pride eventually pushed those thoughts aside. His nation had called him into service, and although it was fractured along racial lines, he was duty-bound to fulfill his obligation. He knew of friends who had been killed in Europe, Burma, and Bataan. They had made the ultimate sacrifice, and Joe had to prepare himself to do the same. Though nervous as he stood with the other inductees on the day he reported, Joe was ready to do his part to fight America's enemies. He couldn't have known it at the time, but Joe would never see a battlefield. His fields would be limited to those with four bases and a pitcher's mound, and he would train not with an infantry or artillery unit, but with the Medical Corps. He often wondered if his army experience would have turned out differently had he scored 118 on his IQ test instead of 149. Was he too smart to be thrown into the fighting?

Joe began his army duty at Fort Dix, New Jersey, where his main job was cleaning the grounds. A transfer took him to the Veterans Administration Hospital in Northport, Long Island, a complex of red-brick buildings on rolling, grassy grounds. Taking in the scene, Joe figured, great, he was a soldier, a guy who was supposed to be defending the country, and he'd probably be ordered to cut the grass. Instead, Joe was assigned to the Physiotherapy Department and told that after he finished his training, he'd be commissioned as a Warrant Officer in the Medical Corps. The patients were veterans with mental disorders, mainly shell shock. Joe learned about catatonics, schizophrenics, paranoiacs, and paranoid schizophrenics. Though he delighted in gaining knowledge in new subjects, he was saddened to see how the minds of healthy individuals had been destroyed. To his disappointment, Joe never became an officer. As manpower needs had increased, the army had decided that male soldiers no longer would be commissioned as officers in the field of physiotherapy.

Joe still found plenty of fulfillment in his stint on Long Island. He enjoyed the company of his fellow soldiers, a group that included Sidney Poitier, who would go on to an award-winning acting career. In 1943, however, Poitier was a troubled sixteen-year-old who lied about his age to join the army, which required enlistees to be eighteen. Joe got to pitch in games at Stewart Field, the air base for the US Military Academy at West Point. Among the batters he faced were Mickey Witek, who was the regular second baseman for the New York Giants in 1942 and '43, and Chuck Connors, who had a brief Major League career and played professional basketball before achieving more enduring fame as the star of the TV series *The Rifleman*.

Joe would admit years later that learning about Negro league baseball and then pitching a few times with the Elite Giants had blinded him to the realities of segregation, which confronted him head-on in the army. He also found that racism on the East Coast was camouflaged, but existed just the same. His was an all-black unit that supported the civilian staff at the VA Hospital, and when they were off duty on weekends, Joe and others would pile into two trucks and ride to the nearby town of Oyster Bay or Huntington. Each town had a small black community with a couple of bars, where the soldiers in Joe's unit could meet women and listen to music.

>>>>>>>>>>

Many years later my dad cautioned me about the company I should keep. I know now he was just looking out for my well-being. When he spoke to me about men, he never put it as don't do this or don't do that. Instead, he always said, "Your body is the only body you have, and that is your gift. I know other women can do whatever with men, but just because they do, doesn't mean you have to do it. Because your body is only yours. You are special."

I think he spoke to me in that manner because of what he did when he played baseball. My dad always said, "God gave you a mind for thinking, a body for working, and a heart for loving. God gave you those things for a reason, so you should use them wisely."

That's how he succeeded. He used what God gave him.

>>>>>>>>>>

Military police officers always accompanied the troopers on their forays into town, just to make sure everyone stayed out of trouble. One night, two of the black MPs patrolling the area stopped at a roadhouse in the white section of Oyster Bay, hoping to get some sandwiches and beer. The place was filled with customers, all of them white, and when the MPs asked the bartender if they could order some food and drink to take out, she told them, "We don't serve niggers in here." They told her they didn't intend to eat in the building. All they wanted was to take the sandwiches and beer out to their truck. "We don't serve niggers in here," she repeated. They asked to speak to the manager and got the same response. So the MPs left to a chorus of customers hooting, laughing, and yelling insults.

After they told the others in the unit what had happened, everyone agreed to return en masse and order fifty sandwiches and beer. They did, and the manager repeated, "I thought I told you we don't serve niggers in here." If the guy planned to say something else, he never got the chance. One of the MPs drove his fist into the manager's nose and then, as Sidney Poitier recalled it, "all hell broke loose." The soldiers tore the place up as customers fled through any opening they could find. The female bartender tried to escape through a window and was helped along by a soldier who booted her in the rear. Within minutes, "the bar was left in shambles," Joe said.

Their captain got mad as a hornet when he learned about the incident the next day and ordered everyone in the unit, all 150 soldiers, to line up on the parade ground. He said he didn't want to punish anyone who wasn't there, so he asked the guilty parties to take one step forward. All 150 soldiers then stepped forward—in formation. Unamused, the captain confined the entire unit to base for six months and threatened everyone with a court martial. But no one squealed and army investigators never did learn who took part in the ruckus.

Joe and his buddies also partied in New York City from time to time, usually heading to the jazz clubs on East 52nd Street. One night, Joe's friend Gervis Tillman began teasing him about drinking Coca-Cola. Joe didn't drink alcohol and was content to sip soft drinks when out on the town. He eventually relented, however, and said he'd order a drink. His buddies suggested beer, but Joe thought that being in a nice club, he should have a mixed drink. Then you should order a Tom Collins, they said, because it didn't have much alcohol and looked like lemonade. It was a favorite of the ladies for that reason. "Sure enough, it did look like a fancy lemonade," Joe thought. He decided to treat it like castor oil. Drink it fast and maybe it wouldn't leave an alcohol taste in his mouth. So he chugged half the glass and found that hey, the stuff wasn't bad. He finished the glass—and then drank four more. He awoke the next morning with a stomachache and felt stiff and sore all over. He dragged himself to breakfast, where another one of his friends, Calvin Smith, remarked, "Man, I didn't know you liked to fight so much."

"What the heck are you talking about?" Joe said.

"Don't you remember having those fights last night?" Calvin asked.

Joe thought Calvin was just messing with him, but Calvin insisted he wasn't joking and told Joe his last encounter had been with an MP at the gate, and Joe had agreed to fight him at four o'clock that afternoon. Joe merely laughed and went about his duties. As he walked back to the barracks after checking out for the day, Smith and Tillman met him and told him the MP and his buddies were waiting. Joe realized then they were telling the truth, so he accepted his fate and donned boxing gloves. As the spectators cheered, jeered, cajoled, and shouted advice, Joe and the MP traded punches. Joe thought his opponent must have tripped, because it looked as though he had been staggered by Joe's blows, so the "Plainfield Puncher" was declared the winner. That night, Joe decided he wasn't a drinker. He'd sip nothing stronger than water, soft drinks, juice, or milk.

>>>>>>>>>>

Most army bases were located in the South or Southwest, which exacerbated tensions for black soldiers. Not only did they have to deal with segregation and subpar facilities on base, they faced hostility and Jim Crow laws in the local communities. Those tensions at times boiled over into riots, some of them deadly. Major disturbances broke out at Fort Bragg in North Carolina, Camp Van Dorn in Mississippi, Camp Stewart in Georgia, Fort Bliss in Texas, Camp Breckinridge in Kentucky, Camp Phillips in Kansas, and March Field and Camp San Luis Obispo in California.

A disturbance at Fort Bragg left one white MP and one black soldier dead; two white MPs and three black soldiers were wounded. Just outside Camp Van Dorn, a black soldier who had been questioned by an MP tried to flee and was shot by the county sheriff. A near-riot ensued on the base and one soldier was slightly wounded when a squad of black MPs fired into a group trying to rush them. The body of a black army private from Fort Benning in Georgia was found hanging in the woods, a noose around his neck and his hands tied behind his back. It had all the appearances of a lynching, but army investigators treated it as a probable suicide and no one was ever prosecuted. At Camp Stewart, one MP was killed and four were wounded during an altercation triggered by a rumor that a black woman had been raped and murdered by white soldiers after they killed her husband. Investigators concluded the riot was brought about by pent-up emotions and long-held resentments among black soldiers.

Even bases in the North were not immune from trouble. Near Fort Dix, New Jersey, where Joe had begun his army stint, a white MP and two black soldiers were shot to death during a disturbance triggered by a dispute over a telephone booth.

Though no violence ensued, one of the best-known incidents involving a black soldier came when Jackie Robinson, stationed at Fort Hood in Texas, defied an order from a white bus driver to sit in the back. Jackie ended up facing a court-martial that he said smelled of a frame-up, but the army judges ruled in his favor.

Joe's next assignment took him to one of those bases in the Southwest, Camp Barkeley near Abilene, Texas. Boarding a train at New York's Penn Station, he understood that by leaving the East Coast, his baseball career with the Elite Giants truly was on hold. But he was serving his country, and as the train chugged out of the station, he noted that blacks and whites rode together. Any satisfaction from that vanished when he changed trains in St. Louis. "Wearing uniforms of the U.S. Armed Services gave you no privileges," he said. All black travelers had to sit in the cars that were closest to the locomotive. Black passengers who wanted to eat in the dining car had to be lucky enough to secure one of the eight seats reserved for them behind the curtain that separated blacks from whites.

Any train traveling south of a Missouri-Ohio-Potomac line was similarly segregated. Cars for blacks often were poorly kept and crowded, while those reserved for whites rolled along with empty seats. Ulysses

Lee, who undertook an extensive study of life for black soldiers during the war, wrote: "Negroes generally argued that the Jim Crow car was always separate but never equal." Joe decided against waiting for one of the few seats in the black section of the diner to open when he got hungry, instead eating "paper thin bologna sandwiches" and fried pies he bought from a vendor. "Constipation is not your best friend the first day you report for duty at your next Army camp," he said.

Camp Barkeley was a sprawling complex named for a Texan who was awarded the Medal of Honor in World War I, David B. Barkley (somewhere along the line, the extra "e" was mistakenly added to the name). It was not a welcoming place for black soldiers. A letter to the *Pittsburgh Courier*, the city's black newspaper, written by black soldiers called Camp Barkeley "the worst camp we have ever been to." They complained that the swimming pool was open to blacks only on Monday and Friday and the only movie theater at the post that blacks were allowed to attend was outdoors. If it rained, there was no show. Only two of the buses to town were reserved for blacks, and even if a white bus had only one passenger, the driver wouldn't stop for black soldiers.

Another letter from the post, written a year later, said all five theaters had been opened to blacks after much protest, but the seating was segregated. The few black buses were always overcrowded, according to the writer, Private Bert B. Babero, and the black living quarters were located just in front of the camp's cesspool. Camp Barkeley also housed German prisoners of war, and Babero was disheartened to see a sign on a latrine stipulating one side for blacks and the other for whites and POWs. "It made me feel, here, the tyrant is actually placed over the liberator," he wrote.

Joe thought he'd be attending Officer Candidate School at Camp Barkeley, but when he presented his papers to the officer of the day, he could tell by the man's body language that something was wrong. After reading the papers, the officer looked up and told Joe he wasn't eligible for OCS, because somehow, Joe had spent sixteen months in the army without going through basic training. The officer assigned Joe to a basic training battalion and he accepted the order without protest, knowing it was something every army grunt had to endure.

So off he went to a routine of early reveille, a barking sergeant, and drills, drills, and more drills. Joe had never hoisted a firearm heavier than a cap pistol or BB gun, so carrying a Springfield rifle on his shoulder was a shock. He thought his shoulder would break from hoisting that rifle in all the drills while marching. Firing the rifle was problematic, too. Joe had no clue about recoil. The rifle kicked so strongly that his first shots flew well above the target. It was almost as embarrassing as his first attempts at hitting in Negro league ball.

Joe spent seven months at Camp Barkeley, and that was long enough. One weekend he had a pass and decided to check out Abilene. He got off the army bus and was headed toward the black and Mexican section of town when he sensed two people walking up rapidly behind him. He glanced back over his shoulder and saw two white men in cowboy hats. The men slowed when they got to within ten feet of Joe, who was in his uniform. He could not be mistaken for a local.

"What is that in that army uniform in front of us? A monkey can't be that big, so it must be one of those northern baboons," Joe recalled one saying.

Joe ignored them. He wasn't afraid to fight, but thoughts of the lynchings he had read about made him dismiss that notion, and he kept walking. He heard one of the men say, "It's Saturday night, he must be going into nigger town for some kitty cat." The other one then said, "If he doesn't turn into colored town, I'm going to stick my boot up his ass."

Though insulted, Joe decided it was, as he put it later, "better to be a living coward than a dead hero." He turned toward the railroad tracks, walked away from his hecklers, and waited for the bus to return him to base. As the bus bounced down the highway, he puzzled over what had just happened. He wore a US Army uniform. He hadn't done anything wrong. Yet he was treated as someone who wasn't quite human. "I kept trying to figure out: Why are they doing this?" Joe never did get to see Abilene. And he never asked for another weekend pass while he was at Camp Barkeley. The incident was one episode in a series of reminders—separate facilities, prejudicial attitudes, substandard amenities—that the United States, which he had once seen as the great melting pot, was actually two societies: one for whites, another for blacks. Joe felt that with segregation dividing institutions like the army and baseball, America seemed to condone racial prejudice. "Is this liberty and justice for all?" he asked.

Once his basic training was completed, Joe expected to be sent to OCS. Instead, the army again assigned him to a medical unit. He attended classes in anatomy, physiology, and histology and learned how to draw blood and give shots. It wasn't what he had anticipated, but it sure beat lugging that Springfield rifle around. Joe didn't remain at Camp Barkeley much longer. His entire battalion packed up in the spring of 1945 and moved to Camp Crowder in the Ozark Hills of southwestern Missouri, near the town of Neosho. Camp Crowder was one of the largest military installations in the Midwest, with more than 47,000 soldiers stationed there at its operational peak. Among them was a young GI named Mort Walker, who later created the Beetle Bailey cartoon strip and based his fictional Camp Swampy on Camp Crowder. Walker came up with the name "Swampy" because the base grounds were prone to flooding. He recalled that one morning he woke up and found "we were in a lake."

>>>>>>>>>>

Just like other bases, Camp Crowder had subpar facilities for black soldiers. One soldier stationed there wrote that his unit lived in a "condemned area" and they had to shave and clean up in a poorly heated hut across the street from their barracks. The German POWs held there "live better than we do," he wrote.

Despite the conditions, Joe found a more relaxed atmosphere at Camp Crowder, devoid of the racial tension he had felt in Texas. Part of the 66th Battalion, Joe was assigned to Company D, which formed a basketball team that played other company teams and nearby colleges. The team featured Hubert Price, who had played for the Harlem Globetrotters and was so good that he was asked to join the post team, which represented the entire base. That delighted Joe, because it meant Camp Crowder had an integrated team. So that spring, after joining his company's baseball team, Joe saw a notice about tryouts for the post's baseball team and assumed the invitation extended to black soldiers. He found, to his dismay, that it did not. He went to a practice, watched from the bleachers for about fifteen minutes to check out the talent, then asked one of the players how he could try out. The player replied that "you people are going to have your own baseball team." Dejected, Joe walked back to the 66th, stung again by the inequalities in his life.

The next day, as he practiced with his company team, for which he was the number-one pitcher, a Jeep stopped at the bleachers behind home plate and two white soldiers got out. They watched practice for a while, and then Joe's coach brought them over to where he was working out, introducing them as Sergeants Neil O'Donnell and Harry Steiber.

"Are you the soldier who came over to the post team for a tryout?" O'Donnell asked. Joe said he was.

"That soldier had no authority to send you away," said O'Donnell, who played minor league ball before the war and would do so again after he was discharged. "What position do you play?"

"I'm a pitcher," Joe replied.

"Steiber is the catcher for the team," O'Donnell said. "Would you mind throwing him a few pitches?"

Steiber borrowed a mitt and Joe fired some pitches. Those few pitches—at the time Joe figured he could pump his fastball in at 100 miles an hour—were enough to convince O'Donnell, who asked Joe if he'd consider showing up for the post team's practice the next day. "He'll be there!" Joe's teammates shouted.

The post team was coached by Tommy Bridges, a Tennessean who at that point had won 192 games in fourteen seasons as a right-handed pitcher for the Detroit Tigers. From 1934 through 1936, Bridges rang up victory totals of 22, 21, and 23 and twice led the American League in strikeouts, relying on a big-breaking curveball. A former teammate, pitcher Elden Auker, said Bridges had the best curve he ever saw. "It was like it rolled off the edge of the table," Auker said. Interestingly, Bridges had pitched against the St. Louis Cardinals in the 1934 World Series, which Joe had seen the men following outside the Plainfield newspaper office. Bridges went 1-1 in that series, throwing a seven-hitter in a 3–1 victory against Dizzy Dean that gave the Tigers a lead of three games to two, which the Cardinals erased by winning the last two games.

Bridges, then thirty-eight and the post team's top pitcher, sized Joe up and said, "Neil and Harry tell me that your fastball makes them think of Bob Feller. If you are one half as good as they claim, it will be good for me because I won't have to do too much pitching."

Bridges then asked Joe if he'd be ready to pitch against Fort Leonard Wood in two days. Joe couldn't say no, so it was settled. He hadn't even practiced with the team and he was already getting his first start.

Many base commanders took great pride in their athletic teams, and they were able to stock them with numerous professional athletes during the war. The Great Lakes Naval Training Station north of Chicago fielded perhaps the best teams in those years. Hall of Fame catcher Mickey Cochrane managed the club, which at one time or another had the likes of Walker Cooper, Billy Herman, Johnny Mize, Gene Woodling, Schoolboy Rowe, and Virgil Trucks. When Cochrane was sent to the Pacific, Bob Feller, back from duty aboard the USS *Alabama*, became the team's manager and top pitcher. Before shipping out to the Pacific, Feller had pitched for the Norfolk Training Station team along with Fred Hutchinson. Phil Rizzuto, Dom DiMaggio, Eddie Robinson, and Tommy Byrne also played for the Norfolk team.

Dom DiMaggio's more accomplished brother, Joe, played for the Army Air Corps base at Santa Ana, California, while the Navy's preflight training program at the University of North Carolina had Ted Williams, Johnny Pesky, and Johnny Sain. Stan Musial played for the team at the Naval Training Station in Bainbridge, Maryland, as did Dick Bartell, Buddy Blattner, Fred Chapman, and Elbie Fletcher. So it was no accident that a player of such repute as Bridges was put in charge of the Camp Crowder team. On game day, Joe was excused from duty early so he could get ready. This time, he didn't have to walk. He was in the army "big leagues" now, so he was driven to the diamond. Once there, he began feeling a little unsettled. Then he realized why: everyone there except him was white. He had played integrated sports back in Jersey, of course, but for the last three years, he had lived in a segregated world of "whites only" here, "coloreds only" there. The Fort Leonard Wood players looked at him curiously. He sensed puzzlement in the looks of the whites in the bleachers. Most of his teammates greeted him with a grunt instead of hello or good luck. He felt all alone in the midst of this white world. If he didn't perform, he might never get another chance.

Then, off in the distance, he heard a chant. "Jody had your girl when you left, you're right. Jody had your girl when you left, you're right. Left. Right. Left. Right. Hup two. Hup two. Count cadence count. By the numbers. Count cadence count. By the numbers. One, two, three, four, cadence count. There's a one, two, threeeee, four. There's a one-two—three-four. 'Cause Jody took your girl when you left, you're right."

As the chant grew louder, Joe smiled and breathed a sigh of relief. Company D of the 66th Battalion had arrived to support their fellow soldier. He promptly relaxed and pitched a four-hitter in Camp Crowder's 6–1 victory. The game did produce an incident that Joe laughed about later. The catcher and other team members used to yell words of encouragement to the pitcher. "Come on, Smitty, hum it in here!" or "Throw hard, babe! Throw hard!" Early in the game, the third baseman ambled over and asked Joe what he should call him.

"I can't say come on, Blackie," the guy said.

"You're right," Joe responded. "Call me Joe."

Joe was so excited about winning that he swapped his spikes for army boots and marched back to Company D with his fellow troopers. Back at the barracks, soldiers greeted him with applause and cheers. Joe talked with fellow athletes Hubert Price and Jimmy Hicks during dinner, and they agreed that once on the playing field or court, color was not an issue. Talent and effort, not race, determined success. Two days later, Tommy Bridges told Joe that he would be the team's number-one pitcher. That would ensure that Joe got plenty of work and he was grateful for that, because his only chance to pitch for the Elite Giants in 1945 came during his two-week furlough.

With the post baseball team, Joe felt accepted, even by the soldiers from the Deep South. He believed that because of his deportment and intelligence—not to mention his fastball—his teammates from the South changed their views of blacks and accepted him as a person. Away from the field, however, Joe didn't socialize with his teammates, because all the facilities were segregated. White soldiers had their areas, blacks had their own, and they didn't meet.

>>>>>>>>>>

The Camp Crowder team generally took an army bus on road trips. When they'd stop to eat, Joe usually would pretend he was asleep. Restaurants displayed their WHITES ONLY signs prominently and Joe wasn't inclined to challenge them. It was easier to make it appear he was too sleepy to go inside. He got something to eat only because teammates brought food to him on the bus. Once, though, during an especially long trip, Joe's teammates felt he needed to get up, stretch his legs, and eat a decent meal. They shushed his protestations, ignored the signs, and walked him into the restaurant. The whole place went quiet when the customers saw Joe, the silence finally interrupted by a booming voice that proclaimed, "We don't serve niggers in here." One of Joe's teammates, who happened to be from Georgia, shouted back, "We don't have any niggers with us. We are all members of the United States Army." Joe wanted the guys to back off and avoid causing trouble, but they were insistent. "We all eat or nobody eats," one declared. Angered by the soldiers' demand, the proprietor ordered all of them to leave. They did—eventually. First, they tore the place apart, Joe said. Tables and chairs flew across the room in a noisy clatter. The smack of fist hitting skin and the yelps of those receiving the blows added to the cacophony. Satisfied they had made their point, the soldiers returned to their bus—tired, bruised, disheveled, and still hungry.

"That was a nice thing to do," Tommy Bridges told his team. "We're soldiers. We're part of the United States Army defending this country. All of us are the same." Bridges let that sink in, then added, "Secondly, I'm proud of you, because you're a team. You acted like a team and you took care of your teammate."

Bridges and the team stood up for Joe during a similar incident at a Kansas City restaurant, where the manager greeted each of Joe's teammates and directed them to a seat. Then he saw Joe and asked, "Who are you?" Before Joe could answer, Bridges interjected, "That's Corporal Black, our star pitcher," he said. The manager mumbled something, then smiled and asked Joe to follow him because the cook would like to meet the star pitcher. They walked into an empty banquet room, where the manager told Joe to sit down and then went to get the cook. The cook was black, and he and Joe talked about the Negro leagues for a few minutes. When the cook left, the manager reappeared with a plate of food and told Joe he'd be more comfortable eating there. Joe looked around at the room, which he estimated could seat two hundred diners, and realized he wasn't welcome in the regular dining room. Angered and humiliated, Joe slid back his chair and stormed out through the restaurant to the door.

"Hey Joe, where are you going?" a teammate asked.

"To a restaurant where I'll be welcome," Joe responded.

Once Bridges saw what was going on, he asked Joe to wait a minute. When he returned, the entire team followed him into the banquet room and they ate with Joe. Segregation still ruled many areas of his life, but Joe was heartened by the knowledge that some whites believed in his dignity as a human being.

Joe enjoyed his time with the Camp Crowder team. Bridges gave him plenty of opportunity to pitch so he could stay sharp. If he couldn't pitch for the Elite Giants, playing ball in the army was the next best thing. He wasn't sure he was becoming a better pitcher, but at least he was pitching. Once, when he was getting ready to bat against a team he was dominating on the mound, the catcher struck up a conversation.

"So they call you Big Joe?" he said.

"Yeah," Joe replied.

"Why?" the catcher asked.

"Because I'm big," Joe responded.

"You're a thrower," the catcher told him.

Joe knew that was so. "That's all I was," he later acknowledged. "I didn't know how to pitch. I just let it go."

Tommy Bridges saw that, too. "If you ever learned to throw a curveball," Bridges told him, "you'd be hard to hit."

Joe would hear that, or something similar, many times in the years ahead.

>>>>>>>>>>

Just as Negro league players like Joe were called into the service, so too were players from the white Major Leagues, including top stars. These included not only Bob Feller, Ted Williams, Joe DiMaggio, Stan Musial, and Phil Rizzuto but also Yogi Berra, Pee Wee Reese, Hank Greenberg, and Enos Slaughter. The mass movement to the armed forces left the sixteen Major League teams desperate for bodies to stock their rosters. In many cases, that's about all they were—bodies. Players who were too young or too old and too untalented wore big-league uniforms during the war years. In ordinary times, they never would have been there.

The mighty Yankees were reduced to using players like catcher Mike Garbark and shortstop Mike Milosevich. Garbark batted .244 with a grand total of two home runs in 1944 and '45, his only seasons in the majors. Milosevich hit .241 in those same seasons with no home runs and only seventeen extra-base hits.

Brooklyn Dodgers coach and scout Clyde Sukeforth suited up in 1945 at the age of forty-three and appeared in eighteen games. Babe Herman, a popular player among the Dodgers' "Daffiness Boys" of the 1920s, returned after a seven-year absence from the majors to play in thirty-seven games for the Bums. Jimmie Foxx came out of retirement to play for the Philadelphia Phillies in 1945 and belted the final seven home runs of his Hall of Fame career, which produced 534 round-trippers. Also that season, Gus Mancuso caught seventy games for the Phillies at the age of thirty-nine. The Detroit Tigers won the American League pennant and World Series in 1945 with a double-play combination of two thirty-five-year-olds—second baseman Eddie Mayo and shortstop Skeeter Webb. Outfielder Doc Cramer played in 140 games for the Tigers that season, at age thirty-nine. The 1945 Cincinnati Reds had three pitchers at least forty years old, including forty-six-year-old Hod Lisenbee, who had last played in the majors in 1936.

At the other end of the age scale, Joe Nuxhall pitched a game for the Reds in 1944 at the age of fifteen years, ten months, and eleven days. The Dodgers brought up shortstop Tommy Brown at the age of sixteen and used him in 103 games in 1944 and '45. Pitcher Carl Scheib was four months shy of his seventeenth birthday when he debuted with the Philadelphia Athletics in 1943. Infielder Eddie Yost, who would go on to play eighteen seasons, was seventeen years old when the Washington Senators put him on the field in 1944. Perhaps the most famous war-time fill-in of them all was Pete Gray, the one-armed outfielder who hit .218 in seventy-seven games for the St. Louis Browns in 1945. The majors were so watered down that the lowly Browns won the American League pennant in 1944, after finishing in the first division only once in the previous fourteen seasons.

Yet with the Major Leagues so desperate for players during the war years, not one team tapped what could have been a rich resource—the Negro leagues. Raw teenagers and old-timers long past their prime, not to mention a one-armed outfielder, were signed over the likes of Satchel Paige, Josh Gibson, Roy Campanella, Sam Jethroe, Verdell Mathis, Ray Dandridge, Pee Wee Butts, Luke Easter, Lennie Pearson, and Dave Barnhill. "Shoot," pitcher Chet Brewer huffed, "the only thing a one-armed white man can do as good as a two-armed black man is scratch the side that itches."

All the while the lords of baseball continued to insist there was no rule, written or unwritten, that banned blacks from the Major Leagues. After the Communist Party newspaper the *Daily Worker* quoted Dodgers manager Leo Durocher as saying he would sign black players if baseball allowed it, Commissioner Kenesaw Mountain Landis hauled Leo into his office. Landis, a determined foe of integration, emerged from that meeting in July 1942 to say that Durocher had been misquoted and to proclaim, in all seeming sincerity, that baseball had no "understanding, unwritten, subterranean, sub-anything" against signing black players. Overseas, blacks fought—and died—alongside white soldiers. But at home, Landis's remarks notwithstanding, they were not allowed to play alongside whites on a Major League baseball field. "I can play in Mexico, but I have to fight for America where I can't play," Negro league pitcher Nate Moreland complained.

Oh, there was talk of tryouts for black players—and some were even held, though the two most widely known were forced upon the big-league teams. In early April 1945, sportswriter Joe Bostic arrived unannounced at the Brooklyn Dodgers spring training camp at Bear Mountain, New York, with Negro leaguers Dave "Showboat" Thomas and Terris McDuffie and demanded they be given a tryout. Thomas, a slick-fielding first baseman, was a veteran of more than twenty years in black baseball, while McDuffie had been a top-notch pitcher. But both were in their thirties, past their prime, and Dodgers general manager Branch Rickey was irate at having the tryout thrust upon him. He gave the two players a cursory look and then sent them away. Later that month, the Boston Red Sox, under pressure from sportswriters and city councilor Isadore Muchnick, allowed Jackie Robinson, Sam Jethroe, and Marvin Williams to try out. None was invited back.

Roy Campanella had his hopes of playing big-league baseball recharged in 1942 when he was told the Pittsburgh Pirates wanted him to attend a tryout along with pitcher Dave Barnhill and infielder Sammy Hughes. Campy waited and waited and eventually received a letter from Pirates President William Benswanger that "contained so many buts that I was discouraged even before I had finished reading" it. Benswanger told Campanella that he'd have to start at the bottom of the farm system and work his way up, he would not be paid much, and there was no guarantee that he'd make it. Still, Campy wrote back to say that he would be happy to start in the low minors. All he wanted was a chance. When it was reported that the tryout would be August 4 and the three players were named, Benswanger denied setting a date and knowing the names of the players to be invited. Campanella never heard another word from the Pirates. No wonder he lamented in his autobiography, "As far as I was concerned the big leagues were in Siberia."

It wasn't until after the war ended and Commissioner Landis had died that the color barrier finally broke with the Brooklyn Dodgers' signing of Jackie Robinson. The war years had exposed the nation's hypocrisy in race relations—blacks fighting for freedoms they were denied at home—and helped accentuate the push for integration. Jackie's signing would take it to a new level.

A little more than a week after news of Rickey's bold move flashed across the country in October 1945, Joe Black received a letter from a Boston Red Sox scout named Joe Becker, who had umpired some of the games Joe pitched for Camp Crowder. Joe impressed Becker with his velocity and rangy build. Becker saw a potential Major Leaguer and let Joe know that in his letter.

"You have the one thing that we are looking for in a Major League prospect—the fast ball," Becker wrote. "You have a good, in fact, a fine physique. In other words, you have the fundamental qualifications of a Major League ball player."

Becker continued, "You have a lot to learn about pitching, as far as the Major Leagues are concerned. But, that is no drawback. We all have to learn our ABCs before we can put the letters together so we can read them and know their meaning. I am interested in your future in baseball and if the proper arrangements can be made, will be more than glad to get you the opportunity in organized professional baseball."

Thus, two pieces of paper—Jackie's minor league contract and the letter from Becker—rekindled Joe's dream of playing Major League baseball and made that dream seem reachable. As it turned out, Jackie's signing carried much more weight. Whether Becker didn't follow through on recommending Joe to Red Sox management or whether the Red Sox simply weren't interested, Joe never found out. He heard nothing from the club that would be the last in the Major Leagues to put a black player on the field. It didn't happen until Pumpsie Green ran for Vic Wertz in the eighth inning of a game against the Chicago White Sox at Comiskey Park on July 21, 1959, a full twelve years after Jackie debuted with the Dodgers.

Joe didn't have to wait that long, but in 1945 his date with white baseball was still years away. He was discharged from the army in March 1946 and within a month, he was a professional baseball player again, working out with the Elite Giants in spring training. He went about his drills with a new vigor, because after pitching in those army games, he was convinced he had what it took to become a Major League pitcher.

9

Joe to the Rescue

July 1952

As Joe got stronger and more dependable, many of his teammates—the pitchers in particular—struggled with an assortment of ailments. Ralph Branca had injured his back in spring training when he landed on a Coke bottle after a metal folding chair collapsed. The fall knocked him out of alignment and he developed a sore arm, which limited his work and resulted in a stint on the thirty-day disabled list. By the end of June, Branca had pitched only ten times and worked just forty-seven innings. He started against the Philadelphia Phillies on July 1, then did not pitch again until September 2. He would end up pitching a mere nine innings in the final month. Preacher Roe, at age thirty-six, was having back problems. Though he took a 7-0 record into July, Roe wasn't eating up innings at the rate he had the year before. He'd pitch only two complete games after June 24 and finish with a modest 159 innings.

Branca and Roe both had been staff stalwarts in 1951. Branca went 13-12 while giving the club 204 innings and pitching thirteen complete games, but would be remembered only for the home run ball he had served up to Bobby Thomson. Roe had racked up nineteen complete games and 258 innings in 1951 while posting a glittering 22-3 record.

Reliever Clyde King had developed a sore arm near the end of his superb 1951 season and hardly pitched in the early weeks of 1952. Through the end of June, King had worked only nine and two-thirds innings and was ineffective, allowing fifteen hits and five earned runs. Only one year earlier, King had gone 14-7 and led the National League with thirteen victories in relief. King said he wore out late in the year—he pitched only nine innings in September and allowed twelve runs as the Dodgers vainly fought to stay ahead of the Giants—and felt he'd be able to pace himself better in 1952. Earlier in the '51 season, King had been so effective that team president Walter O'Malley tore up his contract and gave him a raise.

Clem Labine also developed a sore arm and Johnny Rutherford had a shoulder problem. Labine would finish 1952 with a 5.14 earned run average and more walks (forty-seven) than strikeouts (forty-three), yet he still managed an 8-4 record. But he'd win only once after July 11. Rutherford would pitch just four innings in July after working just six and one-third innings in June, but got stronger down the stretch when manager Charlie Dressen moved him into the starting rotation.

Carl Erskine was gutting his way through his starts with a sore elbow, which required applications of pain-deadening salve so he could pitch. That was nothing new for the gritty right-hander, who pitched in pain for most of his career but still won sixty percent of his games, notched two no-hitters, and set a World Series record by striking out fourteen while beating the New York Yankees in game three of the 1953 Fall Classic.

"For some reason, the Dodger pitching staffs during the late 1940s and into the 1950s had tremendous arm troubles," said the man Dodger fans knew as Oisk. "I don't know why exactly. I fought an arm injury almost my whole career, but nobody knew how to deal with it. Where's it hurt? It wasn't bleeding, it wasn't swollen, it wasn't bruised. They'd look in your eyes and imagine it's all in your head. A bone wasn't sticking out, so you must not be hurt. There wasn't a real sensitivity to pitchers then. They were seen as necessary evils. You had to have them, but they were stupid."

The Dodger pitchers weren't alone in their infirmities. Some everyday players were banged up as well, including catcher Roy Campanella, who was knocked around in collisions at home plate, got hit in the left hand with a pitch, and got his right hand tangled up in an opponent's bat while making a throw.

Campy took his first blow when Toby Atwell of the Chicago Cubs crashed into him at the plate in a May 3 game at Wrigley Field. Campy held on to the ball after taking a throw from right fielder Carl Furillo and Atwell was out, but the Brooklyn backstop had to sit for a game two days later in Cincinnati. Less than two weeks later, a pitch from the Pittsburgh Pirates' Ron Kline hit Campy in the left hand. He took his base, scored on Duke Snider's triple, then left to have his hand x-rayed. The bruised hand kept him out of the next three games. Campy returned in time to catch Joe's first victory, a two-inning stint on May 22, but the very next night in Philadelphia, the Phillies' Jack Mayo crashed into him at home plate as he was thrown out by Andy Pafko and Campy caught his thumb in Mayo's shirt. He stayed in the game and hit a grand slam the next inning, but didn't catch again until June 4, missing ten games in all behind the plate. The injury at first was thought to be a sprain. Doctors later determined Roy had chipped a bone.

His most bizarre injury occurred July 11 at Wrigley Field, and it again involved Atwell. Atwell was batting when Campy snapped a throw to first base and whacked his right thumb on Atwell's bat. Roy finished that game, missed the next one, then played five more games before the pain became too much and the thumb was put in a cast, causing him to miss ten games. Campy said he kept playing even when hurt because that's what he'd had to do in the Negro leagues. "You just didn't get hurt in that league," he said. "If you didn't play, you didn't get paid, so you just had to play no matter what happened to you."

Billy Cox, the master fielder at third base, was plunked in the left arm above the elbow by the Cincinnati Reds' Frank Smith on May 21, sending him to the bench and ending his consecutive game streak at 115. Billy didn't play again until June 15, when he ran for Dick Williams against the Reds at Ebbets Field. Cox had started off hot, hitting .396 in April, but he played in only twenty-seven games in May and June and batted just .240 in those months.

Carl Furillo, meanwhile, was struggling mightily at the plate. After batting .295 with sixteen home runs and ninety-one RBIs in 1951, Furillo began July hitting .239 with six homers and thirty-six driven in. His average later would drop to .232 at one point and his on-base percentage would tumble to a measly .285. Gil Hodges wasn't hitting for average, just .235 at the end of June, but he had clubbed fifteen home runs and driven in fifty-one.

Playing so many games without Campy was tough on a pitching staff that already was fragile, because his knowledge of opposing hitters and ability to coax pitchers through tough spots was second to none. "When a pitcher gets in a jam, he gets mighty lonely standing out there," Campy said. "He needs confidence and I try to give it to him." When Campy walked out to talk to a pitcher, Pee Wee Reese said he usually hustled in to listen, because he didn't want to miss anything the catcher might say. "He's funnier than Bob Hope," Pee Wee said in a 1954 interview. Pee Wee recalled a time that Campy signaled Don Newcombe for a fastball and got a curve instead. So Campy trudged out to the mound and, according to Pee Wee, asked Newcombe, "How come you give me the local when I call for the express?"

Even with their steadying influence on the bench, the Dodgers plodded on in first place. Without Willie Mays and Monte Irvin, the Giants were hard pressed to mount a serious challenge. The St. Louis Cardinals had dug themselves into a hole by going 18-22 in April and May. The Philadelphia Phillies were getting solid years from pitchers Robin Roberts, who'd end up winning twenty-eight games, and Curt Simmons, but lacked consistent hitting and power. Only the last-place Pirates would hit fewer home runs. And the Dodgers had Joe, who strolled in from the bullpen time after time to prop up the pitching. "Whatever that magic was, what Joe did, he just shut everybody down," Carl Erskine said. "He did not have what I call overpowering stuff, but he had an unusual delivery. Not so much the delivery, but the way the ball moved. He had great control. His curveball wasn't a big breaking curveball, but he could throw it in a teacup that year."

From the press box, Roscoe McGowen of the *New York Times* said it was hard to tell the difference between Joe's fastball and curve, because the curve had such little bend. But that wasn't a problem, because Joe usually could put either pitch where he wanted it. "Charlie says to get the ball over and take a chance they'll hit it safely," Joe said of his manager. "So I get it over. That's better than walking them."

>>>>>>>>>>

The Giants did manage to chop the Dodgers' lead to just two games with a 4–3 victory at Ebbets Field on July 3. Entering the game with his team trailing 4–2, Joe gave the Dodgers a chance by blanking the Giants over the final two innings in relief of Billy Loes. But the Bums managed only one run in the eighth despite putting four runners aboard, and Hoyt Wilhelm, a knuckleball wizard even then as a rookie, closed it out for the New Yorkers in the ninth. The Dodgers won the next three, however, to push their lead back to four and a half games, and Joe saved the last of those victories for Ben Wade, entering in the eighth inning with the bases loaded, two runs in, and the Dodgers leading the Boston Braves 5–2. He fanned Sid Gordon to end the inning, then pitched a scoreless ninth after the Dodgers had tacked on three more runs for an 8–2 victory. As both leagues paused for the all-star break, Joe could look with great satisfaction on some sparkling numbers. He was 3-0 with five saves and had allowed only seven earned runs in thirty-eight and two-thirds innings. He may not have been a second Don Newcombe, but he was doing just fine as the first Joe Black.

Dodger blue and white dominated the National League's all-star roster. Jackie and Campy both were selected, along with Carl Furillo, Gil Hodges, Pee Wee Reese, Duke Snider, and Preacher Roe, who was replaced by the New York Giants' Jim Hearn so he could visit his seriously ill father. All eight pitchers chosen for the game at Philadelphia's Shibe Park were starters, so Joe and Hoyt Wilhelm got a short vacation. It's unlikely they would have been used anyway. Rain shortened the game to five innings and the National League won 3–2 on Jackie's solo home run and a two-run shot by Cubs slugger Hank Sauer.

Joe might have been better off without his brief respite. In the Dodgers' first game after the break, Charlie Dressen needed Joe quickly, because Carl Erskine failed to retire any of the first five batters he faced against the Cubs at Wrigley Field. As a result, Brooklyn's early 3–0 lead had become a 3–3 tie, and another run came in as Joe got three straight outs to finally end the inning. The Dodgers came back to tie it on Duke Snider's home run in the third inning, but Joe faltered. He got banged around for three runs and four hits in the fourth—by far the worst pounding he had taken all season—and suffered his first loss after working five innings. He might have escaped with a victory if Gil Hodges could have handled a Johnny Klippstein grounder that would have been the third out in the fourth inning. Instead, the ball got through, it was scored a hit, and the Cubs went on to get their three runs, all of which became earned.

Less than a week later, Joe began a stretch that would define his—and the Dodgers'—season. From July 16 through July 30, Dressen summoned Joe ten times to bail out a pitcher in trouble, and the big guy delivered. Joe went 3-1 in that stretch, with three saves. In seven of those appearances, he did not allow a run. And he came through in some hairy situations.

Joe relieved Ben Wade with two outs in the ninth inning at Cincinnati's Crosley Field, a run in, two runners on, and the Dodgers leading 5–3. He promptly fanned Bobby Adams for a one-out save, his sixth of the season. The next night, also at Crosley Field, Joe worked the final two and two-thirds innings of a 1–1 tie and picked up the victory when Carl Furillo singled in the tie-breaking run in the eleventh. Joe had relieved Preacher Roe in the bottom of the ninth with runners on first and second and one out. He ended the inning quickly, retiring Hank Edwards on a popup and Bob Borkowski on a fly ball. The very next night, at Pittsburgh's Forbes Field, Joe replaced Billy Loes in the bottom of the ninth with the bases loaded and one out. He struck out Clyde McCullough and retired Harry Fisher on an easy grounder to Jackie at second base to end it and notch his seventh save. "If we were ahead by a run in the late innings, we always looked over our shoulder to see whether Joe was warming up," Jackie said in a 1953 interview. "His attitude was, 'Don't worry, they won't score,' and it was contagious."

When Dressen summoned Joe to replace Ben Wade in the seventh inning at Forbes Field on July 20, it was his fourth appearance in five days. The Pirates had a runner on and one run in, and there were two outs with the Dodgers leading 5–3. Joe needed only one pitch to get Dick Groat on a comebacker to end the inning and he finished the game, which the Dodgers won 8–5. Joe gave up two harmless runs in the eighth after the Dodgers had gone up 8–3, one of them on a double by—who else?—Joe Garagiola. It was enough for save number eight, but it renewed his frustration over handling the pesky, loquacious catcher. "I wish there was a special course that would tell me how to pitch to Joe Garagiola," Joe said. "I do all right against the sluggers like Sauer and Kiner, but Garagiola, a .250 hitter, murders me." The victory in Pittsburgh completed an 8-1 Western swing that boosted the Dodgers' lead over the Giants to seven and a half games. Joe had a hand in half those victories, three saves and a win. Ben Wade won three times on that trip and Joe saved two of them. When someone congratulated Wade for winning those three games, he smiled and said, "You mean me and Joe."

Back home two days later, Dressen called on Joe again, this time in a tight game against the Cincinnati Reds. Ted Kluszewski's two-run triple off Preacher Roe had tied the score at 2–2, and the muscular first baseman, who played in short sleeves to show off his enviable biceps, stood at third with one out when Joe came on. He retired Andy Seminick on a bouncer back to the mound, walked left-handed-hitting Grady Hatton to get to the right-handed-swinging Roy McMillan, and got him on a grounder to Pee Wee to preserve the tie. But he couldn't do it again in the tenth after the Dodgers went down in order in the bottom of the ninth. The Reds lit him up for four hits and three runs and, for once, Joe had to be relieved. Billy Loes gave up a run-scoring hit, the run being charged to Joe, before getting out of the inning. But Joe got off the hook for the loss when his teammates scored five times in the bottom of the tenth to win 7–6. The game ended when Rube Walker, who caught when Campy was on the bench, got hit by a pitch with the bases loaded. Rube had taken one for the team.

Joe's ugly line—one and one-third innings, four hits, and four runs—hiked his earned run average from 2.17 to 2.82, still an impressive figure. But he was never cuffed around like that in a relief appearance for the rest of the year. He would work in relief twenty-seven more times, often for three or more innings, and give up only thirteen earned runs. He had become so reliable, journalist Stanley Frank wrote, that it seemed Dodger fans rooted for a rally by the opponent when their team led. Because that meant Dressen would have to bring in Joe.

By this time, the Dodgers had come to respect and appreciate Joe's performance on the mound, because he did his job. If the Dodgers led, he protected that lead. If they trailed, he kept the opponent in check to give the Dodgers a chance to rally. It was everything a manager and team wanted out of a relief pitcher. "He gunned them down, I know that," Andy Pafko recalled. "I don't know what he threw, but I was glad to be on his side." Pafko saw a fierce competitor when Joe pitched and that was to be expected. After all that Joe had endured to get to the big leagues, he wasn't about to let up against anyone, not even his friends.

Once while facing the New York Giants, Joe became annoyed when Bobby Thomson twice asked the umpire to look at the ball. He thought the Giants were implying that he was throwing spitballs and felt their manager, Leo Durocher, was behind the ploy. So when Campy signaled for a fastball, Joe said he aimed it at Thomson's left elbow. Thomson tumbled out of the way and Joe got him out a couple of pitches later. Hank Thompson batted next and he and Joe were friends, but friendships didn't matter when the Dodgers met the Giants. Joe walked halfway toward the plate and yelled, "Hank, if you ask to look at this ball, so help me, I'm gonna knock you on your butt!" Thompson backed out of the box, looked back and forth between the mound and Durocher a couple of times, and then said, "It ain't me, it's Leo. He wants me to look at the ball." As Joe recalled it, he wound up, fired an inside fastball, and down went Thompson. "He got up slowly, looked at me and stepped back into the batter's box," Joe said. "But with less enthusiasm than he had originally."

The Dodger players also liked Joe personally. He was unpretentious and easy to be around. Teammates could tell he appreciated his opportunity to play Major League baseball. "He was a neat guy," utility infielder Rocky Bridges said. "I liked him very well. He didn't put on any airs. He just came to play."

"He always spoke highly of everybody," Andy Pafko said. "He was grateful to be on the big club because of Jackie. He had a high regard for Jackie Robinson. They were real close friends." Carl Erskine said when talking to Joe, it quickly became evident he had gone to college. "That was a rarity in those days. There were very few college men in the Major Leagues," Carl said. "Joe broke the mold somewhat. He was intelligent, he was very well spoken, he had a very polished demeanor about him. He carried himself with some dignity. He didn't have it that easy, but he kept that [dignity] throughout the years that I knew him."

Joe neither smoked nor drank. He had enjoyed watching the female students walk by in college and didn't mind the admiring glances from women in Cuba, but he was no partier, Roy Campanella said. "His control over himself is just as good as it is on the ball," the stout catcher reported. "He and I are roomies because we don't play cards, and I know all that man wants to do is pitch and watch television." Reporters also liked Joe, because he was approachable and, what they call in the business, a good quote. *New York Times* columnist Arthur Daley found Joe to be "just bursting with class." To Daley, Joe was "far more intelligent than the average ball player, better educated . . . and has a sharper sense of humor." Roger Kahn once wrote that Joe spoke "polysyllabically." Need to fill some space? Joe Black was your man.

Those attributes were not lost on BBDO advertising executive Tom Villante, whose clients included the two sponsors of the Dodgers television and radio broadcasts, Schaefer Beer and the American Tobacco Company, maker of Lucky Strike cigarettes. Because his agency handled those two accounts, Villante became the executive producer of the team's telecasts and broadcasts, and he noticed that Joe not only expressed himself well but was attuned to life beyond baseball.

"I've been around ballplayers all my life," said Villante, who was a batboy for the New York Yankees in 1944 and '45. "They really don't know what the hell is going on. But there were some, Tommy Henrich was always tuned in to what was going on. He was very much aware. Another was Carl Erskine. And Joe Black. Joe knew what was going on. He would sense things and just know. He had a wonderful voice and was a great storyteller. He would just hypnotize you with his stories."

Villante figured Joe's talents could be put to use on behalf of Lucky Strike, so he pitched an idea for a weekly column called Lucky Strikes by Joe Black. The column, which ran in black newspapers such as the *Baltimore Afro-American* and *Chicago Defender*, included Joe's thoughts on some aspect of baseball or the Dodgers, and those musings cleverly weaved into a plug for Lucky Strike cigarettes—sort of like a blog with an advertising pitch.

Villante would pick Joe's brain for ideas, write the column, and then get Joe's approval. They wrote about everything from baseball slang and superstitions to the pennant race to the base-stealing wizardry of Jackie Robinson and Pee Wee Reese. Some columns were short features on players. Joe shared tidbits about Gil Hodges ("one of the nicest guys I've ever met"), Roy Campanella (outstanding mentor for pitchers), Carl Furillo ("He plays that tricky right-field wall at Ebbets Field as though he built it"), and Jim Gilliam ("makes hard plays look easy").

In a column about pinch hitting, George Shuba told Joe, "If you don't live under a horseshoe, don't be a pinch hitter." Another column talked about how players joke around to relieve the tension. Joe mentioned the time some sparkling catches by Duke Snider saved a pitcher who was getting hit hard. When the inning ended, Charlie Dressen asked the pitcher if he was tiring. "No, I'm not," the pitcher replied. "But I think Snider is."

Handsome and photogenic, Joe also appeared in ads for Lucky Strike cigarettes, telling readers, "You can take it from me, Luckies taste better." Joe didn't actually smoke, but the extra money from those ads was surely welcome, because Joe's baseball salary—and that of many other players—wouldn't even amount to minimum wage today.

Though no one could have foreseen it then, Lucky Strikes by Joe Black became a precursor to the By the Way columns Joe would write for Greyhound in his later years, commentaries for which he would be lauded in some circles and reviled in others. "Joe got such favorable press, that kind of set the tone for where he might end up," Villante said.

>>>>>>>>>>

Neither Joe's intelligence nor his pitching helped the Dodgers the last week of July, when they hit their worst slump of the season. After that ten-inning victory over the Reds extended the Brooks' winning streak to nine, they proceeded to lose seven of their next eight, ending that stretch with five straight defeats. Joe pitched scoreless ball in relief appearances against the Reds and Cardinals to give his team a chance, but the Dodgers lost both games by a run. In another appearance against the Cardinals, Joe surrendered a two-run single to Billy Johnson that gave St. Louis a 5–3 victory and dropped his record to 4-2. The fifth straight loss was the worst of all, a 7–1 setback on July 29 to the lowly Pirates, who beat the Dodgers for the first time that season after thirteen losses. Campy was sidelined all during that stretch because of his latest thumb injury, and Jackie Robinson appeared only as a pinch hitter in three of the losses because of sore ribs. Yet the Dodgers were still four games ahead of the Giants and eight and a half in front of the Cardinals. Even so, they needed a spark to reverse their slide, and they got it from Joe and his fishing buddy, Carl Furillo.

The Pirates led the Dodgers 3–2 at Ebbets Field on July 30 when Joe came out to start the ninth inning. He held them scoreless and his team rallied. Campy's home run in the bottom of the ninth tied it and Furillo's two-out run-scoring single in the tenth won it, lifting Joe's record to 5-2.

Charlie Dressen called on Joe again the next day in another extra-inning game against the Pirates, the opener of a doubleheader. Joe was the nineteenth player to appear for the Dodgers in the game and he blanked the Bucs in the tenth and eleventh innings. He got the victory when George Shuba walked with the bases loaded—a walk-off walk—for a 7–6 win after the Dodgers had trailed 6–0. Brooklyn won the nightcap 4–1 behind Joe Landrum, a twenty-three-year-old right-hander who had been called up from Brooklyn's Double-A farm club at Fort Worth after Ralph Branca was put on the disabled list. Landrum went 15-10 with eight shutouts and a 1.94 earned run average at Fort Worth, but couldn't duplicate that success in the big leagues. He would go 0-3 in four more starts before finishing the season in the bullpen. Landrum would never pitch in the majors again after 1952, and that July 31 game against the Pirates would be his only victory. But like Joe, Landrum had prepared for a life outside baseball. He had skipped the 1951 season so he could finish his work on a degree in architecture from Clemson University, where he had pitched two seasons before signing with the Dodgers.

Though his time was brief, Landrum had helped gain a key victory that enabled the Dodgers to take some momentum into August. Could they keep it going? So much of that answer would depend on Joe Black. It was strikingly clear that he was their workhorse, and they were going to ride him as long as he could hold up.

10

Throwing Heat in Havana

Cuba 1950–52

As the Elite Giants' 1950 season wound its way toward an end, Joe started to think about winter ball. He liked both the extra money he could make in Latin America and the chance to work on his pitching, not to mention weather that was far balmier than that of Baltimore or Plainfield. So he asked the pitching coach for the New York Cubans, Rodolfo "Rudy" Fernandez, to keep him in mind if he learned of a team that needed a player. Fernandez, who pitched for the Cubans in the 1930s, had been a fixture in Latin American baseball for years and was a coach for the Almendares team in the Cuban League. When he learned that Cienfuegos needed a pitcher, he recommended Joe to the manager, Salvador Hernandez. Hernandez agreed to bring Joe on board.

Joe joined the Cienfuegos "Elefantes," or Elephants, in November after barnstorming with a Negro leagues all-star team headed by Cleveland Indians slugger Luke Easter. For that trip, Joe—much to his relief—had Willie Mays backing him as a teammate instead of robbing him of extra bases. Once in Cuba, Joe found a nation rich in baseball tradition and fever.

Baseball was introduced in Cuba in the 1860s, and by the turn of the century, both black and white players found the island an attractive locale for the winter season. For blacks, Cuba had the added advantage of a more tolerant racial climate. Fans flocked to games by the thousands, and they were rabid. Covering Jackie Robinson and the Dodgers when they trained in Havana in 1947, Sam Lacy of the *Baltimore Afro-American* wrote, "I had heard that Cubans are a deeply religious people. In two days here I have learned that baseball is their religion."

The year before, American player Dick Sisler became an instant icon in Cuba when he smacked three home runs in a game on January 24, all off Sal Maglie, who would become one of the National League's best—and most feared—pitchers with the New York Giants. So many fans mobbed Sisler while trying to get his autograph that league officials had to assign three policemen to escort him from the clubhouse to a taxi. People surrounded him when he walked down the street. Shop owners refused to let him pay for his purchases. In 1950, Sisler hit one of the most memorable home runs in Philadelphia Phillies history, a tenth-inning shot against the Brooklyn Dodgers in the last game of the season to clinch the National League pennant. "But I doubt that it was appreciated by the Philadelphia fans as much as my three homers in that one game in Havana were by the Cubans," Sisler recalled during a 1952 interview.

Another player from the States, outfielder Marv Rickert, captivated Cuban fans without even hitting the ball. As he settled into the batter's box, Rickert—known in US ball as "Twitch"—would wiggle one hip, then the other, then throw in an extra shake for good measure. Fans loved it. They nicknamed him "Meneito"—a Cuban dance with lots of hip grinding.

Players of all shades plied their trade in the Cuban League. Author Peter C. Bjarkman, who wrote a detailed history of the sport on the island, called Cuban baseball an "unparalleled racial proving ground." White Major League teams regularly toured Cuba in the early years of the twentieth century until the commissioner, Judge Kenesaw Mountain Landis, halted the practice in 1923. Landis ruled that intact Major League teams could not face black teams on barnstorming tours in Cuba or anywhere else. Individual Major Leaguers continued playing there, however, and many prominent Negro leaguers found success in the Cuban League, including Josh Gibson, Cool Papa Bell, Willie Wells,

Oscar Charleston, and Rube Foster, who brought black baseball into a new era when he organized the Negro National League in 1920. Negro league stars Buck Leonard, Dave "Showboat" Thomas, Sam Bankhead, and Ted "Double Duty" Radcliffe also played in Cuba.

Cuban baseball featured many home-grown stars, too, beginning with Jose Mendez, a right-handed pitcher known in his homeland as "El Diamante Negro," or "Black Diamond." The five-foot-eight Mendez established himself as a giant among his peers when, at the age of twenty-one, he dominated the visiting Cincinnati Reds in November 1908. He first pitched a one-hit shutout, followed that with seven innings of hitless relief, then blanked the Reds again in a complete game for a total of twenty-five straight scoreless innings. One writer said of the Reds, "The only way they could have caught up to his fastball was with a time machine." When John McGraw took the New York Giants to Cuba, he was so impressed with Mendez that he thought the dark-skinned hurler would be worth $50,000 if he had been allowed in the Major Leagues. Mendez later played and managed in the Negro leagues.

Cristobal Torriente became Cuba's greatest power hitter and also starred in Negro league ball, while right-handed pitcher Dolf Luque became the first great Cuban Major Leaguer, winning 194 games over twenty seasons, including a 27-8 mark for the Cincinnati Reds in 1923. Luque was fair skinned with blue eyes, so he could avoid the barrier that kept black Cubans out of the majors. Cuban fans followed his Major League career diligently, the way blacks did with Jackie Robinson when he joined the Brooklyn Dodgers. Because of that, they developed a loyalty to the Cincinnati ballclub, "nuestros queridos rojos" or "our beloved Reds."

Luque also pitched and managed in the Cuban League in a career that spanned forty-two years. As a manager, he apparently expected his pitchers to be workhorses. Author Donn Rogosin, in his book *Invisible Men: Life in Baseball's Negro Leagues*, related a story involving Luque when he was managing the Almendares club and pitcher Terris McDuffie. Luque, the story goes, wanted McDuffie to pitch on only two days' rest, but McDuffie refused. Luque then reached into his desk, pulled out a handgun, pointed it at McDuffie, and asked if he was ready to pitch. "Gimme the ball," McDuffie is said to have replied. He pitched a two-hitter.

Perhaps the most renowned Cuban player of them all in the first half of the twentieth century was Martin Dihigo, who certainly was the most versatile. Robert Peterson, in his groundbreaking work on black baseball, *Only the Ball Was White*, put his biographical sketch of Dihigo in the outfielders section, but acknowledged it was purely "an arbitrary decision" because the Cuban star could play any position, including pitcher, and play it well. Homestead Grays owner Cum Posey said Dihigo's "gifts afield have not been approached by any one man, black or white." Dihigo played mostly in the infield when he started his Negro league career in 1923. He began to pitch more often as he matured, but would play elsewhere in the field when it wasn't his turn in the rotation. Dihigo also played in Mexico, Venezuela, Puerto Rico, and the Dominican Republic, and is the only player to have been inducted into baseball halls of fame in the United States, Cuba, and Mexico.

>>>>>>>>>>

The Cuban League had played its first championship season in the winter of 1878–79. When Joe reported in 1950, there were four teams: Almendares, Havana, Marianao, and his own club, Cienfuegos. Turk Lown, who would pitch eleven seasons in the Major Leagues with the Chicago Cubs and White Sox, was among Joe's teammates. Also on the team from organized baseball in the States were pitchers Red Hardy, Tommy Fine, and Al Epperly, outfielder Bob Addis, and infielder John Sullivan. Another teammate, shortstop Silvio Garcia, was a veteran of both the Cuban and Negro leagues. Leo Durocher, who was Jackie Robinson's first manager with the Brooklyn Dodgers, raved about Garcia after watching him play. "I've seen a shortstop in Cuba blacker than my shoes," he told friends, "and Marty Marion can't carry his glove." Marion was one of the game's top shortstops in the 1940s while playing for the St. Louis Cardinals.

Joe's catcher was Ray Noble, a former Negro leaguer who had just helped Oakland win the Pacific Coast League championship and would join the New York Giants in the spring. A Cuban, Noble was a smart receiver and skilled with a bat. In that 1950 PCL season, Noble hit .316 with fifteen home runs and seventy-six RBIs in 110 games. And any runner steaming toward home with Noble astride the plate ran the risk of a damaging collision—for the runner. Writing in the *Sporting News*, Ken Smith described the five-foot-eleven, 210-pound catcher as "built along the general lines of an Army tank." Piling on the adjectives, Smith called Noble a "broad-beamed, barrel-chested, wrestler-necked human oak." It might have been easier to try to knock down an outfield wall.

For Joe, Noble became a valued friend who shared his baseball knowledge and made sure Joe felt at home in his new surroundings. Noble and Minnie Minoso, who played for Marianao and had begun a Major League career that would span five decades, showed Joe the sights and helped him learn to speak and read Spanish. Joe learned to speak it well enough to have a short conversation with a young lawyer who eventually would become one of the world's most recognized figures.

Fidel Castro had pitched for his high school baseball team as a senior (though he was reported to be better at basketball and track) and was a big baseball fan. Joe recalled seeing him at games frequently. One day, Castro watched Joe warming up with Noble and noticed that Joe threw from ten feet behind the rubber, a practice that would puzzle many observers through the years. Joe felt he had good reason for his madness. Warming up from seventy feet away enabled him to stretch his muscles and then, when he toed the rubber at sixty feet, six inches, the plate would look that much bigger. Hearing that explanation, Castro looked at Joe and said with a shake of his head, "You're loco." That would not be Joe's only encounter with the future Cuban leader. They later hooked up in a one-on-one game of basketball and Joe came away impressed with Castro's ability, confirming the stories that Castro was indeed more skilled in basketball than baseball.

>>>>>>>>>>

All four Cuban teams were based in Havana and played their games at Gran Stadium, which opened in 1946 and seated thirty thousand. Also called Cerro Stadium after the neighborhood in which it was located, the ballpark was the showplace of Cuban baseball and would remain so for many years. Havana at the time was a playground for Americans, a city rich in glittering nightlife. Players could enjoy casinos, clubs, tropical drinks, gourmet restaurants, and hot music, all at modest cost by US standards. The ballplayers lived rent free in modern apartments and received living expenses—$250 a month for a single player, $350 for those who were married. The Cuban ballclubs also paid their travel expenses to and from the island. Joe was paid $600 a month in salary his first season in Cuba and $1,000 a month in his second. The season ran from early October to mid-February, and teams played only three or four times a week, giving players plenty of time to golf, fish, swim, and soak up the city's delights. It was a wonderful way to spend the winter—as long as you produced. A player whose performance on the field suffered because he indulged too much in his free time would find himself on a plane headed back home. Fans in Latin America had a term for such a player: "paquette grande." It meant he was a big package about to be shipped back to the United States.

Joe felt the league was on par with Triple-A baseball in the United States, and the two seasons he spent there became his stepping stone to the Major Leagues, the final chapter of his drive to realize a dream that once seemed impossible. Joe made a splashy debut in Cuba with a performance so impressive it drew Grantland Rice–type prose from a local sportswriter. The story, translated from Spanish, began:

"On a gray, cold and sad afternoon, a pitcher named Joe Black made his debut. He took charge of the pitching assignment of Cienfuegos and gave an extraordinary, a very impeccable, a very inspirational performance that resulted in a victory of 9–1.

"So—a star is born, a new star in the professional championship. Black comes without fanfare. He comes, takes the ball and starts throwing!"

Joe gave up only five hits and allowed just one walk in that victory over Marianao, which was the league's hottest team at that point. Despite that effort from Joe, Cienfuegos was stumbling badly as the season went on, losing fourteen of its first twenty-two games. That cost manager Salvador Hernandez his job. On December 7, he was replaced by Billy Herman, a move that turned out to be as critical as any in getting Joe to the Major Leagues. Herman was a smooth-fielding second baseman in his playing days with the Chicago Cubs, Brooklyn Dodgers, Boston Braves, and Pittsburgh Pirates. He was the Pirates player-manager in 1947, managed the Minneapolis Millers in 1948, and played with Oakland in the Pacific Coast League in 1949. Later, he'd manage the Boston Red Sox and gain induction into the Hall of Fame.

But in December 1950, Herman was looking for a scouting job when Robert Maduro, who ran the Cienfuegos club, contacted him at baseball's winter meetings in St. Petersburg, Florida. With his team buried in last place and showing no signs of getting out, Maduro offered Herman the manager's job. Herman, who had visited Cuba as a player with the Louisville Colonels in 1930 and expressed a desire to return, promptly took it. His hiring produced immediate dividends. The previously moribund Elefantes won six of their first nine games under Herman's tutelage and eight of their first twelve. The *Sporting News*, which had correspondents reporting on all the Latin winter leagues, called it a "complete reversal of form." While Herman had been an infielder throughout his career, he seemed to be at his best working with pitchers. Raul Lopez, a left-hander in the Giants system, did not win a game before Herman arrived. Herman pulled Lopez out of the bullpen and made him a starter, and the veteran responded by reeling off three straight victories.

Luis Aloma and Al Epperly also began pitching better, and Joe "has started to click," the *Sporting News* reported. Backed by a twelve-hit attack that included Ray Noble's two-run homer, Joe pitched his team to a 5–1 victory over Marianao on January 21. With Cienfuegos playing .595 ball since Herman took over, going 16-11, the club named him its manager for the 1951–52 season. He had sparked so much optimism that many felt the Elefantes could contend for the pennant in the following season. Herman's magic wasn't enough to pull Cienfuegos out of the cellar, however, and the team finished 28-44, a hefty twelve games out of first and the only club in the league with a losing record.

Havana and Almendares, which had faced each other in the very first Cuban League game in 1878 and became known as "Los Eternal Rivales," tied for first, forcing a one-game playoff. Havana won 4–2 behind former New York Giants lefty Adrian Zabala, who had been a .500 pitcher during the season.

It seems only fitting that later in 1951, the National League's own eternal rivals, the New York Giants and Brooklyn Dodgers, would stage a dramatic playoff of their own for the pennant.

Joe went 5-7 for Cienfuegos, hardly a sterling record, but he faced some of the best competition of his career. Opposing hitters such as Minnie Minoso, Don Thompson, Ray Dandridge, Dick Williams, Steve Bilko, Johnny Jorgensen, Sandy Amoros, Bert Haas, and Cuban star Pedro Formental could challenge even the best pitchers. Thompson, who finished second in the league with a .343 average, would become one of Joe's teammates with the Dodgers, as would Amoros and Williams. Amoros was voted the league's top rookie.

>>>>>>>>>>

My father enjoyed his time in Cuba. He was respectful of the culture and learned to speak Spanish. He later enjoyed talking with the Latin players in Spanish at White Sox games in Chicago. Castro wrote friendly letters about baseball to my father when he joined the Dodgers in 1952, and all of them were in Spanish. The US government at the time had become suspicious of Castro and what he was doing in Cuba, and started tracing his communications to our country, including the letters he wrote to my father.

One of my dad's friends from his years in Havana was Minnie Minoso, who is Cuban and played in the Major Leagues over five decades, starting in 1949. People know him as "Mr. White Sox," because he spent most of his career with the team, and he still visits with White Sox fans, players, and front office staff. Fans love it when they get a chance to meet him.

Minnie and I were talking one day when he told me a story about his time playing against my father in Cuba. Minnie said he always had trouble hitting my father, so he went up to him and asked, "Chico, Chico, how do you get me out? How do you get me out?" They were opponents, and pitchers aren't known to share that kind of information with a hitter. But my father cherished his friendship with Minnie, so he offered his theory. Minnie used to grip his bat so hard he couldn't swing properly. My father told him, "Loosen your grip and I guarantee you can hit better." And he did.

>>>>>>>>>>

During his first season in Cuba, Joe wondered why many of his teammates made $1,000 a month while he was paid only $600. The difference, he learned, was in their minor league experience in the States. Joe had none. The $1,000 figure was the going rate for those who had played at the Triple-A level. As the 1951–52 Cuban season approached, Joe was coming off a summer in Triple-A ball, having split the 1951 season between the Brooklyn Dodgers' farm clubs at Montreal and St. Paul. So when it came time to talk salary, he could command $1,000 a month, the most he had ever been paid to play baseball. The negotiations with the club—he again would play for Cienfuegos—were quick and easy. "I merely mentioned the words Triple-A," he said.

Joe did little to excite the Dodgers brass with his Triple-A pitching, going 7-9 at Montreal and 4-3 at St. Paul for a combined 11-12 record. If he was going to get called to the big club, he had to make a good showing in Cuba. Luckily, he had willing helpers in manager Billy Herman and catcher Ray Noble, back on the island after helping the New York Giants win the National League pennant. Noble patiently explained to Joe how Giants ace Sal Maglie set up hitters so they couldn't get the fat part of the bat on his curveball. He encouraged Joe to adopt Maglie's philosophy: the corners of the plate belonged to the pitcher and if he had to pitch high and tight, that was his prerogative.

Maglie, who went 23-6 for the Giants in 1951, had been influenced by Cuban ace Dolf Luque, who was Sal's manager when he played in Mexico and Cuba. Luque told Maglie a pitcher had to keep hitters off balance so they couldn't get comfortable at the plate, even if that meant brushing them back. "Luque believed in protecting the plate and I became a believer, too," Maglie said. Sal would go on to brush so many batters off the plate with "close shaves" that he gained the nickname "the Barber." With hitters ready to bail in fear of Maglie's brushback pitch, they became susceptible to a sharp-breaking curve on the outside corner.

Noble thought Joe could become even more intimidating than Maglie, because he threw harder. So Joe spent hours pitching to Noble, who'd hold his mitt first on the inside black strip on the plate, then on the outside strip, then move to the inside strip again. Thanks to that practice, hitting the corners became natural for Joe. He no longer had to aim at Noble's mitt. He simply could rear back and fire and still hit his spots. Thus, when he threw his sharp-breaking curve, batters were reluctant to step into it, because it might be an inside fastball. And with Joe Black throwing, they certainly didn't want to get in front of it. "Yes, I have hit some batters," Joe acknowledged. But he was quick to point out that not every inside pitch is a bean ball. "A bean ball," he emphasized, "is one that is thrown at a batter's head, not chin." A batter might not see much difference between the chin and the head, but that wasn't Joe's concern. His improved control and greater willingness to pitch inside imbued Joe with a new sense of confidence.

Herman shared that confidence. He felt Joe, Pat McGlothin, and Johnny Rutherford all could become big winners during the Cuban season if the defense held up. He said the infield was faster and the outfield stronger. There was no reason the Elefantes couldn't challenge Havana for the pennant. "This is a much better team than Cienfuegos fielded last year," Billy declared.

Joe set the tone for his season in the opener, shutting down Marianao on four hits in a 4–0 victory before a Ladies Day crowd of eighteen thousand. He followed that outing with a five-hit, 2–1 win over Havana, a Johnny Jorgensen home run spoiling his shutout. The Havana Reds jumped on him in his next start, when Joe wilted in the hot, humid weather and lost 8–5. Jorgensen, a third baseman who had played for the Dodgers and Giants, again took Joe deep, this time on his very first pitch of the game. But Joe bounced back to beat Havana on a four-hitter the next time he took the mound, then helped himself by belting a home run in a 5–2 victory over Almendares. He went the distance in both games.

Yet the team remained mired in last place, winning only six of its first nineteen games. Joe had four of those victories and the Dodgers noticed. He had pitched forty-four and a third innings at that point, giving up just ten runs and twenty-seven hits. Of the thirty-six players from organized baseball in the Cuban League that season, fourteen were Dodger farmhands. Brooklyn executives visited the island in mid-October and came away particularly impressed with Joe and Walter Moryn, a left-handed-hitting center fielder who had batted .299 with twenty-four home runs at Mobile in 1951 and was playing for Almendares. Moryn eventually would play eight years in the majors, starting with the Dodgers in 1954, and was a National League all-star with the Chicago Cubs in 1958.

Joe got his league-leading fifth victory with a five-hit, 2–1 win over Almendares on November 14. His team had won only three other games, but then got hot, winning seven of eight to pull within two and a half games of first place. Johnny Rutherford reeled off four straight victories and Joe contributed a win to the surge, 1–0 over Marianao, to improve to 6-2. His extensive work with Noble, along with Herman's advice and encouragement, was paying off. Herman helped Joe understand the importance of keeping himself in shape and maintaining his concentration so he could bear down on hitters from start to finish. Noble taught him a pitcher must believe that *he* owns the plate, not the batter. For all his time in baseball, Joe had considered himself merely a thrower, albeit one who could throw hard. In Cuba, he was becoming a pitcher.

Two of the league's most prominent figures, managers Mike Gonzalez of Havana and Dolf Luque of Marianao, called Joe one of the winter season's best pitching prospects in ten years. Dodgers vice president Buzzie Bavasi also liked what he was seeing, not only from Joe, but from Almendares pitcher Bob Alexander, who was coming off a 15-9 season at Montreal. Bavasi suggested both could make the big club in 1952, and said they would "get the chance of their lives to prove to us they can stick along with the club all summer." Alexander, however, would not reach the big leagues until 1955, and it would be with the Baltimore Orioles, not the Dodgers.

Joe's outing against Havana on December 10 was especially impressive. In a duel between the two men who would become the National League's best relievers in 1952, Joe bested Hoyt Wilhelm 2–1, backed by home runs from Ray Noble and Oscar Sierra. Wilhelm would enjoy a spectacular rookie season with the New York Giants in 1952 and become one of baseball's preeminent knuckleballers, a pitch that would enable him to stay in the big leagues until he was forty-nine years old.

As the calendar flipped to 1952, Cienfuegos went on another tear, winning nine of ten to climb eight games over .500 and pull to within a game of league-leading Havana. During a five-game winning streak, Joe beat Marianao and then, foreshadowing what he'd soon do for the Dodgers, he relieved Pat McGlothin and held Havana hitless over the last three innings to save the victory for the former Brooklyn right-hander.

Just before starting its January surge, Cienfuegos signed a young shortstop named Don Zimmer, who had played for the Dodgers' Class A farm team in Elmira, New York, the previous summer. The team needed to replace Gene Mauch, who then was a six-year Major League veteran and wanted to return to the United States before spring training. Zimmer had been recommended by Chicago White Sox general manager Frank Lane, who had seen him play at Elmira. "You won't regret signing him for the rest of the winter," Lane said. "He'll win a lot of games for you." Zimmer was at home in Cincinnati when Dodgers scout Al Campanis called on a cold, miserable day to ask if he wanted to spend the rest of the winter in Cuba. "I said, 'Yeah, my goodness,'" Zimmer recalled. Zimmer and his wife Jean hopped on a plane the next day and within hours, they stepped into Havana's tropical warmth. "At that time, I thought it was heaven," Zimmer said. "It was a resort. I mean, what a gorgeous place."

In 1952, Zimmer was a baby-faced twenty-one-year-old nicknamed "the Kid." Because he didn't look his age, he was mistaken for a youngster seeking an autograph when he reported to the club. But he provided an immediate spark, smacking a three-run homer to cap a five-run rally that produced a 6–3 victory over Havana. As the Elefantes continued winning, Zimmer fielded well and delivered some timely hits. Lane had not sold him short. Nearly sixty years later, Zimmer was still in baseball; he served as a senior adviser with the Tampa Bay Rays until his death in 2014.

January also brought news from the States: Dodgers coach Clyde Sukeforth was parting ways with the club and Billy Herman was hired to replace him. Sukeforth was the one who told manager Charlie Dressen during that fateful playoff game with the New York Giants the previous October that Carl Erskine had bounced his curveball in the bullpen, but Ralph Branca was throwing hard and looking strong. Whereupon Dressen summoned Branca to pitch to Bobby Thomson, who then hit the most famous home run in baseball history. Dressen had always blamed Sukeforth for sending him the wrong pitcher. Sukeforth shrugged it off as Dressen being Dressen—taking the credit when things went well, blaming someone else when they went wrong. As for Herman, he was happy to be back with a big-league club and felt his work with Cienfuegos helped him land the Dodgers job. That was good news for Joe, because Herman had become one of his biggest supporters and he'd be in a strong position to advocate for Joe with the Dodger brass.

>>>>>>>>>>

In late January, facing Marianao, Joe turned in his most dominating performance of the season. He just missed the $1,000 prize that went to a pitcher throwing a no-run, no-hit game, allowing only a Texas League single by Damon Phillips in a 3–0 victory. Joe was 12-6, leading the league in victories and strikeouts. Even the Cuban writers were speculating that he might fill the hole in the Dodgers' rotation created by the absence of Don Newcombe, who was being called up by the army and would miss the 1952 season. "He depends mainly on his fast ball," Pedro Galiana wrote in the *Sporting News*, "and while his curve isn't much, Manager Billy Herman has been teaching him when and how to use it." Joe paid attention. He won six of his last seven decisions to finish with a league-high fifteen victories against only six losses. Of all those who had pitched in the Cuban League through the years, only two others had won more than fifteen games. Ray Brown set the league record with twenty-one victories in 1936–37, and Tommy Fine had won sixteen times during Joe's first season in Cuba. Joe also topped the league with seventy-eight strike-outs and a 2.42 earned run average. He certainly looked like a big-league pitcher in the making, and Herman kept the Dodgers informed, sending the club regular reports on how well Joe was progressing.

Joe felt those reports convinced the Dodgers to invite him to spring training with the big club. "Herman was the first one who ever told me how to set up hitters for my best pitches," Joe said. "I learned how to pitch the way a kid learns to read. The letters on the page look like hen tracks until they suddenly run together and make sense one day. That's how it was with me and pitching after I listened to Herman for a couple of weeks." In Billy Herman, Joe had a staunch ally.

Herman's generosity in sharing his knowledge went beyond his work with Joe and other Cienfuegos pitchers. One day, Herman was introduced to an eighteen-year-old Cuban lad who wanted to try out for the team. The kid looked like a ballplayer, but he didn't have a glove. Herman smiled at the young man's eagerness, got him a uniform, borrowed a glove, and sent him out to shortstop. He then hit a succession of grounders—to the youngster's right, to his left, and straight at him. Joe was impressed with the kid's agility, range, arm, and soft hands. So was Herman, who bought the young man a glove and invited him to practice with the Elefantes whenever they had a game. Four years later, that young man, Humberto "Chico" Fernandez, was playing shortstop for the Brooklyn Dodgers.

As Joe racked up the victories down the stretch, so did his team. On February 10, after winning fifteen of seventeen games, Cienfuegos moved into first place by half a game over Havana, which had led all season. Then the pitching fell apart and Cienfuegos lost its last four games. Herman sent Sandy Ullrich to the mound for a February 11 game against Almendares, whom Ullrich had defeated 1–0 in his previous start. But Ullrich gave up a fourth-inning grand slam to Frank Carswell and lost

6–4, dropping the Elefantes into a tie for first. With the final games tightly bunched, Herman had to improvise with his pitching staff and started Al Epperly, a reliever, the next day against Marianao. Epperly pitched respectably, but Eddie Yuhas, who was in the St. Louis Cardinals organization, shut down the Cienfuegos hitters and won 3–1. Now, the Elefantes were half a game out of first.

They were still half a game behind when they met Havana on February 15 in what would be the deciding game of the race. While Cienfuegos was struggling, Joe and his teammates were confident, because they had defeated Havana six straight times and they were starting Pat McGlothin, a right-hander from Tennessee. McGlothin was a career minor leaguer except for brief appearances with the Dodgers in 1949 and 1950, but he had beaten Havana seven consecutive times. Whatever spell he held over the Reds dissipated on that day, however. Havana knocked him out in the fifth inning and built a 10–0 lead before settling for a 10–5 victory that moved the Reds one and a half games in front with two to play. Cienfuegos' fate was sealed the next day by an 8–1 loss to Almendares, giving Havana its twenty-eighth Cuban League pennant. So it didn't matter when the Elefantes' final game was rained out. They finished 39-32, two games out of first.

The team's late surge after its miserable start earned for Billy Herman the league's manager of the year award, while Ray Noble edged Joe, ten votes to eight, as the outstanding player for Cienfuegos. Havana's thirty-eight-year-old Bert Haas, who had appeared in his first Major League game with the Brooklyn Dodgers in 1937, was a unanimous choice as the league's most valuable player after winning the batting title with a .323 average. Joe and Noble split the second-place votes, and both were named to the all-star team. Haas played his final Major League season in 1951. In what turned out to be his last at-bat, he belted a pinch-hit home run for the Chicago White Sox, who released him the next day. One of nine brothers who played professional baseball, Haas would hang on in the minor leagues until he was forty-four years old.

Joe's Cuban experience made him a better pitcher and turned him into a legitimate Major League prospect. His time there and in other Latin American countries also taught him something about human relations. In the United States, he had played baseball in a segregated league and served in a segregated army. He cringed at the insulting Jim Crow laws that made him feel like a second-class citizen. The contrast south of the border was striking. He saw blacks, Latinos, and whites intermingling freely. In Havana, he found white women from the American South enjoying the company of black men. To Joe, it was heartening to discover "that all societies don't use skin pigmentation as an evaluation tool."

Joe had another reason to feel encouraged: the Dodgers had sent him a telegram in late January inviting him to spring training in Vero Beach, Florida, this time with the big club. Between that invitation and the confidence he gained from winning the pitching championship, Joe was in high spirits when he flew to Norfolk, Virginia, to join his wife, Doris, who was visiting her parents, Frank and Mamie Byrd. While he was there, his contract arrived in the mail. It was a St. Paul contract and would pay him $600 a month. Joe was crestfallen—and a bit angry. He knew he was no star, but he had just turned twenty-eight, Doris was pregnant, and he felt that not only did he need more money than that, he deserved it. Joe put the contract down and left it there.

About a week later, the phone rang. It was Buzzie Bavasi from the Dodgers asking if it was true that Joe had not signed his contract. It was true, Joe said, and before he could say anything more, Bavasi reminded him that he had been invited to train with the Dodgers, not one of the minor league clubs, but he couldn't report until he had signed his St. Paul contract.

"Why won't the Dodgers send me a contract?" Joe asked.

"You'll have to make the team," Bavasi replied, "and then we'll purchase your contract from St. Paul and renegotiate your salary. That's why you'll have to sign your St. Paul contract."

Joe had spent the last ten years working—and praying too—for this chance, and now here it was. Yet the money offer was so disappointing. Bavasi, he thought, must have sensed his inner struggle, because he went on: "Listen, if you are as good as Billy Herman claims, then you don't have to worry about the St. Paul contract. That would merely be a formality. So sign the contract and come on down to Vero. You know, the longer you stay away, the other players will be getting ahead of you."

Joe finally relented and said he'd sign the contract and send it along. Doris was pleased and proud. Frank, however, could read the dejection in Joe's demeanor and asked if he could say something.

"Joe," he said, "all those years that you pitched in the Negro league and those Spanish countries you were hoping that one day you could play in the majors with Jackie Robinson and those other colored guys. So don't be foolish. This is your chance. Sign that contract and go on down to Florida and become a Dodger!"

Joe thought about what his father-in-law said, but not for long. Two days later, he was on a train, headed for Vero Beach.

11

Dominating in the Dog Days

August 1952

BACK IN SPRING TRAINING, MANAGER Charlie Dressen called Joe over one day for a chat. Dressen had run hot and cold on Joe at Vero Beach. He was the one who staged the demonstration that resulted in Joe being compared to Don Newcombe, the twenty-game winner who had gone into the army in February. But at other times, Charlie had said he wasn't sure about Joe or suggested that Joe had to show him more before he'd earn a spot on the team. And Dressen had seemed ready to give up on Joe after he faltered at the end of a seven-inning stint against the Philadelphia Phillies—until Joe pointed out the unfairness of being judged on seven innings of work when other pitchers had been asked to go only four or five innings. On the day he called Joe over, Dressen had been impressed with how Joe carried himself. "You throw great, Joe," journalist Roger Kahn recounted Dressen as saying. "Just throw where I tell ya. When we want it high, throw it high—and tight. When we want that hard curve low, throw it down—and away. When I want you to brush a hitter, I want you to go right at his head. I want to see his bat go one way, his cap go another and his ass go somewhere else. Do what I tell ya, Joe, and you're gonna be a big leaguer and the hitter will be whoops,

Goodbye Dolly Gray." Joe simply nodded in agreement. "OK, number seven," he replied, referring to the manager's jersey number.

Joe took Dressen's words to heart, though throwing at hitters wasn't something he relished. Still, he had to concede the high inside heater could be useful at times. For one thing, it reminded the hitter that pitchers believed they, not the batter, owned the inside corner of the plate. Anyone crowding that area needed to be taught to back off. "Pitchers are paid to quiet the bats of hitters, not to throw the ball and let the free swingers hit it far and often," Joe wrote in 1983. "Not too many of today's players would have been able to stand the heat of yesteryear's pennant races. When a pitcher throws high and tight today, it usually ignites a fight. The hitters should realize that if a pitcher wanted to hit them with the ball, it could be done."

He also found a few knockdown pitches useful in silencing race baiters. Once, while warming up against the Cincinnati Reds, Joe heard some of the Reds players start to serenade him: ". . . I hear those gentle voices calling Old Black Joe." The Reds had no black players at the time and wouldn't until 1954, when Chuck Harmon and Puerto Rican Nino Escalera played their first game. Joe said he tried to stay cool, but admitted that inside, "I was seething." As tempting as it might have been to storm into the Cincinnati dugout and grab one of the taunters, Joe kept reminding himself of Jackie's admonishment: "We don't fight." But Joe did have a way to retaliate: with his pitches. Author Peter Golenbock recounted that Joe fired a high hard one at the head of each of the next seven Cincinnati batters. That stopped the singing.

Even more than Dressen's talk in spring training, Joe said Giants manager Leo Durocher was the one who eroded his reluctance to dust off hitters. As Joe remembered it, Durocher mumbled something as he trotted past him on the pitcher's mound en route to the third base coaching box, where most managers operated in those days. Joe later told Campy he thought Durocher merely was talking to himself. But he listened closely the next inning and said he heard Durocher say: "Look out before I spit on you." Joe couldn't keep quiet. "Yeah," he retorted. "And I'll kick your butt, too." The next inning, Durocher began his ploy of telling his hitters to ask the umpire to look at the ball, prompting Joe's knockdowns of Bobby Thomson and Hank Thompson. "Yep, Leo Durocher helped me to beat his Giants and other National League teams," Joe said.

>>>>>>>>>>

In the dog days of August, Joe not only beat teams, he dominated them. August turned out to be his strongest month of the season. He pitched thirteen times and finished eleven games, going 5-0 with three saves. Joe allowed only five earned runs in thirty-six and two-thirds innings, for an earned run average of a miserly 1.23. In eight of his appearances, the opponent didn't score at all against him. And they weren't just the one-inning jobs that today's closers undertake. Eight times the Dodgers needed Joe to work at least two innings.

In his first appearance of the month, August 5 against the Giants at the Polo Grounds, Joe worked almost the equivalent of a complete game. George Wilson had just pulled the Giants into a 4–4 tie with a one-out solo home run off Billy Loes in the seventh inning when Dressen signaled for Joe, who retired the next two batters to end the inning. Leo Durocher brought in his own rookie relief ace, Hoyt Wilhelm, to start the eighth. The two standouts, one with the blazing fastball, the other with the dancing knuckler, threw blanks for five straight innings in as intense a game as the two rivals would play all year. Wilhelm was lifted for a pinch runner after reaching on an error in the bottom of the twelfth, when the Giants loaded the bases with only one out, putting Joe in a jam. An unusual double play saved him. Whitey Lockman hit a grounder to Jackie, who threw to Campy at the plate for one out. Campy then fired the ball to first in time to double up Lockman. Joe had a chance to win it when Andy Pafko homered leading off the fourteenth for a 5–4 lead. But with two outs in the Giants' half and Bob Elliott at bat, Joe put too much of a pitch over the plate and Elliott drove it off the upper-deck facade in left field for a game-tying home run.

The Giants finally won it in the fifteenth inning, the last that could be started under a 12:50 AM curfew. First, the Dodgers went up 6–5 on Pafko's sacrifice fly, but they would pay for leaving the bases loaded when Carl Furillo flied out to end the inning. Joe finally was relieved after giving up a one-out double to Bobby Hofman, and the Giants rallied against Chris Van Cuyk after Jackie Robinson's error on what should have been the third out left the door open. Bobby Thomson's RBI single tied it, the run being charged to Joe, and Dusty Rhodes raced around all the way from second with the winning run on Don Mueller's high chopper.

Van Cuyk fielded the ball cleanly, but it took so long to come down that he had no time to get Mueller at first. The thrilling game, played out before a throng of 43,373, lasted four hours and fifty-nine minutes and didn't end until 1:31 AM. Writing in the *New York Times*, Joseph M. Sheehan called it an "epic contest" that "packed everything possible in the way of thrills," and called Joe "a brilliant performer in relief." Joe's line showed eight innings, four hits allowed, one earned run, six strikeouts, and two walks. Other than maybe wanting back that pitch to Elliott, Joe did everything possible to keep the Dodgers in it. And while Durocher had to use five pitchers, Joe's performance allowed Dressen to save the fragile arms of his staff.

The victory drew the Giants to within five and a half games of the Dodgers, and they had yet another reason to be encouraged, because Monte Irvin's broken ankle was healed. He had returned July 27 for a pinch-hitting appearance, and though it would be late August before he played regularly, having him in uniform and available to hit was an emotional lift. On the downside, pitcher Sal Maglie had hurt his back in St. Louis on July 16 and would be out for a month. A back injury also would hamper Larry Jansen, who'd go winless after July 26. Jansen had been a consistent winner since joining the Giants in 1947 and posted a 23-11 record in 1951 to share the league lead in victories with Maglie. But the team wouldn't be able to count on him down the stretch. So, like the Dodgers, the Giants were depending heavily on their star reliever to get by. Manager Leo Durocher said if Hoyt Wilhelm had not been so reliable, "you could stick a fork in us right now. We'd be done. He's been a life saver." During a thirty-two-game stretch that ended with the marathon against the Dodgers, Wilhelm pitched eighteen times, going 3-0 with five saves. "I haven't wanted to use him like I have," Leo noted, "but he's been the only one of the relievers I could count on."

The Dodgers certainly counted on Joe. Two days after his eight-inning stint against the Giants, Joe relieved Ben Wade in the fifth inning of another game against the New Yorkers and pitched the final four and two-thirds innings. He came in with two runners on and surrendered a three-run homer to Whitey Lockman, but blanked the Giants the rest of the way and got the victory in the Dodgers' 7–5 win. Writer James P. Dawson called Joe's work "supercharged pitching" in the *New York Times*. Joe won again on August 11 in Philadelphia, allowing just a single run over the final four and one-third innings in relief of Joe Landrum. The Dodgers trailed 4–3 when Joe came in, but home runs by Gil Hodges, Jackie, and Campy powered a six-run sixth inning that resulted in a 9–5 victory and a split of their doubleheader. Joe had hiked his record to 8-2 and the Dodgers' lead over the Giants had grown to nine games. The next day, August 12, marked the one-year anniversary of the date the Giants began their remarkable run to the pennant, and Leo's boys were closer to Brooklyn in 1952 than they had been a year earlier. But they had lost five straight and eleven of sixteen. Combine those struggles with their pitching woes and the Giants were in no position to mount another charge. Or so it seemed.

>>>>>>>>>>

The Giants' losing streak reached six when Joe thwarted them in the first game of an August 13 doubleheader at Ebbets Field. He relieved Carl Erskine in the eighth inning of a tie game and got the final out, then pitched out of a bases-loaded jam in the bottom of the ninth after the Dodgers had taken a 5–4 lead on Pee Wee's run-scoring single. Dressen sent Joe back out in the eighth inning of the nightcap with the Dodgers trailing 5–4, but it might have been a case of going to the well once too often. The Giants got to Joe for three hits and two runs, and Chris Van Cuyk had to come in to get the final out of the inning in a game the Dodgers ended up losing 8–4.

Still, Associated Press sportswriter Ralph Roden felt compelled to bring up the Newcombe comparison again in the wire service's daily wrap-up of Major League games, saying Joe "has contributed as much to the Dodger cause as big Newk did in the past." Roden also pointed out: "It's doubtful if the Dodgers would be leading the National League by nine games today of it weren't for Black." Which was something the Dodgers and their fans already knew.

Joe faltered again six days later at Cincinnati's Crosley Field. In the eighth inning of a tie game, he gave up a two-run triple to the Reds' big bopper, Ted Kluszewski. The two baserunners had reached against Johnny Rutherford, however, and he took the loss.

Along with steely nerves and confidence in his pitches, a reliever has to have a short memory. He can't dwell on a bad outing. He has to forget it because he could be back on the mound as soon as the next game. So it was with Joe. He shrugged off the Kluszewski triple—somehow the big fella managed to leg out eleven three-baggers that season, by far the most of his career—and in a four-day span starting August 22, Joe won a game and saved three others. Joe got the victory with three and two-thirds innings of relief in a 9–3 win over the Pirates, then saved games for Clem Labine, Preacher Roe, and Ray Moore, who had been called up from St. Paul at the beginning of the month in yet another attempt by the club to bolster its pitching. Labine, still dogged by arm trouble, was sent down to St. Paul at the time, only to be recalled three weeks later. The victory that Joe saved was Labine's first appearance since returning and he was sharp, giving up two runs and five hits in a 3–2 victory over the Pittsburgh Pirates at Forbes Field.

The Dodgers added a position player during that series in Pittsburgh, one who would later leave an indelible mark in Brooklyn lore. Edmundo "Sandy" Amoros, a swift twenty-two-year-old outfielder from Cuba, had been lighting up American Association pitchers at St. Paul. Amoros was hitting .337 with twenty-four doubles, ten triples, nineteen home runs, and seventy-eight RBIs when the Dodgers called him up, in part at the urging of coach Billy Herman, who felt additional outfield depth would help the club avoid a repeat of the 1951 fiasco. Herman had watched Amoros closely while managing in the Cuban Winter League. "With the first look I got of him, I knew he couldn't miss making the Major Leagues," Herman told reporters. "He can outrun anybody in the Dodger organization and perhaps anybody in the majors." Amoros spoke only Spanish and that's where Joe came in. Joe had learned Spanish during his playing days in the Latin American leagues, so he met Amoros at the Pittsburgh airport and agreed to interpret for him. To make room for Amoros, the Dodgers shipped pitcher Chris Van Cuyk to Pueblo of the Class A Western League. Van Cuyk ended up in St. Paul in 1953 and never again pitched in the majors.

The very night Amoros arrived from St. Paul, the Dodgers got a look at his speed. Charlie Dressen sent the newcomer up to bat for Dick Williams with the Dodgers leading the Pirates 7–2 in the ninth inning and Gil Hodges on second. Amoros, blessed with powerful wrists, singled sharply up the middle, and when the ball got past center fielder Brandy

Davis, he kept running. Dressen waved him around from the third base coaching box, and he crossed the plate not all that far behind Hodges.

As impressive as that sprint around the bases may have been, Amoros made his most memorable play three years later at Yankee Stadium. He robbed the Yankees' Yogi Berra of an extra-base hit with a spectacular running catch that he turned into a double play in the seventh game of the 1955 World Series. The Dodgers led 2–0 at the time and ended up winning by that score to capture the series.

Joe's save for Ray Moore on August 25 completed a doubleheader sweep of the Cardinals in St. Louis. With the Giants losing 3–0 in Cincinnati, the Dodgers' lead ballooned to ten and a half games. There was still a month to play, but it was looking more and more like this, finally, was going to be the Dodgers' year. Just as encouraging, Johnny Rutherford had pitched a gem in the first game of that doubleheader, allowing only two hits in a 3–1 victory over a team that had come in riding an eight-game winning streak. Rutherford showed no sign of the shoulder ailment that had bedeviled him earlier and kept him out for six weeks in June and July. In Chicago three days later, Joe became the National League's leader in winning percentage, running his record to 11-2 in a 9–6 victory before 40,311 at Wrigley Field. He was far from perfect, allowing the Cubs to tie the score at 5–5 after relieving Clem Labine at the start of the fifth inning. But he limited the Cubs to one run the rest of the way and the Dodgers gave him a nice cushion by scoring four times in the seventh. With the victory, Joe became the first Brooklyn pitcher to beat each of the league's seven other teams. "Rubber-armed Joe Black" the AP called him. It was Joe's forty-fourth appearance of the season.

Number forty-five came two days later against the hated Giants at Ebbets Field, but his two perfect innings weren't enough. The Dodgers stranded a runner in each of the eighth and ninth innings and lost 4–3, Sal Maglie going the distance for the Giants to earn his fourteenth victory against five losses. They bounced back the next day to beat the Giants 9–1 on Billy Loes's four-hitter, returning their lead to nine games as the calendar turned to September, the month that had produced so much misery for Brooklyn in each of the past two years.

The Giants' September surge and the Dodgers' fade in 1951 may have hurt the worst, but the final month of the '50 season also had been painful for Brooklyn loyalists. As September 19, 1950, dawned, the Dodgers were stuck in third place, nine games behind the league-leading Philadelphia Phillies. Complacency then set in with the Phillies; the Dodgers got hot and when they beat Philadelphia 7–3 at Ebbets Field on September 30, they trailed by only one game. If the Dodgers could somehow win the season finale the next day, they'd force a playoff and have a chance to get to the World Series, something even the most delirious of Flatbush fans couldn't have imagined just two weeks earlier. As so often happened with the Dodgers, though, it was a case of hopes building, only to be crushed.

Each team put its ace on the mound for the big game, Don Newcombe for the Dodgers, Robin Roberts on only two days' rest for the Phillies. Each had won nineteen games and each did his job, because it was 1–1 going into the bottom of the ninth. That's when the Dodgers mounted a threat. Cal Abrams walked leading off and moved to second on Pee Wee Reese's single. When Duke Snider singled sharply to center, third base coach Milt Stock waved Abrams home. Ralph Branca remembered thinking, "No! Don't do that! Ashburn has him beat on the play!" That would be center fielder Richie Ashburn, who made a perfect throw to home, and Abrams was tagged standing up, several feet short of the plate. While manager Burt Shotton, Dressen's predecessor, defended Stock for sending Abrams, columnist Arthur Daley demurred, calling the decision "an exceedingly foolish and disastrous bit of strategy."

Still, the Dodgers had a chance. With runners on second and third, Roberts walked Jackie Robinson intentionally to load the bases with one out, but Carl Furillo popped out and Gil Hodges flied to right, stranding their three teammates. Dick Sisler then belted a three-run homer off Newcombe in the top of the tenth, Roberts retired the dispirited Dodgers in order in the bottom half, and the Phillies had their first pennant in thirty-five years. The Dodgers' stretch run had started just a little too late.

As September 1952 got underway, the Dodgers hoped that, for once, they could avoid all that late-season drama. In the end, they did—but only after things got a little dicey.

12

From a Royal to a Saint

1951

IN MOST RESPECTS, THE MONTREAL Royals' International League game at Rochester's Red Wing Stadium on April 21, 1951, was nothing more than a routine early season minor league matchup. It was a chilly Saturday afternoon, the type of weather the city's baseball fans could expect at that time of year, and a slight breeze blew off Lake Ontario. But with the game to be played during the daylight hours, a fan who dressed properly could stay comfortable. Montreal had split the two games of a season-opening series at Baltimore and stopped in Rochester for another two-game set as the club worked its way north toward home after spring training in the warmth of Florida. Rochester had won the International League pennant in 1950, finishing seven games ahead of second-place Montreal, the Brooklyn Dodgers' top farm club. The two teams also would end up 1-2 in the league when the 1951 season ended, only with Montreal on top by an eleven-game margin. That was too far down the road to be thinking about in April, however. Mainly, the league's managers just hoped to avoid the spring rainouts that force makeup double-headers and wreak havoc on a pitching rotation.

For one player, though, the game was about to produce one of those moments that when it comes, you can hardly believe it's happening. Joe Black, told all those years ago that colored guys don't play baseball, was going to play his first game in organized ball. Montreal manager Walt Alston had tabbed Joe as his starting pitcher, and with his first pitch, Joe would break his own personal color barrier. He could only hope his debut came close to matching what his good friend Jim Gilliam had accomplished in the Royals' opener at Baltimore three days earlier.

Gilliam was an absolute terror at the plate in that game, going 4-for-6 with a double and a home run. He drove in six runs and scored two. The quiet second baseman belted his home run batting left-handed and his double batting from the right side of the plate. Obviously, the work he had done learning to switch hit at the urging of George Scales during his days with the Elite Giants had paid off. In Rochester, it would be Joe's turn to show what he could do. He had as much zip on his fastball as anyone. If he could control it and keep batters off balance with that "nickel curve," he just might succeed. It was what he expected of himself, and it was what Alston expected when he put Joe in the starting rotation after breaking camp. Joe knew he had a solid team behind him. But he also knew that ultimately, his fate—and his future in baseball—depended on how he and he alone performed.

>>>>>>>>>>

Once Joe became a full-time player with the Elite Giants, baseball turned into a year-round pursuit: Negro league ball in the spring and summer, Latin American ball in the late fall and winter, then a return to the States for spring training to start the process again. It was a vagabond life, to be sure, and there was little down time. But the paychecks kept coming and his skills stayed sharp. Besides, if he wasn't playing baseball, Joe would have had to find a real job. He wasn't ready for that yet. He still had a dream to pursue, and in 1951 he had inched even closer to making it real. Joe was going to spring training not with the Elite Giants or any other Negro league team, but with the Brooklyn Dodgers organization in Vero Beach, Florida. If all went according to plan, he'd spend the season with the Dodgers' Triple-A team in Montreal, one step from the Major Leagues. His years in the army and hop-

(left) Young Joe in his high-top sneakers.

(below) Joe's mother, Martha Black, was a major influence in his life.

(above) Showing the form that made Joe a successful pitcher with the Baltimore Elite Giants.

(right) Joe's big season with the Cienfuegos Elefantes in the 1951–52 Cuban Winter League helped propel him to the Major Leagues.

(right) A happy pitcher relaxing in the Dodger clubhouse.

(below) Teammates surround Joe (in the center) after his victory over the New York Yankees in game one of the 1952 World Series.

Joe and Jackie Robinson chat before a game.

Joe felt he made a difference as a teacher and coach at Hubbard Junior High School in his hometown of Plainfield, New Jersey.

Even on a teacher's salary, Joe was a sharp dresser.

During his career at Greyhound, Joe's name became so closely linked to the company that he was known as Mr. Greyhound.

Joe worked at becoming the best father he could be for Chico and Martha Jo.

Joe, who was being honored on this night, always took time to listen to Martha Jo.

(right) Joe and Casey Stengel as friends rather than opponents.

(below) Many years later, Sandy Koufax remained grateful for Joe's help during his first spring training with the Brooklyn Dodgers.

scotching across the country with the Elites had fortified his resolve to take that final step.

Joe and Jim Gilliam agreed to meet in Baltimore, where they'd catch a train and ride the rest of the way to Vero Beach together. They were chatty as the train rolled along on its southward journey, just what you'd expect from two friends embarking on a new adventure. But as the train drew closer to Florida, doubts began to creep in. Who would meet them at the station? Would their teammates accept them? A lot of them probably had never played with black teammates. "Was the scar of integration still a festering wound?" Joe wondered.

They also worried about what would happen if they didn't make it in organized ball. Negro league ball no longer was an attractive option. The Elite Giants would limp through the 1951 season playing most of their games on the road. The Negro American League would barely function as an organized entity. As fans and the black press turned their attention to the black stars in the Major Leagues, Negro league teams sold more and more of their top players to organized ball to make a quick buck. It became increasingly harder to replenish that talent, because Major League organizations were signing the best of the black players coming out of high school, college, and semipro teams.

It was always easy to say that Jackie Robinson's move to the Dodgers triggered the demise of the Negro leagues, but Joe disagreed with that thinking. Joe recognized that Jackie playing for the Dodgers gave hope to thousands of young blacks, himself included. But he felt Negro league owners precipitated their own collapse by their failure to go all-out in an effort to affiliate with the majors. They had discussed that possibility in the mid-1940s, but without a strong leader who could rally the clubs to a common cause, nothing came of those talks.

Looking back years later, Joe thought the black leagues could have survived if the owners had gone to Major League Baseball and offered to develop players and help them learn to play in an integrated setting. "Instead of that," he said, "they just called up and said, 'I have two players here. They are very good. Why don't you come and look at them. How much? Give me 5,000 [dollars].' So you start selling your better players. Now you have nothing left but the older players and young guys who came up and never played baseball. Nobody was going to pay money to see mediocre baseball."

They would pay to see blacks in the big leagues, though, and Joe was certain his young friend had the tools to make it, even if he still wasn't sure about his own chances. Thus, Joe felt it was his responsibility to convince Gilliam that he was as good as any infielder trying to make the team. He reminded Junior of all the game-saving double plays he and shortstop Pee Wee Butts had turned with the Elite Giants. Sharp execution comes from skill and practice, he pointed out. A person's skin color has nothing to do with it. Gilliam knew Joe had grown up playing sports in a mixed environment, so Joe figured his words carried the weight of credibility.

One of their worries vanished as soon as they stepped off the train in Vero Beach, because parked at the depot was a bus with DODGERTOWN painted in bold letters on the side. A middle-aged white man approached and asked, "You the two boys coming to spring training?" Hmmm, Joe thought, some people still can't tell the difference between a man and a boy. The bus dropped them off at the administration building, where they checked in and received their instructions. They had been so eager to get to camp that they were several days ahead of the Montreal reporting date. So when they were told to report at 9 AM the next day to Bobby Bragan, that gave them pause. Didn't Bragan manage the Dodgers' Double-A farm team at Fort Worth? That was not what they had bargained for. Fort Worth played in the all-white Texas League, which also had teams in Dallas, Houston, San Antonio, and Beaumont, Texas, as well as in Tulsa and Oklahoma City in Oklahoma and in Shreveport, Louisiana. Joe had seen what Texas could be like for blacks during his army stint at Camp Barkeley near Abilene. Jim Crow laws still held firm in Louisiana. As for Oklahoma, that state would be the site of one of the ugliest racial incidents ever on a football field. That fall, Oklahoma A&M defensive lineman Wilbanks Smith slugged Drake University's black star, Johnny Bright, in the face while another Drake player ran with the ball on the other side of the field. The punch broke Bright's jaw and ended his season. A photo sequence of the incident won a Pulitzer Prize for the *Des Moines Register* photographers who had captured it on film.

Joe and Jim had to wonder: were they being asked to emulate Jackie Robinson's pioneering spirit and integrate the Texas League? Branch Rickey had moved on to the Pittsburgh Pirates, but they thought maybe his views on integration had trickled down to the current Brooklyn administration. They knew that Jackie, Roy Campanella, Larry Doby, Don Newcombe, and Satchel Paige had opened eyes and shown that black players could excel in the white majors. Organized baseball shedding its whites-only persona was becoming a question of not *if* but *when*. Still, they saw a host of potential obstacles. They could not envision a warm reception in the Texas League when two black players trotted onto the field. They knew from their travels through the South in Negro ball that public facilities were segregated. They remembered how black Major Leaguers had trouble finding a place to stay when their teams played exhibition games en route north from spring training. Joe told Gilliam they had to ask themselves if their desire to reach the Major Leagues would give them the discipline they'd need to cope with the abuse they'd be sure to encounter. They agreed that yes, they were determined to play Major League baseball, and yes, they could turn the other cheek.

Joe then let out a little laugh and said they were allowing fear to get the best of them. They should just let the next day bring what it may. What it brought was a bunch of curious faces staring at them as they made their way through the breakfast line at the dining hall. What had they gotten themselves into? Once in the clubhouse, Joe and Jim quietly undressed and prepared to change into their uniforms, again with players staring at them from across the room. They unfolded their jerseys and looked at the large, blue script letters across the front: MONTREAL. Their relief was palpable. They didn't have to become pioneers after all. Bragan told them they were ticketed for Triple-A ball in Montreal, just as they expected, but they'd work with the Fort Worth candidates until the Montreal camp opened.

Warming up on the field, Joe tried to ease Jim's anxiety by telling him to forget the hostile stares and unwelcoming atmosphere. They were unknown competition, he said, and those other guys were just trying to size them up. Two coaches jumped in and spared Joe and Junior the embarrassment of having to play catch with each other. Joe felt he surprised the other pitchers with his speed as he bounded off the mound to cover first base on balls hit to the right side. He'd glance over at the infielders occasionally and see a coach trying to show Gilliam how to pivot on a double play. Joe had to laugh. No one needed to teach Jim Gilliam the intricacies of turning a double play. Though just twenty-two years old at the time, Gilliam already was a master of the twin killing.

Amid the laughter and chatter in the clubhouse after the workout, Joe occasionally heard the word "colored" sprinkled in the conversation coming out of the shower room. When Joe and Jim went in, all conversation stopped and the others finished up quickly and hurried back to their lockers. Joe could only shake his head. Those guys didn't have anything to fear. He and Gilliam were just two guys trying to make the team.

Spring training gave Joe a chance to refine the techniques he had learned from Billy Herman in Cuba. He worked on improving his control and relying on more than just his fastball, or "muscle ball," as Joe called it. Too often in the past when he absolutely needed an out, Joe simply would pump his arms and let go with a 98-mile-an-hour heater. That was fine against a weak hitter who couldn't catch up to a fastball. But throw a pitch like that over the heart of the plate to a good hitter and the ball comes right back at you—or sails over the fence. If Joe was going to get to the big leagues, setting up a hitter for his "out" pitch had to become second nature.

Gilliam impressed the Fort Worth coaching staff with his speed, agility, and intensity. Joe also showed some speed, even though he carried 215 pounds on his six-foot-two frame. Of the thirty-five players in camp, only Gilliam and three others beat him in time trials. He also was faster than the others with his pitches. But most of the talk among the staff and the other players concerned Joe's age. He was twenty-seven, old for someone just breaking into organized ball, though not too old to keep him from playing in the minors. Seven players who would suit up for the Fort Worth Cats in 1951 were at least thirty, including thirty-seven-year-old pitcher Chink Zachary and thirty-six-year-old catcher Mickey Livingston. Bobby Bragan, who was thirty-three, would not only manage the team but play in 103 games that season.

Joe understood how his age might work against him, but he felt that as long as he could control his fastball and maintain his velocity, he could realize his dream.

His time in the Fort Worth camp was not without a reminder of racism. It seemed that every time he and Gilliam walked together, they'd hear someone yell, "Hey, Blackie!" They thought the remark was addressed to them, and they let off steam by talking about it in their room so they wouldn't do anything foolish. But they were determined to figure out if they were facing racial slurs.

They found out there was nothing racist involved when a man they had seen around walked up and introduced himself. He was Blackie Sherrod, a reporter for the *Fort Worth Star-Telegram*, and he asked if he could interview them. Sherrod's gentlemanly approach helped ease some of the tension Joe and Jim felt, as did the attitude of the other players, who became friendlier each day. Still, they were glad when it came time to join the Montreal candidates. They found a more welcoming group that included Tom Lasorda, Walt Fiala, Dick Teed, Al Epperly, and Mal Mallette, all veterans of minor league play and, in Lasorda's case, a future Los Angeles Dodgers manager. Another who was destined to manage the Dodgers, Walter Alston, managed the Montreal club.

It would be left to Dave Hoskins, a star Negro league outfielder who had become a pitcher in white baseball, to integrate the Texas League. Hoskins would win twenty-two games for Dallas in 1952 and become a major drawing card wherever he pitched. Following that season, his appearances on the mound were estimated to have added 92,850 fans to the attendance figures, and he was hailed as "the savior of the Texas League."

>>>>>>>>>>

When camp broke, Joe, Jim Gilliam, and Hector Rodriguez, a black infielder who had starred in the Cuban League, headed north as members of the Montreal Royals. According to Montreal general manager Guy Moreau, Rodriguez spoke just three words of English, albeit useful words on a baseball field: "I got it."

Joe found Montreal to be a beautiful city, a place where he and Gilliam felt welcomed by the fans and residents. The parent club's three black stars in 1951, Jackie Robinson, Roy Campanella, and Don Newcombe, all had passed through Montreal on their way to the Dodgers, so fans were accustomed to watching and cheering black players. "There were many blacks in Montreal," said Jacques Beauchamp, who wrote for the *Montreal Matin*. "Nobody made a fuss over them." Joe and Jim also enjoyed the companionship and guidance offered by Herb Trawick, the first black in the Canadian Football League. Trawick, a popular two-way lineman for the Montreal Alouettes, sought out and befriended every black who played for the Royals. Long after his playing days had ended,

Joe wrote of his regard for Trawick, who showed the black players where they could find the conveniences that would make their stay in the city enjoyable and comfortable.

Though a more tolerant city for blacks than many in the United States, Montreal wasn't entirely without prejudice and discrimination. As popular and as talented as he was on the gridiron, the only job Trawick could find during the off-season was as a restaurant doorman, even though he had a college degree in science and physical education. But for the most part, it was as pleasant a city as Joe could have wanted for his debut in organized baseball. Two other Canadian cities, Toronto and Ottawa, joined Montreal in the International League, along with Buffalo, Rochester, and Syracuse in New York; Springfield, Massachusetts; and Baltimore.

Before settling in his new city, though, Joe had to deal with the Rochester Red Wings on their turf. Part of the St. Louis Cardinals' organization, the Red Wings were a formidable club, even if their roster included no one who had been or would become a Major League star. Opposing Joe on the mound was Jack Faszholz, a big right-hander who had gone 5-3 in twenty appearances with Rochester in 1950. Faszholz, who would enter the ministry when his playing career ended, was in his seventh season of minor league ball, so he certainly had the edge in experience. As the seventeen hundred fans settled into their seats, some had to be curious about the Royals' black righty. Was this another Don Newcombe on the rise? Or would he flame out and never be heard from again? Both were legitimate questions.

Joe gave the Royals what would be regarded today as a "quality start," though at that time it was more a case of not quite getting the job done. He went eight innings and gave up five hits and three runs, striking out five and walking four. Within an out of taking the loss, he ended up with no decision, thanks to Walt Fiala, who batted for Joe with two outs in the top of the ninth and Montreal trailing 3–2. Fiala singled in the tying run to get Joe off the hook, and the Royals won 4–3 when Jim Gilliam scored on Johnny Welaj's bases-loaded fly ball in the tenth.

It was eight days before Alston sent Joe to the mound again and this time, he delivered a victory for the Royals with his bat as well as his arm. Joe stifled Rochester on three hits in a 1–0 victory in a seven-inning game at Montreal. His walk-off, run-scoring single in the bottom of the seventh ended the game after he had broken up lefty Freddie Hahn's no-hit bid with a bunt single in the sixth.

Used mostly as a starter, Joe went on to win five of his first six decisions, including a complete game six-hitter in a 3–1 victory at Buffalo on May 10. He pitched five times in relief during that stretch and got one of his victories coming out of the bullpen, replacing Ross Grimsley with two outs in the second inning and working five and two-thirds innings in a 9–8 win over Springfield. It was the kind of stint Joe would be summoned for frequently in another year. Joe also saved a victory for Mal Mallette with three and one-third innings of relief, and he got the Royals out of the fifth inning against Syracuse after the team's starter, twenty-three-year-old lefty Tom Lasorda, gave up six hits and seven walks.

Joe was becoming a dominant figure on the mound, so perhaps it was inevitable the press would make the comparison. Like Don Newcombe, who went 17-6 for Montreal in 1948 and won nineteen games for the Brooklyn Dodgers in 1950, Joe had a commanding presence. He was big and he threw hard. Thus, after Joe beat Rochester in that April 29 game, the Associated Press declared: "The Montreal Royals have the makings of another Don Newcombe in Joe Black, husky Negro hurler who is making his debut in organized baseball with the Brooklyn Dodgers' International League affiliate this year." An AP staffer thought the comparison so apt that the wire service used it again after Joe's May 10 victory at Buffalo. That story began: "Maybe the Brooklyn Dodgers have a new Don Newcombe coming along in Joe Black of their Montreal farm in the International League." It would not be the last time someone hailed Joe as the next Newcombe, because the comparison would follow him into the big leagues. Joe understood he'd be better served if he just worked at being himself. Still, the comparison was flattering.

Not so flattering was an ugly incident at Buffalo, whose team was affiliated with the Cincinnati Reds. Joe was pitching, and from about the third inning on, he remembered hearing invective spew from the Buffalo dugout: "Niggers!" and "Dumb niggers!" and even "Monkeys and niggers all belong in Africa!" Joe could tell that one player did all the yelling and managed to figure out where he sat, but he couldn't identify him. Late in the game, Joe laid down a sacrifice bunt, and as he trotted back to his dugout, he could hear his tormentor yell something, but all he could make out was "like your dumb mother."

This time, Joe caught a glimpse of the guy, and now he was really steamed. It was one thing to insult Joe Black. Insulting his mother was going too far. "I wanted that man," Joe recalled.

After getting two quick outs in the ninth, Joe ran the count to 2-2 and shook off his catcher until he got the sign for a fastball. Joe unleashed his pitch and started for the dugout before it even reached the plate. He was crossing the first base line when the umpire yelled "strike," ending the game. Joe brushed past players in his path and saw the guy he wanted just as the Buffalo player said, "Ah, they're just a bunch of dumb niggers!"

"Well," Joe declared, "This nigger is going to kick your ass."

The guy reached into a cooler and pulled out what Joe took to be an ice pick. "Come on nigger," he said as he turned to face Joe. Joe threw his glove at the guy, then leaped toward him, grabbed him, and drew back his arm, angry enough to punch the Buffalo player senseless. Just then, Gilliam grabbed his arm and shouted, "No! No! You're going to mess it up for us." Alston and other Montreal players joined Gilliam and pulled Joe away before he could throw a punch. Back in their room, Joe apologized to Junior for losing his cool and almost blowing their opportunity. Jackie had accepted all that abuse in 1947 without lashing back because he knew that if he retaliated, it would be just what many whites expected—"Those colored boys can't control themselves, you know." The great experiment would have been over and who knows how long it would have been before another black player was brought to the Major Leagues. The Buffalo incident gave Joe yet another reason to appreciate what Jackie had endured so that he and others would have a chance to follow him.

>>>>>>>>>>

With his strong start, Joe was on his way to becoming one of the league's top pitchers. But it didn't last. As mid-June approached, Joe began to falter. He'd do well early in the game, then lose his stuff. After lasting only three and two-thirds innings in a 7–5 loss to Baltimore on June 10, he pitched three times over the next ten days, losing twice and winning once. The victory came in the second game of a doubleheader at Buffalo, an 11–4 win that was part of a huge day for Jim Gilliam. Junior went to bat eleven times in the doubleheader and reached base on all eleven trips to the plate. He singled four times, walked twice, and scored twice during a 7–2 victory in the opener. In the nightcap, Gilliam walked, singled three times, and belted a grand slam to back his buddy. Joe got into the act on offense as well, driving in a couple of runs and scoring once. The Royals led the league by four games at that point and, despite Joe's recent struggles, the two former Elite Giants were making key contributions. Joe was 6-3 with a save, while Gilliam was hitting .332. The team's third former Negro leaguer, Hector Rodriguez, was also coming up big with a .329 average and forty-six RBIs. He and Gilliam ranked 1-2 in the league in hits.

Joe stumbled in his next appearance, however. Relieving Ross Grimsley in the seventh inning as Montreal led 3–1 at Rochester, Joe couldn't keep the Red Wings at bay and they scored four runs en route to a 5–4 victory. Alston seemed to lose faith in Joe after that. Over the next five weeks, Joe made only three starts. He did fashion a complete game seven-hitter in a 4–1 victory over Springfield, but he lasted only three and a third innings in his next start, and when he finally was given another start two weeks later he was lifted after four innings. A little support in either game would have helped. Montreal was shut out both times.

Joe no longer showed much promise as a reliever, either. In eight relief appearances between June 20 and July 22, Joe went 0-4 with just one save. Though he had a couple of good stints, Joe gave up the winning run in the eighth inning of one game, the ninth inning of another, and the fourteenth inning of a third. That extra-inning game, a 9–7 loss to Ottawa on July 22, turned out to be Joe's last of the season with Montreal.

The Dodgers shipped pitcher Dan Bankhead to the Royals after the former Negro league star struggled mightily with the big club—posting a record of 0-1 with fourteen walks in fourteen innings and a 15.43 ERA. Someone had to go and that someone was Joe, who was sent to St. Paul, the Dodgers' other Triple-A farm club, in the American Association. Joe left with five straight losses, a 7-9 record, and a 3.85 earned run average. Neither figure was what you'd call sparkling, but Joe didn't think he was shipped out for pitching poorly. Instead, he always believed the Dodgers and Montreal had an unwritten agreement that no more than three black players would be assigned to the Royals at any one time. Gilliam and Rodriguez both were among the league's top hitters, so they weren't going anywhere. They had been so impressive that league president

Frank "Shag" Shaughnessy crowed in late June, "I never saw two hungrier ballplayers than Hector Rodriguez and Junior Gilliam. They make the Royals go." That left Joe as the odd man out.

Joe had been dogged by soreness in his shoulder, which he had knocked out of whack while showing a player how to make a tackle way back when he was at Morgan State. He never mentioned it to anyone, because he feared the Dodgers would release him. While he usually managed to work around it, the shoulder sometimes tightened up on him in Montreal and he felt it reduced his effectiveness as the game wore on. As a result, Joe said the organization tagged him as a pitcher who couldn't go nine innings, and that label stuck when he went to spring training in 1952.

Joe wasn't happy about going to St. Paul, because it was a demotion. But he had no choice if he wanted to remain with the Dodgers, so he caught a train to Columbus, Ohio, to hook up with his new team. The Saints were managed by Clay Hopper, who had been Montreal's manager during Jackie Robinson's season there in 1946. Hopper was Deep South all the way. He was born in Mississippi, grew up there, and lived there during the off-season. Montreal reporter Jacques Beauchamp said Hopper once told him that if his father were alive, "he would probably kill me for managing a black player." In the end, though, Hopper had been praised for his steady hand in guiding Jackie through his first season in organized baseball, so Joe figured he'd get a fair shake.

With a solid club that included Jim Pendleton, Don Hoak, Danny Ozark, Jack Cassini, Johnny Rutherford, and Pat McGlothin, the Saints would finish second in the American Association to the Milwaukee Brewers and reach the finals of the league playoffs. Joe would do his part, going 4-3 with an impressive 2.25 ERA in the regular season and picking up two more victories in the playoffs.

Hopper used Joe twice in relief in late July—he pitched effectively both times—then moved him into a rotation headed by Rutherford and McGlothin. Al Epperly, Joe's teammate at Cienfuegos the previous winter, had been sent from Montreal to St. Paul in May and had established himself as the Saints' bullpen ace. Joe made seven starts for the Saints and pitched five straight complete games during one stretch, winning four. He was proving that he could go the distance after all. Then trouble surfaced. Joe felt a stabbing pain in his right elbow during an August 24 game against Milwaukee. It was so severe that he asked Hopper to take him out of the game. He felt as though the area around his elbow was as swollen as a flexed bicep. Joe did not throw for the next seven days. He soaked the elbow in a whirlpool, put a heat lamp on it, and had the trainer massage it. The rest and treatment worked. The arm started to feel better and he finally returned to action on September 6 against the Kansas City Blues, a New York Yankees farm club.

Joe looked strong and appeared headed for his fifth victory, leading 2–1 after six innings while allowing only one hit, a home run by Andy Carey. But he gave up a two-run homer to light-hitting Roy Partee in the seventh and lost 3–2.

St. Paul finished the season three days later at 85-66, nine games behind first-place Milwaukee, and lined up against red-hot Louisville in the first round of the playoffs. The Colonels had won their final fourteen games to edge Minneapolis for the fourth and final playoff spot. There was reason for the Saints to be confident, though, because they had gone 16-6 against Louisville during the regular season.

Rain halted the first game of the series with the score tied 5–5 in the eighth inning, so the two teams had to replay it from the beginning two days later. Joe started and pitched well before being lifted for a pinch hitter, and Louisville won 7–5 in eleven innings. But the Saints quickly shook off that loss and swept the next four games to win the series, Joe getting the third victory in that run with eight sharp innings.

Milwaukee promptly dashed that momentum by winning the first two games of the championship series and eventually took the series four games to two. Joe got the victory in game three, with help from reliable reliever Al Epperly, and, with his team facing elimination, got the start in game six on only two days' rest.

He looked good for a while on a damp, cold, dismal night, blanking the Brewers through the first two innings in front of a mere 829 shivering fans at Milwaukee's Borchert Field. But Joe ran out of gas and so did the rest of the St. Paul pitchers, who were pummeled mercilessly by the Milwaukee hitters. The Brewers rolled to a 17–2 victory that sent them to the Little World Series against International League champion Montreal, Joe's former team. Milwaukee also won that series.

>>>>>>>>>>

Joe had not killed his chances of getting a shot at the Major Leagues with his first season in organized ball, nor had he done a lot to enhance that opportunity. Between Montreal and St. Paul, he went a combined 11-12 with a 3.28 earned run average. He gave up 150 hits in 170 innings, striking out 84 and walking 61. Not the kind of numbers to raise eyebrows, but also not so poor that the Dodgers would dismiss him outright.

If anyone had put up numbers to impress a Major League team, it was Epperly. He had worked seventy-one innings with the Saints, almost all of them in relief, and fashioned a 13-4 record with a 3.80 ERA. In five games with Montreal at the beginning of that season, he had gone 2-0 with a 2.25 ERA.

But Epperly was thirty-three years old and had already had two brief stints in the majors—twelve years apart. He pitched in nine games for the Chicago Cubs in 1938 and five for the Dodgers in 1950. After pitching three mop-up innings for Brooklyn in a 7–2 loss to the Philadelphia Phillies on July 7, 1950, Epperly never appeared in another Major League game. He'd hang on in professional ball until calling it quits at the age of thirty-six and embarking on a thirty-year career in law enforcement in his home state of Iowa.

As unlikely as it appeared in September 1951, it was Joe Black, not Al Epperly, who in 1952 would become the Dodgers' relief ace and save their season.

13

First a Threat, Then a Pennant

September 1952

JOE WAS RELAXING IN THE VISITORS' clubhouse at Braves Field in Boston reading his fan mail while his teammates dressed and manager Charlie Dressen talked to reporters. As usual, some of the conversation concerned Joe and whether he could continue his remarkable relief work in the stretch drive. Dressen shuddered to think where the Dodgers would be without him. Third place? Fourth place? "We could be in real trouble if he should have a bad stretch," the little manager said. The night before, September 3, Joe had picked up his eighth straight victory with six shutout innings of relief in the Dodgers' 6–5 win over the Braves. Jackie had scored the winning run on Duke Snider's bunt in the eighth inning and Joe pitched out of a bases-loaded, one-out jam in the ninth. Joe had been ordered to intentionally walk Jack Dittmer to fill the bases, because the pitcher, Warren Spahn, was up next. Spahn was a decent hitter, batting .333 one season and cracking thirty-five home runs in his long career, so manager Charlie Grimm let the left-handed swinger bat for himself. Joe struck him out and that brought up Sam Jethroe, a good hitter in the clutch. Jethroe worked the count to 3-1 before missing with a big swing on Joe's fastball. The small crowd of 6,756 fans cheered loudly as Joe prepared for the payoff pitch. Jethroe popped it into short right-center, but Snider had a bead on the ball. He caught it, held it high in his glove and then kissed the ball. Roscoe McGowen wrote in the *New York Times* that the game might have been Joe's "finest hour."

The victory lifted Joe's record to 12-2. He also had eleven saves, his earned run average had dropped to 2.01, and the Dodgers led the Giants by eight games. Joe Black's world was spinning nicely, better than even he could have imagined when he was a youngster pretending to strike out the St. Louis Cardinals' Gashouse Gang hitters while throwing at that brick wall in Plainfield.

Those warm feelings vanished when he opened an envelope that carried a postmark from Bronx Central Station in New York. The message in the letter was composed of letters cut from a magazine, like something from a B-grade cop show. But the words they formed were chilling:

> Joe Black: I have bet my life savings on the Giants winning the pennant. I consider you to be the main reason why they are eight games out of first place. If you come in to pitch at the Polo Grounds Saturday, Sunday or Monday, Sept. 6, 7, 8, it will be the last time you ever appear on any baseball mound. I live in a project overlooking the Polo Grounds and you would be an easy target standing alone on the mound. I will watch your every move.

Joe had received a death threat. It was one thing to stand up to the racial taunts that had been hurled at him. Those were just words. While there was nothing overtly racist in the letter, it implied something far more sinister than being called Old Black Joe or a monkey. Still, Joe thought it was nothing more than a joke from a disgruntled Giants fan. Everyone who followed baseball knew Joe was the main reason the Dodgers led the National League. And he had been especially effective against the Giants. At that point, he was 2-0 against Leo Durocher's crew and had given them only two earned runs in twenty-one and two-thirds innings. And his best and most critical effort against the Giants was still to come. "He had great control," said the Giants' Bobby Thomson, who managed only two hits in ten at-bats against Joe that year. "The ball just moved. And it wasn't just me. A lot of guys I talked to would say the same thing—what the heck is it?"

Joe showed the letter to Dressen and he too thought it was a prank, but he notified authorities just the same and revealed the contents of the letter to reporters that night. Warren Spahn had been threatened earlier in the year and was given a police guard in Chicago. Pittsburgh Pirates slugger Ralph Kiner and Philadelphia Athletics pitcher Bobby Shantz also had been threatened. Nothing happened in any of those cases, but with the Dodgers in the final stages of a drive they hoped would take them to the pennant, Dressen wasn't about to take any chances with his most valuable arm.

Dressen called on Joe again to pitch that night, and whether he was distracted by the letter or just didn't have his best stuff, he couldn't keep the Braves at bay. He allowed six hits over four and two-thirds innings, the last a run-scoring single by Sid Gordon in the bottom of the eleventh inning that gave the Braves a 6–5 win, their first in fifteen games with the Dodgers that season. The Dodgers had another game in Boston the next day, but Dressen sent Joe back to Brooklyn as a precaution, figuring he'd be safer in his own home. The Braves beat the Dodgers again on September 5 by a score of 3–1 in a game that Dressen entrusted to left-hander Ken Lehman, who was making his Major League debut. The Dodgers brought Lehman up from their St. Paul farm club at the end of August in their continuing effort to plug holes in the pitching staff. Lehman had gone 3-1 at St. Paul following his discharge from the army, which had kept him out of baseball in 1951. He gave the Dodgers seven decent innings, surrendering two earned runs and three runs total. But Brooklyn couldn't get much going against the Braves' big right-hander, Jim Wilson, who scattered six hits while collecting a couple of hits himself and scoring a run.

The loss, coupled with the Giants' 5–4 victory over the Phillies, cut the Dodgers' lead to six games heading into a five-game series at the Polo Grounds that could decide if the Dodgers would run away with the pennant or be forced to fight off the New Yorkers until the end. Aware of the series' importance—and of the friction between the two clubs—the National League split up two umpiring teams so it could put the four best arbiters possible on the field for those games. The result was a crew of Jocko Conlan, Bill Stewart, Al Barlick, and Lee Ballanfant. In the end, they earned their pay.

Joe was the subject of much attention because of the threatening letter. Two police detectives escorted him from his home in Brooklyn to the Polo Grounds. According to newspaper reports, twenty other detectives and two lieutenants circulated in and around the ballpark. The two rivals started the series with a day-night doubleheader, and Joe knew it would be an emotional three days. He once wrote that a game between the Dodgers and Giants was like the "Fourth of July, Christmas and a homecoming football game wrapped into one package." Giants star Monte Irvin said it was likely a few batters would hit the dirt to avoid brushback pitches, because both clubs followed the same credo: "If you knock one of our guys down, then two of your guys are going to get it."

"Those Dodger-Giant games weren't baseball," Andy Pafko noted, "they were civil war."

When he looked back on that series years later, Joe could see the humor in the follow-up to the letter. Teammates yelled "VIP" and "Public Enemy Number One" when Joe walked into the clubhouse with his two bodyguards. He recalled Gil Hodges ambling over and saying, "Chico, let's switch uniform tops. Maybe the killer will be so far away that he won't know the difference." Joe laughed and continued putting his uniform on. He had agreed to appear on a pregame television show hosted by actress Laraine Day, who happened to be married to Giants manager Leo Durocher. Naturally, the subject of the threatening letter came up and Sam Lacy recounted their conversation in the *Baltimore Afro-American*.

When Joe said he wasn't worried about the threat, Day replied, "Well, I got a threat, too, in the morning's mail. A Dodgers fan said he'd be watching me from the upper stands and if anyone shot you, he would shoot me."

Joe: "Gee, then I certainly hope nobody tries bothering me."

Day: "That's nice of you, Joe. You're a nice fellow and I'd like to see you do well, providing the Giants are doing well at the same time. Of course, I could be a little prejudiced, since I'm the manager's wife."

Joe: "Yeah, that Leo does sorta have you over a barrel."

>>>>>>>>>>

Despite his best attempts to shrug off the threat, Joe still had to make the long walk from the clubhouse, located in deep center field, to the dugout. It was nearly five hundred feet from there to home plate, so Joe had to cross a lot of open ground inside the gaping U-shaped stadium. He left three detectives behind in the clubhouse and made the walk by himself, striding directly over the middle of the field before cutting across the diamond to the dugout. He kept his focus straight ahead, the *Times* reported, never once looking to his left or right. Then, shortly before the game started, Joe had to walk back across the field to the visitors' bullpen in deep left-center field, so far from the plate—nearly 450 feet—that the players sat in fair territory. Before making that trek, Joe said Dressen told him, "If you're lucky the guy's roof will be on the left-field side and you'll have that high wall to protect you." As he began trotting that way, he heard his manager yell, "Hey! Get against the wall and stay there!"

Joe didn't pitch in that doubleheader, which the Giants swept. The Dodgers committed four errors and hit into three double plays, losing 6–4 in the opener, which dragged on for three hours and thirty-eight minutes, then the longest nine-inning game in Major League history. In the nightcap, the Giants pounded Johnny Rutherford and Ben Wade for thirteen hits in a 7–3 victory. At that point, the Giants had won five straight and ten of fourteen. The Dodgers had lost four in a row and their lead, which stood at ten and a half games on August 26, had shrunk to four games. Joseph M. Sheehan wrote in the *Times* that Dressen and the Dodgers "can't help being haunted by their 1951 collapse." The Dodgers had to find a way to stop their skid. Their problem was that all season long, they never had a starting pitcher they could legitimately call a stopper. Dressen had decided he would go with Preacher Roe the next day, though he tried to deceive everybody, Leo Durocher in particular, into thinking he had someone else in mind. In Charlie's view, the ploy worked. Many others, however, insisted they knew what he was doing all along.

Dressen had the recently summoned rookie, Joe Landrum, warm up on the side for everyone to see, and he even made out three lineup cards with Landrum as his starter, handing one to the Giants, one to the public address announcer, and another to the reporters. Meanwhile, he had Roe, Joe, and a couple of others throw in the bullpen, and he listed Roe as his starter on the lineup card he gave to the umpires, making it official. Roe had completed only six of his previous twenty-two starts and had not beaten the Giants in over a year, but he was magnificent on that Sunday afternoon before a crowd of 40,037, subduing the Polo Grounders on three hits in a 4–1 victory. Gil Hodges, Pee Wee Reese, George Shuba, and Billy Cox backed the gangly left-hander with solo home runs in a victory the Dodgers desperately needed, one of their most important of the season. It hiked their lead back to five games.

A couple of incidents in that game set the stage for what would happen the next day. After Reese homered off Sal Maglie in the third inning, the Barber dusted Jackie Robinson. When Roe hit Monte Irvin in the elbow the next inning, the umpires called Dressen and Durocher in for a meeting and reporter James P. Dawson said umpire Jocko Conlan could be heard shouting at Dressen: "I'm warning you. I don't want any more of this." In the eighth inning, Hodges took out second baseman Davey Williams with a rolling block on a double-play ball. Williams injured his back on the play and had to leave the game. It was no surprise that Williams got hurt. Hodges was a ruggedly built six-foot-one two-hundred-pounder. Williams was five foot ten and weighed 160. "Gil is a mild-mannered man," journalist Arch Murray wrote, "but when he hits, you stay hit."

Afterward, the two managers carped at each other like schoolboys arguing on the playground.

"I really showed up that Durocher, didn't I?" crowed Dressen, obviously proud of his lineup card shenanigans.

"In a pig's eye he did," Durocher shot back.

"You should have seen his face when I made that last-minute switch to Roe," Dressen went on. "He nearly had a fit. But he was hornswoggled. There was nothing he could do."

Dressen believed he forced Durocher to start more left-handed batters to play the percentages against the right-handed Landrum. So when it was Roe who took the mound, the advantage swung to the Dodgers. Durocher, however, asserted that he knew Roe would pitch and if he had wanted to change his lineup, he had plenty of time to do it. "But why should I change?" he said. "I've been winning with it." If Dressen was looking to the newspapermen for support that he had fooled Durocher, he didn't get it from Dawson, who wrote the Landrum-Roe move "baffled no one at all."

While Joe continued to receive a police escort to and from the ballpark, he had not been forced to show himself on the field during the first three games. That changed on the final day of the series, another day-night doubleheader. Starter Ken Lehman got into trouble in the second inning, when the Giants loaded the bases with one out. Though the Dodgers led 5–2, Dressen feared the Giants were on the verge of a big inning so he called on Joe. It was one of the longest walks he'd ever made. Joe recalled that he could hear the buzz of the crowd as he strode across the spacious outfield, but it seemed to get quieter with each step. By the time he got to the infield, Joe felt enveloped by silence. "It was eerie," he wrote in his autobiography. As he reached down to pick up some dirt, he noticed his hand was shaking. Pee Wee Reese then strolled over and asked, "What's the matter, Chico, are you scared?" Joe straightened up and replied, "Pee Wee, if someone claps their hands loudly, I'll drop dead." That brought a laugh from the Dodgers captain. "Man," he told Joe, "get over there and warm up."

Joe did and the Giants never had a chance. He ended their threat with two quick outs and blanked them the rest of the way, allowing six hits over the final seven and two-thirds innings of a 10–2 victory. But even in a game that wasn't close, it was still the Dodgers playing the Giants, and things got nasty. Hoyt Wilhelm hit Hodges with a pitch in the fifth inning, and when Carl Furillo followed with a double-play grounder, big Gil took out his second infielder in as many days. He spiked Bill Rigney, who had started in place of the injured Davey Williams, and opened a gash that required five stitches to close. Then came the tit for tat.

Joe sent George Wilson sprawling with what he later called the most intimidating duster he ever threw. Wilson's cap hung in the air momentarily as he ducked to avoid Joe's heater and the ball shot by between the cap and his head. "There were no helmets in those days," author Donald Honig said. "If it had hit him, it would have killed him." Roger Kahn called it "the single most terrifying pitch I have ever seen." Joe said Wilson had never done anything to aggravate him. He just happened to be at bat when Joe felt it was time to send a message. "George turned pale, temporarily," Joe wrote, "and when he looked at me, I stared back at him. The knockdown loses its effectiveness if a pitcher shows remorse. Besides, when a hitter's line drive makes a pitcher duck, the hitters never apologize."

Somehow, Wilson managed to collect himself for another pitch and made contact, popping out to Hodges in foul territory. Later, the Giants' Monty Kennedy sent Hodges to the dirt and twice narrowly missed Joe, one of the pitches carrying all the way to the grandstand backboard and prompting a warning from home plate umpire Lee Ballanfant. The next New York pitcher, Larry Jansen, plunked Andy Pafko in the eighth inning and was ejected after hitting Billy Cox with two outs in the ninth. The beanball battle proved costly for the Giants. Durocher was suspended for two days, his third suspension of the season, and fined one hundred dollars. Jansen was fined twenty-five dollars, but it was rescinded because of his otherwise good conduct. Monty Kennedy was socked with a fifty dollar fine even though he didn't hit anyone. Neither Joe nor anyone else with the Dodgers was fined. And nothing happened to Joe, other than those two pitches from Kennedy he had to avoid. Evidently, the threatening letter was nothing more than a prank—or at the most an ominous attempt to rattle Joe into a bad performance. At that, it failed miserably.

Sal Maglie outpitched Billy Loes to give the Giants a 3–2 victory in the nightcap, the last meeting between the two that season. The Giants had taken three of the five games in the set and won the season series with the Dodgers 14–8, but they had gained only one game on their rivals and trailed by five with nineteen to play. As difficult as the New Yorkers' plight seemed, they still made the Dodgers sweat. And for a few days anyway, it looked as if they might even manage to make the irrepressible Dressen eat his words.

>>>>>>>>>>

The weekly issue of the *Saturday Evening Post* that hit the newsstands on September 10 included a story with a headline blaring, THE DODGERS WON'T BLOW IT AGAIN. The author was none other than Dressen himself, sharing his thoughts with writer Stanley Frank. "I'm confident," Dressen said in the article, "that this year the Dodgers will be up top when the season ends." Those words had to ring hollow for some, because any fan who picked up the magazine that day could see Brooklyn's lead had shriveled to four games after a 7–1 loss to the Chicago Cubs the day before. The Giants had shaved six and a half games off the lead in just two weeks, and they actually were closer to the Dodgers than they had been exactly one year ago, when they trailed by five and a half games. Durocher had joked a few days earlier that if the Giants pulled off another pennant-winning comeback, "there'll be 100,000 suicides in Brooklyn."

Dressen said he didn't regret agreeing to the story and didn't feel he had gone out on a limb. "If anybody says I opened my big mouth and put my foot in it, that's all right with me," he told reporters. "It's my foot and my mouth and this is still my ballclub." Besides, Dressen felt the Dodgers were much better equipped for the stretch drive than they had been in 1951, pointing to the contributions of five players who weren't with the team the year before—Joe, pitchers Billy Loes and Ben Wade, and reserves George Shuba and Bobby Morgan, who was a utility infielder. "If any two of those five newcomers had been with the team last September, we would have breezed to the pennant," he said in the story.

Dressen's bravado seemed even more misplaced when the Giants crept another game closer. Four times they sliced the lead to three games, which is where it stood on September 17 after the Dodgers lost to the Pirates and the Giants beat the Cubs. During that stretch, when the Dodgers scuffled along at a .500 clip, Joe continued to pitch well. He picked up his fourteenth victory with six innings of relief against the Cardinals on September 12, worked a couple of two-inning stints in which he didn't give up a run, and got a four-pitch save against the Pirates on September 16, striking out Frank Thomas with two outs and two runners on to preserve Jim Hughes's first big-league win.

In his win over the Cardinals, Joe tied a team record by finishing his thirty-seventh game in relief, a mark that an earlier ace reliever, Hugh Casey, had set in 1947. The Cardinals' Stan Musial capped a 4-for-4 performance in that game with a home run and single off Joe, which led to an amusing exchange afterward. "You know, Stan," Joe said, "I didn't mind you hitting that one out of the park, but you didn't need that single." Musial, who had encouraged Joe after he had been taunted during that June game in St. Louis, responded good naturedly. "I've been trying to hit you all year, Joe," he said, "and I wasn't going to pass up another chance." Joe broke Casey's record for finishing games by pitching perfect eighth and ninth innings in an 11–5 victory over the Reds on September 15.

More recognition came Joe's way when he was honored by his hometown. September 9, the day after his clutch performance against the Giants, was "Joe Black Night" at Ebbets Field. Some one thousand fans from Plainfield, New Jersey, turned out to honor their native son, who was cheered as he stood on the field with his wife, Doris. The city's mayor, Carlyle W. Crane, presented Joe with a check for $2,000, and the

Plainfield High School band marched and played the national anthem. Joe didn't pitch that night, which turned into a downer for the Dodgers because they lost to the Cubs 7–1 while the Giants were beating the Pirates.

In that September 17 loss to the Pirates, Joe failed to keep it close. He came on in the eighth inning with the Dodgers trailing 2–1 and gave up a home run to George Metkovich on his first pitch. The Pirates nicked him for another run in the ninth and won 4–1. The next day, the Giants announced they would start accepting World Series ticket orders, the first team to do so. The Dodgers had played twenty games in September and lost twelve of them, hardly the pace you want in a pennant race. But that race was about to turn.

First, the Dodgers got a break when a Leo Durocher gamble backfired. Trying to give his weary staff a rest, Durocher sent Jack Harshman, who had just arrived from the Giants' farm club in Minneapolis, against the Chicago Cubs' Warren Hacker at the Polo Grounds on September 16. Harshman was a one-time first baseman who didn't start pitching regularly until earlier that season. Hacker, meanwhile, had allowed only eight earned runs over his previous fifty-three and one-third innings, a stretch that included two complete game victories over the Dodgers. Hacker throttled the Giants on three hits, Harshman was lifted after walking the first two batters in the third inning, and Durocher ended up using three other pitchers in a 9–0 loss.

Though the Giants trailed by only three games at the time, Durocher reasoned it was pointless to waste an ace against a pitcher like Hacker who was likely to win the game. Few others agreed. With only 7,637 fans in the massive stadium, one could be heard yelling, "Are you giving up, Leo?" Reporters from the New York papers wondered the same thing and roundly criticized the fiery manager. A "shameful giveaway," Jim McCauley wrote in the *Daily News*. An "inexcusable boner," Ken Smith wrote in the *Mirror*. Smith went on to say the Giants were "visibly let down" by their manager's move and "played a spiritless game." Durocher had "apparently conceded the race," Ed Sinclair said in the *Herald Tribune*.

Three days later, the Dodgers got another break when the Boston Braves' Sam Jethroe swung at one of Joe's pitches. It was the eighth inning at Braves Field and rain was approaching. The Dodgers led 4–2 and Joe was in for his fifty-fourth time in relief, tying the club record set by Les Webber in 1943. There were two outs when Jethroe swung at a 2-1 pitch and grounded out to Pee Wee at shortstop to end the inning. Right after first baseman Gil Hodges caught Reese's throw, the skies opened and it rained so hard the umpires declared the game over. If Jethroe had taken the pitch and the game had been stopped then, the score would have reverted to the end of the seventh, when it was 2–2, and the two teams would have been forced to play a doubleheader the next day.

Roscoe McGowen called it "the most timely swing any opponent has made this season." Some Boston writers questioned why Jethroe was swinging when it was about to rain. But while their press box vantage point afforded a view of the rain rolling in from the west, it wasn't as apparent down on the field. "When a man is up there facing a pitcher like Joe Black, he has no time to be a meteorologist," Boston manager Charlie Grimm said in defending his player. Jethroe said he was just trying to get a hit. "I didn't know the rain was coming," he said. "I was watching that pitcher. I couldn't be looking at the sky and hoping to see what Black was throwing at me."

The victory—which came with Joe's fifteenth save—started a four-game winning streak, a run that capped a surge of six victories in seven games, nailing down the pennant for the Dodgers. Joe saved three of those wins and got the victory in another, when Charlie Dressen tipped his hand on what he might do in the World Series. On September 21, two days after Joe induced that critical swing from Jethroe, Dressen started his bullpen ace in the series finale with the Braves. Joe proved to be just as effective as he had been coming out of the bullpen, though he caused his manager some consternation before taking the mound. Dressen was startled to find Joe sitting in the dugout ten minutes before the game. He had yet to warm up and Dressen demanded to know why. "I told him I wouldn't know what to do with ten minutes' warm-up," Joe said. "In the bullpen, I'd warm up with twenty throws." Joe threw for seven minutes, then went out and stopped the Braves 8–2 with a neat three-hitter.

Not only had Joe shown he could start and go the distance, he'd assured his team of at least a tie for the pennant. He had played a huge role in keeping the Dodgers in the lead during the season, then made sure that's where they'd finish on the final day. Of course, the Dodgers had wound up in a tie at the top on the final day of the 1951 season and everyone knew what happened after that, so they still had a piece of unfinished business. They took care of it two days later in the next game, beating the Phillies 5–4 behind Johnny Rutherford in the first game of a doubleheader at Ebbets Field. That hiked the lead to six and a half games with six to play. The Dodgers had clinched the pennant with a cobbled-together pitching staff and what *New York Times* columnist Arthur Daley termed Dressen's "prodigious use of the prodigious Joe Black."

Although Carl Furillo, Gil Hodges, Pee Wee Reese, Billy Cox, Jackie, and the oft-injured Campy all experienced a drop-off in hitting from 1951, the Dodgers still led the league in runs, home runs, and stolen bases. And it certainly didn't hurt the Dodgers' cause that their closest rival, the Giants, lost Willie Mays to the army and had to play much of the season without Monte Irvin, who came back from his injury to hit .310 but couldn't play enough to make a difference. "You just can't lose a guy like that for four months and hope to take it all," Durocher conceded.

Daley had suggested in a column in mid-September that Joe certainly was the Dodgers' most valuable player and maybe the MVP of the entire league. Dressen had said a few days earlier that in his view, the MVP race was between Joe and the Cubs' Hank Sauer, who was leading the league in home runs. The MVP award winner would not be announced until November, and it would stir some controversy. In the meantime, Joe received a major honor from the *Sporting News*, the publication known as "the Baseball Bible," which named him the National League's Rookie of the Year. The newspaper called Joe the "stalwart mainstay" of a "faltering mound staff." So how had Joe done it? Easy, Dressen said: "He throws hard and he throws strikes." Joe felt it was a little more complicated than that and tried to explain it to Sam Lacy of the *Baltimore Afro-American*:

> Let the other people explain it any way they wish, but I'll give you the real dope. I'm lucky. Lucky I can get the ball over and lucky I can pitch to Campy. Campy's smart, Sam, the smartest. He talks to you all the time, keeps your mind on your work and doesn't for one minute lose track of any situation. Because of him, I'm breaking my curve better, and because of him, I'm mixing it in with a little fast stuff and the old curve, the one that broke about so much. The new one, I call it Campy's curve, is about two inches bigger and it stops the hitters from crowding the plate like they had started to do on my original curve. The more I pitch to the

> guy, the more I realize how little I know about this game. Watching him, no one can possibly know how much he means to a team and to a pitcher, the way he gives you confidence, sets up the hitters and all that. Actually, Campy is like a guy taking a blind man by the hand and leading him across an unfamiliar street.

When Campy wanted to pitch a hitter a certain way, that's exactly how Joe pitched him. Lacy related a conversation that occurred after Joe fanned the Cubs' Bob Addis twice in a game in late August. Dressen wanted to know what he threw to get the Chicago outfielder, who had been a personal nemesis for Joe and usually hit well against the Dodgers. "Just fastballs low and away, like Campy told me," Joe replied. Dressen countered that the consensus among everyone in the league was to pitch Addis high and tight. That's when Campy broke in. "Skipper," he said, "I've been begging you for two seasons to pitch him low and away, but you wouldn't pay any attention. So today, when you said we could call our own plays, that's what I did. We got him out." Lacy didn't say if Dressen had a retort.

Joe made one more start after the Dodgers clinched, and it didn't go nearly so well. The Braves' Jack Dittmer and Eddie Mathews each rocked him for two-run homers and Joe left after five innings of an 11–3 loss at Ebbets Field on September 27. But the game was meaningless, and though a player tells himself to bear down in those situations, it's too easy to coast. Even with that subpar effort—five runs and five hits in five innings—what Joe did over the last two months of the season was remarkable. From July 30 through September 23, when the Dodgers needed him the most, Joe pitched twenty-five times in fifty-eight games. During that span, he went 11-1 with seven saves and compiled a 1.22 earned run average, allowing just eleven earned runs in eighty-one and one-third innings. The Dodgers went 33-25 in that stretch, meaning Joe had a hand in more than half those victories. When the team returned to New York after a late-season road trip, a photographer caught Joe, nattily dressed in a double-breasted blazer, holding two suitcases as he stood in front of some fans. One held a sign that read, OUR CHERCE: IKE FOR PRESIDENT, JOE BLACK MOST VALUABLE PLAYER.

If Joe had been running against Dwight Eisenhower in the presidential race, Ike wouldn't have stood a chance in the Brooklyn precincts.

On the season he won fifteen games against only four losses and saved fifteen more while appearing fifty-four times in relief, starting twice, and working 142⅓ innings. His earned run average, a stingy 2.15, was the best among the league's regular pitchers, but he fell 11⅔ innings short of qualifying for that "title," which went to the Giants' Hoyt Wilhelm at 2.43. During the 1947 pennant race, New York Yankees manager Bucky Harris would lift a glass and toast his outstanding reliever: "To Joe Page." Charlie Dressen and the Dodgers had their own toast in 1952: "To Joe Black." "Without him," the Brooklyn skipper declared, "I would've been dead."

The Dodgers ended the regular season with a 5–5 tie against the Boston Braves at Ebbets Field on Sunday, September 28. The game was called after twelve innings and meant so little that home plate umpire Al Barlick left after the tenth so he could catch a train to his home in Springfield, Illinois. Tom Gorman finished up behind the plate and amused the smallish crowd of 9,453 by imitating Barlick's "stee-rike" call and gesture. Preacher Roe drew a cheer when he coached first base in the eighth inning. There was no work for Joe that day, because Dressen had other plans. After Joe's first start, Dressen had declared, "Now that Joe has proved to me he can pitch nine innings, he is my number-one pitcher." He went on to say that Joe would start the opening game of the World Series, Carl Erskine would go in game two, and Preacher Roe would pitch the third game.

At that point, the American League pennant was still up for grabs. The New York Yankees, who had won the last three World Series, were finishing strong, but the Cleveland Indians stayed right with them. Then, when the race finally was decided, all the Indians could do was sit and watch. The Yankees secured a tie for the pennant with a 3–2 victory over the Boston Red Sox on September 25 and clinched their nineteenth flag in thirty-two years by beating the Philadelphia Athletics 5–2 in eleven innings the next night. The Indians weren't scheduled either day, rendering their final two games of the season moot. The Yankees won by two games.

So it would be a Subway Series again, the fourth between the Dodgers and the Yankees, who had beaten the Bums in each of their previous meetings, most recently in 1949. But the flame of hope glowed forever bright in Brooklyn, and besides, the Dodgers had Joe Black, who had been so good and so reliable that when he was on the mound, anything seemed possible. If there was someone who could make the mighty Yankees look human, surely it was Joe.

As it turned out, that was asking just a little too much.

14

Career Change

Joe knew he had done the right thing when he retired from baseball in 1957. If he had any hope of continuing, he'd need frequent cortisone shots or surgery on his arm, and Joe wanted no part of either. Even with treatment, there was no guarantee he'd be good enough to stick with a Major League club. At thirty-three, he was a man without a job—a fact that hit him as he relaxed with Jim Gilliam and Willie Mays after a workout at the Harlem YMCA.

Junior and Willie were surprised when Joe told them he was quitting baseball, because they thought he pitched well on their postseason barnstorming tour. When Joe reminded them he had to find a doctor to give him a cortisone shot every time he was scheduled to pitch, they understood. Then they asked what he planned to do. That's when it finally dawned on Joe that he had no plans.

He needed to find work.

But how hard could that be? He was an ex-ballplayer who had been popular with his teammates, writers, and fans. He was well known. He was smart, articulate, and had a college degree. Joe remembered people he met telling him that when he got out of baseball, he should look them up. They might have something for him. He was confident he would have no trouble finding a job.

Joe put together a list and said he called on twelve people in Manhattan and Brooklyn. Each visit, he said, played out the same way: They were all happy to see him and they talked baseball for a few minutes before Joe explained why he was there. Then the excuses came. He was a great guy, but business was a little slow at the moment. After making a big-league salary, it would be embarrassing to accept what the business could offer. The owner's partner was on vacation and they couldn't make a decision until he returned. "I must have written my phone number in invisible ink," Joe wrote, "because the phone never rang."

Joe got the picture. Being a former ballplayer didn't carry the weight he'd thought it would. He'd leave home confident and jovial, and return frustrated and dejected. He sulked and found himself mad at the world as the apologies and rejections continued. He yelled at Doris and Chico for no reason.

When Joe sought a job with the Brooklyn Dodgers' broadcasting team, he was rebuffed in that effort, too. According to Joe, he was told the team didn't pick the announcers, the sponsors made that decision. So he went to Schaefer Beer. Executives there told him they knew he was articulate and college educated, but the flagship radio station made the decision. He went to the station and was told the ballclub chose the announcers. "That's three strikes," Joe said after relating his run. "I said, 'Geez, I guess I can't sit up there and say it's a sunny day here in Brooklyn and looking down, big Newcombe's warming up.' I guess I couldn't say that."

Joe was disheartened at what he viewed as getting the runaround, but evidently, he did not talk to the right person. As executive producer of the Dodgers' telecasts and radio broadcasts, Tom Villante chose the announcers in those days, subject to approval by the ballclub. He said Joe should have checked with him first, though in the end it probably would not have made any difference. While Joe would have been an excellent analyst in the studio, Villante said, he likely would not have done well at running commentary.

"Joe spoke very slowly," he said. "It wouldn't have worked in play-by-play, especially radio. You need more of a, not rapid-fire, but you've got to get it out quickly. If you don't, something else is happening. When you analyze, slow is good. Play-by-play, it's very awkward. But Joe was really insightful. In today's world, he would have been terrific in the studio."

There were no such shows when Joe was looking for work. If he was going to talk for a living, he'd have to find another venue. And he did.

Joe knew he couldn't sell cars or insurance. That wasn't his kind of talking. But he figured he could teach.

Joe had given teaching a whirl in 1950, after getting his degree from Morgan State. He quit baseball and found a job teaching general science and health education at the Sollers Point School near Baltimore. He enjoyed the work, but quickly realized he couldn't make it on a teacher's salary. He guessed he could make $10,000 pitching in Latin America in the winter and with the Baltimore Elite Giants in the summer, so he quit three weeks into the school year and caught on with Cienfuegos in the Cuban Winter League, an important step in his climb to the majors.

This time, Joe did not have the option of playing in the Negro leagues or going to Cuba. So he dug out his degree and college transcript and went to the Plainfield Board of Education to see the superintendent, Vic Podesta, who had been a teacher and assistant coach at Plainfield High School when Joe went there. His timing was perfect. The district had an opening at Emerson Elementary School because a sixth-grade teacher had just resigned. Joe was hired and assigned to a midlevel class, designed for average-to-above-average students. He spent a week observing before taking over the class and noticed something right away: Students no longer respected—or feared—the teachers as they had when he was in grade school. They were loud and boisterous. He recalled three students strolling into the classroom singing doo-wop songs and wondering when the teacher would make them stop. He said they went on for five minutes. Joe realized then that he'd have to establish discipline before he could do any teaching.

His first day alone in the class was a big moment. He had stood by himself many times on the pitcher's mound while an array of fearsome hitters paraded to the plate, but in the end, baseball was just a game, a form of entertainment. In the classroom, he was charged with shaping and enhancing the minds of youngsters who represented his country's future. Joe appreciated how he had benefited from a hunger to learn in his youth. His job was to foster that in those students sitting in his classroom, a task he knew he could not approach lightly.

Joe printed Mr. Black on the chalkboard in large letters before the students arrived. He thought they were especially orderly and quiet as they filed in, maybe because he was new and because at six foot two and 240 pounds, he was an imposing figure. Then came his first challenge.

"Good morning boys and girls," Joe said.

"Good morning, Mr. Black," most responded.

One boy, however, piped in with, "Hi, Joe."

Well, time for his first lesson. Patiently, Joe explained that he was a baseball player last year, and if one of them had asked for his autograph, it would have been perfectly fine to call him Joe. But as a teacher, a figure of authority, his position demanded the respect of being addressed as Mr. Black.

With that issue settled, Joe started in. For two weeks, he said, he stood in front of the class and lectured. He had been in an adult world for so long, he just assumed the students knew what he was talking about. Eventually, he realized he wasn't really teaching. "I'm just running at the mouth," he recalled.

That became clear when he devised what he thought was a simple math exercise. If twelve inches equal one foot and three feet equal one yard, one yard must equal how many inches? He called on five or six students and none gave the correct answer. Joe remembered that he was thinking, "How dumb can these kids be?" when a boy raised his hand and asked, "Mr. Black, you're asking us when you're supposed to be teaching us."

Joe was taken aback by the comment, but it helped him understand that he needed a different approach. He began interacting on a more personal level with the students by complimenting them on their appearance, telling a girl the blouse she wore was really pretty, or remarking how sharp a boy looked that day. Joe also played up his baseball connections. He felt the boys respected him because he was on a first-name basis with Willie Mays, Yogi Berra, Pee Wee Reese, Roy Campanella, and Sandy Koufax. He sensed the girls thought he was cool because he had traveled to so many big cities and had been to places like Cuba, the Dominican Republic, and Hawaii. Joe saw his rapport with the class improve, which he believed made him a better teacher.

Two distressing incidents, however, almost drove him out of the profession.

A female student who was a couple of years older than the other sixth-graders accused Joe of wanting to have sex with her. That landed Joe in the principal's office, where he faced the girl and her mother. When the girl said Joe tried to hold her hand, he explained that all he had done was extend his hand for a handshake. The girl backed down and the mother apologized, saying her daughter had convinced her that Joe had made sexual advances.

Despite the apology, Joe was livid as he left the principal's office, feeling he had been defamed. He knew that even when disproved or retracted, accusations of that nature can stain a reputation. He cooled off once he got to his classroom and saw the faces of his students, eager for their next lesson.

A few weeks later, though, Joe was in hot water again. He kept a girl in his class after school because she had been disruptive, then saw her walking along the street as he drove to his mother's house. The girl didn't live in that area, and when Joe asked why she hadn't gone home, she told him she was going to a girlfriend's house. Sensing she was hesitant to go home, Joe offered her a ride and drove to the police station, hoping that one of his friends, officer Sal Velard, would talk to her. When he went into the station to find Velard, the girl fled.

Joe and Velard assumed she had gone home, so he left, only to find himself ordered into the principal's office—again—the next morning. The girl was there with her grandparents, who said the girl told them Joe had hugged her and started driving her to his apartment in Newark. She escaped when Joe stopped for a red light, the grandmother said. Joe had to defend himself again, and he fought back his anger as he explained what had happened. The girl admitted she had been afraid of getting spanked at home and burst into tears as she apologized for fabricating her story.

The apology did little to assuage the anger that Joe again felt, and he told the principal, Charlie Detgen, that maybe he should get out of teaching. Joe had learned he would be teaching at Plainfield High School the next year. If elementary girls had made sexually tinged accusations against him, what could he expect from high school students? Detgen urged him to stay, telling Joe he had become a good teacher and reminding him that young girls were impressionable and he could see how they imagined themselves falling for a big, good-looking former baseball player. When they realized there could be no relationship, they made things up to cover their disappointment, Detgen said.

Joe stayed, and the students in the Plainfield school system benefited from that decision.

>>>>>>>>>>

He taught physical education and health at Plainfield High for a year, a period in which he renewed acquaintances with faculty members Jack Liddy, Henry Banta, and William Sette, to whom he remained grateful because they had gone out of their way to help him get into Morgan State. The hardest thing, he said, was getting used to calling them by their first names.

Joe found high school students to be more challenging, because he felt many were set in their ways and reluctant to change or examine something in a new light. To Joe, it appeared they felt they were grown up and knew as much as, or more than, adults.

He continued to work hard at enforcing discipline. Joe felt physical education was important to the overall development of a student and those who didn't take his gym classes seriously were told they could make it up after school. "Happy Hour," he called it, though about the only thing happy about it for the students was when the session ended.

In truth, it lasted only twenty-five minutes, but they were twenty-five rigorous minutes as Joe put them through calisthenics and conditioning exercises. One involved picking up a tennis ball. The student trotted the length of the gym and Joe rolled the ball to him at different spots. The student had to pick the ball up while continuing to trot and throw it back—almost like an infield drill in spring training. The student had to do ten pickups before Joe let him stop.

Joe thought the drill was good for the legs, respiratory system, and abdominal muscles. One of his nephews had to do it one time and thought otherwise. "Mama, your son is crazy," he told Joe's mother. "Today he tried to kill me with a lot of dumb exercises."

When Joe moved to Hubbard Junior High School for the 1959–60 school year, he took Happy Hour with him. Because the high school was getting crowded, the Plainfield school system moved freshmen into two junior high schools with seventh- and eighth-graders. Joe was assigned to Hubbard as a physical education and health teacher amid speculation that the school's principal wanted teachers who would maintain discipline.

Joe certainly did that.

"The kids said he was rough on them," said Joe's sister Phyllis, who continued to live in Plainfield. "He'd make them do push-ups." But when Phyllis saw his former students, "They also said he made a different person out of them. He was trying to keep them on the right track."

>>>>>>>>>>

Not long after Joe got out of baseball, he and Doris separated and eventually divorced. Their son, Chico, went with Doris, though Joe had visitation rights and remained engaged in Chico's life. Chico lived with Doris's family in Virginia for several months while she settled in and got established in a job in Brooklyn. Doris also became an educator, teaching physical education and biology in Brooklyn before moving into counseling and then school administrative work.

Once back in Brooklyn, Chico attended Catholic schools, which sometimes had different breaks from public schools. When he stayed with Joe during those breaks, Joe took Chico to Hubbard Junior High School, sat him in the back of the classroom, and had him do his homework. When his students came in, the first thing Joe told them was, "OK, before you ask, that's my son in the back. His name is Chico. Now turn around and let's get to work."

Chico remembered his father commanding respect in the classroom. "They paid attention to whatever he was teaching," he said. "It seemed like all the boys wanted to hang around him. They'd sit and listen to what he had to say. I don't know if it was because of who he was, but I know they paid attention."

It never bothered Chico to split time with his parents. He stayed with Joe every other weekend and every other holiday break. Doris told him the nuns at his school could tell when he had spent time with his father. "They said when I'd come back to school on Monday after being with my dad, my attitude would change," he said. "I didn't know that. Maybe I was a little bit more forceful, aggressive. If I was with my mom, maybe I was a little more laid back. But my mom would tell me, 'Yeah, the nuns could tell when you were with your dad.'"

>>>>>>>>>>

My father's relationship with Chico was so strong that after Greyhound transferred him to Phoenix, Chico eventually settled there, too. By this time my dad was in his midfifties and he weighed around three hundred pounds. I went with him one day to drop off something at Chico's apartment. It was located on a cul-de-sac, and there was a car parked in front of the complex facing toward the street when we pulled up. We were going to be there for just a couple of minutes. Then two men came out and started screaming at my father, cursing at him and telling him to move the car. My dad found their language offensive and told them so. "You must have lost your mind," he said. "Don't speak like that. My child's in the car." One of the men swore again and said he didn't care who was in the car. My father told them to wait, because it would only take a minute and then he would move his car. They were looking at him like yeah, right, what are you going to do, old man? They quickly found out. My dad picked one of the men up and threw him onto the hood of their car. That took the fight out of him and the other one ran off.

>>>>>>>>>>

At Hubbard, Joe felt he grew into the job and flourished as a teacher. He thought he became more humane and more patient. Hubbard had a diverse student body, with a black-white ratio of 60-40. Incomes in the district ranged from welfare families to the ultra-rich, adding to the challenge facing teachers. Joe saw it as his job to make all students feel important, regardless of their race or economic status. He believed that once students developed a feeling of self-worth, they were more likely to show up for school every day.

He spent a lot of time talking to students, asking about their hopes and dreams. He thought young blacks too often reverted to fighting to prove their worth. He tried to convince them that, as he had learned in his younger days, education, not fighting, was the path to getting ahead.

Joe said he often received notes from parents asking him to talk to their son. The youngster wouldn't talk to them, they said, but they were sure he'd listen to Joe. When he saw them at a PTA meeting, he asked why they sent the note.

"They said, 'He's always saying, Mr. Black said, Mr. Black said.' So I talked to the kids."

One of Joe's former students was Steven Selzer, whose father, Nathan, had given young Joe a baseball all those years ago. The younger Selzer recalled that his old classmates at Hubbard often named Joe as their favorite teacher, because he cared about them and encouraged them to learn. He was strict but approachable, Selzer said. Joe's door was open when a student wanted to talk. And Joe cut a striking figure at the front of the classroom, regularly wearing "beautiful suits," Selzer said.

Joe never hesitated playing up his baseball experience if it helped him reach students. When girls would ask him who was cuter, Sandy Koufax or Mickey Mantle, he'd describe the physical attributes of each and let them make up their own minds. But one question from boys always gave him trouble: Who was the better center fielder—Mantle, Willie Mays, or Duke Snider? Joe mused, "That's almost like asking 'which is worth more, a one-thousand-dollar bill or ten one-hundred-dollar bills?'" All three could run, throw, field superbly, hit for average, and hit for power. In the end, he gave the edge to Mays. After all, who else could have run down Vic Wertz's long fly ball to the deepest reaches of the Polo Grounds in the 1954 World Series?

"Other teachers used to ask me why I didn't have the same trouble controlling kids that they did," Joe said in a 1964 interview. "I guess it was because they knew I had been in baseball and they sort of looked up to me."

At the start of each school year, Joe picked a handful of students who became his "unofficial pets." He'd check on their progress throughout the year, and if he heard they had slacked off in class, he stepped on their toes in the hallway or gave them a nudge with his elbow, just to let them know he was watching. Eventually, the students got wise. If they knew they had done something to get Joe's attention, they turned and walked the other way when they saw him coming.

Joe also worked to soothe misunderstandings between whites and blacks. If white students thought blacks were always looking to fight, Joe tried to explain why. Maybe they had come to school without breakfast and didn't have enough money for a decent lunch. He remembered the times that all he could manage for lunch was an onion sandwich. He didn't care how rancid his breath smelled afterward. He just needed something in his stomach.

With blacks, he pointed out that it really didn't do them any good to beat up white kids, because after it was over, they were just as poor as they had been before the fight. Again, he used his own youth as an example. His family relied on government relief to get by, but he took his school work seriously and used his education so he didn't have to live in a house infested with roaches or rats. Use your brain instead of your fists, he implored.

Chico got the same lesson. It grew out of what Jackie Robinson had told Joe back in the spring of 1952: "We don't fight."

"We were still having racial tensions in those days and he said, 'What would happen if this guy fought you?'" Chico said. "'You'd probably win. Then this guy fought you. You'd probably win. And so on and so on. My point is, they know what you can do with your hands. They're more afraid of you when you use your mind. So therefore, use your mind. That's what's going to get you ahead, your mind, not the physical part.'"

Joe refused to play favorites in the classroom. He once gave a black student an "F" and overheard the student's mother complaining to the principal about teachers routinely failing black students. Well, the principal said, your son's teacher is right here.

"You're colored," Joe remembered the woman saying.

"Yeah, I'm colored," Joe responded.

"Then what are you doing failing him?" she demanded.

"Because he didn't do anything," Joe answered.

Joe said the youngster swore to him he'd never get another "F"—and he didn't. Years later, Joe said, the junior high boy he had flunked became a dentist.

In one of Joe's health classes, all the students were black. In another, they were all white. When he gave a major test, three-fourths of the white students earned a "B" or better, but all the black students flunked. He chewed them out the next time they had class, telling them that just because he was black didn't mean they could expect any favors. He would not, he said, allow them to develop a mentality of expecting something for nothing. Joe Black did not owe them a good grade. They had to earn it. And they did. By the end of the year, Joe said every student in that class achieved a better-than-average grade.

Joe also tried to incorporate life lessons in his physical education classes. He arranged wrestling matches to try to show that brains and agility could win out over brawn. To illustrate, he faked an attack on a five-foot-six, 120-pound eighth grader, who promptly grabbed Joe by the arm, turned, and flipped him over his shoulder. The other students oohed and aahed as Joe slammed onto the mat, unaware he had worked with the student on that move for several days so he could make his point.

Boxing matches became another favorite activity. The combatants wore oversized gloves, headgear, and mouthpieces for maximum protection; rounds lasted only one minute. Through those matches, students who were shy and usually gave in to bullies developed the courage to stand up for themselves. Joe staged the wrestling and boxing matches after learning that some black students had been extorting money from some of the Jewish students. After a few weeks of the one-on-one bouts, the extortion stopped. "The Jewish kids found out that because a guy is black doesn't mean he's tough," Joe said, recalling those days. "The black kids found out that because a guy is Jewish doesn't mean he's chicken." When students were matched on equal terms, Joe felt they understood each other better.

>>>>>>>>>>

Joe never strayed far from baseball after leaving the sport, and it only seemed natural that he was tapped to coach the Hubbard Junior High team. He had a scrappy bunch that lacked power and had to scratch for runs. He forbade his pitchers to throw curves, screwballs, and sliders, much to the consternation of their parents. How could their son become a top-notch pitcher if he couldn't throw a breaking ball? Joe was holding them back, they complained.

But Joe was concerned about protecting their young arms. Throwing a curveball can strain the muscles and tendons, and if anyone could understand what happens when a pitcher wrecks his arm, it was Joe. So he emphasized control, which had been so important in his big 1952 season, telling them that if they could keep nine of every twelve pitches low and on the outside corner, they'd succeed.

Joe stressed fundamentals and discipline in his coaching. One of his better hitters tried to stretch a single into a double by leaping, spikes high, into the fielder's chest. Joe ordered the player to apologize. When he refused, Joe kicked him off the team.

Steven Selzer, who played on the team, recalled the time Joe introduced them to New York Yankees manager Casey Stengel at Yankee Stadium. Joe told the grizzled skipper that his team was struggling. They had lost sixteen of eighteen games and he wondered what he should be teaching them. "Lost sixteen of eighteen you say?" Selzer remembered Stengel saying. "Well, first you better teach 'em to lose in the right spirit."

Joe's right arm remained sound enough for him to pitch occasionally. He played semipro baseball in East Orange, New Jersey, for a while and even pitched a game in the waning days of Negro league ball, taking the mound for Newark against the Brooklyn Stars in Albany, New York, in July 1959. Brooklyn left-hander Miguel Sanabria struck out eighteen in handing Joe and his team a 5–1 loss.

The Los Angeles Dodgers invited Joe to pitch batting practice for them before a couple of East Coast games, and he made several appearances when clubs staged an old-timers game, always in a Brooklyn Dodgers uniform. Joe wore the Brooklyn flannels when he helped the Los Angeles hitters tune up before a 1961 game against the Phillies in Philadelphia, an appearance that touched a nostalgic nerve in *New York Times* writer Robert L. Teague, who crafted half his game story about Joe.

"Although weighing a portly 249 pounds, Joe seemed to be one of the few 'real' Dodgers present," Teague wrote. "While strangers cavorted in gray road rompers, Joe stood out in the same well-worn white flannels he had sported in happier days at Ebbets Field." Teague described Joe's uniform as "rather grimy" and torn at the left knee. "Still," he continued, "as he winged in his high fat one to the Dodgers, one could almost believe that time had suddenly gone in reverse."

Several players from the club's Brooklyn days were still with the team, including Jim Gilliam, Gil Hodges, Roger Craig, and Sandy Koufax, all of whom had appeared in the Brooklyn Dodgers' last game, a 2–1 loss to the Philadelphia Phillies at Connie Mack Stadium on September 29, 1957. It was Koufax who recorded the final out by a Brooklyn pitcher, fanning Willie Jones to end the eighth inning.

Joe showed up in his Brooklyn whites again when the Dodgers played the New York Mets at the Polo Grounds for the first time on May 30, 1962, a game that stirred memories of the old Dodgers-Giants donnybrooks.

Fans began gathering outside the cavernous ballpark at seven o'clock in the morning for the doubleheader, which drew 55,704 and resulted in a Dodgers sweep against a team that would lose 120 games. Joking with reporters before the game, Joe said, "If you see a guy as fat as I am, that will be Ralph Branca."

"I'm to pitch in the first game, if I can survive batting practice," countered Branca, also wearing a Brooklyn uniform. "But I'm nowhere as big as you are, Joe." Joe was a large man at the time, weighing in at 250 pounds. But he had been dieting and was down from 287. Weight would be an issue for Joe for the rest of his life.

During an old-timers game at the Polo Grounds in 1963, Joe came full circle in his baseball life when he pitched against his childhood idol, Hank Greenberg. Greenberg was fifty-two at the time and all he could manage off Joe was a popup that Sal Yvars caught in foul territory. Pitchers had not been so lucky when Greenberg was in his prime.

Writers also waxed nostalgic when Joe pitched on Old-Timers' Day at Yankee Stadium in 1959, a two-inning game between former Yankees and former players from their World Series rivals. Sportswriter Tom Meany said that game, which featured Joe DiMaggio, Bill Dickey, Allie Reynolds, and Dizzy Dean, was his greatest thrill of the season. He remembered especially the thunderous ovation that arose when Roy Campanella, by then confined to a wheelchair, appeared on the field. "All of a sudden," Meany wrote, "yesterday was today."

In April 1960, Joe showed up for Jersey City's International League opener, just in case the Cincinnati Reds' farm club needed a batting practice pitcher. He ran into journalist Harold Rosenthal, and while they talked, Joe revealed he was thirty-one days short of the five years of Major League service he needed to qualify for a pension. Rosenthal later wrote that Joe's situation "has to stand out as one of the major inequities to develop since the plan was instituted." Joe didn't need the eighty-eight dollars a month to get by. "Still," Rosenthal added, "if ever a fellow warranted inclusion, it was Black."

Joe told Rosenthal he could name several others who were just short of qualifying. When the writer suggested one of the Major League clubs should carry him for a month so he could qualify, Joe waved him off. "No," he said, "I wouldn't want it that way."

>>>>>>>>>>

Joe's satisfaction in coaching went beyond winning. He enjoyed watching Al Gordon, a four-foot-ten, ninety-pound pitcher, rely on his control to become a good reliever. He liked the heart and hustle that five-foot-four Bobby Duchin brought to the team. He marveled at the athleticism of a youngster named Vic Washington, who could hit and outrun anyone. Joe thought Vic had a chance to become an outstanding player and looked forward to watching his development.

To Joe's disappointment, the swift youngster gave up baseball for football and track, but he did alright for himself. Vic Washington became an All-American at the University of Wyoming, then played pro football, spending three seasons in Canada and six in the NFL.

Joe believed he earned the respect and, in many cases, even the friendship of students during his time at Hubbard. They looked out for him. When a student stole a watch from Joe's desk, he returned it the next day, saying other students had threatened to beat him up if he didn't put it back. After a Plainfield police officer was grazed with a bullet, investigators suspected a Hubbard student had fired the shot and asked for Joe's help. Joe said he wouldn't turn anyone in, but he'd get the gun. He talked about the incident in his classes, and when he opened the bottom drawer of his desk at the end of the day, the gun was there.

Teaching filled Joe with a sense of accomplishment, even if it didn't always fill his bank account to the extent he would have liked. "It helped me grow as a person and the young students made me feel that I was needed," he said. "I'd like to think that I made a positive contribution to their growth and development."

One of Joe's most satisfying moments occurred years later when Steven Selzer and his family visited Joe at his home in Phoenix, Arizona. Selzer, who had become a lawyer in the Washington, DC, area, wanted his two sons to meet Joe, because he had talked in such glowing terms about "Mr. Black" that they didn't believe such a person really existed. "They said, nobody's like that," Joe said. "So they came and he said, 'There he is.'"

As much as he enjoyed being around young people, Joe knew he had to do something to better himself financially. He worked part-time at a department store to earn extra money and took graduate courses at Seton Hall and Rutgers during the summer. If an opportunity in another profession came up, Joe would have to consider it.

It came, fittingly, at a baseball game.

15

Dodger Disappointment—Again

1952 World Series

....

For all of Charlie Dressen's bluster—and there usually was plenty when the Dodgers skipper was involved—he did a masterful job handling the team's crippled pitching staff. He juggled the rotation to try to get the best matchups, dipped into the farm clubs for help, kept the bullpen constantly on call and, of course, relied on Joe time and time again. Gayle Talbot of the Associated Press went so far as to call the Dodgers "the pitchless wonders." Another AP account said that other than Joe, "nobody can predict with any confidence what any Brooklyn thrower will do on any given day." By season's end, Dressen had used seventeen pitchers, fifteen of whom had recorded at least one victory. Dodger starters pitched only forty-five complete games, after going the distance sixty-four times the year before, and Joe was the top winner with his fifteen victories. In those days, it was rare for a team to win a pennant without a twenty-game winner on the pitching staff. Of the sixty-four pennant winners in the two leagues from 1920 through 1951, only ten did not have a pitcher with twenty victories. Somehow, the Dodgers had matched the ninety-six regular season victories recorded by the 1951 club, which had Preacher Roe with twenty-two wins, Don Newcombe with twenty, and Carl Erskine with sixteen.

A key was the Dodgers' ability to beat up on the second-division teams. They went 8-14 against the Giants, 10-12 against the Phillies, and managed to only break even (11-11) with the Cardinals. But they piled up a 19-3 edge against the Pirates, went 18-3 against the Braves, and won 17 of 22 from the Reds. That more than negated their struggles against the top clubs, and the Dodgers coasted in with a four-and-a-half-game cushion over the Giants. Just as Charlie had said, the Dodgers didn't blow it. And then, when Dressen rolled the dice by starting Joe in the World Series opener against the New York Yankees and Joe came through with his historic victory, the little guy looked like a genius.

"Charlie was a different kind of guy," said Rocky Bridges, the utility infielder. "He had a hunch, I guess, and his hunch was good. Joe did a heck of a job. I guess he surprised everybody. The Yankees, too. They hadn't seen his type. He basically had two pitches, but he had phenomenal control." While Joe had professed to being calm before the game, insisting it was just one more pitching assignment, he admitted afterward his stomach had churned with butterflies. He also felt he had pitched better games during the season, even though he surrendered a mere six hits and stopped Casey Stengel's hitters cold with runners in scoring position, leaving them 0-for-6. "I've been faster, I know, but my curveball was coming in there pretty well and I had control," Joe said. Joe also was quick to point out: "It wasn't easy. Don't ever let anybody tell you that." Dressen, meanwhile, spoke with smug satisfaction. "First, I was second-guessed for that magazine article in which I said we wouldn't blow the pennant again," he said. "Then I was second-guessed for starting Black. The boys had to swallow both."

Something did trouble Joe after the game, however. A small cross, which dangled from a long, thin gold chain around his neck, had fallen off while he was pitching. So he told the grounds crew and they dug around the pitcher's mound until they found it. Years later, Joe gave the chain to Martha Jo when she went to college.

>>>>>>>>>>

As a teenager I was like almost everyone else—I loved to talk on the phone. But my father had a rule in his house: no one should call past 10 PM. If someone called after that hour, my father would answer the phone and remind them that I wasn't to get any calls after ten, because I had school the next day. I got my own phone when I was fourteen, and that gave me a way to keep talking past ten. If I was talking when my father came in to say good night, I simply hid the phone under the covers, pretended I was getting ready to go to sleep, then got the phone back out when he left.

But there wasn't much you could get past my father. Clove cigarettes were a big deal when I was in high school, and one day—I was sixteen—I was smoking one while I was out with some friends. We were standing outside Jack-in-the-Box, which was located on a busy street. There was a lot of traffic going by. The next day, as my dad and I were walking into the house, he said, "You know what, kid? Smoking is not good for you." I said, "I know, Dad." He said, "Well, I just wanted to remind you of that." He didn't smoke, and after that episode, I never smoked again. He could either read my mind or someone must have told him they saw me smoking. I couldn't get anything past my father, which upsets you when you're in high school.

I remember another incident involving a club called Tommy's. It was a twenty-one-and-over club in the front, but the back was a non-drinking club for teens only. I went there one weekend with my girlfriends when I was sixteen and we had a lot of fun dancing. I was excited when I got home and told my dad, "It was great. We danced all night. There were cute boys." My dad said, "OK. Glad you had a good time, kid."

The following weekend, I told my dad we were going to Tommy's again and he said, "Oh no you're not." Then I asked if I could spend the night with my best friend Charisse, and of course my dad said it was OK. But when I got to Charisse's house, we decided to go to Tommy's anyway. My Dad drove by Charisse's house that night and all the lights were off, because her mother was asleep and we were out. My dad didn't stop and ring the doorbell. He just drove by—and went right to Tommy's. He walked in and saw me dancing with a boy. My friend Charlene said, "Your dad is here," and I said, "Oh, shut up," thinking she was teasing. The next thing I know, my dad is picking me up by the back of my shirt. Charisse was out in the parking lot talking to a boy and when she saw my father, she hid behind a car, because she knew she'd be in big trouble, too, if he saw her. My dad, whose hands were twice the size of mine, smacked me on the butt and said, "I can't believe you lied to me!"

He hauled me out to the car and drove us home. I cried all the way, because I was embarrassed that it happened in front of my friends. The next morning he told me I was grounded for a week and he took away the phone in my room. That episode was the only time I've ever been spanked, but my friends to this day still tease me about my father storming into Tommy's and hauling me out.

>>>>>>>>>>

The two teams remained at Ebbets Field for game two, and the Dodgers had the veteran Erskine going on five days' rest against Vic Raschi, who went 16-6 during the season with four shutouts and a fine 2.78 ERA. Winning the series opener had been unprecedented for the Dodgers. Bob Considine of the International News Service called it a victory that "shook the baseball wacky borough to its foundation." A Dodgers victory in game two would be outrageous. Win that and the Bums would need just two more victories to claim their first World Series championship. A United Press article said the Dodgers already were "in the driver's seat" because of their win in game one. "They've beaten the best that Casey Stengel could throw at them," the story noted.

With Oisk next up on the mound, Dodger Nation had to be feeling confident. The tenacious right-hander won his last three decisions of the season to finish 14-6, he led the staff with 206⅔ innings despite his sore elbow, and his earned run average of 2.70 would turn out to be the best of his career. But as usual with the Dodgers, something crazy happens just when things are starting to look up.

In the training room before the game, Erskine banged his knee on a heater as he stepped down from a small ladder he had climbed to look out a window. It had been raining and Carl wanted to see if it had stopped. He grabbed the knee, sat down on a trunk and promptly passed out. Then Dressen walked in. "Here's his starting pitcher absolutely out cold as a mackerel," Erskine related. "He didn't know what was going on."

Carl woke up and assured his manager that he could pitch, so Dressen sent him out there. Erskine felt he had good stuff, but he struggled with his control, walking six as the Yankees touched him for six hits and five runs en route to a 7–1 victory behind Vic Raschi.

So the series moved to Yankee Stadium knotted at one game apiece. Preacher Roe, the colorful, crafty left-hander, got the call for the Dodgers against Eddie Lopat. Dressen said Joe would watch from the bullpen, ready to come in if things got tight. It turned out he wasn't needed, because Preacher went the distance with a six-hitter and the Dodgers got a big assist from a passed ball.

With Brooklyn clinging to a 3–2 lead in the top of the ninth, Yankees catcher Yogi Berra couldn't handle an inside fastball from Tom Gorman and two runs scored as he scrambled after the ball, securing what became a 5–3 win for the Dodgers. They were back on top, two games to one, and Joe would pitch the next day, even though he had thrown nine full innings only three days before.

"If we were leading three games to none, I'd still pitch Black," Charlie declared. "He's the biggest, strongest fellow we have and I know he can do it." Stengel had hoped to start Ewell Blackwell and give first-game starter Allie Reynolds another day of rest. But with the Yankees trailing in the series, the manager known as the Old Perfessor felt he had to go with his ace. Joe had outpitched Reynolds in the opener. Could he do it again?

Meanwhile, something disturbing was happening among the Dodger regulars: first baseman Gil Hodges was hitless through the first three games. "I'll get one tomorrow," Gil predicted. If only he had.

>>>>>>>>>>

A crowd of 71,787 filled Yankee Stadium for game four on Saturday, October 4, and they saw Allie Reynolds at his best. Joe pitched well himself, giving up only three hits and one run. But his control was a bit off—he walked five—and Reynolds was sensational. The Chief struck out ten and allowed only four harmless singles as the Yankees won 2–0 to even the series. Stengel had started big Johnny Mize at first base after seeing Joe Collins go hitless in the first three games, and the move paid off. The lead-footed thirty-nine-year-old slugger wasn't much of a fielder, but he still had some pop, as he had shown with a home run the day before. Batting in the fourth inning, he lashed a high inside fastball into the lower deck in right field, about twenty rows up, for a 1–0 lead. Joe was lifted for a pinch hitter in the eighth, and the Yankees added a run in their half of that inning when Mickey Mantle tripled to deep center off Johnny Rutherford and went around to score when Pee Wee overthrew third on the relay. Reynolds then retired the Dodgers in order in the top of the ninth and the series was all even again.

Earlier, an alert Billy Martin, the Yankees' scrappy second baseman, had helped Reynolds get out of a jam. The Dodgers had Andy Pafko on third and Gil Hodges on second with one out in the fifth inning and Joe coming to bat. Martin, who had played for Charlie Dressen at Oakland in the Pacific Coast League, saw the squeeze play was on, so he shouted a warning to Reynolds. Reynolds put everything he had on a fastball, Joe had no chance to make contact, and Pafko was an easy out at the plate. As Gil McDougald, the Yankees' third baseman, related it, Dressen "was doing a crazy dance in the coaching box and nobody had a clue to the sign." McDougald said Martin remembered the squeeze sign was part of that dance, but Charlie had changed it since Martin had played for him. "At the last second, Billy glanced at Joe Black," McDougald said. "From Black's bug-eyed look, he was sure the squeeze was on." Joe was even more stunned by the speed of the pitch from Reynolds. "Listen, that pitch I tried to bunt was the fastest pitch I ever saw," he said. "Reynolds just reared back and let go. I'm amazed the cover didn't come flying off the ball." Jackie also had been blinded by Reynolds's velocity and was called out on strikes three times. According to Roger Kahn, Jackie shouted at the writers in the clubhouse, before they could even ask him a question, "You can't hit what you can't see!"

The failed squeeze had to be especially discouraging for Dressen, who had drilled the club frequently on squeeze bunts in spring training. The Dodgers skipper had also undertaken a novel ploy by bringing in miler Leslie MacMitchell, who once shared the world indoor record, to teach his players how to run. Dressen may have been full of himself, but he looked for every edge he could find for his club.

Joe was disconsolate over the way he pitched, even as writers approached him sympathetically. "I threw that long ball," he moaned. "I'm always failing." No way, countered Pee Wee, who knew full well Joe was the main reason they were playing the Yankees in the first place. "What's the guy want to do? Pitch a shutout every time he's in there?" the Dodgers captain said. "Always failing? My gosh."

But Joe had been sent out there to win the game and he didn't, so in his own mind, anyway, he failed. If that's the case, the Brooklyn hitters failed even more. The heart of the order, Duke Snider, Jackie, and

Campy, went a combined 0-for-11 with five strikeouts against Reynolds. "My fellow was just wonderful out there today," Stengel said. And who could argue? Dressen would leave it to Carl Erskine in game five to get the Dodgers back on top in the series. And he'd call on Joe if he was needed. Stengel wouldn't have minded a day of rain so he could come back with game-two winner Vic Raschi, but he opted for Ewell Blackwell, obtained in August from the Cincinnati Reds.

>>>>>>>>>>

Game five fell on Erskine's fifth wedding anniversary and he pitched like a man eager to celebrate, shutting down the Yankees through four innings as the Dodgers built a 4–0 lead. But the Yankees roared back with five runs in the bottom of the fifth, forcing Dressen to send Joe sprinting to the bullpen in far left field. Charlie headed for the mound while Joe warmed up, though he said later he had no intention of removing Erskine. Carl recalled that Dressen took the ball from him and then, to his surprise, asked if it was his wedding anniversary and if Betty, his wife, was in the stands. Erskine said she was, Dressen asked if he would take her out that night to celebrate, and Carl said he probably would. Dressen then slammed the ball back into Erskine's glove and said, "Well, see if you can get the side out before it gets dark."

Carl not only got out of the inning, he retired the final nineteen batters in a superb display of pitching mastery and the Dodgers won it 6–5 in eleven innings to again go up in the series, three games to two. "You don't know how it feels for a manager to stick with you like that," Erskine said. "I was determined to pitch my arm off for Chuck after that."

And so the Dodgers were one victory from their first World Series championship. Better still for the Bums, the series was going back to Ebbets Field, the cozy ballpark where they always felt more comfortable. They had split the first two games of the series there and another split was all they needed to become the kings of baseball. It would be Billy Loes for the Dodgers going against Vic Raschi, and the game would feature one of those bizarre plays that would leave fans shaking their heads and muttering, "Only in Brooklyn."

>>>>>>>>>>

Loes was a twenty-two-year-old right-hander who grew up in Queens and signed with the Dodgers out of high school for what was an enormous bonus at the time, $21,000. Another in the line of Brooklyn's colorful characters, Loes once said he didn't want to win twenty games because then he'd be expected to do it every year. Before the '52 World Series, he supposedly predicted the Yankees would win in six games. When reporters finally ran him down to ask if it were true, Loes told them he had been misquoted. "I never told that guy the Yanks would win in six," he said. "I said they'd win it in seven."

He began his first World Series start pitching like an ace, blanking the Yankees through six innings and getting a 1–0 lead when Duke Snider homered leading off the bottom of the sixth. Then came the fateful seventh and an incident for which Loes would always be known: he lost the ball in the sun. And not a fly ball, but a low liner that glanced off his knee. That was after he was called for a balk because he dropped the ball while his foot was on the rubber as he set to pitch to Irv Noren.

The balk sent Gene Woodling to second base, and he represented the go-ahead run because Yogi Berra had homered to tie it leading off the inning. "I was trying to grip the ball for a curve and it just squirted out of my hands," Loes said. "My hands weren't sweaty," he added. "It was just one of those things."

Loes settled down to fan Noren and retired Billy Martin on a popup before Raschi smacked a pitch back through the box. The ball banged off Loes's left knee and shot past Gil Hodges into right field, enabling Woodling to score for a 2–1 Yankees lead. Loes said he never saw the ball, because—and he said this in all seriousness—he was blinded by the sun. As unlikely as that seemed on a ball that low, Carl Erskine said he understood how it happened. At a certain time of the day in October, "probably no more than a couple of minutes' time," he said, the sun would shine right between the Ebbets Field decks. He noted that while everyone laughed at Loes's explanation, "if you ever pitched in Ebbets Field, you know that's possible in October with a ball that's hit with a little bounce on it."

Loes escaped the inning without further damage, and he gave the Dodgers some hope when he singled with two outs in the bottom of the seventh. Then, for reasons that only he knew, Loes stole second. "I just saw nobody was watchin' me, so I ran to second and got there ahead of anybody," he later explained. His bold—some would say foolhardy—

move put the tying run in scoring position, but Billy Cox struck out to end the inning.

The teams traded solo home runs in the eighth, Mickey Mantle cranking out a four-hundred-foot blast for the Yanks and Snider answering for the Dodgers, his second of the game and fourth of the series. Snider's shot left the Dodgers trailing 3–2, and when George Shuba doubled off Raschi one out later, Casey Stengel felt he had no choice but to bring in Allie Reynolds to face Roy Campanella. "If I'd held him off for tomorrow, there might never have been a tomorrow," Stengel said later. "What would I have been savin' him for then, the junior prom?" Reynolds fanned Campy to end the inning, then got the final three outs in the ninth. The Yankees had a 3–2 victory and the series was tied once again. Game seven would decide it. The Dodgers still had a chance—but then so did the Yanks.

Stengel had wanted to start Reynolds if there was a seventh game, but after being forced to use him in relief of Raschi, the Yankee skipper insisted he wasn't sure whom he would tap. Dressen had no such doubts. "Black will start, of course," he said, "and the Preacher will be ready to help if he is needed, which we hope he won't be."

The Dodgers' long-held hope of winning a world championship would rest squarely on Joe's broad shoulders.

>>>>>>>>>>

Tuesday, October 7, arrived along with a cold front. The temperature dropped into the fifties, nearly twenty degrees cooler than the day before. Joe would be pitching on two days' rest for the second time in the series. Forty-five years later, when the Cleveland Indians' Jaret Wright prepared to start the seventh game of the 1997 World Series on three days' rest, Joe couldn't see why it was such a big deal. "In the old days, we all pitched on three days' rest," he said. "Now it's four days and eighty or ninety pitches . . . if they just let him go out and pitch, he'll do fine. But if you put it in their head that they have only three days' rest, that's not going to help them." As Joe recalled, he felt confident going out for that final game. "I never thought about the word fatigue," he said.

Stengel finally decided to go with left-hander Eddie Lopat, who lost to Preacher Roe in game three.

Neither starter would make it to the end.

Joe cruised through the first three innings looking strong and allowing only a walk. The Dodgers touched Lopat for two hits, but they couldn't score, either. Then Joe was done in by the long ball and Johnny Mize, who had tormented the Dodgers throughout the series. Mize punched a single into left field in the fourth to score Phil Rizzuto, who had doubled and advanced to third when Mickey Mantle grounded out.

The Dodgers countered in the bottom half by loading the bases with no outs, prompting Stengel to rush Reynolds into the game before things got out of hand. Gil Hodges, still hitless in the series, hit a fly ball long enough to bring in one run to tie it, leaving runners at first and third with one out. The Dodgers still had a chance for a big inning, but Reynolds quashed the threat by striking out George Shuba and getting Carl Furillo to ground out.

Gene Woodling belted a pitch from Joe over the screen in right field to start the fifth inning, but the Dodgers came back to tie it again on Cox's double and Pee Wee's single. Joe, however, was wearing down. He might not have thought about fatigue, but he was entering his twenty-first inning in seven days. All those pitches had taken a toll. He remembered Campy calling for a fastball "and I let it go, but it didn't feel right. It all caught up to me."

He knew he was in trouble when he threw an outside pitch to Rizzuto and the Yankees shortstop pulled it. Fortunately for Joe, the ball went right to Pee Wee for the first out of the sixth. But then the switch-hitting Mantle, batting left-handed, drove a fastball over the scoreboard, a titanic blast that carried over Bedford Avenue. When Mize followed with a single, Joe was finished. Preacher Roe replaced him and got out of the inning, then gave up a run-scoring single to Mantle in the seventh for a 4–2 New York lead. But the Dodgers weren't through yet.

With Vic Raschi pitching for the Yankees in the bottom of the seventh, Carl Furillo drew a walk, Billy Cox singled after an out, and Pee Wee walked. Suddenly, the bases were loaded and up came lefty Duke Snider, who already had slugged four homers and driven in eight runs in the series. The Ebbets Field crowd was on its feet cheering wildly when Stengel summoned little-known left-hander Bob Kuzava to face the Brooks' power hitter. Kuzava had been in the big leagues since coming up with the Cleveland Indians in 1946, but he was a journeyman at best.

He had pitched only four times in the final month of the season and until this point, had not pitched at all in the World Series. Stengel was playing yet another hunch.

Snider wrote in his autobiography that as Kuzava warmed up, he told Jackie Robinson, "I'm not going to try to overswing against this guy. I'm just going to try to hit one hard somewhere. I don't care where it goes." Duke said he was confident that if he didn't get a hit, Jackie would deliver.

Sadly for Joe and the Dodgers, neither came through.

Snider worked the count to 3-2, fouled off several pitches he felt he should have hit, then took a big swing that produced nothing more than a popup that third baseman Gil McDougald caught for an easy out. Kuzava then jammed Jackie with an inside fastball and he hit a towering popup to the right side, between the pitcher's mound and first base. Kuzava seemed to freeze and so did first baseman Joe Collins. With two outs, Furillo, Cox, and Reese all took off with the pitch. If the ball dropped, at least two of them would score.

But it didn't.

Billy Martin charged in from his position at second base, stuck out his glove, and caught the ball just above his shoelaces. As Rizzuto described it years later, Martin ran "like Groucho Marx but as fast as Mel Patton, reaching out like a guy trying to keep something from falling off a truck . . ."

Martin's catch took the steam out of the Dodgers, and they went down meekly in the eighth and ninth. The Yankees won 4–2 and they were world champions again, for the fourth straight year and fifteenth time overall. Twice the Dodgers were on the verge of winning the series and twice the New Yorkers denied them.

"I felt bad because I came out losing 3–2," Joe said. "I didn't feel I had let the guys down. I wanted to win as much as they did. But you wanted to be known as World Champions. We also wanted to be known as the team that beat the Yankees." If there was some consolation for Joe, it came from Mantle, who later said the home run he hit off Joe in the sixth inning was his most satisfying. The next time he saw Mickey, Joe had to ask why. According to Joe, Mickey told him, "You were the first pitcher who intimidated me."

Though Joe may not have had his best stuff in that last game, no one could fault his effort in the series. In terms of starting assignments, Joe had been the most inexperienced pitcher ever to start the first game of a World Series. After starting just twice in the regular season, he made three starts in seven days on baseball's biggest stage and performed well. In twenty-one and a third innings against the game's most storied team, Joe allowed only six runs and fifteen hits. While he gave up four home runs, all were solo shots, and the Yankees batted only .200 against him. All he had needed was a little more support.

Only Duke Snider and Pee Wee Reese solved the Yankees' pitching with any consistency. Campy batted just .214 in the series with only one RBI. Jackie, Carl Furillo, and Andy Pafko all batted under .200, and Furillo did not drive in a run. And Gil Hodges suffered through one of the worst weeks of his life, finishing the series 0-for-21 with one RBI. In the seventh game, when one key hit might have broken it open, the Dodgers stranded nine baserunners and went 1-for-7 with runners in scoring position. They couldn't even take advantage of the Yankees' four errors. "Our big men didn't have the punch when we needed it," Charlie Dressen said in a perfect summation of the game—and the series.

Years later, it still gnawed at Erskine that the Dodgers couldn't get any runs off the left-handed Kuzava, who had a career earned run average of 4.05 and won just forty-nine games in a ten-year Major League career. "Jiminy Christmas. I want to throw up," he told author Peter Golenbock. "We used to eat left-handers alive. But those were the kind of things that happened against the Yankees. Honest to God. Unexplainable. Un-ex-plain-able."

The 1952 Dodgers yearbook cover, playing off their fans' common lament of "Wait till next year," featured a cartoon of the Bums character nailing up a poster that read, THIS IS NEXT YEAR.

It almost was.

16

Mr. Greyhound

THE GREYHOUND BUS PULLED OUT of the Atlanta terminal on a spring Sunday and turned west, headed for Birmingham, Alabama. It was May 14, 1961, Mother's Day that year. Among the passengers were nine civil rights activists known as Freedom Riders, a group of whites and blacks, most of them college students, who had set out to test a US Supreme Court ruling that declared segregated waiting areas, washrooms, and restaurants at stations serving interstate bus passengers were illegal. Despite that 1960 decision, many cities in the South continued to enforce Jim Crow laws that created separate areas for blacks and whites in those facilities. The Freedom Riders set out to defy those laws.

The original group of thirteen Freedom Riders left Washington, DC, on May 4, planning to follow a route through the Deep South that would end two weeks later in New Orleans. Riders joined and left the group along the way, and they endured only minor hassles through the first ten days. One rider was punched by whites when he tried to enter an all-white waiting room in Rock Hill, South Carolina. Two riders were arrested in Winnsboro, South Carolina. But those incidents were nothing like the terror that awaited the passengers out of Atlanta.

When the bus reached Anniston, a city fifty miles into Alabama and about sixty miles from Birmingham, the station was closed, locked up, and eerily quiet. Suddenly, a mob of whites—by some estimates up to two hundred strong—surrounded the bus, smashed the side with clubs and pipes, broke windows, and slashed the tires. Police finally arrived and cleared a path for the bus, but made no arrests. As the bus limped out of town, many in the mob hopped into cars and pickup trucks and followed it. They didn't have to trail behind for long.

About six miles southwest of Anniston, a tire on the bus went flat, forcing the driver to pull off the road. Angry whites again descended on the bus, and someone hurled a firebomb through one of the broken windows. As flames and thick black smoke spread through the bus, some in the mob tried to block the door so the passengers couldn't escape. "Oh my God," rider Genevieve Hughes screamed, "they're going to burn us up." But everyone managed to scramble off before the vehicle was engulfed, their assailants driven back by the intense heat. Some crawled out windows. Others got out through the door. The attackers finally dispersed when highway patrolmen called by a passing motorist fired shots into the air.

Photos of the burning bus, the racing Greyhound symbol clearly visible on its side and smoke billowing from the windows, appeared in newspapers around the country. Many people were shocked and sickened that such violence could occur in the United States. The Reverend Billy Graham, whose distaste for segregation was well known, called the attack "deplorable," and said the instigators should be prosecuted "to the full extent of the law."

Joe Black also saw the photos and read the news accounts. He felt sorry for the riders and disgust for the perpetrators of the violence, but beyond that, he was ambivalent. He characterized himself as "indifferent to the whole situation." He was comfortable in his teaching and coaching jobs at Plainfield's Hubbard Junior High School. Why should he get riled up about something beyond his control?

Yet those photos—and the emotions they provoked—ultimately sent Joe to the next stage in his life.

>>>>>>>>>>

While Joe wasn't spurred into action by the violence in Alabama, the incident rattled Greyhound executives at company headquarters in Chicago. The burned-out hulk of one of their buses was not the image they wanted to portray, especially among blacks. For cash-strapped black families, bus travel was affordable. The Greyhound folks welcomed that business and didn't want to lose it. Because it was an interstate carrier, Greyhound did not practice segregation. Its passengers could sit anywhere they wished. In light of the unrest in the South, company officials wanted to make sure that message got out, and felt they needed to hire someone to deliver it. That person turned out to be Joe, but only because of a chance meeting at a baseball game.

Joe was sitting with his Hubbard baseball team at Yankee Stadium when he heard someone say, "Hey, I know you." Joe turned and saw a man who smiled and asked if he was Don Black. Joe laughed. Don Black pitched for the Cleveland Indians and Philadelphia Athletics in the 1940s, well before Joe reached the majors. He was also white. The man quickly realized his mistake, called Joe by his correct name and introduced himself as Warren Schwed. They chatted, and Joe told him he was a teacher and he enjoyed his work. True, he didn't make a lot of money, but most of the merchants in Plainfield gave him a discount, he had a part-time job in a clothing store, and he was well-known and respected in the community. Besides, he felt he had something to offer the students.

Schwed was a vice president at Grey Advertising, which handled Greyhound's account. He said he remembered Joe as a smart, articulate player, one of the few who had graduated from college, and thought Joe could do better financially than what he made as a teacher. So he handed Joe his card and said he'd be in touch if he heard of something. Right, Joe thought. Just another glib backslapper who would conveniently forget they ever talked.

But Schwed fooled Joe. He called.

Schwed knew Greyhound was looking for someone to reach out to the black community, and he thought Joe was right for that job. Just a few weeks after they talked at Yankee Stadium, Joe and Schwed were flying to the company's corporate headquarters in Chicago to meet with Greyhound executives. They explained to Joe that they needed someone who could convince black Americans that the company did not condone the white-instigated violence in the South. They said they were in a touchy position, because they operated a national company in an area that still adhered to local segregation laws. Could Joe help them work through that? He said yes, and the Greyhound men welcomed him aboard. They hired Joe as a "special markets representative," his market being the black community.

Joe thought he got the job for two reasons: He had become a national, well-known figure pitching for the Brooklyn Dodgers, and not only was he black, he was dark black. Businesses in those days didn't want to be accused of hiring only those who were, as he put it, "light, bright, damn near white." Whatever the reasons, Joe Black had to reinvent himself again, this time as a business executive. He later told an interviewer, "Athletics may have been instrumental in me getting my job, but it's my education that can keep me there."

>>>>>>>>>>

Joe would work only part time for Greyhound at first. He'd continue to teach during the week and spend weekends, holiday periods, and summer vacations with the bus company. He would give up most of his free time, but Joe didn't mind. He could make more in his stints with Greyhound than he could in an entire year as a teacher. So with a mixture of eagerness and trepidation, Joe reported for work at the Greyhound Travel Bureau in midtown Manhattan. He looked forward to starting a new venture, yet wondered how he'd be accepted. Joe wasn't sure whom he'd report to—or if whoever that was even knew to expect him.

He needn't have worried. A desk had been readied for him. And it even had a nameplate:

JOE BLACK
Special Markets Representative

The desk sat on the first floor, right in front of a window looking out on the busy Avenue of the Americas, or Sixth Avenue as New Yorkers know it. Anyone walking by could see that Greyhound had a black man working at a desk job. Was Joe to be nothing more than a token, a showpiece so Greyhound could say, look how racially aware we are? As Joe put it once, he felt like "the spook who sat by the door."

He didn't stay there long. When Raymond F. Shaffer, a tall, strapping executive who ran Greyhound's Eastern Division, saw Joe in front of the window, he demanded to know who put him there. Hearing his shaken office manager stammer that he thought the company wanted Joe to be seen only intensified Shaffer's anger, and he promptly had Joe moved to an upstairs office. "And that is how I got my first spacious, drape-windowed, air-conditioned office," Joe recalled. He believed then that with Shaffer's backing, he had a chance to become much more than a token and could make special markets an important cog in the company's operation. Greyhound gave Joe an opportunity—and he ran with it.

Once he got comfortable talking to a crowd, that is.

Greyhound arranged a speaking tour for Joe in major markets like New York, Philadelphia, Chicago, Detroit, and Los Angeles to introduce him to the public. Joe would attend a luncheon, then give a short talk. There was just one hitch: he was as nervous as a fledgling actor at his first screen test, which, in a sense, is what the tour was for Joe. It was one thing to stand in front of a classroom and lecture. He had gotten used to that. But now he had to shine before an audience that might be thinking he was just another ex-ballplayer trying to cash in on his fame. The speech class he had taken at Morgan State was nothing but a faded memory. Joe remembered looking out at his audiences and thinking, "It seemed as though each pair of eyes was challenging me to say something meaningful."

When it came time to talk, Joe grabbed the podium with both hands, took a deep breath, and stared out over the audience, because he was afraid to look anyone in the eye. He didn't care for the script the public relations staff had written, but he dutifully memorized it. He was a rookie again, so he went along. The script had him talking about being a former pitcher, wearing two hats—teacher and ballplayer—and hoping he didn't throw any curves. He had to keep himself from groaning as he delivered those remarks. Joe would go on to become a prolific speaker for Greyhound—and after this first tour, he wrote his own speeches.

>>>>>>>>>>

When my dad wrote speeches for his appearances at colleges, I could help him, because I knew all the latest music and all the fads and trends. He didn't want to sound like he was old and out of the loop, so he would ask me: What's the latest song? What's the latest dance? I would tell him the things that would resonate with college students.

>>>>>>>>>>

As Joe became more involved in Greyhound's affairs and more comfortable as a public speaker, he saw the opportunity it provided, so he gave up his job at Hubbard. It wasn't a decision he made lightly. Joe liked working with the youngsters. He felt he had earned their respect and made a difference in their lives. At Hubbard's year-end assembly in 1963, his baseball players gave him an attaché case and pen/pencil set for his new career, bought with their own money. Joe choked up momentarily, but managed to thank them. He knew he had succeeded as a teacher when several students told him, "Hubbard School won't be fun anymore because we kids won't have you for a friend." In an interview later that year, Joe called his teaching stint "the six happiest years of my life."

Greyhound promoted Joe to director of special markets in September and moved him to the company's headquarters in Chicago. He started his first community relations project, a Woman of the Year luncheon. His department grew in stature after Raymond Shaffer moved to Chicago in 1965 as executive vice president of Greyhound Corporation and Gerald H. Trautman was elected the corporation's president and CEO. Joe felt they understood that blacks were a key segment of Greyhound's business, and that companies such as theirs could help blacks succeed economically.

Trautman gave Joe the go-ahead to develop a Greyhound-funded scholarship program for students at historically black colleges and set aside $5,000 for the first grants. The program started in 1966 with three schools. A few years later, Joe announced to a large gathering that 126 students at sixty-seven universities were receiving Greyhound scholarships. Over time, the scholarship fund grew to $2.3 million, involved more than two hundred schools, and helped Latinos, Native Americans, and underprivileged whites as well as blacks. "I was able to give back something," Joe said, "because the black people riding those buses put me in the job in the first place."

Joe's duties took him to conferences organized by civil rights groups such as the National Urban League, the NAACP, the Southern Christian Leadership Conference, and the Congress of Racial Equality, which had organized the 1961 Freedom Rides. He met and stayed in contact with the nation's top black leaders—the Reverend Martin Luther King

Jr., James Farmer, Whitney Young, Roy Wilkins, and the Reverend Jesse Jackson. With Joe becoming a leading voice for the company, Greyhound did not draw the ire of black activists who promoted boycotts of businesses for not doing enough to hire and promote minorities. The very fact that a black man was a top executive in the company indicated that Greyhound was committed to equal opportunity and was deserving of respect.

>>>>>>>>>>

After my dad died, a woman who had worked at Greyhound in the 1980s came to my father's house to pay her respects. While she was there, she explained to me why she came. "Your father was so helpful to me," she said. "If it wouldn't have been for your father, I wouldn't have gone back to school. He encouraged me to study and said he would help me get a scholarship from Greyhound for college. I got my bachelor's degree and now I have a master's degree, too." It was one of the many reminders of how my father gave back to the community.

>>>>>>>>>>

While his fame as a ballplayer had opened doors and helped Joe make contacts, he was determined to prove he was much more than an ex-jock getting by on his name. He had one such opportunity early in his career, when he addressed two hundred Greyhound executives at the 1964 World's Fair in New York. Joe was irked because everyone kept asking if he would talk about baseball, so during his presentation, he never once mentioned the sport that had made him famous. He talked about his job and how it involved sales, advertising, and community relations. He used visuals to illustrate what the black market meant for the company. He showed newspaper clippings and photos from Woman of the Year luncheons, and told the audience he was available to help them with sales or problems involving black communities. Joe was proud of his presentation, but he left the podium to silence. The other speakers had been warmly applauded. All Joe heard was . . . nothing.

Melvin C. Frailey, the company's president at the time, then stepped to the podium. Joe had just delivered one of the best presentations ever made at one of their meetings, he told the gathering, so he understood why they were so surprised and silent. "Well," Frailey said, "we told you that Joe Black was a college-bred professional who happened to play baseball. I am glad that he is on our team." Within seconds, thunderous applause broke out as everyone rose to their feet. The vice president of advertising and public relations was the next speaker, but there was no way he would follow Joe right then. He promptly adjourned the meeting for lunch.

Later, a company executive told Joe he had committed a major faux pas: he was so good that he had shown up the boss. According to Joe, at the next four annual meetings, his photo was placed on the stage while the vice president of marketing read remarks Joe had prepared. It seemed that Joe had been too good for his own good. Not that it held him back. In the spring of 1967, Joe was named vice president of special markets for Greyhound Lines, becoming the first black executive to hold a vice president's position with a major transportation company. Two years later, he was promoted to vice president of special markets for the Greyhound Corporation, the bus line's parent company.

Another incident, this one in Richmond, Virginia, showed Joe that even though he wore a suit and held a title, some places still judged him on his skin color. Executives from Greyhound and its subsidiaries met in the Virginia capital for a marketing conference, and when Joe arrived, the hotel desk clerk told him he couldn't register because he was black. It didn't matter that Joe was dressed just like his colleagues. Or that he had earned a master's degree and was a corporate vice president. He was the wrong color.

Gerald Trautman was already in his room when Joe tried to check in, and when he heard what had happened, he stormed into the lobby and ordered the Greyhound people to pack up and move to another hotel. When one of the executives warned the hotel might sue to collect the cost of the lost reservations, Trautman was said to have responded, "Great. That will publicize their attitude toward blacks and they'll never get another convention." As they left, one Greyhound executive was reported to have said it was the only time they had seen Joe "so deeply moved that he could not speak."

Through the years, Joe's Woman of the Year luncheons grew into major events. At each location, Greyhound saluted three black females who helped improve their communities. But Joe didn't look for well-known women to honor. He chose instead to recognize those who flew under the radar and accomplished their good works out of the spotlight. One honoree was a woman in her fifties who brought up nine children left abandoned on her doorstep. She did housework to earn the money she needed to feed and care for the children. Why did she do it? "I thought that's what God wanted me to do," she said when accepting her award. Another woman honored was a minister who worked with her church and a school to find and educate young people who had hearing and speech handicaps. A woman crippled by polio was recognized for spending eighteen years leading a Girl Scout troop of disabled youngsters. Her legs had been so ravaged by the disease that she couldn't climb the steps to the podium to receive her award.

Joe later started Father of the Year luncheons, hoping to counter the image that black men were irresponsible fathers who wanted nothing to do with their children once they were born. He and his associates decided to pick the recipients after reading letters from children explaining why their father should be honored. They expected those letters to come from youngsters. Instead, many came from sons and daughters in their twenties and thirties. Joe felt the program gave children a platform to tell their fathers how much they loved them, something they might have neglected to do while growing up.

The program took on even more significance for Joe when he became a parent again—at age forty-five. His wife, Mae Nell, gave birth to a girl in July 1969 and they named her Martha Jo—Martha after Joe's mother, Mae Nell adding the Jo. The pregnancy wasn't planned, at least not by Joe, but he doted over his daughter and spent countless hours with her as she grew up. When Joe and Mae Nell divorced, he fought for and won custody of Martha Jo, who was three years old when the divorce proceedings began and five when Joe gained custody.

Joe's son, Chico, was in high school when Martha Jo was born and he still lived with his mother in New York. Joe visited whenever he could, once arriving unannounced at one of Chico's high school basketball games. At one point, Chico trotted over to grab a ball that had rolled out of bounds. When he straightened up, he was startled to be looking into his father's face. "What are you doing here?" he exclaimed. They smiled at each other, then went to dinner after the game.

For Chico, it was sometimes hard being Joe Black's son, especially when he played baseball. He made his high school team as a freshman and heard fans talking when he pitched. "That's Joe Black's son," they'd point out. "That used to really bother me, because I just wanted to be myself," Chico said. "So I switched sports. I played basketball, and I did well." But even in basketball, establishing his own identity could be difficult. His senior year, his high school team won a major tournament, the Queens Invitational, and Chico came home with a handful of trophies. "The next day, my mom got the paper and there it was: In 1952, Joe Black did his thing on the mound. Well, last night in the Queens Invitational tournament, Joseph Black . . . and I said, 'What did he have to do with this? It was me.' My mom had to sit me down and explain, 'You're going to have to go through this your entire life.'"

Joe also tried to help Chico understand that such comparisons were inevitable, and all he wanted was for Chico to be himself. "He used to sit me down and say, 'Just do things because you want to do them and don't worry about what other people say. It's a tough road. Some people can handle that, some can't. Right now you can't because you're getting it from all directions. But I can see that growth in you. You're going to be fine. But one thing, I don't want you to try to be like me.'"

>>>>>>>>>>

Buoyed by the success of his luncheons honoring women and fathers, Joe looked for additional ways to reach out to the black community. He put on career opportunity luncheons for young people, usually with four or five black professionals attending to answer questions, and Joe hoped they would serve as inspirations for the youngsters. His department organized drug/alcohol abuse seminars at luncheons, again aimed at the youth audience. He also found nontraditional ways to help. He got four prostitutes in Chicago off the street by giving them jobs washing buses, offering them $275 a week. A couple of months later, Joe noticed four women in the reception area after he returned from lunch. It took a moment, but then he recognized them: the four women he had hired to wash buses. "They had cleaned themselves up," Joe recalled. "They didn't even look the same." The women explained that they used to beat their children, but stopped after Joe gave them jobs. They ditched the men who had hung around with them, pooled their money, and rented a house. They just wanted to thank Joe for what he had done for them.

Anyone who knew Joe would not have been surprised by that episode. "Joe was a doer," former Dodger pitcher Don Newcombe said. "He wanted to get things done. I think he made his mind up that he was going to make change and be involved in change."

Joe also stayed close to baseball. He always felt that excitement on the basepaths was part of the game's appeal, having come up through the Negro leagues, where speed was an essential element, and having played alongside Jackie Robinson, a master at tormenting pitchers by dancing off a base. So Joe persuaded his bosses at Greyhound to sponsor a stolen base award, which was given yearly to the top base stealer in each league. He continued to appear at old-timers games and spoke often of what the game had done for him.

"It's such a wonderful thrill to be a big-league player," Joe said in one interview. "Baseball was the kind mother, the indulgent but stern father. People think I'm talking nonsense when I say how much I owe to baseball. But I owe everything to baseball. It gives me a humility and a sense of pride when I say my name is Joe Black and people remember me. They don't think if I'm black or white, not to make a pun. But I feel like a great man, and when you can feel that way, you have the world and everything that's in it."

Joe spoke out, too, saying baseball needed to break down another barrier and hire a black manager. It was fine that some teams had blacks as coaches, Joe said in a 1966 interview, but that wasn't the same as putting a black man in charge. "A baseball coach is little more than a player," he added. Speculation in the mid-1960s centered on Joe's good friend, Jim Gilliam, as possibly the first black manager. Gene Baker and Maury Wills also were mentioned. But it didn't happen until 1975, when another of Joe's friends, Frank Robinson, took over as manager of the Cleveland Indians.

By then, Joe was living in Phoenix, Arizona, where Greyhound relocated its corporate headquarters in 1971. Before the move, Joe had become friends with Jesse Owens, the four-time gold medalist from the 1936 Olympics, and his wife Ruth. After Jesse and Ruth moved to Phoenix, settling into a house just a five-minute drive from Joe's, they became almost a second set of parents for Martha Jo. Such was their friendship that Joe delivered the eulogy at Jesse's funeral in 1980, remembering the indignities his friend had suffered because of his race, and reminding the crowd that Jesse Owens, the man who shot down Adolph Hitler's dream of promoting Aryan supremacy, was much more than a great athlete. "His vibrant personality and charisma made him a man for all people," Joe said. "I don't know anyone who better epitomizes the philosophy: reach out, touch a hand, and make a friend."

>>>>>>>>>>

While I was growing up, I spent a lot of time visiting Jesse and Ruth Owens. Jesse always said, "I'm your godfather. Call me Uncle Jesse." I enjoyed hearing his stories and playing at their house, but he would discipline me if I did something wrong, as would Auntie Ruth. Their house was like a second home for me, but I had to behave, just like I did at home. I knew he had been in the 1936 Olympics, which impressed me.

My dad and Uncle Jesse had come from Chicago, which was predominantly Democratic. Arizona was strongly Republican. They loved to play golf, but they began to wonder: how were two Democrats going to get into those clubs? Even though they both were athletes whom people recognized, they realized that the state was heavily Republican and they had to figure something out. So they changed political parties on their membership applications. The day they switched that one line from Democrat to Republican, they got into every golf club they wanted to join.

It might sound strange to say this, but I would say they took Phoenix over. Everyone knew who they were. We never went to a restaurant where we had to wait to be seated. My dad was always greeted by name. So was my Uncle Jesse. When they switched to Republican, we noticed a lot of things changed. They received more opportunities and people didn't question them.

>>>>>>>>>>

Once entertainer Bill Cosby met Joe, they became fast friends. The two had much in common, including a strong belief that the path to a better life had to start with education. Cosby once watched Martha Jo when she was a youngster in his hotel suite while Joe made a public appearance. Fans of *The Cosby Show* saw Joe and Frank Robinson on an episode as former Negro league players who showed up one day to reminisce with Cosby's character, Cliff Huxtable. Cosby held Joe in such high regard that when he was inducted into the NAACP Image Awards Hall of Fame in 2007, he talked not about himself but about Joe, who had died five years earlier.

>>>>>>>>>>

My first memory of Bill Cosby goes back to when I was eleven. It was 1980, and my dad and I went to Las Vegas, where he would play in a golf tournament as a celebrity. My dad took me to Vegas often, and we always went to shows. We saw Bill Cosby's show the night before my dad played golf and went backstage to visit with him after the show. My dad mentioned he was going to put me in child care at the Hilton, where we always stayed, and Cosby said, "No, bring her to my suite when you leave for the tournament in the morning." His suite was on the top floor of the hotel and it looked like a home. Camille, his wife, and their kids would be coming later that morning. So I got settled in, Cosby turned on the big-screen TV and put on a cartoon channel. Then he went into the bedroom to go back to sleep. I was enjoying the cartoons and Fat Albert *came on. Fat Albert was one of the characters from Cosby's popular comedy sketches, which were made into a cartoon. Cosby was on the show and talked before the cartoon began. I did not realize the program was filmed earlier, so I was thinking Cosby had left me and gone to the studio for the show. There I was in his huge hotel suite, my dad was playing golf, and Bill Cosby had left to do his show. I was thinking I was all alone and I became nervous. So I walked over to the room he was sleeping in and the door was open a crack. I peeked in and Cosby must have heard me open the door because he said, "I'm here. Don't worry, I didn't leave you." Was I ever relieved. I said, OK, went back to the front of the suite, sat down in front of the TV, and watched the rest of the show.*

>>>>>>>>>>

In the spring of 1968, many American cities were in flames, the result of violence that erupted after the Reverend Martin Luther King Jr. was gunned down on the balcony of his Memphis, Tennessee, hotel on April 4, sparking a wave of anger in the black community. Joe had not been moved into action by the burning bus in Alabama seven years earlier, but King's death dealt him a much harder blow. As he traveled the country, Joe sensed a desire for revenge in some of his black audiences, but saw resignation and defeat in the faces of others. They had lost one of the most eloquent, dedicated leaders in the history of black America. Who would fill that void? Joe decided then that he needed to add his voice to the conversation. King had done all he could. Joe reasoned it was up to everyone else, himself included, to use their minds and talents to carry on King's legacy.

Joe had just started his Greyhound career when he joined more than two hundred thousand others in the March on Washington, one of the seminal events in the civil rights movement. A mass of humanity walked from the Washington Monument to the Lincoln Memorial, where they heard King deliver his stirring and oft-quoted "I Have a Dream" speech. Jackie Robinson, Don Newcombe, and Monte Irvin also walked the route on that warm August day in 1963, as did basketball stars Wilt Chamberlain, Bill Russell, Elgin Baylor, Walt Bellamy, and Al Attles.

King's resolve and passion impressed Joe, and he understood why the civil rights leader preached a doctrine of nonviolence. It was the same point Jackie had made in spring training back in 1952: no matter how much hate spews from fans and opponents, we don't fight. But when Joe saw King at the Newark airport in 1964, he confronted the famous pastor and, for reasons Joe himself never quite understood, asked him why he wouldn't fight back. Both had plenty of time before their flights, so King sat Joe down to explain.

"Brother Black," Joe remembered King saying, "if you should strike me, what would I gain by swinging back at you? The pride of showing that I am not afraid of you? Would that be a victory? However, if I don't resist you and you continue to lash out at me with your fists, sooner or later your conscience will start to bother you and you'll pause and wonder why you are beating on me. You'll stop punching me because you'll feel like an uncontrollable bully, and I will have gained a lasting victory."

Besides, King said, if activists fought back, their tormentors could rationalize their violence. But how can you rationalize beating and killing people when they're not fighting back? Joe nodded his understanding and promised to become more involved. King said the movement needed all the help it could get, but suggested Joe might be more valuable in a role other than marching. "I don't think you have the strength to non-violently accept the violence that we confront," King told him. Joe wasn't offended. But he *was* motivated. Joe always had viewed the civil rights movement from an outsider's perspective, wondering what "they" wanted. After talking to King, Joe realized he was part of "they."

Joe learned of King's death after speaking at a dinner in Tulsa, Oklahoma. He flew to Atlanta for the funeral and served as an usher during the service at Ebenezer Baptist Church, where King and his father were pastors. Hundreds of blacks had massed outside the church, and as Joe stood at the door he saw entertainer Sammy Davis Jr. trying to make his way through the crowd. "My people, my people," Joe heard Davis cry out. Joe then waded into the crowd and helped Davis, a diminutive figure next to Joe's imposing bulk, get into the church. "Am I glad to see you," the breathless Davis exclaimed as he hugged Joe.

Back in his Greyhound office, Joe again thought about how he could speak directly to the black community. He believed he could add a voice of reason and experience to the debate, so he decided to write editorial messages urging blacks to take charge of their own lives and work to improve themselves and their communities. He titled his columns By the Way.

In one sense, Joe adhered to a philosophy that rang of conservatism. He believed that education, initiative, and hard work were the keys to getting ahead, and that blacks shouldn't expect to be given something just because they were black. Joe certainly understood the indignities that had been heaped upon black people through discriminatory laws and practices over the years—he had been subjected to them himself—but that didn't mean they should sit back and rely on handouts. "Life is tough," he once told a reporter. "There are no shortcuts, no gimmicks. But you only go around once, so get the most out of it while you can. Life is too short to nurture hate."

Joe tried to make that point—and many others—in his messages, which ran in *JET* and *Ebony* magazines and in black newspapers. He also recorded his columns for broadcast on radio stations serving black communities, telling listeners he was "just one small voice asking humbly for a little more sanity, a little more honesty, and a lot more thinking through of what we are doing and the methods we are using to realistically solve the problems of our black community."

"Everybody read *Ebony*," said Len Coleman, a former National League president and one of Joe's closest friends. "When you looked in there, there was Joe's picture. In the barber shops, people sat there and read *JET* and *Ebony* while they were waiting, and they always saw Joe's picture in there with his column."

His columns stressed the importance of education, responsible parenthood, and avoiding the temptations of the street. Joe chided parents who used their welfare checks to buy luxuries for themselves instead of food and clothing for their children. "Parents are responsible for the well-being of their children," he wrote. "And when a Black parent uses welfare money for the benefit of his children, it's a good example of responsibility. And love."

Joe's family had relied on welfare to get by when he was a youngster and would have suffered greatly without it. But he believed that welfare should be a stopgap to carry a family through tough times, not a way of life. Too many families, he said, allowed the welfare system to "rob them of their responsibility, their dignity, and their pride. And the tragedy is the fact that this loss of initiative and ambition has been passed down to their children. Black America," he continued, "I ask you if receiving something for nothing is really worth risking the loss of some potential future leaders of our community and this nation."

Many of Joe's columns touched on the black nationalism that arose in the 1960s. Young blacks began wearing traditional African clothes and colors. They wore their hair in unique styles. "Black is beautiful" became a popular catchphrase. James Brown sang "Say it loud, I'm black and I'm proud," lyrics that became a mantra for many. The clenched fist became a symbol of black unity and the battle against oppression. It was never more prominently displayed than at the 1968 Olympics in Mexico City, where US sprinters John Carlos and Tommie Smith stood on the medal stand with heads bowed, Carlos raising his black-gloved right hand in a clenched fist salute, Smith doing the same with his left hand.

Joe wrote that it was fine for blacks to sing "We shall overcome," to strive for greater equality, but added it takes ambition to make that happen. "The attitude starts in the schoolroom," he said. "Education is part of what Black power is all about. Without it, Black power becomes Black powerless." Later, he wrote that true power comes from being strong economically—owning more businesses, qualifying for more high-paying jobs, and spreading wealth throughout the community. That can be accomplished only with education and training, he added. "A clenched fist is almost powerless if it is empty when opened," he wrote.

Joe also railed against the acceptance of "black" English. He bristled at hearing blacks say "foteen" instead of "fourteen," "dis" instead of "this," "Jooly" for "July," and "axe" instead of "ask." "There is no reason why every other ethnic group can migrate to this country and master English and we, who are born here, cannot," he wrote. He went on to note that in a job interview, "you very often make it or fall flat on your face the first time you open your mouth. So, start working on your communication system."

Fatherhood was another subject Joe felt needed attention in the black community. He worked hard himself at trying to be the best parent he could for Martha Jo and despaired at seeing black men who were too lazy or too proud or too indifferent to fill that role. "A Black man's responsibility and contributions to his family does not stop with producing children and sharing an occasional paycheck," he wrote. "It takes much more. It takes involvement. Interest. Understanding, caring and love."

>>>>>>>>>>

My brother, Chico, is seventeen years older, and I grew up as an only child. My dad had five brothers and sisters, so he knew how to play with others. Since I didn't have that option, he made sure I played with our neighbors' kids. He knew I needed to learn how to share and get along with others. That's one reason he played with me when I was playing with my Barbie dolls, which was all the time. If he had the blonde Barbie and I wanted her, he'd say, no, we're going to share and take turns. He taught me that I had to be respectful of what others wanted, too. If you just go to school and then come home and stay by yourself, you never learn how to interact with others and develop social skills. When my father took me to Las Vegas, he'd leave me in the child care center while he played in a golf tournament, and I had to play with other kids. He made a point to put me in situations where I had to learn how to socialize.

He also took me places to expose me to other environments, such as New York City, London, and Hawaii. In New York, we attended Broadway shows and opera. We took a bus trip up the Pacific Coast from Los Angeles to San Francisco and back. At home, we went to see the Phoenix Suns, Arizona State football, and hockey games. My dad took me to spring-training baseball games, the rodeo, and the state fair. The best part about the state fair was the Indian fry bread with beans or honey or powdered sugar. When my father took me to the opera in

Arizona, most of those who attended wore jeans and my father told me, "That is not how you dress for opera." My father wore a navy suit—blue was his favorite color—and a tie, and I wore a dress. He wanted me to experience all facets of life so I would be comfortable no matter where I went.

>>>>>>>>>>

To succeed, Joe believed, blacks needed to fit in. He thought cornrows, plaits, and braids were fine for singers and entertainers, but not for someone trying to make it in the business world. "My young friends," he wrote, "are you making it easy for 'the man' to keep so many of you on the unemployment rolls? Remember, employers can and will enforce a dress code." He was disturbed that radio stations serving black communities were heavy on music, but scant on news and informational programming. "So while we are doing the boogie, the world is passing us by," he wrote.

Often, Joe took his message on the road. He told graduates of Dillard University in New Orleans at their commencement that they had the power to change long-entrenched attitudes hampering black progress. But, he added, "Changing our hair and clothes style and rapping about how all of our woes are to be blamed on a racist society won't do it." Joe also felt that black college students too often took courses just to get by instead of classes that would help them get decent-paying jobs in a competitive labor market.

Many of Joe's messages sprang from personal experience—living on welfare as a youngster, dealing with racist attitudes in baseball, and the value he placed on his education at Morgan State, where he first gained an appreciation for black history and culture. Joe feared for the future of historically black colleges like Morgan, sensing that many were struggling financially and that black students often regarded them as inferior. But Joe still saw a role for those schools. "A Black college or university can effectively reinforce a Black student's identity," he wrote, "and it can also make it possible for more inner city educated Black youths to attend college. So if Black is truly beautiful, then it is about time for some Black people to find out just how beautiful black colleges can be." To that end, Joe urged graduates to open their wallets and donate to the schools that set them on their career paths, even if it meant giving as little as twenty-five dollars a year. "You know," he said, "the school that we save may be your own."

Few subjects were untouchable for Joe, even baseball. He contended in one column the game had become too staid and overregulated. It lacked the verve he remembered from earlier days and wasn't fun anymore. "Let the athletes do their thing," he implored. "Let 'em give what they've got in an atmosphere free from rules that inhibit individuality, flamboyance and the things that made baseball thrilling in the first place." And if a pitcher wanted to throw a spitter once in a while, what was wrong with that?

Joe wanted to provoke a reaction from blacks with his columns, and he certainly succeeded. Many readers and listeners responded angrily, calling Joe a sellout, a tool of whitey, an Oreo—black on the outside, white inside. "There were a lot of people he met through the years who either liked him or disliked him. There were very few in between," said Angela Phoenix, who worked with Joe at Greyhound. "People challenged him. They would go up to him and say, 'I disagree with what you said on the radio the other night' and try to argue the point. Joe would never back down. He always had a valid argument."

Joe definitely had his detractors. In one letter Joe received, the writer said his commentaries belonged in *Time* or *Newsweek*, not *JET*. "Don't ever put that trash in a black magazine again," the letter said, because blacks "didn't want to hear that dumb kind of Oreo thoughts that you have to give." Some readers threatened to shoot Joe. Others cussed him out. How, some asked, could Joe know anything about blacks when he didn't live in the ghetto? Joe was called an "Uncle Tom," a "Grand Coon," and a "sick man." And that was just in one letter. "I really feel shame for you and if you have children or grandchildren, I pity them," the letter said. Some took Joe to task for failing to place greater blame on racism for problems in the black community. His response: "I deeply believe in the importance of uniting people of good will more than I do dwelling on those things that divide them." But if people wanted to criticize him and call him names, well, that meant he must be doing something right. "At least someone out there is reading and thinking," Joe said.

He also received many encouraging responses to his messages. One letter saluted Joe for urging blacks to use their talents for learning and working. "Keep up the good work," the writer said. Another thanked

Joe for his commentary on blacks often having misguided priorities. The thirty-seven-year-old man said Joe's words encouraged him to begin saving and planning for his future. "You are truly a great and remarkable man," the writer stated. Joe found additional motivation to keep prodding the black community when he heard from a seventy-four-year-old letter writer who was upset because at a time when blacks had more opportunities than ever, young people weren't taking advantage of them. "The ones that are guilty of stealing, snatching pocketbooks, smoking dope may wake up too late to find out they can't make it that way," the writer said.

"You may rest assured that as long as one voice calls out for help," Joe wrote, "I shall continue to challenge black people to get our heads out of the proverbial sand."

Joe spoke out in arenas beyond his columns. He took on the administration of President Gerald R. Ford in 1976, accusing the government of failing to crack down on major corporations for violating minority hiring laws. "If they would make a couple of examples, all of this would stop," he said. At a news conference in Tallahassee, Florida, Joe claimed the administration had prevented the Equal Employment Opportunity Commission from moving against such corporations. Though he did not name any companies, Joe suggested they escaped sanctions because they had influence and contributed heavily to political campaigns. He also said major corporations eagerly hired blacks in the 1960s, when hiring laws were being enforced, but "now they have their so-called quota and are no longer interested in hiring qualified blacks."

Author and Negro leagues historian Larry Lester said that kind of bluntness from Joe rubbed some the wrong way. Lester, however, found it refreshing.

"I enjoyed talking to Joe because when you'd ask Joe a question, he'd give you an honest answer, not the politically correct one," Lester said. "He didn't dance around the issues. He gave you his opinion. If you had a shirt and asked him what he thought of it, he'd say, 'I think it's ugly' if that's what he thought. He had a shoot-from-the-hip approach. That was great with me. He was a man among men basically."

When Greyhound was criticized over its minority-hiring practices in Atlanta, Joe stepped in and worked with bus company president J. L. Kerrigan on a response. In an agreement that Joe helped hammer out with the black activist group Operation Breadbasket and the Metropolitan Atlanta Summit Leadership Conference, the company said it would hire ten to twenty black drivers in the coming year, bring in minority workers to fill office and other staff positions to achieve racial balance, open accounts with black-run banks, and increase financial support of area colleges. Joe's effort in those negotiations didn't generate the headlines of a World Series victory. But for someone who got one of those jobs, it was just as significant.

>>>>>>>>>>

During Joe's time in Chicago, a young attorney occasionally saw him entering or leaving the Greyhound offices. Brooklyn native Jerry Reinsdorf had cheered along with the rest of Dodger Nation as Joe worked his wonders on the pitching mound in 1952. "We were all incredibly depressed at the end of the '51 season. That was about as low as you could get," Reinsdorf said, remembering the agony of Bobby Thomson's pennant-winning home run for the New York Giants. "So we go into the 1952 season, everybody's very, very depressed, and out of nowhere comes this guy. All of a sudden he's saving games, he's winning games. They don't win the pennant without Joe Black."

As pleasant as that memory might have been, Reinsdorf hesitated to share it with Joe. "I didn't know him. And I wasn't going to walk up to him, a perfect stranger, and say, 'Hi, Joe Black. I knew you from Brooklyn.' I was too shy. I figured people were doing that to him all the time." Later, when both lived in Arizona, Reinsdorf was introduced to Joe. "I was thrilled, of course," he said. "We became instant friends."

Once he got to know Joe, Reinsdorf marveled at his network of friends. He remembered a conversation with Michael Jordan, who mentioned that his mother wanted to buy a house in Arizona so she could spend the winters there. "So I said if it's OK with you," Reinsdorf said, "I'd like to introduce your mother to a friend of mine who I think can get her more established in the community, could introduce her to a lot of people. He said, 'What's your friend's name?' I said, 'Joe Black.' He said, 'Oh, I love Joe Black.' I didn't even know he knew Joe Black. Where the heck did Michael Jordan get to know Joe Black? Everybody knew Joe Black. It was amazing."

It was easy to see why, said Len Coleman, who had Joe accompany him to dozens of baseball-related functions. "He was naturally likable," Coleman said. "He had that smile and that laugh. As soon as you met him, you liked him." Coleman, Joe, Frank Robinson, Don Baylor, and former Major League umpire Paul Runge were together so often that journalist Claire Smith dubbed them "the Posse." Joe enjoyed the give and take of his friendships. He liked ribbing his friends and they teased him right back, often about two of his passions—golf and food. "He'd do anything to play golf," Coleman said. "You mention golf and his bag was packed." He held his own on the course, too, usually shooting in the eighties in the annual baseball players golf tournament.

Could it be because he knew how to communicate with the ball? Coleman always chuckled when Joe approached the tee, looked at his ball as he held it, and started talking to it. "He'd tell the ball what he wanted it to do," Coleman said. "When he was putting, he'd tell the ball what to do, how it was supposed to break. When he missed the putt, he'd say, 'I didn't tell you to do that, I told you to break over there.' He didn't hit it that long, but when he got around the green, he was in attack mode. He could smell that hole."

Joe was just as dedicated when he sat down to eat, especially at dessert time. "We used to go to a Chinese buffet," Jerry Reinsdorf said. "It was all you could eat Chinese food. Man, did he get his money's worth." One time, Reinsdorf said he wanted to eat light, so Joe took him to a restaurant that had a long salad bar. They made their salads, paid, and had just sat down when Joe said he'd be right back. "He comes back with a plate loaded with pasta," Reinsdorf said. "Because on the other side, there was a pasta bar. I didn't know there was another part of the restaurant. So he comes back with all kinds of stuff. Then after that we had dessert and cookies. He could really eat."

During the memorial service for Joe after he died in 2002, the Reverend Mark Anderson talked of all that Joe had been in his life, then smiled when he told the congregation they were celebrating a man who "could eat a whole chocolate cake by himself." "That alone," he added, "is an accomplishment worth mentioning."

He was just as crazy about coconut cake. Once after a round of golf, Joe, Len Coleman, and Frank Robinson lingered over lunch for an hour and a half, teasing each other and swapping stories. Robinson drove that day, so when he got up to leave, Coleman also stood. Before Joe got up, a waiter came out with a big coconut cake to put on the dessert tray. Robinson and Coleman promptly sat back down, because they knew what was coming. "Joe saw that cake and Frank and I didn't have a chance of getting out of there," Coleman said. "He had to have that coconut cake."

In 1998, Coleman took Joe with him on a baseball promotion trip to Japan and remembered Joe asking about what they'd eat.

"I don't know," Len said. "Whatever the commissioner says we're going to eat, that's what we're going to eat."

"You know I don't eat any of that sushi stuff," Joe reminded his friend.

Naturally, the first place they went was a sushi restaurant.

"They bring nine different courses, petite things, and we go through the courses," Coleman said. "Over a couple of hours they bring all this sushi and I look over and Joe is eating *everything*. We got in the car afterward and I said, 'Joe, I thought you don't eat sushi.' And Joe said, 'I thought you said we had to go along with the program, so I went along.'"

The one person Joe didn't talk back to was John Teets, who became Greyhound Corporation's CEO in 1982. Teets could be blunt, and he didn't tolerate fools. He also admired, respected, and genuinely liked Joe. "We talked frankly with each other," said Teets, who promoted Joe to senior vice president for urban affairs in 1986. "Something's on his mind, he'd speak up. If something was on my mind, I'd do the same. But one thing about Joe, he was always up. He was never down. I don't think he ever had a bad day."

While Joe's baseball days were long past, it seemed that anyone who had been a Brooklyn Dodger at some point in his career was never forgotten. So it was with Joe, but he also made a name for himself with Greyhound, because, like the company's buses, he went everywhere. He spoke at churches, banquets, annual meetings, black consumer seminars, black history conferences, marketing conferences, commencements, and high school assemblies. Joe never urged his audiences to ride Greyhound buses or use the company's products. But in focusing on the benefits of education and self-reliance, promoting tolerance and civility, and stressing the dangers of drugs and gangs, Joe helped foster a positive image for the company. He was so visible he became known as "Mr. Greyhound."

Because of his national prominence, Joe usually got what he wanted at Greyhound when he proposed a new program or suggested that the company back a certain project. The self-assurance and notoriety that resulted from his successes carried over into other areas, even to something as minor as getting the right table at lunch. Anderson, Joe's pastor in his later years, remembered arriving early for a lunch appointment with Joe and indicating he wanted a table for two. He was told to wait and then nothing happened—until Joe arrived. "He walked in almost like he owned the place," Anderson said. "They said, 'Over here's your table.' He said, 'I don't like that table, I like that one over there.' He didn't do it in an officious or arrogant way. He just did it because that was what he wanted and that was the way it was going to be. He had this presence about him. I thought, I'm just going to walk behind him and follow in this presence, this confidence."

Even as he succeeded at Greyhound, Joe found himself failing at something else: he couldn't control his weight. Martha Jo remembered her father not as the solidly built athlete who threw 95 miles an hour, but as a warm, loving man who tipped the scales at three hundred pounds or more. "I don't enjoy having a 300-pound body," Joe wrote in his autobiography. But he learned to live with his size, and he believed that as long as his blood pressure and heart checked out, he'd be fine. Joe even found a way to capitalize on his girth, John Teets said. "He always left an impression because of his pure size," the former Greyhound boss said. "People listened to him. He was a very talented guy. Obviously, he was famous. People wanted to see him and talk to him and set up places where they could meet him. He was just one big, likable guy."

His friends may have joked about how Joe enjoyed eating, but they also worried about his weight. Jerry Reinsdorf said he often begged Joe to lose weight, but got nowhere. Joe did try in earlier years. Sam Lacy, the noted sportswriter for the *Baltimore Afro-American*, saw Joe at Yankee Stadium during the 1963 World Series and pointed out that Joe looked nothing like the pitcher he remembered from 1952. True, Joe said. "But you should have seen me a few months back," he added. "I had ballooned up to 292 pounds and was talking to myself: 'Joe,' I said, 'what are you training for, the New York football Giants or to fight Sonny Liston?' Right away I started taking [it] off and I'm down to 255 now, but there isn't anything that has come harder to do."

Keeping his weight down became even more difficult for Joe after a phone call from his sister Phyllis in 1964.

"Sonny, come on home," she said in a sad voice. "Momma's gone."

Martha Black had been sick for a couple of months, but Joe had not prepared himself to hear that she had died, and he was overcome with grief. Joe had been motivated to succeed because he knew it made his mother happy. Even at age forty, he still looked to her for advice. He remembered the time early in his Greyhound days when he called his mother to complain that his fellow workers seemed indifferent to him. "Sonny," she told him, "you went there to work, not socialize." As usual, his mother, with her grade-school education, knew exactly what to say to her college-educated son. So why, he wondered, would God take someone as wise and kind and loving as his mother when the world had so many criminals and people who were just plain nasty?

Once he was back in Plainfield, Joe sat beside his mother's casket each day at the funeral home and talked to her. He thought about all the hours she had worked yet still found time to offer love, guidance, and support to her children. He thanked her for all she had given him, and he said a prayer of thanks that he had been able to see the sparkle of pride in her eyes when he graduated from college, won that World Series game, and became a teacher.

"When my mother died, I leaned over into the coffin and kissed her," Joe said in an interview in 2000. "I became a different person. I could feel something. I guess it was my mother's spirit coming to me. After that kiss, I thought more about other people and I wanted to share. She was the biggest influence in my life."

Joe wept openly at her funeral, stunning his twelve-year-old son, who hugged his father and cried, "Daddy! Daddy!"

"That was the first time I saw my dad cry," Chico said. "That took me by surprise. Wow, he's crying. I didn't really understand. Later on in life, I understood. That was his mom."

Joe never drowned his sorrows in alcohol, because he didn't drink. So in times of depression, he went to a bakery instead of a bar. Joe loved sweets, and eating pastries was the only way he felt he could cope. After his mother died, Joe's weight went from 245 to 285 pounds in less than six months. He could skip a meal, but he couldn't pass up something sweet. It was a habit he never broke.

Many sad occasions followed his mother's death. Joe's father and oldest sister, Ruby Elizabeth, also died. Gil Hodges, the quiet pillar of strength who played first base for the Dodgers, died in 1972.

At Hodges's funeral, Pee Wee Reese remembered Jackie Robinson sitting by himself at the front of the church. Jackie had been ailing from diabetes. The body that had enabled him to succeed in whatever athletic endeavor he tried was failing him. A leg was giving him trouble and he was going blind. "I saw him and said, 'Hey, Jack, how're you doing?'" Pee Wee said. Jackie didn't say anything, just continued to stare straight ahead. "Later," Pee Wee said, "he came over and said, 'Pee Wee, I'm sorry. I couldn't tell who you were.'"

Joe, Jackie, and Pee Wee were together again when Jackie was honored before the second game of the 1972 World Series at Cincinnati's Riverfront Stadium. As Joe stood with them in the tunnel leading to the field, he heard Jackie tell Pee Wee that all he could see of him was a blur. What he heard next rocked him.

"That's nothing," Jackie said. "On Tuesday, I'm going to have my leg cut off."

"What the hell did you say?" Pee Wee asked incredulously.

"I told you I'm going to have my leg cut off," Jackie said.

"You got to be crazy," Pee Wee exclaimed. "You can stand there and calmly say you're going to let them cut your leg off?"

"It doesn't do me any damn good," Jackie said. "They might as well cut it off."

That was Jackie's last public appearance. He died of a heart attack nine days later.

Joe remembered his days playing baseball in Venezuela, where fans thought he looked like Jackie Robinson. Evidently, they still resembled each other in 1972, at least in the eyes of one woman. Joe was standing near Jackie's coffin when the woman approached, looked down at Jackie's body, looked at Joe, looked at the coffin again, and then returned her gaze to Joe. "What's going on?" she cried. "Who are you kidding? They told me Jackie Robinson was dead. No, you're Jackie. You're standing right there." It took Joe a few minutes to calm her down and get her to believe that it truly was Jackie in the coffin.

Throughout his life, Joe never passed up a chance to explain what Jackie had meant to him, to baseball, and to the entire civil rights movement. Without Jackie Robinson in baseball, he often remarked, there would have been no Joe Black. "I owe a lot to Jackie," Joe said. "I have a good job, a nice house. A lot of doors opened for me. If Jackie Robinson had failed, the doors would never have opened. When I look at my house, when I look at the grass around my house, I say, 'Thank God for Jackie Robinson.'" Joe saw Jackie as a hero who never acted like one. "He used to wake me up to go and speak to the kids at schools," Joe said. "The schools did not call him. He looked them up in the phone book because he knew the importance of education. He never used his status to make himself seem better than anyone else."

As often as he saluted Jackie's contributions, Joe felt the same deep appreciation for the man who had the foresight to bring Jackie into the Major Leagues: Branch Rickey. "I hate to imagine what life would be like without Branch Rickey," Joe told an interviewer in 1997. "The man was a hero. People talk about Rosa Parks, but she was just too tired to move to the back of that bus. She didn't realize the impact of it and how she would become a symbol for the movement. I've got a feeling Mr. Rickey knew all along just what would happen. I bet he's upstairs smiling right now because not only did he leave baseball better off, but the entire world."

Joe was a pallbearer at Jackie's funeral, along with Pee Wee, Bill Russell, Jim Gilliam, Don Newcombe, and Ralph Branca. "I really hope the world will mourn the passing of a man, not just an athlete," Joe said at the time. "I don't want him to be a martyr, but I want people to know that they've lost a battler."

Joe would repeat much the same message twenty-five years later, when Major League Baseball recognized the fiftieth anniversary of Jackie's first appearance with the Brooklyn Dodgers. "He allowed all young men to dream and to make it come true," Joe said. "The 50th anniversary will be a waste of time if people remember he stole bases and won pennants and don't remember he helped race relations."

Jackie's passing "was the loss of a great friend," Joe recalled, but another death later in the decade hit him even harder. In 1978, Jim Gilliam, his best friend in baseball and Chico's godfather, passed away. "Gilliam's death was like losing a brother," Joe said. Billy Cox, the slick-fielding third baseman, died the same year. Two years later, Jesse Owens's death left Joe with an emptiness he couldn't describe, the same feeling that had struck when he learned of Gilliam's passing.

>>>>>>>>>>

Joe retired from Greyhound in 1987, after Martha Jo graduated from high school. He left with an appreciation for the support he received for his work from executives like John Teets, Gerald H. Trautman, and Raymond F. Shaffer. To Joe, Trautman and Shaffer were the power behind his special markets operation, because "they believed in people and opportunity." If they were the engine, then Joe turned out to be a most skillful driver.

"What I've always told people is Joe had the world figured out," Jerry Reinsdorf said. "He understood people better than anybody I've ever known."

First as a teacher, then as a business executive working with the black community, Joe spent thirty years trying to help and make a difference. Yet in a way, he was just getting started.

17

A Question of Value

November 1952

THE REGULAR SEASON WAS OVER, the World Series was in the record books as yet another Yankees triumph, and the Dodgers and their fans began their annual wait for the next year to roll around. Yet Joe had much to savor. He had saved his team's season and established himself as one of the game's elite pitchers. Joe often shrugged off his success as luck. He had come to the right place at the right time, entering the big leagues with a team that had lost its ace and desperately needed a stabilizing force for its pitching staff. He had a wise hand in Campy as his catcher and one of the majors' best defensive teams behind him. "I've been lucky, real lucky," he kept telling Sam Lacy of the *Baltimore Afro-American*.

Yes, Joe had a great support system. But he was the one who had to deliver, the one who had to get the ball over the plate without serving up anything good to hit, the one who had to summon the courage and single-mindedness to face down a batter with runners in scoring position and the game on the line, to muster the confidence that he, not the hitter, was master of the situation. And he did that time and time again. As Jackie Robinson put it, "His efforts on our behalf were beyond description."

In late September, after the Dodgers had clinched the pennant and he had been named Rookie of the Year by the *Sporting News*, Joe sent a bottle of champagne to each of the writers who traveled with the club, telling them it was a "small token of gratitude for having written so many nice things about me this season." Roscoe McGowen of the *New York Times* noted that Danny Litwhiler, then with the Cincinnati Reds, was the only other player anyone could remember making such a gesture. Litwhiler, a sure-handed outfielder who batted .281 in his career, sent a bottle of whiskey to the sportswriters in each of the cities in which he played—Philadelphia, St. Louis, Boston, and Cincinnati—to thank them for the stories they wrote about him.

In Joe's case, maybe the writers should have been the ones expressing their gratitude, because Joe was what they call in the business "good copy." He was accommodating, intelligent, and well-spoken. And his was a compelling story—growing up poor, being told he couldn't play in the big leagues because he was black, slogging through all those seasons in Negro ball, and then appearing out of nowhere to become one of the biggest stories of the 1952 season. How hard could it have been to write positively about that? And write they did, which kept Joe's wife, Doris, busy, because she collected all the clippings she could find about her husband and put them in a scrapbook.

Joe had met Doris Saunders in 1946 when both were students at Morgan State. As Doris recalled it, she learned who Joe Black was after she challenged her political science teacher about her grade, a B-plus.

"Did you see Mr. Black's paper?" the teacher asked Doris.

"Who's Mr. Black?" she shot back.

"How long have you been in school? You don't know who he is?" the teacher said.

"No," Doris replied. "Should I?"

"Mr. Black," the teacher said, "pass your paper up to her."

Doris said she looked at Joe's paper and then at hers. "I had the same answers he had," she said. "But he filibustered. I wrote one or two sentences and he had like a whole paragraph. But my answers were correct. That's how we met. I challenged the teacher. I figured I was smart, too." Joe, she saw, had received an A.

At the time, Doris was tall and thin. She said guys used to laugh at her and call her "skinny." But not Joe. "He started talking to me because he felt sorry for me." Talk led to dating and dating led to marriage, a union that eventually would end in a divorce. Doris later would have a thirty-five-year career in Brooklyn as a teacher, guidance counselor, and school administrator.

>>>>>>>>>>

Joe rarely brought the game home with him, Doris said. She didn't go to many games and Joe usually didn't say much about them. If you didn't know him, she said, you wouldn't know if the Dodgers had won or lost or if he had done well or poorly. "He just left it alone," Doris said. "But I could usually tell by his mood if the game was either good or not so good."

Game seven of the World Series was one of those that wasn't so good. "I believe that we had the best team and should have won the World Series," Joe said. "But fate decreed otherwise." If he had just located those home run balls he served up to Gene Woodling and Mickey Mantle a little differently. If only Billy Martin had been a half-step slower beginning his charge to catch Jackie's bases-loaded popup. If, if, if, there are always so many when a series is as tightly contested as the one the Dodgers and Yankees had just finished. But there were no do-overs, of course, and if anyone deserved a vacation it was Joe. For the last two years, he had been a full-time baseball player without a break: spring and summer of 1950 with the Elite Giants, a barnstorming tour in the fall followed by the winter season in Cuba, then spring training at Vero Beach, a summer in Montreal and St. Paul, another winter season in Cuba, spring training with the Dodgers, and then a full big-league season.

But three days after the series ended, Joe was back in uniform in Charlotte, North Carolina, playing with a barnstorming all-star team headed by Roy Campanella, who scheduled a series of games in the South that stretched into early November. Campy assembled most of the top black players in the majors for his team, including Hank Thompson and Monte Irvin of the Giants; Luke Easter, Larry Doby, and Harry "Suitcase" Simpson of the Cleveland Indians; and George Crowe of the Boston Braves. The Giants' Willie Mays managed to join the team on a furlough from the army and Campy found a spot for twenty-year-old Wes Covington, who had hit .330 with twenty-four home runs in Class C ball that summer and later would star for the Milwaukee Braves in the

1957 World Series. Like previous barnstorming ventures, the tour gave fans in places like Knoxville, Tennessee, Birmingham, Alabama, Little Rock, Arkansas, and New Orleans a chance to see Major Leaguers up close and personal. A Negro American League all-star team provided the opposition at most stops. Joe pitched well and everyone pocketed some extra money. For Joe and Campy, that money was on top of the $4,200.64 each collected as his World Series share.

Even when he was back home in Brooklyn after more than three weeks of travel that must have reminded Joe of his Negro league days, the whirlwind continued. In early November, he crowned the young woman selected as the queen of the Capital City Classic football game between Morgan State and Virginia Union at Griffith Stadium in Washington, DC. A week later, Morgan State honored him during its homecoming weekend. As part of those festivities, Joe gave the school the last ball he threw in his historic game-one victory over the Yankees, plus another ball signed by all the Dodgers. That second ball went to coach Eddie Hurt, who was asked to present it to the athlete Hurt and his assistants chose as the most outstanding player in the homecoming game against Hampton. If that wasn't enough, Joe played a few games with a touring basketball team called the Broadway Clowns. When the team played in Baltimore, Joe received a citation from Morgan State students and alumni. He also appeared with the Clowns when they played in Norfolk, Virginia, Doris's hometown.

In mid-November, United Press named Joe as one of the pitchers on its National League all-star team. Campy, Pee Wee, Jackie, Duke Snider, and Gil Hodges also were named to the Dodger-heavy honor squad. It was around that time that Joe became the first of the Dodgers to sign his 1952 contract, though the club would not announce that it had come to terms with its star pitcher until the winter meetings got underway in Phoenix, Arizona, in early December. His negotiations with general manager Buzzie Bavasi were quick, painless, and fruitful for both sides. Joe got a nice raise and the Dodgers got off paying him less than what he probably could have demanded.

Bavasi, according to journalist Stanley Frank, began the negotiations by pulling out a blank contract and asking Joe to write in what he thought he was worth. Joe put down $10,000. Bavasi then pulled out another contract, this one filled in with the amount the Dodgers intended to pay him. The Dodgers GM said he offered Joe $1,000 more than he asked and attached a stipulation—he had to use the extra money to buy Doris a fur coat. Joe promptly signed, much to Bavasi's relief.

Bavasi had feared that Joe would ask Campy and Jackie what he should seek and they'd tell him to ask for $20,000. Bavasi said the Dodgers would have had to pay it. "After all," he said, "he won the pennant for us." And if Joe had held out, Bavasi felt "the fans would have murdered us after the year he had." Joe later said he wouldn't buy a fur coat for Doris and instead would put the extra money toward a house. "A fur coat will keep my wife warm," he said, "but it's going to be awfully cold for those two kids and me if my control goes haywire."

The *Baltimore Afro-American* speculated that the Dodgers wanted to get Joe's negotiations out of the way before the Most Valuable Player vote was announced, because if he won—and many thought he would—they'd have to fork over even more money. If the Dodger brass had been worried about that, any fretting would have been for naught.

Though the consensus held that the Dodgers wouldn't have finished anywhere near first place without Joe, the National League MVP award went, in a surprise vote, to outfielder Hank Sauer of the fifth-place Chicago Cubs, an announcement that left many writers aghast. They would have understood if the twenty-four-member panel of writers had chosen Philadelphia Phillies ace Robin Roberts ahead of Joe. Roberts, after all, had gone 28-7 with a 2.59 earned run average and a league-high thirty complete games. He pitched in thirty-nine games, started thirty-seven, and got a save in the two games he didn't start. But Sauer, a .270 hitter for a team that didn't even make the first division and finished ten games behind the fourth-place Phillies?

Columnist C. M. Gibbs of the *Baltimore Sun* called the award to Sauer "slightly on the comic side," and it would go down as one of those episodes that keep fans from taking awards too seriously. United Press columnist Oscar Fraley chimed in: "What happened to the lame is debatable, but there can be no doubt today that the halt and the blind voted baseball's most valuable player awards this year." Fraley went on to say that anyone who "knows the difference between a bunt and a punt must be completely flabbergasted at the selection of Hank Sauer." Another writer, who was not identified, said in an Associated Press story the voting panel "made a farce of the whole thing."

To his credit, Sauer did share the National League home run lead with Ralph Kiner at thirty-seven and led the league with 121 RBIs. The Cubs, generally picked for seventh or eighth before the season, improved by fifteen games over 1951. In mid-June, the Cubs were fifteen games over .500 and trailed the first-place Dodgers by only four games. But Sauer tailed off badly after a fast start. The big left fielder hit only three home runs and managed just seven RBIs in September. After homering off the Dodgers' Ben Wade on September 11, Sauer did not go deep the rest of the season. He batted just .103 in that stretch with no extra-base hits and only one RBI.

No one could argue that Sauer carried the Cubs early. On June 11, he slugged three homers against the Phillies to run his season totals to eighteen home runs and fifty-eight RBIs. He was batting a lusty .352 and was on pace to top Babe Ruth's record of sixty home runs in a season. But over the final 104 games, Sauer batted only .226 with nineteen home runs, and the Cubs went 46-58 to finish at 77-77. "I was trying too hard for those long ones during the last month of the season and wound up hitting nothing," Sauer acknowledged.

Roberts, meanwhile, was sensational down the stretch, winning his last eight games, seventeen of his last eighteen, and twenty-one of his last twenty-three to help the Phillies finish within nine and a half games of the Dodgers.

Joe, of course, was used more and more as the season went on. He pitched in twenty-two of the Dodgers' last fifty-one games as they were fighting off the Giants, and went 7-2 with seven saves in that stretch. The second of the losses came when he started a meaningless game against the Boston Braves after Brooklyn had clinched the pennant. "Minus Black, the Bums would have been minus, period," C. M. Gibbs wrote.

What seemed especially befuddling was that three writers left Joe off their ballots entirely. The MVP awards were voted on by twenty-four writers—three from each city in the league. They selected ten players and ranked them in order of who they determined to be the most valuable, with fourteen points awarded for a first-place vote, nine points for a second-place vote, and so on down to one point for a tenth-place vote. So three writers decided that Joe Black, who rescued a crippled pitching staff on the pennant-winning team, didn't even deserve to be among the top ten candidates for the award. Sauer was left off one ballot and that, too, was unjustified. While Sauer might not have deserved the award, he should have at least been among the leading candidates. One writer also left Roberts off his ballot.

Sauer and Joe each received eight first-place votes, while Roberts had seven. The remaining first-place vote went to Duke Snider, who tied Pee Wee Reese for eighth in the balloting. Sauer finished with 226 points, Roberts with 211, and Joe with 208, one of the closest three-way races ever. With five second-place votes and five more for third place, Joe was listed on more top three ballots than Sauer, who got six votes for second and three for third. But Sauer beat Joe by getting two votes each for fourth, fifth, and sixth. Joe received one vote for fourth, one for eighth, and one for tenth.

Sauer had his share of defenders, led by his manager, Phil Cavarretta, the 1945 National League MVP. "I wouldn't trade Sauer for both Roberts and Black," Cavarretta said. "If I did, I should have my head examined. No pitcher could possibly have been as valuable to us last season as Hank was." Writer John C. Hoffman noted that the Dodgers missed the pennant by just one game without Joe in 1951 and had been picked to win the NL in many quarters in 1952, long before anyone knew what Joe could accomplish. "To many, despite the gnashing of teeth by Eastern critics, Sauer was the most logical choice," Hoffman wrote. Chester L. Smith of the *Pittsburgh Press* pointed out that Sauer had "made a respectable team out of the Cubs, who had been consigned to the basement."

Gayle Talbot of the Associated Press suggested that Sauer benefited from the votes of Midwest writers who "stuffed the ballot box," while Eastern writers generally divided their votes between Joe and Roberts. "You could have cut the moral indignation [among the Easterners] with a bat," Talbot wrote. Talbot also brought up the salient point in the MVP voting: how exactly do you determine who's the most valuable? It's supposed to be the player who made the most valuable contributions to his club, not necessarily the best player on the best team, and that's always a judgment call. There's also the matter of comparing everyday players to pitchers, especially starters who appear only once every four or five days. How do you determine who does the most for his team?

The Cy Young Award for pitchers did not exist in 1952, so if a pitcher was to be honored, it had to be as the MVP. Only a handful of pitchers had received that distinction, including Philadelphia Athletics pitcher

Bobby Shantz, the 1952 American League MVP. Before that, a pitcher had won the American League award only four times, and three of those came during the talent-depleted war years. The NL award had gone to a pitcher six times, including in 1950 when it went to Philadelphia Phillies reliever Jim Konstanty. "If Jim Konstanty of the Phillies rated the award in 1950, Joe Black rated it in '52," wrote United Press sportswriter Steve Snider. "They did the same job."

Was Joe denied the award because of racism? There were a total of six writers from St. Louis and Cincinnati, and neither city was particularly welcoming to blacks. But Jackie had won the award in 1949 and Campy had been voted the MVP the previous year. If any bias was involved, it was more likely that some writers believed everyday players were more deserving than pitchers. Yes, Shantz did win the American League award, but no AL hitter that season had the type of big year that would command attention. Yankees pitcher Allie Reynolds finished second in the AL voting, ninety-seven points behind the Athletics' ace, while teammates Mickey Mantle and Yogi Berra were third and fourth.

The outcry that resulted from the NL voting was unfortunate for Sauer, a genuinely good guy who was so popular with Cubs fans that he became known as the Mayor of Wrigley Field. All he did was try to do the best he could to help his team. The day the award was announced, his wife, Esther, gave birth to their second child, a son they named Hank Jr. Though the derision over his selection was directed mainly at the writers, it ricocheted and stung Sauer at what should have been one of the happiest and most satisfying times of his life. A particularly cruel dig came from Gibbs, the *Baltimore Sun* columnist, who wrote: "You wonder if Hank will ever be able to explain to junior how his dad won the MVP award despite a stretch run sag into mediocrity and such tremendous opposition as Joe Black offered."

Publicly, Joe said all the right things. He was honored to finish so high in the voting, he hoped he would justify that with another strong season in 1953. Years later, Joe said he didn't need the award to boost his ego, nor did he have any ill feelings toward Sauer, who went 1-for-10 against him in 1952 with three strikeouts and no RBIs. Joe had assumed that Roberts would win the award and that if he didn't, the writers would follow the tradition of selecting someone from the pennant-winning team. Yet Joe evidently did feel cheated, because thirty years after the fact, he pointed to an Arthur Daley column in the *New York Times* to sum up what he thought about the voting.

Under a headline that read A QUESTION OF VALUE, Daley wrote that there is no accounting for taste, but "that still can't explain or excuse the selection of Hank Sauer" as the MVP. He went on to scold the three voters who left Joe off their ballots and the one who omitted Roberts. "These omissions bespeak either bias or ignorance," Daley wrote. "Neither can be excused." He also said Sauer's selection exposed "fundamental flaws" in the voting system that undercut the award's value. "How," Daley asked, "could anyone in conscience disregard Black and Roberts?"

Joe did get some consolation. The day after Sauer was announced as the MVP, Joe learned he had been voted the NL's Rookie of the Year by a wide margin—by the very same group of writers who selected the MVP. Each writer voted for only one player as Rookie of the Year and Joe received nineteen votes, with three going to the Giants' Hoyt Wilhelm and one each to Eddie Mathews of the Boston Braves and Dick Groat of the Pittsburgh Pirates. Joe was pleased by the recognition, because he felt the award might go to Wilhelm, who had a slightly better winning percentage and won the ERA title. Others, however, saw it as a makeup vote for the award Joe should have won. The *Afro-American* said it could be seen as the baseball writers' attempt to "soften the disappointment" of those who felt Joe should have been the MVP. Baltimore columnist C. M. Gibbs wrote that for Joe, receiving the Rookie of the Year award must have been as gratifying as "ordering waffles and bacon and having to be satisfied with toast and coffee."

Yet even a die-hard Dodgers fan like Jerry Reinsdorf could understand why the voting turned out as it did. "It was very tough for a starting pitcher, let alone a reliever, to be an MVP," he said. "If Sauer hit a lot of home runs that year, then I can understand that. Clearly [Joe] should have been the Rookie of the Year, and he was."

>>>>>>>>>>

The flap over the MVP vote triggered a discussion over possible changes in the selection process and intensified the debate over whether a separate award should be established for pitchers. Three members of the Baseball Writers' Association of America (BBWAA) were appointed to a committee, headed by J. Roy Stockton of the *St. Louis Post-Dispatch*, to solicit ideas on what, if any, changes should be made. One thought was reducing the voting panel to eight—one writer from each city. One writer suggested starting the process by picking one player from each team. There also was a suggestion for two rounds of voting: after the first vote was tabulated, the writers would vote on the top five.

In the end, no changes were made and the BBWAA accepted the committee's recommendation against creating an award for pitchers. The *Sporting News* had started honoring the top pitcher in each league in 1944 and made it an annual award in 1948. The newspaper often editorialized in favor of a baseball writers' award for pitchers, acknowledging the difficulty—"and often the injustice"—of trying to pick a pitcher as the MVP over an everyday player. It would not be until 1956, the year after pitching great Cy Young died, that an award for pitchers was established in his name. By then, Joe would be near the end of his career. At first, the Cy Young award was given to honor the top pitcher in all of Major League Baseball. The award would be expanded in 1967 to recognize a pitcher in each league.

>>>>>>>>>>

The recognition for Joe didn't stop with the Rookie of the Year Award. He received the annual achievement award from the Harlem branch of the YMCA. The *Afro-American* named Joe its black athlete of the year. The New York Bible Society gave Joe and civil rights activist Channing Tobias its Brooklyn Awards of the year—leather-bound, gilt-edged Bibles. Joe was especially touched by that honor, saying he cherished it more than any of the others he had received. "If you have watched me pitch," he told the audience at the ceremony, "you may have noticed that the third baseman holds the ball a little longer than usual before he returns it to me. That is because he knows I say a prayer before every important pitch to a batter."

Finally, in late December, Joe had time to relax. He took Doris and Carolyn to Cuba for a week in late December, leaving young Chico with Doris's parents in Norfolk. The trip took Joe back to the place where his pitching had propelled him to his sensational 1952 season. Sadly for Joe, his more leisurely trip would not have the same impact in 1953.

18

A Single Parent

MARTHA JO WAS A SURPRISE, AT LEAST to Joe. He was forty-five when he learned his wife, Mae Nell, was pregnant; he was working in a job that ate up much of his time and required frequent travel for speeches and meetings. He was going to be a father again? At his age? That had not been on his radar. Martha Jo suspects she wasn't such a surprise to her mother, who may have felt a child would ensure that she'd have a permanent attachment to Joe and the comfortable life he could provide.

When Chico was born seventeen years earlier, Joe had panicked when Doris's water broke and screamed that she was urinating all over him. The doctor had to control his laughter when Joe called in a tizzy. When Mae Nell went into labor late on the Fourth of July in 1969, Joe knew exactly what was going on. He hustled her into the car, sped away from their apartment in Hyde Park on Chicago's South Side, and headed for Northwestern Memorial Hospital, which is on the north side of downtown.

As Joe peeked in and looked at his little girl for the first time, Roberta Flack's voice floated softly through the hospital's speaker system and Joe caught the words: "The First Time Ever I Saw Your Face." The lyrics touched him as he gazed at his daughter's tiny face, and it became his and Martha Jo's special song.

Joe and Mae Nell lived on Forty-Seventh Street in a high-rise apartment building that faced Lake Michigan. It was a neighborhood rich in culture and diversity that has been home to, among others, Enrico Fermi, Clarence Darrow, Dick Gregory, Hugh Hefner, Muhammad Ali, and, more recently, Barack Obama. Mae Nell thought the location was perfect. Their building had a grocery store on the first floor. It was easy to catch a bus or train to get downtown. They had none of the responsibilities that come with owning a house. Joe agreed the high-rise was great for a couple, but not for a couple with a young child. He insisted that Martha Jo needed a house with a basement and a yard so she could play outside and run around.

They found that house on Yates Avenue, in a mixed residential neighborhood seventy or so blocks south of their apartment. They lived there for fewer than two years. When Greyhound moved its headquarters to Phoenix, Arizona, in 1971, Joe and his family relocated to the desert, settling into a one-story southwestern-style house in a new subdivision in north Phoenix. They had escaped the fierce Chicago winters, Joe was on his way to becoming known as "Mr. Greyhound," and far from being a drag on his life, fatherhood was a blessing. But his marriage unraveled. He and Mae Nell divorced in 1974 and the custody battle ensued.

>>>>>>>>>>

Divorces can be messy, custody battles even more so. I know, because I was right in the middle of both. That's why I found myself sitting in front of a judge one day—when I was five years old.

My father and mother had divorced, and my father had moved out of the house. He had given up on the marriage, but not on being a parent, so he asked the court to grant him sole custody of me. He had a prestigious, well-paid job at Greyhound Corporation and could afford to provide me with whatever I needed. He was a respected figure in his profession. We lived in a spacious house in a growing community. But he believed that being a father went far beyond providing a support check. He never argued that my mother was unfit to care for me. Instead, he made the case that a child needs a parent's love, time, guidance, and loyalty, and he felt he was in the best position to provide that.

There seemed to be little chance that a single African American man, soon to be fifty-one years old, living in conservative Phoenix, Arizona, in 1975 would be awarded custody of his five-year-old daughter. Custody cases were rarely settled that way. My father's attorney, Nicholas Udall, warned that his request was a long shot and my father shouldn't get his hopes too high. Right or wrong, judges almost always sided with the mother.

Because my mother and father argued over custody, the judge handling the case decided to ask me about it. So there I was, not even in grade school yet, sitting in the office of a judge who would, in a way, decide my future.

"Who do you want to live with?" he asked.

"I want to live with my dad," I replied.

When the judge asked why, I told him it was because my dad played with me all the time. He talked to me. He joked around with me. It didn't have anything to do with what he could buy me. He just spent so much time with me.

Growing up I was such a tomboy. I'd get dirty while I was playing and come inside, and my mother would be wearing beautiful white linen pants. I'd be ready to jump on her and she'd say, "Oh, no, Poopsie. I don't want to get dirty." That's what she called me, Poopsie. My dad could come home from work in a suit and I'd jump on him and he was OK with that. I saw my father as somebody who was always there regardless of what was going on. With my mother, I had to be pretty. My hair had to be done. I didn't want any of that then. Now, yes. But then, I just wanted to play. So when the judge asked me who I wanted to live with, the answer was easy.

My father.

I would like to think what I said influenced the judge. How much, I don't know, but I'm sure he took it into consideration. Because when Nicholas Udall called my father on that day in January 1975, he was able to say, "Joe, you're not going to believe this, but you won custody of your daughter." All my dad could say was, "Thank God." He wasn't saying, "Thank God I got her away from her mother." That was not how he felt. He was just happy the judge listened to him. He tried to counter the stereotype that African American men were irresponsible fathers. He argued that nothing other than custom says the mother automatically should get custody of the child. He put it so well in his autobiography: "God never said that only females have the ability to be a parent."

My father was never too embarrassed to say he loved me or he was proud of me. He was everything a parent should be—and more.

>>>>>>>>>>

It was not Joe's first divorce, nor would it be his last. Joe married seven times, tying the knot for the first time on a bet, and all seven marriages ended in divorce. He married women older, younger, and much younger, and it didn't make any difference. The marriages all fizzled. Joe's friends puzzled over why a warm, gregarious person who seemed so interested in the welfare of others could not stay married.

"Maybe he didn't choose well," Jerry Reinsdorf said. "Maybe he chose to marry the women that he wanted to sleep with, but that's not necessarily the right thing." At Reinsdorf's invitation, Joe spoke to the Chicago White Sox players one spring about what it meant to be a Major League player. He warned them about people who might want to take advantage of them, the pitfalls they should avoid, and the women who might make themselves available. "He just knew," Reinsdorf said. "He knew who the good guys were and who the bad guys were. That's why it's so incongruous that he had all these marriages. Outside of that, his ability to size up people was terrific."

Joe could be stubborn and insistent on doing things his way. Chico said that might have contributed to the breakdown in his father's marriages. "He was a dominant kind of person," Chico said. "I knew all the wives. Did he somehow just get tired of all of them? I don't think so. Maybe his wives got tired of him."

According to Joe, some of his wives could not understand that even though he associated with celebrities, politicians, and top business executives, he was a homebody. He didn't want to be part of the social scene of parties and dances and big events. He preferred taking his wife to a movie or a play where they could sit and hold hands, or maybe just spend a quiet evening at home. Not all his wives were content to do that, and the friction that resulted ruined the marriages. One marriage ended after he returned from a business trip in 1964 and found his wife had taken all her clothes and left. When Joe finally reached her by phone, she told him—much to his puzzlement—that her family urged her to leave him because his complexion was too dark.

In the end, Joe conceded that neither he nor his wives worked hard enough on the marriages. "We were not willing to take the bitter with the sweet," he wrote in his autobiography. He also felt it was hypocritical to stay in a failed marriage just for the sake of appearances. If it wasn't working and couldn't be reconciled, they should split. Why should two people stay together if they're just going to bicker and be angry all the time, a point on which his sister Phyllis concurred. "I knew all of his wives. I got along with all of them," she said. "I don't have anything detrimental to say. But there's no need living in misery if you can't get along."

Joe knew the judge's decision in the custody case would not be popular in some circles. At the time, a little more than a third of all black parents nationally were raising children by themselves, and only 3 percent of those single-parent families were headed by men. Joe shrugged off the thought that women might stare at him and think, "How dare you take a child from her mother," or that men might shake their heads and think he was crazy for giving up his freedom to care for a little girl. He felt no joy in "defeating" his former wife in court and understood her disappointment in the outcome. Joe also believed that Martha Jo needed to maintain a relationship with her mother, so he allowed her to spend time with Mae Nell beyond the dates spelled out in the decree. If Mae Nell wanted to see Martha Jo, Joe usually was fine with that.

With the custody battle settled, Joe started out on a new phase in his life. He had become a single parent, and was ready—no, more than ready, he was eager—to meet the challenges that responsibility would bring. "You can bet I was a proud man when my daughter and I walked into our home," he wrote later.

>>>>>>>>>>

There were rough times, too. One of the most embarrassing episodes in Joe's working career occurred in Chicago while he was speaking to about two hundred people at one of Greyhound's Woman of the Year luncheons. It was a Saturday in June 1976, more than a year after he and Mae Nell divorced. Joe noticed Mae Nell entering the room with three men, and two of them walked to the podium, forcing Joe to excuse himself to the audience and stop in the middle of his speech. One of the men identified himself as a Cook County sheriff's deputy who had a warrant for Joe's arrest. Mae Nell was suing him for divorce, which stunned Joe, because their divorce had been finalized in Arizona. And if that wasn't enough to ruin Joe's day, the deputy added that he would have to go to jail until a court hearing on Monday—unless he posted a $20,000 bond.

Joe did well financially, but there was no way he could come up with that kind of money on short notice. One of the luncheon sponsors knew the judge, so he called him and the judge agreed to reduce the cash requirement to $10,000 if Joe could find an attorney to file a request for the reduction. Another friend found an attorney, and Joe's call to Greyhound president Raymond F. Shaffer brought the Chicago terminal manager to the banquet hall with the $10,000 in cash. Joe avoided jail time, but he had to comply with the court date. His own attorney, Nicholas Udall, flew in from Phoenix and enlisted a local attorney to represent Joe in court.

Mae Nell had been upset with the divorce settlement because she did not receive any alimony, and Joe believed her friends had persuaded her to "get Joe Black." The local attorney, Samuel Patterson, showed the judge the Arizona divorce papers and the case was dismissed. Joe then went to Mae Nell and pleaded with her to stop harassing him. His name had already been splashed across the newspapers because of the warrant for his arrest. With any more bad publicity, Greyhound might consider him a liability and fire him. If that happened, how could he afford to take care of their daughter? As Joe recalled, Mae Nell retorted: "That's just like a black man. He doesn't want to support his children."

Another dispute caught Martha Jo in the middle. Mae Nell moved to Chicago after the divorce and Martha Jo visited her there occasionally. During one of her visits, when Martha Jo was ten, Joe returned from a business trip five days after his daughter was supposed to have been back in Phoenix, only to find she was still in Chicago. Angered, Joe called Mae Nell, they argued, and Mae Nell said she was keeping Martha Jo there. So Joe flew to Chicago, drove to the brownstone Mae Nell shared with her mother and an aunt, and yelled as he stood outside, "Mae Nell, send her down! We're leaving!" Martha Jo wanted to go to her father, but Mae Nell kept her inside. Joe finally called the police, who escorted Martha Jo to her father.

It wasn't the first time police got involved in Joe's squabbles with Mae Nell. Back when they first divorced, Mae Nell called the police so they'd be at the house to make sure Joe moved out. They waited at the door while Joe packed some belongings, then escorted him to his car.

>>>>>>>>>>

Losing the custody case hurt my mother. She had a hard time coping with the fact that her daughter was in someone else's care, especially when it was a man with whom she had a falling out. Not long after my father moved back to the house and my mother moved out, she pulled up in her car as our housekeeper, Sandy, was about to drop me off at kindergarten. My mother walked up to me and said, "Oh Poopsie, look what I have for you." I started to go to her and Sandy said, "Martha, you need to go inside."

I said, "No, no, it's my mother."

"No," she insisted, "you have to go inside."

I went to my mother's car anyway, and she opened the back and it was filled with boxes and boxes of Barbie toys. I was thrilled. I couldn't even begin to think what I was going to do with all those toys. "Let's go play," my mother said. "You don't need to go to school. You can go tomorrow." Sandy knew what my father would think about that, so she grabbed me, put me in the car, locked the door and started to drive away. My mother pursued us, but Sandy kept driving. The area where the students were dropped off wasn't paved. It was gravel, and my mother fell. I was crying because she had fallen on the gravel and I didn't understand what was going on.

Even with all the bickering between my mother and my father, I never lost my feelings for her. After living in Chicago for a while, she moved back to Phoenix and worked at a bank. But she was unhappy in that job, so when we needed a new housekeeper, I told my father he should hire her. Amazingly, he did. He ended up paying my mother to look after me, and she lived at our house for free. My father gave her money for groceries and because she was such a good cook, it was a win-win situation. But only for a while.

When the woman who turned out to be my father's last wife moved in with three of her four children, my mother moved out because we no longer needed a housekeeper. He told me he was going to marry this woman and she would be living at our house with her children. I had been an only child for so long that I knew I couldn't handle other children being around, so I moved out, too, and went to live with my mother. We moved to an apartment in Scottsdale, about ten minutes from the house. I was sixteen, and it was the most difficult time I ever had in my relationship with my father. Maybe it was teenage jealousy, but I no longer felt as though he put me first. I had been spoiled by all the attention he had lavished on me and now someone else was getting it. I didn't know how to accept that. It hurt. We didn't speak to each other for a year and a half other than an occasional phone call to say hi, how are you, what have you been doing?

My dad told my Aunt Phyll, "I wish Martha would allow me to be happy, to be with a significant other." It's something you don't necessarily see when you're younger, but now I understand how he felt. We eventually worked out our differences, of course. By the time I went to college, my father was divorced again—for the final time.

I got along well with my mother. My father gave her money to help pay for what I needed. It wasn't required legally. He just felt it was the right thing to do. My mother also spoiled me in a way with her cooking. I wish I would have learned more from her. My friends were having sloppy joes for dinner. I'd have steamed lobster and broccoli—and figured that was normal. I thought most people had that.

My mother had to be a fighter because she was diagnosed with cervical cancer a month after I was born. She had treatment and got better, but the cancer came back thirty years later. I had just learned about that when my father visited and took me out to eat. I started to cry and, between sobs, told him I was scared because my mother was sick and would die soon. I was realizing that my parents wouldn't be with me forever, and that's a frightening thought. My dad took my hand and tried to assure me that my mother would be OK and nothing was going to happen to him, though he probably had cancer at the time and didn't know it. But my nightmare scenario became reality. My mother died March 15, 2002, and my father died two months later.

>>>>>>>>>>

While Joe never expected to have Martha Jo in his life, she arrived at a point in his Greyhound career when he needed an extra nudge. The same had been true when Chico was born during his rookie season with the Dodgers. Both careers had their own pressures, which sometimes left Joe tired and frustrated. As he put it, all it took was a "grin and gurgled ga-ga" from Chico or Martha Jo to revive him.

Children also can disappoint their parents, cause them grief and pain, and leave them heartsick. A phone call in 1979 did that to Joe. The caller delivered some of the worst possible news: Chico had been arrested. "For a while, I couldn't breathe or talk," Joe recalled. He got up, walked over to his office door, closed it, then sat back down at his desk and put his head in his hands as the magnitude of the news overwhelmed him. Joe remembered feeling too shocked and hurt to cry as he kept asking himself, how could this have happened? It must be a mistake.

But it wasn't. Joe hired an attorney, then watched with a gnawing pain in his heart as his son was convicted of burglary and assault and sent to prison.

"I took some drugs," Chico said. "It made me do some stupid things and I ended up doing seven years. Everyone knew, 'That's not you,' they'd say. I know, I'd tell them. It's not me. I paid for what I did." Chico knew the person he hurt the worst was his father. He apologized and asked for his forgiveness. "I think he forgave me," he said. "I ask for his forgiveness every day. Later on, I realized I didn't just tarnish his name, I tarnished him. Because I knew all his friends knew what I had done."

Chico went to prison in the fall of 1979 and was released in 1986. He started his term in maximum security, then was moved to medium security before being allowed to finish his sentence as an outside trustee. "That's something that's behind me," he said. "I don't dwell on the past. The only thing I've got to do is worry about now and the future. The only thing the past can help me with is you learn from it. Then you don't do it again. That's what the past is for."

>>>>>>>>>>

Fathers in general seem especially protective of their daughters, and that certainly was truc for Joe, who remained involved in Martha Jo's life even after she established herself in a career. She never found him to be suffocating, only concerned. And oh, did he get concerned when he learned that she was dating Chicago White Sox pitcher James Baldwin. He lit up like a threat sensor on a fighter jet. "She's not going out with a player," he told Len Coleman. "I've been in too many locker rooms. It's not happening."

Coleman told Joe to lighten up, that Martha Jo was a grown woman and could take care of herself. But that didn't stop him. His mind was made up: that relationship wasn't about to go any further. White Sox slugger Frank Thomas, who's now in the Hall of Fame, got wind of Joe's impending visit and teased Baldwin, "Better watch out when Big Daddy comes. This ballgame is going to change."

Joe went to Chicago and was sitting with Martha Jo in the press box when she pointed Baldwin out. After Joe noticed a woman and a little boy waving at him, Martha Jo explained that was Baldwin's son and Sharon, the boy's mother. Joe took that in and said he would be at the ballpark early the next day because he wanted to talk to some of the players. When Albert Belle saw him walk into the clubhouse, he knew what was coming and turned to Baldwin.

"JB," he said, "the real man is here to talk to you, I'm sure."

"I'm not scared," Baldwin said.

"Well," Belle cautioned, "wait till you meet him."

Joe's message wasn't "stay away from my daughter." Instead, he told Baldwin he should marry his child's mother. And he did. James and Sharon's son, James Baldwin III, starred in three sports at his father's high school in Southern Pines, North Carolina, and was drafted by the Los Angeles Dodgers in 2010.

>>>>>>>>>>

I think James reminded my father too much of himself, and dads don't want daughters to date people like them. James was a nice guy. My father talked to him all the time.

My father was never selfish with his counsel and advice. His nature was to share, and he did so willingly. When my cousin, Bridgette Greer, failed the bar exam on her first try in 1988, Dad sat down at his typewriter and composed a letter to her, starting by apologizing for typing his thoughts instead of writing them by hand. His penmanship wasn't as neat as it had once been, he explained.

"Your failing is not a reflection on your intellect," he wrote. "However, it is a test to see if you are a competitive person who maintains the faith that you can overcome." He reminded her of his experience being told that colored guys didn't play Major League baseball and wrote, "You are now challenged to prove to yourself that you can accept adversity as well as accolades. Follow the suggestion of Nehemiah 8:10 and 'Do not grieve, for the joy of the Lord is your strength.'" My father closed with "Love from an uncle who believes in you." Bridgette took the exam again, and passed. She is now a deputy county attorney in Maryland.

My friend Charisse Andrews was distraught when our dear friend Leslie Allen died of meningitis in 1999. She couldn't stop crying, so I asked my father to write to her. He told her it was OK to cry and to wonder why a friend was taken. "Mourn for Leslie; miss Leslie; and use her memory as a weapon to overcome other challenges in your life," he wrote. "It has been said that God does not take away without a plan to give something in return." He reminded Charisse of the Bible verse, "Blessed are those who mourn, for they will be comforted."

"You can best honor and revere Leslie by continuing on the path of goodness as you strive to reach out to others as you seek the mountain top," he continued. "Life is still beautiful so get out of the dark and into the sunshine." He signed the letter, "Martha's dad, Joe."

In 1997, a woman in Joe's church was going through a difficult time. No one asked my father to write to her. He did so on his own, to let her know people cared about her. "I am numbered among the many people who miss you and pray that we will soon be seeing your smiling face," he wrote. "Additionally, I am a little selfish; you see, I need you as my example when I stress to the older adult members that we need to have more young people like you in the congregation. Don't laugh! Don't worry about people whispering behind your back, because you are still a Child of God." My father tried to reassure her with this quote: "God did not create us to laugh or cry alone, that's why He made Friends." He closed by telling her to "hurry home, we all miss you."

Maybe my father missed his calling. For all the good he did as a teacher and at Greyhound, he would have been a compassionate and understanding counselor. I know he was that as a father. I never really gave it a second thought that I grew up in a house without both a mother and a father. I never felt I was missing anything, and that's sad to say because a mother never wants to hear that. But I never felt I was missing a mother because my dad did everything for me.

I'm reminded of something Sigmund Freud once said: "I cannot think of any need in childhood as strong as the need for a father's protection." I'm so very lucky to be able to say I had that.

19

A Star Fades

1953

Joe Black seemed destined for a big season in 1953. After his dazzling success in '52, there was no reason to expect it wouldn't continue. At twenty-nine years old, he still was in his prime as an athlete. He had shown no signs of arm trouble, and with a year of experience, he knew his way around the league. Writer Tom Meany predicted in *Collier's* that if Charlie Dressen used Joe as both a starter and a reliever, he should win twenty games. A story in the newspaper *Grit* said Joe "probably will be the mainstay of the Brooklyn mound staff for years." Pee Wee Reese declared, "Joe Black should be better than he was last year." Those words could not have been comforting to National League hitters.

Joe tried to stay level headed through all the awards and honors, not to mention the glowing copy turned out by writers who found the big right-hander to be such an eloquent, willing source for their stories. But it wasn't easy. "Basking in the sunlight of national publicity and adulation gives one a feeling of importance, and it takes a great effort to keep your feet on the ground," Joe wrote in his autobiography. "It is easy for a person to start believing that he is Mr. Big. Well, I did have my share of moments thinking that the world was mine."

He found a remedy for that in his family. Joe spent a lot of time in Plainfield during the off-season. He saw his mother still doing housework, his sisters and brother working in factories. They still lived in the house on East Fourth Street, next to the railroad tracks. He saw his friends continuing to do whatever they could to try to make it. In such circumstances, Joe knew he had to shed his star persona and just be Sonny Black again. His name had appeared in the sports pages in previous years—though certainly not as it did in 1952—so he tried to go about his business as though everything that had happened was no big deal. He had been lucky, and he knew it.

Joe was also determined to show that his success had not made him complacent. He and Roy Campanella went to Hot Springs, Arkansas, to lose weight so they'd show up at training camp in the best shape possible. Joe shed 13 pounds, dropping to 229. Campy weighed in at 203 pounds after reporting at 221 the year before. Joe returned home to get Doris so they could drive to Vero Beach, and both he and Campy reported early. Joe said he felt the same eagerness and desire that he'd had in 1952, but was more relaxed because he was part of the team, and a key part at that. He wouldn't have to prove himself. He wasn't cocky, he thought, only confident.

Yet an undercurrent of unease ran just below that confident exterior. Whenever a player had a big season as a rookie, it was inevitable that people wondered whether he would fall victim to the dreaded "sophomore jinx," that for whatever reason—ego, laziness, weaknesses finally being exposed—his performance would suffer and he wouldn't match what he had done the previous season. It's never been proven that such a jinx actually exists, but that has never stopped the speculation. And it didn't stop Joe from worrying. The Dodger coaches noticed and they worried, too, fearing their relief ace might lose his confidence. They needed Joe concentrating on getting hitters out, not fretting over whether some mysterious force would rob him of his effectiveness.

Even though Joe's Major League career started late, it certainly seemed he could continue giving the Dodgers double figures in victories and saves for at least a few more years.

Then came the grand experiment and, for Joe, its calamitous result.

>>>>>>>>>>

After his big winter season in Cuba, Joe had spent much of spring training in 1952 working on his control and follow-through. Both he and the Dodgers were rewarded for that work with his spectacular season. But as the Dodgers gathered in Vero Beach to begin preparing for the 1953 season, manager Charlie Dressen thought Joe needed to do more. He insisted that his big right-hander learn a new pitch.

Joe had gotten by just fine the year before with his 90-plus-mile-an-hour fastball, his slider, and pinpoint control. But Dressen didn't think Joe could duplicate his success without giving hitters something else to think about, and it's understandable why he felt that way. Major league hitters are good and they're smart. If the guy on the mound has only two pitches, hitters don't have to do much guessing. They can wait him out until they get the pitch they want. But with his sharp control, Joe consistently put the ball right where Campy held his mitt. He didn't need a changeup or a big sweeping curve to keep the hitters off balance. He did it with location.

The previous fall, Dressen had urged Joe to experiment with a knuckleball during his barnstorming tour. He fiddled with the pitch for a couple of weeks, then gave it up. That winter, according to Joe, Dressen ran into Pittsburgh Pirates first baseman–outfielder George Metkovich, who had hit a meaningless home run off Joe late in the 1952 season. Metkovich, the story went, told Dressen that Joe needed to change his delivery because he was "easy to read."

So Joe began the spring with orders to learn a new pitch. All his instincts told him to ignore those instructions. He thought Dressen and the other coaches should be concentrating on the pitchers who struggled in 1952. He also remembered a warning from Don Newcombe: *don't let them mess with your pitching style.* But Joe wanted to be the good soldier and show he was coachable, so he went along.

That Dressen pressed Joe to try something different surprised no one. "Charlie was always a tinkerer who couldn't leave anything alone," Carl Erskine said. "He had to work at it, he had to change it, he had to have his hand in it," added Tommy Lasorda, the one-time Dodgers pitcher who later spent twenty-one seasons as the club's manager. "You never had to wonder if Charlie was a genius. Right up front Charlie cleared that one up. He told you that he was a genius. Told you so himself." Dressen's proclivity to poke his nose into everything was apparent even to opponents. "Dressen thought he was the best manager in the world," Monte Irvin said.

The Dodgers at the time did not have a former pitcher on their coaching staff. Dressen was an infielder during his playing days. So were all three of his coaches: Billy Herman, Cookie Lavagetto, and Jake Pitler. Erskine always felt pitchers were somewhat disrespected, because no one on the coaching staff really understood them. "It was like this," he said. "The manager comes to the mound and says, 'Look, this guy at the plate is the best hitter in the league. You've got two men on, the score is tied. Now, don't give this guy anything good to hit. But don't walk him.' That's how smart managers were in how to deal with a pitcher."

What happened, Erskine said, is that pitchers usually went to other pitchers for advice or help. Erskine had a slick changeup, so Dressen ordered him to try to teach Joe how to throw it. He told Joe to grip the ball as he would a fastball, then raise his fingers and let the ball roll back until he felt pressure on his knuckles. Delivered with such a grip, the ball rotated like a fastball but with a third less speed. Erskine remembered the conversation.

"I can't do that," Joe said.

"You haven't even tried it yet," Erskine implored.

"No," Joe insisted. "I can't do it."

Then he showed Carl why. Joe had large hands and held both out for Carl to see. "Both index fingers fell limp," Erskine said. "He couldn't hold them out straight."

"So," he added, "we gave up on that pitch."

Joe then tried the knuckleball again. He experimented with a forkball and a sinker. But he couldn't grip any of those pitches properly, either. The coaches worked with him on adjusting his stride, lengthening it at times and shortening it other times. He would stride toward first base when trying to get the ball to sink or throw across his body to try to slow his curveball. If the consequences had not been so serious, Joe thought, it would have been comical. He bounced some pitches halfway to home plate and winged others over the catcher's head.

Finally, Dressen had seen enough and told Joe to go back to his old style of pitching. But by that point, it was too late. Joe felt he had been tinkered with so much, he couldn't remember how he used to pitch. Teammates offered advice and that only confused him even more. He raised up on his toes before pivoting in his windup, one said. Another said he hunched his shoulders as he wound up. Still another said Joe wasn't turning his back to the hitters as much in his windup. His stride was too open, he was told, and that slowed his pitches.

"Spring training went from a fun time to confusion and doubt," Joe wrote years later.

Results were mixed as Joe struggled to sort things out.

One account said he was "roundly cheered" after he allowed only one run and two hits in a five-inning stint against the Philadelphia Phillies in Miami. In his next appearance, a crowd of more than twelve thousand in Miami could see that something wasn't right with Joe. He started against the Yankees and walked three batters in the first inning, throwing ten straight balls at one point. His four-inning totals were anything but encouraging: four runs and seven hits. Joe bounced back with solid outings against the Senators, Braves, and Yankees, then was up and down the rest of the spring as he fought to regain his confidence and control.

Asked by reporters why Joe looked to be out of sorts, Dressen tapped his head and said, "It's mostly up here. Black has been reading so much about the sophomore jinx that he's let it worry him. He had such a great freshman season that he feels he can't escape sloughing off the way most second-year men do."

But on opening day, Dressen turned to Joe after the Pittsburgh Pirates scored four times against Carl Erskine in the fourth inning. Joe held them to one run and two hits the rest of the way and got the victory in an 8–5 win. One game in, and Joe already was a month and a half ahead of his 1952 victory pace. And he kept winning. By mid-June, he was 5–2 with five saves. But those figures belied his actual performance. He didn't dominate batters the way he had a year earlier. They not only hit him, they hit him hard, and his earned run average soared past 5.00. He survived because the Dodgers clubbed opponents with the league's best offense.

Joe gave up eight runs in his next two appearances, which totaled only three and two-thirds innings, and that sealed his fate in Dressen's eyes. He banished Joe first to middle relief, then seemed to forget about him altogether. After the Braves hammered Joe for three runs and five hits in one and two-thirds innings on July 24, Joe did not pitch again until August 21. Dressen moved Jim Hughes into the closer's role, then gave the job to Clem Labine, who was outstanding down the stretch as the Dodgers ran away with the pennant.

"I was not a pitcher," Joe wrote long after he had finished playing. "I was a thrower, without control and confidence. I was nothing. I dreaded being asked to pitch in a game. I felt like a soldier in a war zone without a gun." A pitcher who once exuded an aura of total control turned paranoid. Joe started to imagine that hitters stole Campy's signals. Sometimes he feared batters figured out where he wanted to locate a pitch by reading his eyes. He lamented that hitters he had intimidated in 1952 "were using me for batting practice."

He felt teammates looked on him with pity. Even some opponents felt bad for him and offered advice. Warren Spahn and Lou Burdette, the Milwaukee Braves aces, told Joe his motion wasn't as smooth as it had been the previous year. They also said he looked like a beaten pitcher the moment he entered the game. Cincinnati Reds slugger Ted Kluszewski told Joe that instead of making hitters beat down on the ball, which he had done so effectively in 1952, his pitches were three inches higher, allowing batters to get under them and put more wood on the ball.

New York Giants outfielder Monte Irvin noticed a difference, too. "Joe wasn't mean," Irvin said. "He'd brush you back a little, but he wouldn't try to hit anybody in the head. What he would do was try to keep the ball down and away from you. He was very effective [in 1952]. Then in '53, that's when I started to hit against him in the majors. You could tell he wasn't the same Joe as '52."

Young fans like Jerry Reinsdorf also could see that something had gone wrong with their team's one-time star. "It was apparent he wasn't getting guys out. And we all thought it was because it was Charlie Dressen's fault," Reinsdorf said. "Why did you mess around with a guy that had success? You never try to change a guy who's having success. But Dressen was a self-styled genius, and he felt they had to do it."

Even the great Satchel Paige offered an opinion on Joe's struggles, coming down on Dressen's side. "In the majors, you have to get a new pitch every year," Paige said. "That's why Joe Black didn't have such a good year this summer. He was sensational last year, but once the batters got to know what he was throwing all the time, they murdered him. Now if he'd develop some new pitch, he'd be all right."

>>>>>>>>>>

Carl Erskine said he never saw Joe despondent over his troubles, just mystified, as was Erskine. "We're talking about a mystery here," Carl said. "Nobody figured it out." But one writer saw a despondent figure when he noticed Joe in the bullpen on a damp August night at Ebbets Field.

The Dodgers trailed the Pittsburgh Pirates 2–0 when Bob Milliken entered the game in the top of the ninth inning to pitch for Brooklyn. Joe started to warm up then, and when Milliken walked the first two batters, Joe started throwing harder, noted Jack Hernon of the *Pittsburgh Post-Gazette*. Maybe, Hernon speculated, Joe would pitch for the first time in almost a month. Though Milliken got out of the inning, Joe kept throwing. The Dodgers tied the game in the bottom of the ninth on Duke Snider's two-run homer, and Dressen raced from the third base coaching box to the dugout. Hernon, who called Joe "last year's hero, this year's bum," recounted what happened next.

> He called the bullpen and the next instant, Black was brushed aside and Clem Labine and Glenn Mickens began warming up. Dressen no longer had any faith in Black. Joe pulled on his blue jacket with "Dodgers" written across the front and walked to the bullpen bench along the right field wall.
>
> Black didn't sit there with his back against the fence. He slumped down and was a lonely-looking man out there all by himself.

Labine got the call and did his job, pitching two perfect innings as the Dodgers rallied to win 5–2. By then it had become clear that Labine was the new Joe Black. Roscoe McGowen of the *Times* suggested Joe might be better off going down to Montreal or St. Paul so he could pitch regularly and maybe regain his old form. Joe had the right to say whether he wanted to go down or stay, McGowen wrote, but as things stood, "Dressen cannot afford to send [Joe] into a close game as long as he has other fellows such as Ben Wade and Jim Hughes, who have shown ability—not always of course—to halt an opposition rally. Therefore, Black well could go along the rest of the campaign without a real chance to prove whether he has come back."

McGowen wasn't alone in that thinking. Buzzie Bavasi went so far as to ask Joe if he wanted to return to the minors to try to straighten things out. Bavasi felt Joe deserved the right to make that decision because of what he had done for the team in 1952. Joe decided to stay, and McGowen was proven to be correct. As the Dodgers charged toward the pennant, Joe pitched only seven times in the season's final six weeks, mostly without distinction.

Dressen's reason for making Labine the closer was never more apparent than on September 4 at the Polo Grounds. Joe relieved in the sixth inning and gave up a game-tying home run to Al Dark. Dressen yanked him and inserted Labine, who retired all ten hitters he faced and got the victory as the Dodgers won 8–6.

Joe couldn't even hack it in an exhibition game against the Cleveland Indians. Dressen wanted Joe to pitch the first five innings of the August 10 game in Cleveland. But he lasted only four, giving up five runs and eight hits, including a double, two triples, and a home run in the 8–6 Indians victory. The *Sporting News* account of the game called Joe the "Dodgers' ace of 1952 and flop of '53."

But that exhibition loss was just a tiny speed bump for the Brooklyn express. The Dodgers reeled off thirteen straight victories from August 7 through August 20. Labine picked up four wins during that stretch and Erskine three. Erskine was 15-5 at that point, and the Dodgers had won thirty-two of thirty-eight. They knew then how the Giants must have felt during their late-season charge two years earlier—that nothing could stop them.

And nothing did. The Dodgers announced on September 10 they would start taking orders for World Series tickets. Two days later, they clinched the pennant with a 5–2 victory over the Braves in Milwaukee behind Erskine's nineteenth victory. It was the earliest a team had ever clinched in a 154-game schedule. In another two days, it was all over in the American League, too, the Yankees clinching their fifth straight AL pennant and their twentieth overall. It would be yet another Subway Series.

Joe had not had much to do with it. He was involved in only two decisions after June 5, losing to the Phillies and beating the Reds. Joe recorded three straight saves from June 10 through June 14, working seven scoreless innings, but didn't have another during the rest of the season. He had flopped, but his team had thrived. The Dodgers won a franchise record 105 games and finished thirteen games ahead of the Braves. They were shut out only once all season, batted .285 as a team, clubbed 208 home runs, and led the league with ninety stolen bases.

The highlight for Joe in the season's final weeks came when he throttled the Cincinnati Reds over the final six innings of a 10–3 victory. Joe gave up just one run and two hits, fueling speculation that Dressen would use him as a starter in the World Series, in part because Billy Loes and Johnny Podres had not been as effective as hoped. Loes had struggled as a starter since mid-July, and Podres had pitched only three complete games.

Then again, there were many who thought it didn't matter who pitched for the Dodgers because their hitting was so potent. Gil Hodges, Duke Snider, and Roy Campanella each drove in at least 122 runs, Campy leading the league with 142. Snider smacked 42 home runs, Campy 41, and Hodges 31. Carl Furillo led the league in hitting at .344, though he missed ten days late in the season after breaking a bone in his left hand while tussling with Giants manager Leo Durocher. Jim Gilliam, who had been called up to the big club in '53, scored 125 runs, walked 100 times, rapped a league-leading 17 triples, and stole 21 bases. He later would be voted the National League Rookie of the Year, the same honor Joe had received the previous season.

If the Dodgers were ever going to win the World Series, 1953 seemed to be the year. "This is the greatest Brooklyn team of all time," owner Walter O'Malley declared. "Their numbers would bend the back of a camel," Yankees star Mickey Mantle marveled. Rogers Hornsby, who was fired as the Cincinnati Reds' manager in mid-September, noted, "If the Dodgers don't beat the Yankees this time, they ought to cut their throats."

No one cut anyone's throat, but the Dodgers stumbled again, losing in six games. And Joe could have just as well gone home early. After starting three times in the 1952 series, he pitched one measly inning in the 1953 classic, mopping up in the ninth inning of game five with the Yankees leading 10–6. He struck out Billy Martin, gave up a home run to Gil McDougald, then retired Phil Rizzuto and Bob Kuzava to end the inning.

Joe couldn't have known it then, but those were the last pitches he would throw in a World Series. His record for the season, 6-3, didn't look bad on paper, but he had only five saves, his earned run average ballooned to 5.30, and Dressen no longer trusted him in a meaningful game. The confidence he had lost while trying those different pitches in the spring never returned. "Except for maybe an inning or two here or there," Erskine said, "it seemed like he never regained that magic he had the year before."

>>>>>>>>>>

Joe again barnstormed with Roy Campanella's all-star team of black players, a tour that took them through the South before ending with games in Hawaii and on the West Coast. They played twenty-six games in thirty days, with Joe pitching, filling in as the right fielder, and serving as road secretary. He struggled early, telling Michael Gaven of the *New York Journal-American*, "I was still aiming the ball like I did all season, scared to death somebody was going to hit it over the fence." He eventually settled in, and Campy returned from the tour to report that Joe had been as fast as ever and his little curve broke as sharply as it had in 1952. "I think the trip did a lot for him," Campy said. "I think he got back his confidence and he'll do a lot better—a lot better—next year."

While that was encouraging, it was hardly the biggest news involving the Dodgers. In mid-October, Dressen left the team in a dispute with Walter O'Malley. Dressen wanted a raise and a multiyear contract. O'Malley insisted on one year. Neither side budged, so Dressen was gone, off to California to manage the Oakland Oaks in the Pacific Coast League. Pee Wee Reese seemed the logical choice to replace Dressen, but he didn't want the job. So the Dodgers turned to Walt Alston, who had managed many of the Brooklyn players in the club's farm system at Nashua, St. Paul, and Montreal. Soft-spoken and unassuming, Alston would be a stark contrast to the talkative, peppery Dressen.

Joe had played for Alston at Montreal in 1951, so he felt he knew what to expect. And it wasn't all positive, at least in Joe's mind. "I just always had the theory that Alston resented you if you were black and had a college education, because he was a college graduate [Miami University in Ohio]," Joe said. "I looked back, he loved Campy, he loved Newk, he loved Gilliam, but he didn't like Jackie. When I was in Montreal in '51, he favored Gilliam and Hector Rodriguez, but he had to tolerate me because they sent him there. I didn't feel any warmth. When I got to St. Paul, I felt more warmth from Clay Hopper from Mississippi than I did from Alston." Then again, after Dressen's tinkering in the spring, maybe a change at the top would help Joe. Campy had said after the tour that while Joe had thrown an effective slow curve, he felt his friend was determined to go back to the two pitches that had served him so well as a rookie.

As the off-season dragged on, some bitterness built up in Joe and he let it get the best of him. It surfaced in some comments that led to a spat with his former manager. Talking about his poor season with *JET* magazine, Joe blamed it on Dressen. "It wasn't the sophomore jinx which ruined me last season," he said. "It was Dressen." Joe went on to say that in trying to learn new pitches, he lost his control. Oscar Fraley of United Press quoted Joe as saying the same thing at the Hickok Award dinner in Rochester, New York, blaming his woes on Dressen's experiment. According to Fraley, Joe said, "I experimented—and completely lost my control." The writer also said Joe told him that Dressen never spoke to him after mid-May. "It got real embarrassing because my locker was next to Junior Gilliam's and Dressen had to come up and talk to Gilliam every once in a while," Fraley quoted Joe as saying. "It got so bad that I had to go to some of the other players and ask them what I was doing wrong."

Joe's slide in 1953 had been one of the great mysteries of the season, so Fraley's story ran in newspapers across the country. BLACK BLAMES FLOP ON DRESSEN, one headline read. Another blared, JOE BLACK BLAMES DRESSEN FOR POOR SHOWING LAST YEAR. The *Oakland Tribune*, a newspaper that covered Dressen's new team, took another tack: JOE BLACK HAPPY AS DRESSEN LEAVES, though nowhere in the story did Joe imply he felt that way.

Dressen quickly fired back, telling the *Oakland Tribune* that Joe had a short memory. "Joe apparently has forgotten that if it hadn't been for me, he never would have had a chance to pitch for Brooklyn in the first place," the former Dodgers skipper told the paper. "If there's something wrong in trying to get a man to improve himself, then I'm guilty as charged." Dressen contended that Buzzie Bavasi and other team officials didn't think Joe would make it in the spring of 1952. "But I thought he had a chance and my hunch paid off," he said. Later, Dressen told another writer, "I had to beg the Brooklyn front office not to send him back to the minors in 1952."

Both men eventually toned down their rhetoric, Joe going so far as to say his remarks at the dinner in Rochester had been misinterpreted. "A lot of people thought I had a sore arm," he said. "I never did, and I guess that while I was explaining that there was nothing wrong with my arm, but that I was unsuccessful in getting a new pitch, somebody got the impression I was blaming Dressen. I'm pretty unhappy about that." As for his inability to learn a new pitch, Joe said, "That wasn't Dressen's fault, but mine." Dressen said he had nothing against Joe and added, "I'd take Black as a pitcher for the Oaks right now if I could have him."

Once Joe and Charlie had made nice, Fraley wrote that he had been accused of twisting the facts, but he stood by his original story from Rochester. He also contended that someone "got to Black and ordered a retraction" because he had made Dressen look bad. "I don't know, or care, what alliances remain between Dressen . . . and the Brooklyn front office," Fraley wrote. "But I have a suspicion there must be some from the way they are striving to save face for Whistling Charlie."

From his vantage point producing the Dodgers' telecasts and radio broadcasts, Tom Villante was convinced that Dressen did, indeed, ruin Joe with his meddling. He was just as adamant on that point sixty years later.

"Charlie Dressen was an egomaniac," Villante said. "He was one of those guys who, you could be sensational, but he wanted to have his imprint on it somehow so he could say he helped make you great. It's like saying to Mariano Rivera from the Yankees that he needs another pitch."

Rivera became baseball's greatest reliever with basically one pitch: a cut fastball thrown in the mid-90s that breaks dramatically. Joe never had a single pitch that effective, but his fastball and slider, combined with his ability to throw those pitches exactly where he wanted, made him a sensation in 1952.

"But Dressen had to tamper with him," Villante continued. "He kept trying to teach him a changeup. It works for some guys, but doesn't work for others. In the meantime, he hurts his arm. With Rivera, you wouldn't tamper with him and say he needs another pitch. The guy's had a phenomenal career with one pitch. I always felt bad about that for Joe. Dressen tampered with him, ruined him in '53 and then, all of a sudden, Dressen's gone."

Roscoe McGowen wrote that, in hindsight, it was a mistake to tamper with Joe's delivery. He had succeeded beyond anyone's wildest dreams in 1952, so why ask for something better? "Dressen did ask for something better," he wrote, "and look wha' hoppen!"

Joe wasn't the first victim of managerial tinkering, nor would he be the last. Monte Irvin suggested that in agreeing to Dressen's request to learn a new pitch, Joe "did a silly thing."

"You'd be surprised at some of these coaches or managers who won't leave good enough alone," Irvin said. "They always want to change somebody. When a guy is doing OK, leave him alone until he isn't doing well."

Regardless of where the blame fell, Joe had to forget about it and rededicate himself to trying to become the pitcher he had once been. "This year I'm going to throw that ball the way I always did and not try to aim it," Joe told McGowen in late January 1954. "If I do that, I don't see how I can miss."

But it didn't turn out to be that easy.

20

Going to BAT for Others

Bobby Bonilla was in a funk. The Florida Marlins third baseman had struggled at the plate for most of the 1997 World Series against the Cleveland Indians, and it wasn't getting any easier with the Tribe's twenty-one-year-old right-hander, Jaret Wright, on the mound in game seven at Miami's Pro Player Stadium. Wright repeatedly jammed Bonilla inside, inducing a groundout to second his first time up and striking him out in his next at-bat, leaving him a paltry 2-for-his-last-23. When Bonilla emerged from the dugout to lead off the seventh inning, the Indians led 2–0 and stood just nine outs from their first World Series championship since the days of Larry Doby, Bob Feller, and Bob Lemon in 1948.

Joe Black watched it all as he sat near the Marlins' on-deck circle with his good friend Len Coleman, the National League president. Professional athletes seem to have this knack for recalling events in precise detail from their past, and as Bonilla swung his weighted bat, Joe remembered how he had handcuffed Mickey Mantle with inside pitches in the 1952 World Series—until the slugging center fielder came to bat in the sixth inning of game seven. Mantle had stepped back from the plate slightly, a move so subtle that neither Joe nor catcher Roy Campanella noticed.

"I threw that same pitch and he hit it out," Joe said. Mantle's blast over the Ebbets Field scoreboard in right field and onto Bedford Avenue broke a 2–2 tie; the Yankees went on to win 4–2 and claim their fourth straight

World Series title. That memory prompted Joe, who at that time was working for the Arizona Diamondbacks, to call Bonilla over and offer some advice.

"If you step back, he's not going to notice that you made an adjustment," Coleman recalled Joe saying. "So Bobby says, 'You know, Joe, I'm going to try that.' Bobby takes a step back, Wright comes in on the inside and bam, right into the stands. When Bobby crosses the plate, he points at Joe and shakes his head."

Bonilla's home run rejuvenated the Marlins and they rallied to win 3–2 in eleven innings and take the series, an improbable championship for a franchise only in its fifth season. "That was Joe. He always wanted to help," Frank Robinson said. "He'd bond with certain players on teams and holler advice during a game. He had a vast amount of knowledge that covered a lot of things and he loved to pass it on."

The television cameras had zeroed in on Joe talking to Bonilla, and Bonilla credited Joe for his advice. Suddenly, Joe Black was a baseball celebrity again—because of a batting tip. Coleman named him the league's honorary batting instructor. American League President Gene Budig joked that Joe wouldn't get an AL pass the next season because he had helped send the league's representative to defeat. "Everybody's been teasing me, saying, 'Are you going to be a batting coach now?'" Joe said about a month after the series. "They say, 'You're a pitcher. What do you know about hitting?' . . . I was in the Diamondbacks office and they were teasing me, saying, 'You got a lot of publicity. You must be important.'"

Actually, Joe already had been an important figure for the Diamondbacks—and for many players no longer in the game.

>>>>>>>>>>

Joe stayed busy after retiring from Greyhound in 1987. He continued to work as a consultant for the corporation, which eventually became Viad, and "was actually with us the rest of his life," said John Teets, the company CEO. "He was still working for us as a consultant when he passed on. He was working with me, in fact. He died with his boots on you could say." Joe also answered the call when baseball sought his help, just as he had done as a relief pitcher coming out of the bullpen all those years ago.

Bart Giamatti, before becoming baseball's commissioner in 1989, had talked about his concern over what happened to players when they left the game. Fay Vincent, who became commissioner after Giamatti died of a heart attack only five months into his tenure, said that concern grew out of a meeting with Mookie Wilson, the fleet center fielder who played for the New York Mets and the Toronto Blue Jays. "Mookie came to see Bart one day and said, 'What do you think I can do when I finish baseball?'" Vincent said, "He was very frightened. He didn't have any real skills. How was he going to get along when baseball ends? That question and that meeting really shook Bart up. He told Mookie he thought education was the answer, he should go back to school and acquire some marketable skills. That never happened, but it was a good wakeup call."

When Giamatti became commissioner, he hired Joe to talk to players about managing their money and planning for a life after baseball. Joe eagerly accepted, saying that getting such a job was "like winning a World Series baseball game." But he soon got discouraged, because the players showed little or no interest in their future. "Ninety percent of them don't think about that," Joe said. "They all think, 'I'm going to play until the day I die.' Then they think if they don't have any money, all you have to do is say 'I used to be a baseball player' and somebody's going to give you a big job. And it didn't work that way."

>>>>>>>>>>

In his later years my dad was a consultant for Major League Baseball and spent a lot of time talking to Major League players, counseling them on making their money go as far as possible and on preparing for a life after baseball. He wouldn't tell players where to invest their money, but he would tell them, "Make some investments. Be smart with your money." He also would tell them, "Go back to school in the off-season. Take some classes in something you like, because this game's not going to last forever in your life. There are not going to be TV and radio jobs for everybody on your team. You have to figure out what you want to do. You have to find something that's right for you."

He believed that getting educated in a business or discipline was essential to succeeding in a post-professional-sports career. He would tell players, "When you go for an interview, are they going to talk to you about your baseball years?

That might get you in the door and it may get you a little bit more money, but you have to prove you can stay there. Because after you meet their twenty clients that they want you to impress and you've impressed them, now what are they going to do with you? You have to do something."

>>>>>>>>>>

Joe, of course, came from another generation, before free agency and seven-figure salaries and long-term contracts. Even the best players in his day had worked off-season jobs. Roy Campanella ran the liquor store he owned in Harlem. Gil Hodges sold cars. Yogi Berra and Phil Rizzuto worked in a clothing store. When Dusty Rhodes, the New York Giants' pinch-hitting sensation in the 1954 World Series, left baseball, he worked on a tugboat in New York harbor. "In one week I made more off that damn tugboat than I did during a whole year in baseball," Rhodes said.

Joe knew that even with their bigger salaries, many players would need a post-baseball career, so he encouraged the younger guys to do something during the off-season to improve themselves. Go to school. Learn computers. "That's the wave of the future," Joe told them. "I said, 'You know, I was in six figures [with Greyhound], but I can't get an entry level job today because I don't know anything about a computer.' They said, 'Really?' I said, 'Yes, you have to do it.'"

Vincent moved into the commissioner's office after Giamatti died on September 1, 1989, and he wanted to keep Joe on as a mentor to the players. By that time, Joe was so frustrated he wanted to give up. "I tried to do the right thing, but I'm a total failure," Vincent remembered Joe saying. "Nothing's happened." Joe told Vincent the players were nice and respectful, but "they look at me as an old fat guy who comes from a different world. They think I'm Uncle Tom. They really don't pay any attention. I haven't gotten a single player to take any action or pick up on what I'm saying. I really feel very bad about it." Vincent encouraged him to keep trying, but Joe eventually threw up his arms in surrender.

What really rankled Joe was the indifference shown by many black players. Generally, he found them far less receptive to his message than white players. "You could get one or two who'll lean this way," Joe noted. "White players will say, 'It makes sense. I don't know if I'm going to do three hours [in a college course], but I'll go to school Monday and take a computer class.'" But "the black players, they all say, 'I'm young. I don't have to think about the future until five years from now.' . . . I said, 'No, you can crash into a wall, you can slide into a base the wrong way and it's all over.' Say you're making a million dollars. If all you're going to do is spend, then you're going to go broke.

"I said, 'Look, I see you've got these funny cars. I can see how you might have a high-priced car, then buy something cheap to drive around. No, you've got three higher-priced cars. You guys build houses that nobody would want when you finish and you can't sell them."

Joe urged the players to meet with financial planners and figure how to stretch their money so they could live comfortably long after their playing days ended. Sure you're making $2 million now, he'd say, but what about in twenty-five years? Will you be making $2 million then? "They'd say, 'Well, I'll have all my money saved.' I said, 'How can you save it? You're spending it.'"

It also puzzled Joe when he found white players more interested in what it was like during Jackie Robinson's day than black players. "I try to sit down with black players, try to talk to them about Jackie Robinson," Joe explained to an audience at Kenyon College in Ohio in 2001. "They'd go, 'Oh, man, if they were spitting on him, why didn't he deck them?' I said, 'Well, if he had, you wouldn't be playing.' They just don't understand that. Because they were saying, 'I thought he must have been a sissy or something because he wouldn't fight.' I said, 'No, he would love to fight . . . but he couldn't.'" For players and fans who have always seen blacks in the game, it can be hard to grasp that there was a time they weren't allowed. Joe always wanted to make sure that time—and what the early black players endured—wasn't forgotten.

"When I think of the way things were, I wonder how we did it," Larry Doby once said. Doby joined the Cleveland Indians in July 1947, less than three months after Jackie debuted with the Dodgers. "I remember sliding into second base and the fielder spitting tobacco juice in my face and I just walked away. *I walked away.* They'd shout at you: 'You dirty black so and so.' There's no way to walk away from that. But I did."

Some understood. Randy Johnson, six foot ten and white, winner of 303 games and five Cy Young Awards, used to talk to Joe about Negro league baseball and asked for Joe's help in getting autographs from Buck O'Neil and Double Duty Radcliffe. Hall of Famer Greg Maddux, who won 355 games, sat with Joe one day and asked, "Tell me, was Satchel Paige really that good?"

"But it's very difficult to get some of the black players to sit down," Joe said. Then he added, "But I make them listen anyhow."

>>>>>>>>>>

Nothing, though, stung Joe more deeply than the words of Vince Coleman, the speedy St. Louis Cardinals outfielder who was asked about Jackie Robinson at the 1985 World Series, on a day Jackie's widow, Rachel, threw out the first pitch to mark the fortieth anniversary of her husband's signing with the Brooklyn Dodgers. "I don't know nothin' about him," Coleman told *New York Times* columnist Dave Anderson. "Why are you asking me about Jackie Robinson?"

Joe cried when he read Anderson's account. So much of the good in his life had happened because Jackie Robinson crossed the line and courageously took the abuse without retaliating so others could follow, and here was a player, a black player no less, who professed to know nothing about the trailblazer. All the rage Joe felt when that scout dismissed him forty-three years earlier boiled through him again. "I was infuriated," Joe said, recalling that time. "I was really angry. I said, this is a bad example. So I tried to find him. I couldn't, so I wrote him a letter and told him, 'It's time you ought to know about Jackie Robinson.

"'There's a coach on your bench named Red Schoendienst. Ask him. If he's not there, go up in the front office and ask a vice president named Stan Musial. Vince Coleman, if it hadn't been for Jackie Robinson, you wouldn't be on that field playing baseball today.' I said, 'You should be ashamed to say I don't know anything about Jackie and don't ask me about him. Your parents, I know, are not proud of you.'"

Several months later, Joe spoke to the Jacksonville, Florida, Urban League and Coleman's parents were in the audience. It was a big gathering, fifteen hundred people maybe, and Joe couldn't help himself. Near the end of his speech, he addressed the Colemans. "I said, 'Your son really hurt me,'" Joe remembered saying. "'He hurt a good friend of mine named Jackie Robinson.' I read the quote from the paper and told them exactly what it said. I said, 'When you see him, you should tell him he should be thankful that there was a pioneer that paved the way for him.'"

Back in Phoenix, Joe said he would occasionally see a cart head his way when he was golfing, then abruptly turn and take off in the other direction. Someone eventually told him it was Coleman, so Joe tracked him down. He said they talked, became friends, and even golfed together. But what Coleman had said still hurt, no matter how often Vince tried to explain what he meant. "You take me," Joe said. "I would never say I don't know Joe Louis. Muhammad Ali was a great fighter. They've got great fighters out there. But Joe Louis, when this man went in the ring, we all felt that we were somebody. When he fought, it wasn't Joe Louis. It was as if *we* were fighting—*we're* going to win tonight. We had our hero. You can't destroy that."

>>>>>>>>>>

Joe found another avenue for his energy when Major League Baseball, responding to concerns that many former players struggled financially, created the Baseball Alumni Team, or BAT. Formed in 1986 and later renamed the Baseball Assistance Team, the group of ex-Major Leaguers raised funds and distributed money to needy members of the baseball family. Most of the help was directed toward ex-players who didn't make huge salaries during their careers, many in such dire straits they couldn't pay rent or basic utility bills. Others had major medical expenses that BAT stepped in to pay. The organization helped one player who had exhausted his savings paying his wife's doctor bills. "When you need money, every day you go to the mailbox and the check isn't there, it's a long, long day," said Ralph Branca, the former Brooklyn Dodgers pitcher and BAT's first president.

After a quarter century of developing programs to help and honor blacks at Greyhound, it seemed only natural for Joe to be drawn to a group such as BAT, and he became one of its vice presidents. It was another chance to make a difference. "BAT was the serious side to Joe," Len Coleman said. "He always put in his time with BAT. He was always worried about this player or that player or somebody in a player's family. He was very committed to that. If somebody was down on his luck, Joe would be the first one on the phone."

Joe worked often with his friend Joe Garagiola, a member of BAT's first board and later its president, and Garagiola marveled at how Joe related to the people they helped. He remembered going to Los Angeles to visit a former player's widow who was afraid of losing her house. "It was amazing," Garagiola said. "Here was this frail old woman and Joe assured her we'd take care of it, which we did. After that, when she felt better, she started talking about dying. She was fearful. And you would have thought you were listening to a minister as we sat on the couch and Joe held her hand and talked to her. It's a shame that's not on tape. It's a shame people don't see how far you go."

The hardest part for Joe was hearing about someone of his generation, a guy he had played with or against. "You think, 'No, not that person,'" he said. "You're shocked." That was how Joe felt when he heard about Sandy Amoros, the former outfielder who played with Joe in Brooklyn and produced one of the iconic moments in World Series history with his running catch of Yogi Berra's slicing liner in the seventh game of the 1955 Fall Classic. Another former Dodger, Chico Fernandez, alerted BAT to Amoros's plight and they found him living in a shabby room over a garage in Tampa, Florida. He wore tattered clothes, his left leg had been amputated at the knee, he couldn't afford a prosthesis, and he had circulation problems in his right leg. BAT paid for a prosthesis and sent him $500 a month for living expenses. Amoros later moved in with his daughter in Miami and was living there when he died in 1992. "But he did leave with a little dignity that he didn't have before," Joe said.

If Joe was shocked at the sight of Amoros living as he did, he was absolutely stunned at what happened when a former player called crying for help for his wife. The man sobbed as he told Joe that his wife had been on a respirator for ten months. The doctors told the man to bring the family to the hospital because they were going to unhook her, and the ex-player refused to accept that nothing more could be done. "I just can't let her go," he told Joe. Joe instructed the man to tell the doctors to keep the machines on for another two months and BAT would pay.

"About six weeks later, he called and said, 'Lord, Lord, Lord, her little finger moved,'" Joe said. "I said, 'No it didn't.' He said, 'Yes it did, I saw it moving and called the doctor and he said the same thing, no it didn't.' So they sat there a while and that finger moved. Three weeks later, the whole arm moved. Two months later, he would take her from the hospital and take her to the golf course and strap her to the cart and ride around while he was playing golf. I'm saying, 'Just think, this lady could have been buried if it hadn't been for BAT.'"

BAT kept the names of its recipients confidential, to protect their dignity and privacy. "What we learned is you'd be surprised who needs help," Ralph Branca said. Some, such as Amoros, talked about the help they received and the organization benefited from those stories.

"We owe Sandy a tremendous debt," said Frank Slocum, BAT's first executive director. "Our debt to him is that he went public. He told people we were helping him. That has been invaluable to us in raising money so others can be helped, too."

One former player BAT helped couldn't afford a wheelchair. His wife wasn't strong enough to lift him, so he remained in bed, on his back, for eighteen months, according to Joe. When BAT heard of his case, the organization bought him a wheelchair, and Joe said it was as though they had given the man a new life. "He says, 'I've been crying. You don't know how good it feels to sit up after 18 months laying on your back.'"

Those kinds of stories heartened Joe and made up for the frustration he sometimes encountered trying to raise money. One such time occurred in the spring of 1991, when he visited Major League camps in Arizona seeking donations for BAT to help former Negro league players. Joe talked to more than two dozen black players and only seven contributed: Dusty Baker, Ken Griffey Sr., Ken Griffey Jr., Andre Dawson, Willie McGee, Kevin Mitchell, and Dave Stewart. The rest all turned him down.

Joe's son, Chico, remembered his father telling about the time he approached a player who had just signed a multimillion-dollar contract to ask if he could contribute $5,000 to BAT. The player said he couldn't do it. "My dad would say, 'That's a shame. These guys didn't make all the big bucks and these old-time ballplayers are hurting. They need a little help,'" Chico said. "It was just a sad thing to hear."

Joe tried to point out to current players that while they were well off at present, they might not be so lucky later in life and there could be a time they need BAT's help, too. Some responded, some didn't. "You should have heard him when he was talking to young black players [about helping Negro leaguers]," Joe Garagiola said. "He would tell them about the obligation they had. Our pitch was, 'Thank God that you never need this money, but the guys getting this money never had anything.' I think he had a lot of minister in him. He would reason and talk to them and he'd get the message across."

Vexed as he might have been about players who refused to help, Joe never regretted getting involved with BAT. "Without BAT, some of these guys would be having severe problems," he said. "It's one of the best things baseball's ever done. It's giving dignity to guys who gave the game of baseball a name and positive identification through the years, and now they're forgotten heroes. Some of them are not just down, they're out."

BAT picked them up, and Garagiola found Joe well suited for the task: a former player successful in his post-baseball career and experienced enough in life to know that not everyone who once played had the same opportunities. "He handled that BAT money like it was his own, and he was fair with people," Garagiola said. "Like the little widow: Don't worry about it. Whatever it is, we'll help. We had wives call us and say, 'I don't have enough money to bury my husband.' Joe's line was, 'You bury him with the dignity you and he deserve and don't worry about it.'

"I'd always kid him and say, 'I don't want your heart if I have to have a transplant. You used it too much.'"

>>>>>>>>>>

When my dad wrote his By the Way commentaries, he was trying to talk to African Americans and encourage them to step above where they were. But a lot of people resented him for what he said. They were into the Black Pride movement. They'd wear dashikis or braid their hair. My dad understood that. He said African Americans should be proud of their heritage, and recognized that we had endured hatred, prejudice, and segregation as a community. But he also suggested that to get a corporate job, you shouldn't go in with an afro and wear a dashiki and think they're going to let you deal with, for example, an oil tycoon. Dressing to fit in does not have to mean you're not showing your pride.

When I went to college in Atlanta, some African American women told me they didn't like my father because of his commentaries in Ebony and JET. They didn't understand what he was trying to do. They thought he was a sellout. I recall he did win Oreo of the Year one time—black on the outside, but supposedly white inside.

But I never felt that my father was ever being a sellout. He was encouraging people to try to advance themselves, and when you advance yourself, bring somebody up with you. I miss the way this country used to live by the credo, I am my brother's keeper. My father explained this credo to mean if you see somebody who needs help, you lend a hand to pull him or her up. When my dad was at Greyhound Corporation, the African American executives from the different companies helped each other. Greyhound Corporation was looking for an African American for its board of directors, and my father suggested John Johnson, who owned Johnson Publishing. John was given a seat on the board, and after he passed away, his daughter, Linda Johnson Rice, moved into that seat on the board.

My father's generation acted as each other's keepers because they understood what it was like to be denied opportunities. My father not only lived through the civil rights movement, he was part of it. He was one of the early blacks who followed Jackie Robinson into Major League Baseball. He worked to help the black community when he was with Greyhound and became an example of what could be achieved when he was named a vice president.

When Barack Obama was elected to his first term as president, I can imagine how my father would have felt. I can picture my father and Jackie Robinson saying that everything they went through was worth it. It took them getting spiked and decked by pitches at their heads on the baseball field, being denied rooms in hotels and service in restaurants, and enduring hate and affronts to their dignity. Every little step taken by those men and women in the 1950s and '60s is how President Obama got elected. I can guarantee that my father would have been sitting next to me on election night in 2008 and he would have been crying for joy.

>>>>>>>>>>

Not every decision Joe made was greeted warmly. When Fay Vincent, as baseball commissioner, decided in 1992 that former Negro league players should be covered by Major League Baseball's health insurance plan, he asked Joe and Len Coleman to work out the details. Joe had pushed for such a move, arguing that it would not cost much and would involve only about a hundred ex-players. "These players don't want charity," he said, "but they should be included in the Players Association medical plan." Vincent's move was seen as the right thing to do, but a problem remained: how do you determine who qualifies? Should the benefits go to everyone who ever wore a Negro league uniform, even into the 1950s after baseball had integrated? Or should there be a cutoff?

Joe recommended including only those who played before Jackie Robinson joined the Dodgers, reasoning that after Jackie, blacks had a chance at the Major Leagues if they were good enough. Before Jackie, they were kept out through no fault of their own. It was left to Joe to explain that decision.

"That turned out to be a very difficult judgment," Vincent said. "I think Joe was right, but it was still a matter of controversy. He did what he thought was right and I agreed with him. It seemed like we had to draw a line somewhere. But a lot of Negro league guys from the early '50s were excluded. They didn't like that one bit."

"Joe was the right guy to do that," Len Coleman said. "He knew everybody. But it sure wasn't the most popular job. Guys would say, 'I played,' and Joe said, 'Come on, you were the bat boy.' It could be a hard thing sometimes."

Later, Joe lobbied for baseball to provide a pension for the former Negro league players, and MLB's executive council responded in January 1997, agreeing to pay $10,000 a year to about ninety black players who weren't in the majors long enough to qualify for a pension or did not have a chance to play in the majors at all. To receive the pension, a player had to have spent at least four years in the Negro leagues or a combined four years in Negro ball and the majors. Again, Joe headed the committee that determined eligibility and again, he took some flak.

"It was a no-win situation for Joe," said historian Larry Lester. "Many of the players did not like Joe for that reason: he had to have a cutoff date. But with any program, you have to have some guidelines."

Lester said there was plenty of room to argue whether all black players had a chance at the Major Leagues after Jackie broke in, because bias still lingered and many organizations were slow to integrate. It was eleven years before the Detroit Tigers had a black player (Ozzie Virgil) and twelve years before Pumpsie Green became the first black to play for the Boston Red Sox. But he admired Joe for standing up for what he believed. "He always wanted to right every wrong he saw," Lester said. "That's why he was instrumental with BAT. He had a firebrand attitude that wasn't always politically correct, but he stood his ground on controversial issues. One of the best things I got from Joe was he never argued about *who* was right, but *what* was right."

Seven years later, in part because of prodding from Democratic senator Bill Nelson of Florida, Major League Baseball established a fund to provide pensions for twenty-seven former Negro leaguers who played after 1947. None covered by the new agreement played in the majors. "Some of those guys in the Negro leagues after Jackie, they weren't good enough to play in the majors," Buck O'Neil acknowledged. "But they still deserved something."

>>>>>>>>>>

Joe also helped in smaller ways, and if he could do someone a favor he would, even for a stranger. Joe called his friends at Christmas and asked if he could send them a dessert or a fried turkey. "He loved to send you those fried turkeys," Len Coleman said. Some of the shopping malls put up Christmas trees hung with cards containing the name of a needy family or child. Shoppers were encouraged to take a card and send food or gifts. Joe often took two or three cards at a time. "I forgot this lady's name," Chico said, "but she had two boys and at Christmas time, he would always make sure they had some clothes, things like that. He always expressed that it's a joy when you can help others. When he was growing up, he didn't have anything. He was fortunate to play ball and become one of the senior vice presidents of Greyhound. He was able to earn some money so he could do that, help other people, because he knew how it was."

One day in the spring of 1999, Joe struck up a conversation with a hotel doorman named Peter McCormack, and they got to talking about the twenty-fifth anniversary of Hank Aaron breaking Babe Ruth's career home run record. McCormack named his infant son after Aaron—Henry Aaron McCormack—and mentioned he had been unable to get the Atlanta Braves to send him a ball autographed by the Hall of Fame slugger. McCormack later wrote Joe a letter telling him he had enjoyed their conversation and asking if he had any suggestions about getting the autograph. Joe did even better than a suggestion. He called McCormack and said he would be in Atlanta soon and would get him the autographed ball. "I was stunned that he would call and do that," McCormack said. A couple of weeks later, a small package arrived at the McCormack home with a note from Joe and a baseball signed, "To Hank, Best Wishes, Hank Aaron."

When he worked at Greyhound, Joe once received a call from a ticket agent who said a guy at the counter had dropped Joe's name, saying Joe had left a ticket for him. The agent said there was no ticket for the guy, a young, nearly broke comedian trying to get his next show. Joe sighed and told the agent to put the guy on the phone.

As Len Coleman related the story, the man pleaded with Joe, saying, "You've got to do this for me. I'm going to be big someday. I'll pay you back. I just don't have any money now, and on and on."

Exasperated, Joe finally said, "Give the guy a ticket. Just put him on the bus."

The guy turned out to be David Adkins, who's far better known by his stage name: Sinbad. Years later, as Coleman sat in an aisle seat on a redeye flight from Los Angeles to New York, in walked Sinbad, who plopped down in the seat across from Coleman. Len decided to have a little fun. "Sinbad," he said, "I was put on this plane to collect the money you owe Greyhound when they gave you that ticket. And he goes, 'You had to be talking to that God damn Joe Black. That God damn Joe Black is the only one who knows that story.'"

>>>>>>>>>>

Phoenix was one of the nation's fastest-growing areas in the 1990s, expanding inexorably into the surrounding desert. The city already had a pro basketball team, the Suns, and several Major League Baseball training sites dotted the area. For many fans, a trip to Arizona in March to watch baseball, get a preview of what might be in store for the season, and evaluate the latest hot prospects was an annual rite of spring. So it seemed inevitable the Valley of the Sun would get its own Major League team, and in 1998 the Arizona Diamondbacks began play. Joe was involved almost from the start, hooking up with the club several months after the franchise was awarded in March 1995.

"We had sort of a small operation," said Rich Dozer, the team's first president. "He was our speaker's bureau all wrapped into one person." Joe spoke to Rotary clubs, business groups, Toastmaster clubs—any organization that wanted to hear about the Diamondbacks. He talked if there were twenty people or a hundred, at breakfast, lunch, or dinner, telling stories of Jackie Robinson and his days with the Dodgers and stumping on behalf of the new team that would hit town in a couple of years. "He had such a passion for baseball and he loved Arizona," Dozer said. "He was a great guy to have, an imposing figure."

Jerry Colangelo, the club's chairman and CEO, relied on Joe's knowledge, because Colangelo's background was basketball. He owned the Phoenix Suns and had gotten to know Joe when both were in Chicago, Colangelo with the Chicago Bulls and Joe with Greyhound. "He was in a sense a mentor to me, because he had been around baseball for so many years and had a lot of history that he passed on to me about the people within the game," Colangelo said. "It was a different culture than what I was used to, and he was a great liaison for me. The other thing is, Joe was an ambassador for the game. You run across certain people who love the game, so when you are looking for people to represent you in the community, he fit that description like a glove. So in beating the drums and trying to create interest and develop a baseball following, we thought Joe would be ideal."

Club executives thought so much of Joe they even looked to him as a possible pitching coach. Joe's days of throwing a baseball were long over, but he still knew what it took to sneak one past a Major League hitter. But he was seventy-four when the Diamondbacks started playing. Would the players listen to someone old enough to be their grandfather? Joe decided they wouldn't and opted for a front office job.

"He told me a story of how he was talking to Bobby Bonds about Barry and Bobby told Dad, 'Barry's going to do what he wants to do. He ain't going to listen to me,'" Chico said. "Dad would say, 'Young players know everything. They're not going to listen.'"

But Joe could charm an audience, so he was ideal for what the Diamondbacks needed at the time. And he worked the club's offices as adeptly as he worked a luncheon crowd. Wherever he went, he drew a crowd—from the office suites to the dugout, where he usually chatted with players and coaches before games. Executives and fellow workers remember Joe filling a room with his personality as much as with his imposing bulk. "He was our Pied Piper," Rich Dozer said, a thought Jerry Colangelo echoed. "You ended up being uplifted after any time with him," Colangelo said. "He had a passion for the game and he transposed that passion to whoever would listen, whoever he was with. His storytelling, whether the stories were embellished or not didn't matter. When somebody is a storyteller or a joke teller, you could hear the same thing over and over again and never get tired of it."

To Casey Wilcox, who started with the Diamondbacks as an intern in 1999, seeing Joe around was like coming upon a page out of baseball's past. "When you shook Joe's hand, you could feel the history," said Wilcox, who became the team's director of player and media relations. "I compare it to shaking Buck O'Neil's hands. There was something surreal about him. He played with Jackie Robinson. He was a part of baseball history."

Rarely a day went by without Joe striding into the office, smiling, and calling out greetings to everyone in a loud, booming voice that carried throughout the complex. When Joe was in the house, you knew it. "It seemed like he never forgot where he came from," Wilcox said. "He always took time out for the little people, and that's what I considered myself. He didn't need to give me the time of day for a million years, but he did. And more. I'm richer for having known him."

The Diamondbacks quickly became contenders, winning the National League West in their second season, 1999, and beating the New York Yankees in the 2001 World Series. The club was loaded with veterans like Luis Gonzalez, Randy Johnson, Matt Williams, and Jay Bell, and Joe fit in easily with that group. Most of those players had an appreciation for baseball history, Gonzalez said, and respected what Joe had accomplished. "He was what I call an impact person," said Gonzalez, who later became an executive with the Diamondbacks. "Everybody always talks about the impact player who comes in and makes a difference on the field—he was an impact person. He made a difference not only on the field, but off the field, too."

Gonzalez had been unaware of Joe's batting tip to Bonilla until being told about it years later, but he wasn't surprised, because Joe had offered him some advice during the 1999 All-Star Game at Boston's Fenway Park. He came to bat against Mike Mussina with one out in the fifth inning after replacing Larry Walker in the lineup in the fourth. Gonzalez was in his ninth full season in the big leagues, but it was his first All-Star Game, so he was nervous, of course. Joe sat in his usual spot near the on-deck circle and leaned over as Luis loosened up. "He told me to relax and have fun," Gonzalez recalled. "I felt it was an honor for him to acknowledge me like that, for him to know I had a little nervousness. He'd been there before as a player. He understood that. It kind of took the edge off a little bit." The relaxed Gonzalez promptly lined a double to left, a hit he'll always remember. "I never heard anybody talk bad about Joe Black," he said. "He was one of those people that everybody loved and everybody loved being around."

Joe even drew a crowd at his church, just by being there. He attended Emmanuel Presbyterian Church on Phoenix's northeast side, often arriving late and usually slipping in through a side door. Sometimes he went just for the sermon. "The door would open, you'd see a shaft of light and then this big silhouette in the doorway," said the Reverend Mark Anderson, who became the church's pastor in 1997. "You just turned around and there he was." Joe often lingered in his pew after the service as members of the congregation gathered around, sometimes to just talk about the weather or current events, but occasionally to seek advice after sharing a problem.

"It was almost like he held court," Anderson said. "He was the closest thing to a celebrity that most people had, but he acted in a very unassuming way. He just sat there and people gravitated to him. Then I'd go over and we would sit and talk and eventually I'd walk him to his car. We'd shake hands—I've got small hands—and my hand would just disappear in his. He had strength in that hand, but also a gentleness, just like the way he was. He was a large, powerful man who never used that power in any pejorative way."

But there are some things even the most powerful and hardened and experienced among us can't withstand, as it would be with Joe when he learned in 2002 that he had cancer.

21

Playing on a Rep

1954–57

Spring training always brings a renewal of optimism, and so it was for Joe and the Brooklyn Dodgers in 1954. Don Newcombe was back from the army, giving the club twenty victories right there, most people figured. Carl Erskine was in his prime and coming off a twenty-win season, Russ Meyer had delivered fifteen wins after coming over in a trade, and Billy Loes, still a youngster at twenty-four, was looking for a third straight season with a double-figure victory total. And then there was Joe. Columnist Arthur Daley suggested Joe could become the team's secret weapon despite his struggles the previous season, when "even the bad hitters belted him all over the lot." Joe told Daley the postseason barnstorming tour had turned him around. "I'm positive I'm back on the beam," he said.

To help mold that staff, the Dodgers hired Ted Lyons as a pitching coach, and he actually had been a pitcher. A good one, too. Lyons won 260 games in a twenty-one-year career with the Chicago White Sox (despite playing on teams that were mediocre at best and often downright lousy), and he was a year away from election to the Hall of Fame. Preacher Roe said Lyons was just what the team needed. "I think [Charlie] Dressen knew more about pitching than any fellow I've known who wasn't a pitcher," Roe said. "But only a pitcher can know about pitchers all the way. It's my opinion that this club needed a pitching coach, and I think it has one in Lyons."

Joe started the Dodgers' exhibition opener against the Milwaukee Braves in Miami and came away with mixed results. He gave up four hits and all three Braves runs in a 3–2 loss, but he didn't walk anyone and struck out five in his three innings. He fanned the side in the second.

As the spring went on, Joe told everyone who asked that he was done experimenting and was going back to the pitches that had carried him through his rookie season: his fastball and what he had come to call a "crazy curve"—crazy because it didn't break enough to be called a real curve and curved too much to be called a slider. He looked at the season as a challenge, a chance to prove to others—but mostly to himself—whether he was a Major League pitcher. Or not. Joe said he tried to fool batters in 1953 and that didn't work. "If I get a batter out on a fastball, I'll keep on throwing him fastballs until he starts hitting them off me," he said. "When that happens, I'll try something else. Why try new pitches when the old ones are good enough?"

The trouble was, the old ones weren't good enough. After he pitched a perfect inning in each of his first two appearances of the season, batters started to tee off on Joe, knocking him around for nine runs and eleven hits in five innings over three appearances. It was obvious he wasn't on the comeback trail, and within a few days, he experienced the cold, unfeeling side of Major League Baseball.

The Dodgers beat the Giants at the Polo Grounds on Sunday, May 30, and were scheduled to leave at ten o'clock that night for a two-week road trip. Joe was home packing when the phone rang. It was Charlie "the Brow" DiGiovanni, who was the team's batboy but was as old as some of the players. Charlie, given his nickname because of his thick, dark, bushy eyebrows, also did favors for the players like finding them rides and running errands. He liked Joe, so he called with a warning.

"Chico, I'll get fired if they learn that I called you, but you're too nice a guy for them to be doing this to you," Joe remembered Charlie telling him.

"Do what to me?" Joe asked.

"Don't go to the station tonight," Charlie said.

"Why not?" Joe inquired.

Charlie told him that someone among the Dodger brass wanted to embarrass Joe and planned to tell him in front of the team that he was being sent down to Montreal. "My ego was shattered and I felt offended," Joe remembered thinking. A future that had appeared so bright less than two years earlier suddenly had darkened. The Dodgers no longer needed him. "Yesterday's hero is as important as yesterday's newspaper—something to discard," Joe wrote years later.

The Dodgers made the official announcement the next day, and manager Walt Alston tried to cushion the blow with encouraging words. "I hope Joe can come back," he said. "Nobody has worked harder. But he can't get the chance to pitch up here, and I think he's a fellow who needs to pitch often."

Joe took a train to Richmond, Virginia, to catch up with Montreal on its road trip, rejoining a team he had never envisioned being a part of again. Max Macon, who pitched, played first base, and was an outfielder during a six-year Major League career, managed the Royals, and he immediately put Joe in the rotation. Joe started against Richmond the day after he reported, giving up three runs and four hits in five innings in a 7–2 loss. He threw 106 pitches, and if he kept that up, he'd certainly get the work Alston thought he needed.

Early in his stint with the Royals, Joe learned what might have caused his struggles: he had torn muscles in his right shoulder. No wonder his fastball had lost some of his zip, he thought. So for the rest of the season, he saw a doctor once a week to get a cortisone shot to deaden the pain. The shoulder stopped bothering him, and as the season went on, Joe felt his velocity returning. He also got a lift from Macon's confidence, because the manager kept sending Joe out to pitch regularly—even after he had been shelled.

Ottawa rocked Joe for eight runs and thirteen hits in three and two-thirds innings in mid-July, but Joe was back on the mound five days later. He also produced some sparkling efforts, including back-to-back complete game victories in which he pitched a five-hitter and then a four-hit shutout. A three-game winning streak straightened him out after a 1-3 start, and he was a .500 pitcher the rest of the way—not sensational, but not horrible, either. Joe was encouraged enough to feel that better days were ahead. Baseball had become fun again.

>>>>>>>>>>

One of Joe's Montreal teammates that summer was a strong-armed outfielder from Puerto Rico named Roberto Clemente, still raw then but clearly talented. As Pittsburgh Pirates coach Clyde Sukeforth often told the story, Joe's presence with the Royals helped the Bucs land Clemente. Sukeforth said Pirates general manager Branch Rickey, the former Dodgers executive, sent him to look over Joe to see if he could help their club. Sukeforth said he spotted Clemente, was immediately impressed by what he saw in the youngster, and forgot all about Joe. The Pirates took the young outfielder in the supplemental draft that followed the season, paying only a $4,000 fee, and Clemente became a megastar in Pittsburgh during a career that put him in the Hall of Fame.

The Dodgers' Buzzie Bavasi was quoted by Clemente biographer David Maraniss as saying the club had been resigned to losing Clemente in the draft anyway. Still, Joe mused as he looked back on that time, "I have wondered if the Dodgers had ever wished they had assigned me to St. Paul rather than to Montreal."

>>>>>>>>>>

Joe finished the regular season 12-10 with a 3.60 earned run average, appearing in thirty-one games and starting twenty-four for a team that finished second, nine games behind Toronto. He worked six more times in two rounds of the postseason playoffs, going 2-1 with a save and pitching superbly in the fifth game of the league championship series against Syracuse: a 7–0 two-hitter with six strikeouts and no walks. One reporter wrote that Joe "showed off the kind of pinpoint control that made him a Brooklyn ace for a couple of years."

Actually, Joe had been ace-like for only one season in Brooklyn, but the performance was another boost for his confidence, which had sagged so severely when he was sent to Montreal. Even better for Joe, his season in Canada, which ended with his team's game-seven playoff loss to Syracuse, was good enough to earn him another shot with the Dodgers.

Again, it looked promising for a comeback. Joe had several strong outings while barnstorming with Roy Campanella's all-stars, and the *New York Times* reported early in 1955 that during his stint in Montreal and then with the touring team "the big right-hander suddenly began showing flashes of the Joe Black of old." Roscoe McGowen of the *Times* wrote early in the spring, after Joe pitched well in an intrasquad game, that maybe he had mastered a new pitch. "I don't know how you'd classify the pitch, whether you'd call it a change of pace," Walt Alston said. "It's a slow curve. He takes a little off his curve and it's effective."

Joe and Campy had gone to Florida early to work out on their own in Miami, where they were joined by a young left-handed pitcher who also wanted to get a head start in his preseason training. Sandy Koufax had signed the previous December as a bonus player, meaning the Dodgers had to keep him on their roster for two years. He was nineteen years old, with a lively arm, no professional baseball experience, and no idea what spring training was about. "I needed help to tell me what the hell to do," Koufax recalled. "I had no clue."

He got that help from Joe. When he saw Sandy wandering out on the field, unsure of what to do next, Joe walked over and said, "Just follow me." Joe's graciousness and companionship left a lasting impression with Koufax, who considered Joe a friend for life.

"Joe helped me a lot," Koufax said. "He led me around and told me what to do, where to go. I didn't even know what to do after batting practice. It made an impact, and I was grateful for what he did that first spring. We were friends after that. Not necessarily close, but when we saw each other, we were friends."

Joe also counseled Koufax when the young lefty was sidelined by a sore back and getting antsy to pitch again. Don't rush it, Joe advised. It would be foolish to pitch with a sore arm or sore back, Joe said, because if he didn't do well, he "would be a bum—and an expensive bum." Koufax bided his time until feeling better, then pitched against a team of the Dodgers' top minor leaguers. He worked two innings, and no one hit a fair ball off him. He faced seven batters, striking out five and walking two. One of those who walked was thrown out stealing. Koufax had shown a glimpse of the otherworldly skill that would put him in the Hall of Fame.

Sandy and Joe would be teammates for just a few weeks, but time doesn't matter when friendship is involved. Joe was walking down Fifth Avenue in New York City one day in 1964—he was working for Greyhound then—when someone sneaked up behind him, put both hands over his eyes and said, "Guess who?" It was Koufax, who had spotted Joe from across the street.

"I didn't even see him," Joe said. "He ran all the way around to get behind me. And this guy was a superstar then. If we didn't have that kind of camaraderie [on the Dodgers], he never would have said a word, because I didn't see him. But he took time out to do that."

>>>>>>>>>>

Joe pitched decently in the spring until he had a terrible outing at Yankee Stadium in the final exhibition game. The Yankees pounded him for six runs and four hits, including two home runs and a triple, in three innings. He also walked four batters. Alston said he wouldn't hold that outing against Joe, yet the Dodgers skipper called on him only once in April. Joe got the victory in that game, and he again became part of a historic win. The 14–4 shellacking of the Philadelphia Phillies in Ebbets Field on April 21 was the Dodgers' tenth straight victory to open the season, setting a modern Major League record. Joe pitched the final six and two-thirds innings in relief of Russ Meyer, allowing two runs and five hits and striking out five. It was reminiscent of the Joe Black in his glory days, and was his first Major League victory since August 29, 1953.

It also would be his last with the Dodgers.

After five appearances in which he gave up a total of three earned runs, Joe received some jarring news—not firsthand from a Brooklyn executive, but while driving home in his car with Jim Gilliam after a game. They were chatting and half-listening to the radio when the announcer broke in with a news item: Joe had been sent to the Cincinnati Reds for cash and a player to be named later.

"Why didn't you tell me, Chico?" Gilliam asked.

"I couldn't," Joe replied, "because I'm just learning about it, too."

Joe was angry because neither Walt Alston nor Buzzie Bavasi had told him in person, and he was disappointed because he had enjoyed the friendships and togetherness he found with the Dodgers. He also would miss the World Series check that seemed likely with the club at 40-12 and already nine games ahead of the second-place Chicago Cubs. And there was something a little eerie about Joe going to the Reds.

He once appeared as a guest star on the popular television show *Name That Tune* and had trouble identifying the song "Sympathy." The emcee gave him a clue: "Suppose it was the last of the ninth, the Yankees at bat, score 4–1 in your favor, the bases full, but Yogi Berra hits a homer. What would you expect?"

"I'd expect to be in Cincinnati next season," Joe replied.

The Reds bought Joe after right-hander Bud Podbielan, a former Dodger, broke his wrist sliding into second base, shelving him for eight to ten weeks. They eventually sent outfielder Bob Borkowski to the Dodgers to complete the deal, Borkowski conveniently changing dugouts when the Dodgers were in Cincinnati on June 14.

>>>>>>>>>>

The deal sent Joe to a club that had some productive hitters, such as Ted Kluszewski, Wally Post, Gus Bell, and Smoky Burgess, and he was reunited with former Dodger teammate Rocky Bridges, an eminently quotable utility infielder who once said of playing for the Reds, "It's a good thing I stayed in Cincinnati for four years. It took me that long to learn how to spell it." Joe Nuxhall, who had made his Major League debut at the age of fifteen in 1944, was the top pitcher on a staff that was otherwise thin on frontline talent.

Joe gave the pitching staff some depth—after a disastrous debut, that is. In just one-third of an inning against the Phillies in Philadelphia, Joe gave up five runs, though all were unearned. He steadied himself after that and, working as both a starter and a reliever, went 5-2 in thirty-two appearances with a 4.22 earned run average. The Reds finished fifth, four games below .500 and twenty-three and a half games behind the first-place Dodgers. After Joe had been shipped away, the Dodgers finally won the World Series, beating the Yankees in seven games. Each Dodgers club member who received a full series share earned $9,768.21, a nice sum for a week's work in any era.

With no World Series check, Joe had to be content picking up extra cash barnstorming with Roy Campanella's team and pitching winter league ball in the Dominican Republic. He was the top hurler on the league's last-place team when he was released in January, further fueling his hopes that he could make a major comeback in a full season with the Reds, who had the look of a contender after adding pitcher Brooks Lawrence, catcher Ed Bailey, and a rookie outfielder named Frank Robinson. As he had done with Sandy Koufax, Joe took Robinson under his wing in spring training.

"He showed me the ropes," Robinson said. "It kind of worked that way back, as we call it, in the day. That's what veterans used to do. They were helped and when they got in position, they helped the younger players, gave them advice on what to do, what not to do. You don't see that now in baseball."

Joe had been around, and Robinson appreciated his knowledge of New York and other cities in the league. "Just him being there gave me someone to look to or go to if I had to ask about something, where to live in Cincinnati, getting to the ballpark, that type of thing," Robinson said.

Joe also unwittingly helped boost his new friend's confidence when they faced off in an intrasquad game. "I squeezed in there, hanging tight over the plate, my bat held back on my shoulder, feeling real comfortable with that new stance," Robinson recalled. That stance became a Robinson trademark. He bent slightly at the waist and leaned out over the plate from the right-handed batter's box, almost as if he was inviting the pitcher to hit him (Robinson led his league in getting hit by pitches seven times). "On the first pitch," he continued, "Black fed me a fastball and I swung and hit the ball on a line 390 feet to the right-center-field fence. It was a good start, and it made me feel that I might belong with this ballclub."

Joe was determined to show he still had what it took to be a top-flight Major League pitcher. He worked on a sidearm pitch in the Plainfield High School gym after being let go in the Dominican Republic, and he reported to camp in Tampa ten pounds lighter than the previous year. Manager Birdie Tebbetts believed he had the league's best reliever in Hersh Freeman, who had gone 7-4 with eleven saves and a 2.15 ERA in 1955, and he felt Joe would strengthen the bullpen behind Freeman.

On May 26 of that year, Freeman and Joe became part of a first-of-its-kind pitching gem, combining with starter Johnny Klippstein to hold the Milwaukee Braves hitless through nine and two-thirds innings. It went down as a nine-inning no-hitter, the first time in baseball history that more than two pitchers had combined on such a performance. Joe came on in the ninth to retire the Braves in order, then got the first two batters in the tenth before Jack Dittmer doubled for the first hit. The Braves won it in the eleventh, 2–1, on Frank Torre's bases loaded single off Joe.

Joe said he threw a spitter once in his Major League career, and he did it against his good friend Jim Gilliam. A switch-hitter, Gilliam was batting left-handed, and he knew Joe liked to throw his little curve in on the wrists of left-handed batters. Joe knew that Gilliam knew, so he hoped to outfox his friend with a fastball low and outside. Right then, some perspiration rolled onto the tips of his index and middle fingers, and it hung there when he grabbed the ball, as if to tempt him: "Come on, Joe. Let us drip onto the ball. No one will ever know. And besides, you need this out." He felt a pang of guilt, but not too much because he was in a jam. Joe was just trying to hang on as a Major League pitcher at that point, while Gilliam was one of the Dodgers' stars. It wouldn't set Gilliam back if he made an out. Catcher Smoky Burgess called for the fastball and Joe let it go. The ball steamed in straight, then dove, by his estimation, about eight inches. Gilliam swung over the ball for strike three and Joe was out of the inning.

As he trotted to his position, Gilliam said, "Great sinker, Chico."

"Thanks," Joe replied with a sheepish grin. "I've been working on it."

>>>>>>>>>>

The Reds became contenders in 1956, thanks to their power and the pitching of Brooks Lawrence, who won his first thirteen decisions and finished 19-10, and Hersh Freeman, who went 14-5 with eighteen saves. The Reds clubbed 221 home runs to tie the National League record. But four straight losses in mid-September squelched their pennant hopes, and though they won eight of their last nine games, they had too much ground to make up. The Dodgers eliminated the Reds by beating the Pirates on the next-to-last day of the season, then beat Pittsburgh again the next day to clinch the pennant, leaving Cincinnati in third place, two games out.

Joe thought the Reds hitters tried too hard to bash home runs late in the season, and questioned why Lawrence, who was black, did not start after winning his nineteenth game on September 15. He called it "incomprehensible managerial strategy," and wondered if the Reds management didn't want to see a black pitcher win twenty games. Lawrence did pitch five times in relief, for a total of four and two-thirds innings, after getting his nineteenth win.

As for Joe, he got off to a rough start, giving up seven runs in his first eight and a third innings, and was rarely a factor through the season. He saved only two games, none after May 30, and went 3-2 with a 4.52 earned run average in sixty-one and two-thirds innings over thirty-two appearances. Birdie Tebbetts had toyed with the idea of moving Joe into the rotation in June after he allowed only two runs during a stretch of fourteen innings in relief. But Joe stayed in the bullpen and never had a stretch like that again. "Playing on my rep," is how Joe once described his stint with the Reds.

Joe got that third victory on June 24 by performing like he did in 1952: he pitched five and two-thirds innings of scoreless, hitless relief. It would be his last Major League victory.

The opponent?

The Brooklyn Dodgers.

>>>>>>>>>>

Joe again joined a barnstorming team after the season, traveling through the South, then into Texas and on to the West Coast with a group headed by Willie Mays. As winter approached, Reds GM Gabe Paul reportedly offered Joe and Smoky Burgess to the Cubs for right-hander Sam Jones, left-handed knuckleballer Jim Davis, and catcher Hobie Landrith. The Cubs instead sent those three players, plus utility man Eddie Miksis, to the St. Louis Cardinals. A month later, the Reds released Joe and sent him to Seattle of the Pacific Coast League. The *Sporting News* called Joe one of the major pitching disappointments of the 1956 season. He would have to work his way back up if he was to pitch in the Major Leagues again.

Though Frank Robinson and Brooks Lawrence became two of Joe's best friends, he found that pitching for the Reds wasn't at all like his days with the Brooklyn Dodgers. Not even close. "Playing with the Brooklyn Dodgers back then was like playing with one happy family," Joe said. "Once they put the uniform on, it was all for one and one for all. Sometimes [after] they'd take it off, they didn't speak to each other. But once they had it on, guys were a family. If a guy was a star and if he needed to bunt, they didn't mind bunting the ball. They'd hit behind the runner to get him over. Visiting a town, we'd go to movies together. We'd sit around in lobbies and chat. They'd come to you if you had a problem. That's what made the Dodgers different." Joe never felt that same camaraderie in Cincinnati, but his desire to continue pitching never wavered, nor did his compassion for others.

At the beginning of February 1957, a month before spring training, Joe was driving in New York City during a snowstorm when he hit a pedestrian. She was not seriously hurt, but Joe drove her to the hospital and waited several hours while she was examined to make sure she was OK. Police did not file any charges.

In March, Joe was in San Bernardino, California, for spring training with the Seattle Rainiers, managed by Lefty O'Doul, who batted .349 over an eleven-year Major League career. Joe knew several of the players, including Bud Podbielan, Bill Kennedy, and Larry Jansen. The team also had a speedy shortstop who would turn base stealing into an art form: Maury Wills.

Joe thought it odd to be sweating in the heat of the San Bernardino Valley while gazing at the snowcapped peaks of the nearby mountains. "I was working hard because I wanted my pitching ability to return me to the majors," he said. "But sometimes, a person's dream will fade away like clouds in the sky."

As the season approached, Joe planned to spend a day in camp working on his control. He warmed up, then told his catcher he was going to cut loose with a fastball. His windup and delivery were normal, but the ball hit ten feet in front of the plate. Joe joked that he was still trying to limber up and fired another heater. The ball again bounced several feet in front of the catcher, who yelled at Joe to quit fooling around. Joe said he had changed his mind and didn't want to work on his pitching after all. But that was a lie. He stopped because he was scared. Here he was, still a strapping six-foot-two 225-pounder, and he couldn't even throw a ball sixty feet. He spent the next few days running, exercising, and playing pepper, but he knew something was wrong with his arm.

Joe went on his own to a VA hospital, where X-rays showed bone chips in his right elbow and a small crack developing in his humerus, the long bone that runs from the shoulder to the elbow. A doctor would have been able to remove the chips, but Joe didn't want anything to do with surgery. Then he made what he later called a foolish decision: he did not tell anyone about his injuries and hoped he could get hitters out with guile and smarts. But the hitters were too good to be fooled, even in the Pacific Coast League, and Joe got whacked around, allowing thirty-four hits and seventeen runs in twenty-three and two-thirds innings. Joe couldn't hide it any longer and admitted he had a sore arm, so O'Doul suggested he go down to Tulsa in the Double-A Texas League. The weather there was hotter and drier than the damp climate of Seattle. Maybe the heat would help his arm.

It didn't.

After pitching in just four games, Joe knew it was over. The old velocity and control never returned and the club released him. Joe Black, once the darling of the Brooklyn fans and reporters, the intimidating pitcher who'd saved the Dodgers' 1952 season, was washed up, finished as a Major League Baseball player.

Well, almost finished.

The long train ride back to New York gave Joe time to reminisce. At first, he felt sorry for himself and cursed the bad luck that had dogged him. Then he thought of the games that defined each season, of his teammates, of the players on opposing teams who became friends, of pitching in the World Series and subduing the mighty Yankees. Joe knew he would miss that, but when he saw his family, he realized his relationship with them was more important than any game. But the thought nagged him: maybe he could pitch again if he just got the chance, even though his arm was still sore. That opportunity came from, of all people, Charlie Dressen.

Charlie had always liked Joe, their dustup after the 1953 season notwithstanding. He appreciated what Joe did for the Dodgers in 1952—and for his own job security—and had hoped that Joe could become a top-notch pitcher again. Carl Erskine remembered the time in 1953 when he was pitching in the fifth inning with the Dodgers ahead and Dressen brought in Joe, depriving Carl of a chance for the victory, because a starter has to go five innings to get credit for a win. Though nothing was ever said outright, Erskine believed Dressen was trying to help Joe by putting him in a position to pick up a victory. "He had more reason to think about Joe's need for a win than me," Erskine said. "I feel like Charlie had a real feeling for helping Joe get back out of his doldrums. That's because Joe was likable. Joe tried. He was never a complainer, never a troublemaker. He was a good, team-spirited guy. Dressen knew he was struggling, and he felt Joe still had it in him, if he could just get it out of him. Dressen went out of his way to try to get Joe on track."

Dressen was an assistant to Washington Senators owner Calvin Griffith in the midsummer of 1957, having been booted upstairs after he was fired as the team's manager in May, and he convinced the club to offer Joe a tryout. Unable to stay away, Joe had returned to Ebbets Field to pitch batting practice for the Dodgers in late July, and he must have helped them get loose, because they banged out twenty-two hits in a doubleheader with the Chicago Cubs that day. He began working out with the Senators shortly after that and signed on August 1, becoming the club's first US-born black player. Washington's two other black players, Carlos Paula and Julio Becquer, were Cubans.

"Never felt so good," Joe said after working out the day he signed. "My arm feels like it did in '52. And I'll tell you, I never met better people than Doc Resta and Doc Lentz. They've really helped me." Dr. George A. Resta was the Senators' team physician, while George Lentz was the trainer. "A week ago, I couldn't lift my arm. I just had no life in it," Joe said. "Well, I went to see Doc Resta and he worked on me. So did Doc Lentz. I started to throw easy in batting practice and the arm felt good. I was throwing sliders and curves and didn't feel any pain at all. The more I threw, the better I felt. I tell you, it does something to you to find something you've lost like that."

Resta found that Joe had osteochondritis, a chronic inflammation of the bone. All pitchers had the condition to some degree, Resta said, adding he had seen worse cases than Joe's, even among the top pitchers in the game. He also said part of Joe's problem was mental, and suggested that hooking up with Senators manager Cookie Lavagetto "could be the greatest therapy that he could have." Lavagetto was on Dressen's Brooklyn staff in 1952, and had succeeded Charlie as the Senators' manager in May.

The Washington Senators in 1957 were the sorriest team in all of Major League Baseball, a far cry from the star-studded club that had supported Joe in Brooklyn. The franchise's most recent first-division finish had come in 1946, and even then the team wound up two games below .500 and twenty-eight games behind the pennant-winning Boston Red

Sox. In 1955, the Senators finished 53-101 and forty-three games out of first place, and they were headed for similar futility in 1957. By the time Joe signed, they already were thirty-one games under .500 and buried in last place, thirty-one games out of first.

Yet Joe was excited because he was a Major League pitcher again, and he was surprised by the hustle and spirit he saw in his new teammates. "I'll guarantee that not even the Dodgers gave it a better try than these fellows," he said. "They've been great to me, too. They all told me they were rooting for me to make good and you know, that makes you feel good." Having Lavagetto as his skipper made it even better. "I never met a finer person or a more patient man," he said. "If I can't do it for Cookie, I can't do it for anybody."

As it turned out, Joe couldn't do it for Cookie, the Senators, or himself.

He had a couple of good outings early, throwing four shutout innings against the Yankees and Boston Red Sox. The first batter he faced as an American League pitcher, the Yankees' Moose Skowron, singled to center, and it was a big hit for Moose because it broke a 0-for-21 slump. Skowron, who then went 0-for-7 before regaining his stroke, talked about that hit for years afterward. "I just swung the bat," he said. "I was happy to get a base hit. I remember I broke the damn bat. When you're in a slump, nobody talks to you. Then you start to hit, and the sportswriters come around. I said, 'Where were you guys when I was 0-for-10, 0-for-20?'"

Jerry Reinsdorf often needled Joe about being the only pitcher Moose could hit during his slump. Joe amazed Reinsdorf by remembering the pitch he threw: a high fastball. "And this was fifty years after the event," Reinsdorf said. "He proceeded to tell me that he had lost the velocity on his fastball and that's why Moose got the hit. But he remembered what he threw."

Against the Red Sox, Joe helped end Ted Williams's seventeen-game hitting streak, retiring the Splendid Splinter on a grounder to first in the fifth inning. But he could sense things weren't the same. "I couldn't throw hard enough to break a pane of glass," he confessed in 1982. "I remember going against the Yankees and Casey [Stengel] told his players, 'Don't let him fool you. He can throw harder than that.'"

But he couldn't.

Pitching to the Tigers' Al Kaline at Briggs Stadium in Detroit, Joe couldn't get much on a fastball and it crossed the plate looking like a changeup. Joe recalled Kaline taking the pitch for a strike, then giving him a puzzled look, as if he was thinking, "This guy is supposed to throw smoke and he serves that up?" Kaline took another pitch for a ball, then drove the next one into the right-field seats.

In what would be his final five appearances as a Major Leaguer, the last coming on September 11 at Washington's Griffith Stadium, Joe was a sore-armed shadow of his former self as batters cuffed him around for eleven runs and eighteen hits in eight and two-thirds innings.

Still, Joe enjoyed his time in Washington. Everyone seemed to pull for him and he liked his teammates, a group that included Roy Sievers, Jim Lemon, Eddie Yost, Camilo Pascual, Pedro Ramos, and the ubiquitous Rocky Bridges, who had been picked up by the Senators in May. "Everybody roots for an ex-champ to come back," Bob Addie wrote in the *Washington Post*. And just by suiting up for the Senators, Joe might have made an impact in a city where segregation persisted into the 1950s, a city whose pro football team, the Redskins, did not have a black player until 1962. James L. Price Sr., who worked for the US Department of the Treasury, was among the Washingtonians who took notice when Joe signed. His son, Clement, said he did not recall his father ever showing much interest in the Senators until they had Joe.

"I remember my father was very proud that Joe Black was pitching for the Senators, and at the same time, my dad was troubled there was so much racial injustice in the society at large and in Washington in particular," Clement Price said. "Washington was a southern Jim Crow town. Joe Black's ascent to the Senators was probably metaphoric of changing race relations in the district. Unless my memory really fails me, my father took me and perhaps my brother to a Washington Senators game, hoping to see Joe Black."

Others also remembered Joe's short stint with the club, which amounted to a mere seven appearances and twelve and two-thirds innings. In 2010, eight years after Joe's death and fifty-three years after he pitched in the city, the Washington Nationals created the Joe Black Award to be given annually to a person or organization that promotes baseball in urban parts of the Washington, DC, metropolitan area.

>>>>>>>>>>

Joe pitched decently at times during a barnstorming tour through Latin America and on the West Coast after the 1957 season. But he faced no Major League hitters and his arm still bothered him. When the Senators sent him a contract for 1958, Joe returned it with a letter asking the club to put him on the voluntary retired list or give him his unconditional release. The Senators opted for the latter, and Joe's professional baseball career was over. In the end, half his career victories in the Major Leagues came in his first season. He finished with a 30-12 record, twenty-five saves, and a career earned run average of 3.91.

Joe Black had been a one-year flash as a Major Leaguer, something he himself knew as well as anyone. And he believed to the end that he was lucky to have been Jim Gilliam's friend, because in Joe's mind, that's why the Dodgers signed him. Of course he was frustrated he couldn't follow up on his big season. Who wouldn't be in that situation? He just wished the whole experiment of trying to teach him a new pitch had been handled differently—by himself and by the Dodgers. To begin with, he should have listened to Don Newcombe, Joe said.

"About midway through my first year, Newcombe says, 'Chico, you're having a helluva year,'" Joe recalled. "Then he said, 'Damn it, next year don't let them mess with you, because they're going to come to you and tell you they're going to make you a better player.' I didn't pay attention." Once the Dodgers saw what the experiment had done to him, Joe felt they should have been more forthcoming. "That's my biggest regret," he said. "Once they change you, admit it. Don't let you stay out there and catch all the heck like you were a one-year wonder and you just lost it suddenly. Say, 'Hey, we tried something and it didn't work.'"

But bitter? No way. Joe had dreamed of pitching in the big leagues, of striking out hitters in the World Series, and he had done it. He made valuable contacts and lifetime friends. Yes, he had to wait until he was twenty-eight years old, until Jackie and Larry Doby and Newcombe and Campy paved the way for blacks, before he got his chance. If baseball had integrated earlier and Joe had come up when he was younger, who knows what might have happened. Perhaps he would have starred for several years. But Joe also understood he got a chance that was denied to so many other black players of his era, players like Butch McCord, one of Joe's Negro league teammates with the Baltimore Elite Giants. McCord spent eleven years in the white minor leagues and batted .300 or better five times, yet never spent one day in the majors, finally calling it quits at the age of thirty-five. Another Negro league star, slick-fielding third baseman Ray Dandridge, batted .318 in four seasons with the Minneapolis Millers and was the American Association's MVP in 1950. He, too, never got the call to the big leagues.

"Some guys will say to me, hey man, you weren't that good," Joe said while reminiscing about his life in baseball. "And I said, right. I admit it. I was an average player. But you forget one thing. I had a friend. You don't ever see me say I got in the big leagues because I threw 10 no-hitters. I got there because Jim Gilliam needed a roommate, Newcombe went into the Korean War and bang, there's another guy from New Jersey. I got the shot and it paid off. That's it. If Gilliam didn't need a roommate, I'd be like the rest of you. I wouldn't have had the chance.

"Like they say, the world works in mysterious ways. I was there, the door was open. What you should be is grateful for those who went before and the memories you have."

And Joe was nothing if not grateful. "Just playing in the big leagues was more than I could have reasonably expected," he once said. Besides, he made his living for years playing a game. Who could ever grouse about that? Joe certainly didn't. As he told Roger Kahn, "If we want to get sad, we can think that I pitched my greatest games in miserable ballparks, in the colored league, with nobody watching. But I'm not a sad guy."

"Joe never looked back as far as being upset or bitter," Frank Robinson said. "He never expressed that to me, I never saw that in him. He was always upbeat and in the moment." For Joe, there was no reason to dwell on the past when he could make a difference in the future.

"He never seemed negative," Luis Gonzalez said. "He was always one of those guys who tried to make a positive out of every day of his life, to try to help somebody every day."

Joe also appreciated baseball for what the sport had done to advance racial tolerance. True, there were no black managers or executives in his time, and two teams—the Detroit Tigers and Boston Red Sox—had yet to integrate when he retired. But he thought the sport fostered better understanding between the races, and showed that blacks and whites could get along on the same field, even though some still clung to their prejudices. "Some of my best friends I made were from the South," Joe said. "Because they admitted that growing up, they were taught wrong. People said, 'Stay away from colored people because they're from monkeys, they're ignorant.' Some of them said, 'Hell, you guys have been to college. I didn't even finish high school.' So baseball did help change the attitudes of some."

Joe could feel good knowing he was part of that. In the bigger picture, twenty-win seasons and World Series rings aren't the only things that matter.

"Like every American, I believe passionately in equal rights," Joe said in a 1963 interview. "It distresses me to see anybody fighting. Whether by accident or design, it all worked out beautifully in baseball. I only wish it could work out the same way in other fields."

22

The Final Inning

On a pleasant Tuesday morning in 2001, Joe Black had important business in lower Manhattan, important because it involved Jackie Robinson. Whenever someone proposed a project to promote Jackie's legacy, the organizers knew they could count on Joe as an eager participant.

Plans were underway to erect a statue commemorating the friendship between Jackie and Pee Wee Reese, the white shortstop from Kentucky who defied the racist traditions of the South to try to make his teammate feel welcome. The proposed statue would capture the moment Pee Wee walked across the diamond and put his arm around Jackie's shoulder to assure him he had a friend amid the taunts and jeers from fans and opponents.

Joe was part of a group that was to look at five models of the statute, then pick the one to be cast in bronze and put up in Brooklyn. Joining him were Rachel Robinson, Jackie's widow; Pee Wee's widow, Dottie, and their son Mark; and Ralph Branca, the former Dodgers pitcher. But they never got a chance to make their choice. They stopped when they heard what sounded like an explosion or crash. And then their world turned upside down.

It was 8:45 AM on September 11. A hijacked jet had just slammed into the north tower of the World Trade Center.

>>>>>>>>>>

My father always wrote a note to me or called when he was about to travel, to tell me where he was going and to give me a phone number in case I needed to reach him. So I knew he was in New York that day. I worked at the law firm Winston & Strawn LLP in Chicago then and was driving to the office on Lake Shore Drive when I heard about the plane flying into the first tower. My initial reaction was to call a friend I had met when I first worked for the Chicago White Sox, because her parents and brother lived in New York City. When I got to the office, I called the hotel number my father had given me. Of course, I couldn't get through because all the lines were tied up. But in my heart, I felt very calm. My dad and I were so close that I could feel when something was going on with him, and I just had this feeling that he was OK.

The firm was closing for the day, because we were in the top floors of one of the city's taller buildings and no one knew if any more skyscrapers had been targeted. I tried calling the hotel again when I got home and couldn't get a connection. Still, I wasn't really worried, because I felt nothing bad had happened to my father. He finally reached me that evening, and while I was happy to hear from him, it just confirmed what I had felt all along. But he had endured a harrowing experience.

He said they heard a boom that sounded like a bus or a truck crashing into a building. After a second boom, they had time to look out a window before security guards hustled them to the basement. Then, once outside, my dad saw people jumping from one of the burning towers. Flames were shooting out as people were jumping. Even though he had been in the army during World War II and heard about the horrors of combat, what he saw that day disturbed him greatly. He was grief stricken and I don't think he ever fully recovered from that day.

My dad and Rachel and the rest were taken to the basement of the building so they'd be safe, and they were watching TV when the first tower collapsed. Eventually, the building security staff escorted them outside so they could return home or go back to their hotels. Smoke and dust choked the area, and one of the most prominent and recognizable structures in the New York skyline had been reduced to a massive pile of rubble. My dad said it was the worst thing he had ever seen.

He told me two police officers then helped him jog back to his hotel, one on each side of him, and they were urging him on: "Come on, we have to run, we have to run." They helped him run through that huge cloud of dust billowing over lower Manhattan. When he got to the hotel, all of his clothes were covered with soot, he had dust in his hair, and his back hurt. He believed he had tweaked his back running; it was a nagging pain that just wouldn't go away.

Anyone who had to travel in the hours and days after the September 11 attacks remembers how air traffic was disrupted; a week went by before my father was able to fly back home to Phoenix. His cancer probably was starting to develop in his body even then. He just didn't know it.

My mother also got sick, and she died of cervical cancer the following March. When I flew to Arizona for the memorial service and saw my dad, he looked really tired and thin—thin in Joe Black terms. Not 330 pounds, but maybe 295, and his back still bothered him. I told him he should go to the doctor. I told him about a friend's father who had prostate cancer, and it was because his back was bothering him that he went to the doctor. He got treated and was fine after that. My father just sort of waved it off. "Yeah, yeah," he said. "I just want my back to feel better so I can stay still during the MRI."

He also went through a period of depression. Seeing people jumping for their lives and dying was probably like war. He didn't sleep regularly. At 6 PM, my dad would be tired, so he would lie down and sleep for a while. When he woke up, he would want to stay up all night. He was not eating well and he started losing more weight. But he wouldn't go to the doctor. "I can't lie still," he'd say. He assumed it was all because of 9/11 and he was never the same after that.

Much later, I learned that my dad was told in November or December 2001 that his PSA was over nine, which is well above normal. I feel he knew he was going to die. He never told Chico or me because I believe he didn't want to alarm us.

>>>>>>>>>>

Joe was also urged by Chico to get checked by a doctor, and those pleadings, too, fell on deaf ears. Chico suggested that perhaps a biopsy would help the doctor determine what was wrong, but Joe steadfastly refused. Joe's mother had died not long after undergoing surgery and because of that, Joe insisted that no doctor would ever cut into him.

Chico tried to explain that doctors don't cut people as much as they used to. "They've got lasers," he said. "And he'd say, 'No, no, no, no.'" He was strong-willed. If he didn't want to do something, he didn't do it.

Friends felt similarly frustrated at Joe's refusal to ask a doctor to check him out.

"Joe was scared to death of doctors, scared to death of them," Len Coleman said. "Frank [Robinson] and I were pushing him to go get exams. Obviously, he didn't go until it was way too late. We couldn't get him to do anything with doctors."

One Sunday shortly after the terrorist attacks, Joe asked if he could talk about his experience at church. Within moments, he had the congregation listening in rapt silence. "He spoke for about ten minutes," the Reverend Mark Anderson said. "You could have heard a pin drop. That was pretty much right before he got sick." Anderson visited Joe several times after that, but did not recall seeing him in church again.

>>>>>>>>>>

Joe's health continued to deteriorate in the spring of 2002. He had started a second memoir, calling it "Beneficiary of Baseball Striking Out 'Jim Crow,'" but memories of the horror he had witnessed on September 11 and the persistent back pain sapped his desire to finish the project. He stopped writing while recounting spring training with the Brooklyn Dodgers in 1952.

His condition reached the point where something had to be done when Chico arrived at Joe's house one day in April and found his father sprawled on the floor. Joe said his back had given out and he couldn't get up. Struggling because Joe was still a big man even after losing weight, Chico got him into a chair, made him comfortable, and stayed with him for several hours, promising to return the next day.

>>>>>>>>>>

I called Dad the next morning and he said, "Oh yeah, Chico's going to bring me a shovel. It will help me get to the bathroom." I said OK but I was worried. Something was wrong. So I called him back thirty minutes later and he didn't answer. Then I called again ten minutes after that and still got no answer, so I called Chico at work and they paged him. I told him, "I just talked to Dad and he said to bring him a shovel." I said he needed to get over there because Dad wasn't answering his phone.

>>>>>>>>>>

When Chico got to the house, Joe was on the floor again and couldn't move. "I said, 'Dad, let me call . . .' 'No, no. Don't you call anybody,'" Chico recalled his father saying. "'Don't you call 9-1-1.'"

OK, Chico said. But he slipped into his father's office, called a neighbor, Tom Livermore, and asked him to call the fire department. When the paramedics arrived, Joe started to yell at Chico, but Chico quickly cut him off. "It was the first time I yelled back at him," Chico said. "I said, 'I don't give a damn what you said. Something's not right. We're going to find out what's wrong with you—now!'"

Tests at the hospital confirmed what everyone had suspected all along: Joe had prostate cancer. And it had reached an advanced stage. If that had not been clear before, it was now.

"He waited a long time before he went to the doctor. I think that was his undoing," Mark Anderson said. "Joe could do things on his own. That's who he was: strong and independent. I think most of us are like that—I work in a hospital [ministering to patients], and I hate doctors. He hated doctors, so he didn't go. For him to go when he did, it must have been pretty bad."

As word of the diagnosis spread, the friends who had been drawn to him over a lifetime because of his intelligence, warm personality, strong work ethic, and kindness jammed the phone lines calling to check up on him. Bill Cosby called almost every day. Joe Garagiola encouraged Chico to call if he needed any help at all. Cosby, Jerry Reinsdorf, and former Los Angeles Dodgers president Peter O'Malley offered to fly Joe anywhere doctors thought he might need to go for treatment. Fay Vincent, Frank Robinson, Hank Aaron, Sandy Koufax, Dusty Baker, Ken Griffey Sr., and Vin Scully all called to find out how he was doing. Joe's sister, Phyllis Greer, came from New Jersey for several days, returning home with a promise that she'd come back to see him in June. Martha Jo took a leave of absence from work and flew to Phoenix to stay with Joe and help care for him. He was back home then, so she bought baby monitors, placing one in his bedroom and one in hers so she could hear him if he called out during the night.

"I saw him when we came out to play the Diamondbacks [in early May]," said Robinson, who was managing the Montreal Expos then. "It was sad, that's the only way I can express it. He looked to me like he had lost a lot of weight, and I was hoping he could beat it. He was still upbeat.

He wasn't dwelling on the past. But I was used to Joe coming out to the ballpark, hearing him talk, seeing him with the players, and replaying the game with him after it was over. He couldn't do it that trip."

Joe agreed to chemotherapy, but he got so sick after his first treatment that Martha Jo had to call 911. He was hospitalized, then moved to a hospice, the same facility where Martha Jo's mother, Mae Nell, had spent her final days. Doctors put Joe on morphine to ease his worsening pain, and while the drug helped make him more comfortable, it scrambled his mind. He slurred his words and talked incoherently at times. John Teets, the former Greyhound and Viad CEO, wept when he saw what the disease had done to his once vibrant associate. Joe got angry at times for no apparent reason. He even snapped at Martha Jo, the daughter he had cared for so tenderly all her years growing up. He had never been like that with her. The drugs, Martha Jo felt, had changed his personality.

"Those were tough days for Joe," Teets said. "I spent a lot of time with him then. He wasn't feeling sorry for himself. He'd say, 'They'll never get me. I'm too big.'"

When Bill Cosby called one day, he asked Joe if he needed anything and the old baseball player in Joe answered.

"I need you on the hot corner," Joe said, referring to third base.

"What's going on?" Cosby asked.

"The bases are drunk and I got two balls and no strikes on him," Joe replied. "I need you on the hot corner."

Joe might not have made sense, but he still understood he had a friend on the line and could ask for his help in a tight situation.

>>>>>>>>>>

Bill Cosby has watched over me ever since I was an adolescent. He was there for me—and for my dad—when my dad got sick. I remember calling Cosby during my lunch break from work to tell him about my father being diagnosed with prostate cancer and becoming very weak. Cosby said to me, "I don't want to upset you, but I think your mother's calling your father from heaven." I said, "That is hard to believe, because they did not like each other very much on earth." Then Cosby said, "Your mother gave your dad the best gift of his life, and that was you."

Cosby called my dad at home as well as at the care center and joked around with him. He tried to make my dad laugh, because he said you should never be miserable even if you are sick and dying. You should always laugh, because life's too short, and at this point, it's even shorter. So you should always have a smile on your face. My dad sometimes would say things that didn't make sense, but Cosby would just keep talking and get him laughing again. Bill Cosby was really, sincerely there for my dad.

After my dad died, Cosby honored him at a Jackie Robinson Foundation dinner in New York the next year, and he was kind enough to invite me to the event. I mentioned to him that I would buy my plane ticket from Chicago to New York the next day. He told me that would not be necessary, because he had a private dinner event in Chicago and I could fly to the event with him. I took a cab from my house to the airport and got on his private jet, The Camille, *which he named for his wife. Her picture hangs in the entryway. Cosby also told me he would take care of my return flight as well as my hotel accommodations in New York City. Bill Cosby was a true friend to my father. He spoils me—just as my dad used to do.*

>>>>>>>>>>

Joe seemed resigned that he'd someday have to deal with cancer, because the disease had claimed so many of his family members. "My mom, dad, sister, aunt and uncle all had cancer," he said in one of his final interviews. "In the back of my mind, I think I always knew it would come to this. Yet, I just didn't believe it would happen to me. They always talked about exploratory surgery, but once they cut you up, it's never the same. It's why I fought them cutting me for so long."

Joe's friends continued to call and visit him at the hospice. He had so many visitors—sometimes fifteen to twenty at a time—that he had to move out to the facility's lounge so there would be room for everyone. "He was holding court again," Mark Anderson said. "He was good at that." Sharon Robinson, Jackie's daughter, visited one day. Martha Jo snuck her into Joe's room, because she had not told him in advance that she was coming.

"To see Joe lying there, it was very sobering—this full-of-life guy who still tried to maintain his dignity and carry on," Jerry Colangelo said. "But some things you can't stop."

Rich Dozer, the Arizona Diamondbacks president, gave Joe one of the club's World Series rings, inscribed with his name. It was rare for

Dozer to make a special delivery like that, but he felt Joe deserved it. "We had three levels of rings, and he got the best level," Dozer said. "Anybody with us since before we started playing baseball got that ring. If you look at it, there are four diamonds on the top of the ring. Those four signify that it took us four seasons [to win the series]. The script on the side of the ring says 'Fastest ever.' No one had ever won it in four years after joining the league."

Even as Joe tried to put up a brave face for his friends, the prognosis was grim. Chico remembered the doctor telling him that he didn't know if it was going to happen in a week, six weeks, or six months, but Joe was going to die because the cancer had metastasized. It already had been decided that no extraordinary measures would be taken to keep him alive. The man who didn't want to be cut wasn't going to be hooked up to any machines, either.

"He always said, 'I'm not afraid to meet my maker, but I don't know if my maker's ready for me,'" Jerry Reinsdorf said.

The date was May 17, 2002, slightly more than three months after Joe's seventy-eighth birthday. A boisterous man with a booming voice in life, he died quietly, with his children at his side.

>>>>>>>>>>

The day my father died, the doctor had come in to talk to him. My dad was in bed, so the doctor asked the nurse to put him in a wheelchair. My brother sat on the window ledge, I sat on the bed. The doctor pulled up a chair, sat down and said, "Joe, you know what? We're going to get you these chemo treatments and you'll be fine. You're not going to be 100 percent better, but you can go visit your daughter in Chicago. You'll be OK."

About ten minutes after the doctor spoke, my dad got antsy. "Dad, are you all right?" I asked. He didn't say anything. He was just listening. But he was nervous and moving around, so the doctor asked the nurse to give him a sedative. Then the doctor left and they pulled my dad up a little bit, closer to me. I looked at him and his eyes were getting droopy and closing. And all I heard in my mind then was the song he said was our song, "The First Time Ever I Saw Your Face." That was the song he said was playing in the hospital the first time he saw me after I was born. And I was hearing it in my head. There was no reason.

It wasn't playing in the facility. It just seemed to start up in my head. I guess I should have known then what was about to happen.

I wish I could explain the connection I had with my father, but it was something you just can't put into words. I'm sure you have heard or read stories of women who knew when their children were hurt or in trouble, and they knew they had to find them and help them. It's the same unconditional love a child has with a parent who has been there for her 100 percent, which is how my father was for me. I had known in my heart and soul that my father was OK in New York on 9/11. But my heart sank when Chico told me he found our dad on the floor and he could not get up.

Chico came back to my dad's room after calling Aunt Phyll, and I told him I thought the sedative was working. The nurses moved my father onto the bed and he was still asleep. We weren't going to give him anything or hook him up to any machines to keep him alive, so there was nothing more we could do. And five minutes later, my dad died.

>>>>>>>>>>

"It just seemed like he didn't want to be a burden," Chico said. "When the doctor talked to him, he said, 'Your kids are doing everything. They're going to get this, get that, they're getting everything set for you.' He was wide awake, and then it was like he was slowly shutting down because he didn't want us to have to do anything else for him.

Friends who had known Joe was sick, who had seen him in his weakened state at the care center, still were stunned to hear that he had died. Joe was such a large man, such a powerful figure, someone who had overcome poverty and prejudice to succeed at whatever he tried, and now he was gone? It didn't seem real. When Mark Anderson visited, Joe had always seemed so positive, never showing for even a moment any doubts about beating his latest foe.

"So it was a bit of a shock when I got the voicemail from Chico," Anderson said. "I was at the church in the sanctuary. It was empty. I checked this call and it said, 'This is Chico. I have to tell you that Dad passed away today.' I think I dropped to one knee. I was absolutely crushed when I heard that and just devastated that I wasn't going to see him again. I didn't realize he was that far along. He never mentioned anything."

Joe's death struck a chord in the baseball world, which saluted a man who used every opportunity he could to promote the game he loved.

"He was one of the best, most fair and strongest men that I knew," said Dusty Baker, who was managing the San Francisco Giants at the time. "Whenever you had a problem, he knew to call you. I may not have talked to him for three months and [when] I needed to talk to someone . . . there he was. It was like an instinct with Joe. He always had the right answers."

"Not only did I lose a friend," Frank Robinson said, "baseball lost a great ambassador, someone who showed the niceness of the game. And the players now miss that knowledge that he passed on to them, that friendly hand reaching out to young players."

Veteran Dodgers broadcaster Vin Scully saw in Joe's legacy "the thought that unheralded players can rise to the heights, that someone who at the time was considered an ordinary athlete could wind up pitching game one of the World Series."

"He made you feel like you've been friends forever," said Roland Hemond, the former Major League executive who became a special assistant to Jerry Colangelo with the Arizona Diamondbacks. "Some people are distant until you prove yourself. Joe made you feel that you were his friend."

Added Jerry Reinsdorf, "He never took. He just gave."

Even former opponents regarded Joe warmly. "I always had a nice feeling about him being the right kind of guy," Dodger-killer Bobby Thomson said. "Except when he was striking me out."

>>>>>>>>>>

The day my father passed away at the care center was the most heartbreaking day I have ever endured. The day seemed unreal and unfair at the time. How could God allow that to happen when my mother had just passed away in March? But I had no time to dwell on what did not seem to be God-like.

I know my dad did not want to be in a wheelchair for the rest of his life. When you're an athlete, you have an ego, because you have to be good. I think my father did not want to be someone who could not take care of himself.

Chico and I went back to our dad's house so I could start working on all the things my father had lectured me about doing after his death. While I was gath-

ering some of my dad's papers, the doorbell rang. Chico answered the door and the last woman my father divorced walked in. She gave Chico her condolences and walked into the kitchen, where I was putting some papers in order.

She looked at me, rolled her eyes, and started belittling me and spewing derogatory comments. Because I had so much anger built up from losing my father a few hours earlier that day, her visit was not welcome. I said to her, "I am not the same person that I was in high school when you met me and I am not intimidated by you."

Then she came after me. She started walking around to my side of the counter and Chico had to block the passageway to keep her from reaching me. He then escorted her to the door. I went back to sorting through my father's affairs, because I knew that's what he had expected me to do.

If I feel sorry for my dad at all, it's because he never married his true love. He said he did have one, but he never married her. I don't know who she was.

>>>>>>>>>>

Mark Anderson's church would not have held even a fourth of the crowd expected for Joe's memorial service, so the service was moved to the Historic First Presbyterian Church in downtown Phoenix. As the pastor looked over the faces staring up at him from the pews, it brought into even sharper focus Joe's impact on those who knew him. And it brought back the feeling that swept over him when Joe's family asked him to lead the service.

He was terrified. Because what could he say about a man "that has not already been said by him in the way he lived his life?"

Yet Anderson summoned the right words and spoke eloquently of his friend.

"Simply by the way he lived, he showed all of us what we can be, and what we can accomplish, that we can fulfill God's will for our lives," he told the gathering. "He could have taken the obstacles, the prejudice, and the racism that were heaped upon him and just given up and spent his life hating. But instead, he turned stumbling blocks into stepping stones, prejudice into opportunity, and hatred into love, helping others as he passed along. In short, Joe lived the Gospel." Then he repeated what someone once told him about Joe: "If we could get one trait from him, we'd all be better people."

Jerry Reinsdorf spoke at another service for Joe a week later, this one in Plainfield, his hometown. Hundreds attended, including Bill Cosby, Sandy Koufax, and former Dodger Don Zimmer.

"Joe's been in heaven for two weeks now, which is long enough for the Lord to figure out there's a new man in charge," Reinsdorf said. "I don't know if there's a heaven, but I guarantee you, if there's a heaven, Joe's in charge."

Joe's body was cremated, and he had asked that his ashes be spread over the baseball field in Plainfield where he learned to play the game, on the ground where Ebbets Field once stood in Brooklyn, and on other locations in New Jersey that were significant in his life. City officials nixed the idea of spreading ashes on the baseball diamond, but Chico sprinkled some there anyway. Some of the ashes were buried next to Joe's mother and father. His sister, Phyllis, sent what was left to Martha Jo.

"A lot of ballplayers come and go," Tom Villante said, "but Joe really made the most of what he achieved."

>>>>>>>>>>

In his later years, Joe often attended games in the Arizona Fall League, which was formed in 1992 to give Major League teams easily accessible off-season competition in the Phoenix area for their prospects. And just as he had done at big-league games, Joe enjoyed talking to the players, offering advice, and hearing of their hopes and dreams. He remembered being a young player once with those same dreams.

"He could see many of these players were going to make it," said Steve Cobb, the league's director. "He wanted them to know what a privilege that is when it happens."

Several weeks after Joe's death, Jimmie Lee Solomon, then the director of minor leagues for Major League Baseball, suggested the Fall League name its most valuable player trophy for Joe. Cobb readily agreed, seeing the trophy as a way to keep Joe's legacy alive in the area. That November, Kansas City Royals prospect Ken Harvey received the first Joe Black Most Valuable Player Trophy after batting a league record .479. Joe Garagiola and Jerry Reinsdorf attended the ceremony, held before the league's championship game.

The Diamondbacks also saw to it that Joe was remembered. They put up a sign at the parking spot he had always used in the employees' garage. They left the nameplate at his seat in the press box and named a room at the ballpark in his honor. A large cutout of a baseball printed with Joe's name hangs from the Chase Field rafters.

"Here's a guy that faced the worst that society could throw at him—racism and exclusion, everything that turns your stomach—and yet he was the sweetest, kindest man you could ever meet," Diamondbacks executive Jeff Munn said. "I can't really grasp what he must have gone through. He wasn't just tolerant of everybody. He embraced everybody."

Joe had been inducted into the Sports Hall of Fame of New Jersey in 2001, joining a group that included Don Newcombe, Larry Doby, Monte Irvin, Len Coleman, Leon Day, Yogi Berra, Phil Rizzuto, and Bobby Thomson. That came six years after his induction into the Brooklyn Dodgers Hall of Fame. Even before Joe's death, Phyllis and other family members thought it was Plainfield's turn to step up and honor its native son, and they redoubled those efforts after he died. They urged the city council and school board to name a baseball field after Joe, preferably the diamond at the Hub Stine Sports Complex, where Joe played during his high school days. It turned into a years-long effort.

The city council in 2004 passed a resolution naming a different field in Joe's honor, but a permanent sign was never put up. The family kept pressing and finally, in 2010, the Plainfield School Board voted unanimously to name the high school baseball complex at Hub Stine the Joe Black Baseball Field.

"This was a labor of love for us," said Bridgette Greer, the niece to whom Joe had written that letter of encouragement after she failed the bar exam on her first try. "We are so proud." Thus, the field where Joe was told he would never play Major League baseball because he was the wrong color now carries his name.

Jim Crow proved to be no match for Joe Black.

"I can just picture him sitting there on his throne in the dugout before our games," former Diamondbacks president Rich Dozer said. "And then on opening day in 1998, one of the things we did was retire Jackie Robinson's number. We had a big round circle with his number on it, and we had his buddy, Joe Black, help unveil it on opening day. I just remember how proud he was that day."

Long after Joe's death, Frank Robinson said his wife Barbara and daughter Nichelle occasionally would mention, completely out of the blue, "We sure miss Number One."

"That's the way we referred to Joe in our group with Len Coleman," Robinson said. "I don't think we ever had a two or a three. We only had Number One, and that was Joe."

>>>>>>>>>>

Because my parents no longer were married, my father had to go above and beyond what he would have had to do if they had been together. I think that's rare for any man to do. I think my father got that from his mother, because of her going to my dad's school and throwing the principal up against the wall because they wanted to put my dad in shop classes.

It wasn't cool in the early '70s to be a black man in Arizona and raise a daughter by yourself. And he was fifty-one years old at that point. You just don't think about doing something like that at that age, but he did. I hope my father can be an example to all people, to inspire them to say, if he could do it, so can I.

I'll always remember this quote, because it applies so perfectly to what I had growing up: "Anyone can be a father, but it takes a real man to be a dad."

BIBLIOGRAPHY

Books

Aaron, Hank, with Lonnie Wheeler. *I Had a Hammer: The Hank Aaron Story.* New York: HarperCollins, 1991.

Allen, Maury. *Jackie Robinson: A Life Remembered.* New York: Franklin Watts, 1987.

Arsenault, Raymond. *Freedom Riders: 1961 and the Struggle for Racial Justice.* New York: Oxford University Press, 2006.

Auker, Elden, with Tom Keegan. *Sleeper Cars and Flannel Uniforms: A Lifetime of Memories from Striking Out the Babe to Teeing It Up with the President.* Chicago: Triumph Books, 2001.

Baker, Kevin. "The Dirty, Underhanded, Compromised, Corrupt, and Perhaps Tertiary Shot Heard 'Round the World." In *It Ain't Over 'Til It's Over: The Baseball Prospectus Pennant Race Book*, edited by Steven Goldman. New York: Basic Books, 2007.

Bjarkman, Peter C. *A History of Cuban Baseball: 1864–2006.* Jefferson, NC: McFarland and Co., 2007.

Black, Joe. *Ain't Nobody Better Than You: An Autobiography of Joe Black.* Self-published, 1983.

———. "Memoirs of Joe Black: Beneficiary of Baseball Striking Out 'Jim Crow.'" Unfinished manuscript, 2001.

Branca, Ralph, with David Ritz. *A Moment in Time: An American Story of Baseball, Heartbreak and Grace.* New York: Scribner, 2011.

Brashler, William. *Josh Gibson: A Life in the Negro Leagues*. Chicago: Ivan R. Dee, 2000.

Buckley, James, Jr. *Classic Ballparks*. New York: Barnes & Noble Books, 2004.

Campanella, Roy. *It's Good to Be Alive*. Lincoln: University of Nebraska Press, 1995; orig. publ. Boston: Little, Brown & Company, 1959.

Craft, David. *The Negro Leagues: 40 Years of Black Professional Baseball in Words and Pictures*. New York: Crescent Books, 1993.

D'Antonio, Michael. *Forever Blue: The True Story of Walter O'Malley, Baseball's Most Controversial Owner, and the Dodgers of Brooklyn and Los Angeles*. New York: Penguin, 2009.

Eig, Jonathan. *Opening Day: The Story of Jackie Robinson's First Season*. New York: Simon & Schuster, 2007.

Erskine, Carl. *Tales from the Dodger Dugout*. Champaign, IL: Sports Publishing, 2000.

Falkner, David. *Great Time Coming: The Life of Jackie Robinson from Baseball to Birmingham*. New York: Simon & Schuster, 1995.

Gaines, Clarence E., with Clint Johnson. *They Call Me Big House*. Winston-Salem, NC: John F. Blair, 2004.

Goldstein, Richard. *Spartan Seasons: How Baseball Survived the Second World War*. New York: Macmillan, 1980.

Golenbock, Peter. *Bums: An Oral History of the Brooklyn Dodgers*. New York: Pocket Books, 1984.

Hauser, Christopher. *The Negro Leagues Chronology: Events in Organized Black Baseball, 1920–1948*. Jefferson, NC: McFarland & Co., 2006.

Hogan, Lawrence D. *Shades of Glory: The Negro Leagues and the Story of African-American Baseball*. Washington, DC: National Geographic Society, 2006.

Holway, John B. *Black Diamonds: Life in the Negro Leagues from the Men Who Lived It*. Westport, CT: Meckler Books, 1989.

———. *Voices from the Great Black Baseball Leagues*. New York: Dodd, Mead, 1975.

Honig, Donald. *The Fifth Season: Tales of My Life in Baseball*. Chicago: Ivan R. Dee, 2009.

Irvin, Monte, with James A. Riley. *Nice Guys Finish First: The Autobiography of Monte Irvin*. New York: Carroll & Graf, 1996.

Jacobson, Steve. *Carrying Jackie's Torch: The Players Who Integrated Baseball—and America*. Chicago: Lawrence Hill Books, 2007.

Kahn, Roger. *The Boys of Summer*. New York: Harper & Row, 1972.

———. *The Era: 1947–57, When the Yankees, the Giants, and the Dodgers Ruled the World*. New York: Ticknor & Fields, 1993.

———. *Memories of Summer: When Baseball Was an Art and Writing About It a Game*. New York: Hyperion, 1997.

Kelley, Brent. *Voices from the Negro Leagues: Conversations with 52 Baseball Standouts of the Period, 1924–1960*. Jefferson, NC: McFarland & Co., 2005.

King, Larry, with Marty Appel. *When You're from Brooklyn, Everything Else Is Tokyo*. New York: Little, Brown, 1992.

Klarman, Michael J. *From Jim Crow to Civil Rights: The Supreme Court and the Struggle for Racial Equality*. New York: Oxford University Press, 2004.

Kuenster, John. *Heartbreakers: Baseball's Most Agonizing Defeats*. Chicago: Ivan R. Dee, 2001.

Lanctot, Neil. *Negro League Baseball: The Rise and Ruin of a Black Institution*. Philadelphia: University of Pennsylvania Press, 2004.

Leavy, Jane. *Sandy Koufax: A Lefty's Legacy*. New York: HarperCollins, 2009.

Lee, Ulysses. *U.S. Army in World War II Special Studies: The Employment of Negro Troops*. Fort McNair, DC: US Army Center of Military History, 1966.

Lester, Larry. *Black Baseball's National Showcase: The East-West All-Star Game, 1933–1953*. Lincoln: University of Nebraska Press, 2001.

Letarte, Richard H. *That One Glorious Season: Baseball Players with One Spectacular Year, 1950–1961*. Portsmouth, NH: Peter E. Randall, 2006.

Liebman, Glenn. *Grand Slams: The Ultimate Collection of Baseball's Best Quips, Quotes and Cutting Remarks*. Lincolnwood, IL: Contemporary Books, 2001.

Loverro, Thom. *The Encyclopedia of Negro League Baseball*. New York: Checkmark Books, 2003.

Luke, Bob. *The Baltimore Elite Giants: Sport and Society in the Age of Negro League Baseball*. Baltimore: Johns Hopkins University Press, 2009.

Mantle, Mickey, with Mickey Herskowitz. *All My Octobers: My Memories of 12 World Series When the Yankees Ruled Baseball*. New York: HarperCollins, 1994.

Maraniss, David. *Clemente: The Passion and Grace of Baseball's Last Hero*. New York: Simon & Schuster, 2006.

McGee, Bob. *The Greatest Ballpark Ever: Ebbets Field and the Story of the Brooklyn Dodgers*. New Brunswick, NJ: Rutgers University Press, 2006.

McGuire, Phillip. *Taps for a Jim Crow Army: Letters from Black Soldiers in World War II*. Santa Barbara, CA: ABC-Clio, 1983.

Moffi, Larry, and Jonathan Kronstadt. *Crossing the Line: Black Major Leaguers, 1947–1959*. Jefferson, NC: McFarland, 1994.

Motley, Bob, with Byron Motley. *Ruling over Monarchs, Giants & Stars: Umpiring in the Negro Leagues & Beyond*. Champaign, IL: Sports Publishing, 2007.

Neft, David S., Roland T. Johnson, Richard M. Cohen, and Jordan A. Deutsch. *The Sports Encyclopedia: BASEBALL*. New York: Grosset & Dunlap, 1974.

Paige, Leroy (Satchel), as told to David Lipman. *Maybe I'll Pitch Forever*. Lincoln: University of Nebraska Press, 1993; orig. publ. Garden City, NY: Doubleday, 1962.

Paper, Lew. *Perfect: Don Larsen's Miraculous World Series Game and the Men Who Made It Happen*. New York: New American Library, 2009.

Peterson, Robert. *Only the Ball Was White: A History of Legendary Black Players and All-Black Professional Teams*. New York: Oxford University Press, 1992; orig. publ. Old Tappan, NJ: Prentice-Hall, 1970.

Poitier, Sidney. *This Life*. New York: Ballantine Books, 1980.

Rampersad, Arnold. *Jackie Robinson: A Biography*. New York: Alfred A. Knopf, 1997.

Ribowsky, Mark. *Josh Gibson: The Power and the Darkness*. Champaign: University of Illinois Press, 2004.

Riley, James A. *The Biographical Encyclopedia of the Negro Baseball Leagues*. New York: Carroll & Graf, 1994.

Rizzuto, Phil, with Tom Horton. *The October Twelve: Five Years of New York Yankee Glory, 1949–1953*. New York: Tom Doherty Associates, 1994.

Robinson, Frank, with Al Silverman. *My Life Is Baseball*. Garden City, NY: Doubleday, 1968.

Robinson, Jackie, as told to Alfred Duckett. *I Never Had It Made: An Autobiography of Jackie Robinson*. New York: Putnam, 1972.

Rogosin, Donn. *Invisible Men: Life in Baseball's Negro Leagues*. New York: Atheneum, 1987.

Schisgall, Oscar. *The Greyhound Story: From Hibbing to Everywhere*. Chicago: J. G. Ferguson, 1985.

Selzer, Steven Michael. *Meet the Real Joe Black: An Inspiring Life: Baseball, Teaching, Business, Giving*. New York: IUniverse, 2010.

Shapiro, Michael. *The Last Good Season: Brooklyn, the Dodgers and Their Final Pennant Race Together*. New York: Doubleday, 2003.

Simon, Scott. *Jackie Robinson and the Integration of Baseball*. Hoboken, NJ: J. Wiley & Sons, 2002.

Smith, Ron. *The Ballpark Book: A Journey Through the Fields of Baseball Magic*. St. Louis: Sporting News, 2000.

Snider, Duke, with Bill Gilbert. *The Duke of Flatbush*. New York: Kensington, 1988.

Tygiel, Jules. *Baseball's Great Experiment: Jackie Robinson and His Legacy.* New York: Random House, 1984.

Zumsteg, Derek. *The Cheater's Guide to Baseball.* New York: Houghton Mifflin, 2007.

Newspapers & Wire Services

Arizona Republic
Associated Press
Baltimore Afro-American
Baltimore Sun
Christian Science Monitor
Des Moines Register
Grit
Hayward (California) Daily Review
International News Service
Los Angeles Times
Lowell (Massachusetts) Sun
Neosho (Missouri) Daily News
New Albany (Indiana) Tribune & Jeffersonville Evening News
New York Daily News
New York Herald Tribune
New York Times
Newark Star-Ledger
Oakland Tribune
Redlands (California) Daily Facts
Sporting News
Syracuse Post-Standard
United Press International
Wall Street Journal
Washington Post
Washington Times

Magazines and Other Periodicals

Baseball Digest. Filler item regarding Joe Black's appearance on "Name That Tune." October 1992.

Breslin, Jimmy. "The Dodgers' New Daffiness Boy." *Saturday Evening Post,* August 22, 1953.

Brioso, Cesar. "Baseball in Cuba." *Cigar City Magazine* 18 (September/October 2008).

Creamer, Robert. "With Mirrors, Flat Gloves and Sawed-Up Bats." *Sports Illustrated*, June 3, 1963.

Dressen, Charlie, as told to Stanley Frank. "The Dodgers Won't Blow It Again!" *Saturday Evening Post*, September 13, 1952.

Frank, Stanley. "Can He Do It Again for the Dodgers?" *Saturday Evening Post*, April 4, 1953.

———. "Nobody Loves Baseball More Than Campy." *Saturday Evening Post*, June 5, 1954.

Henry, Patrick. "Jackie Robinson: Athlete and American Par Excellence." *Virginia Quarterly Review* 73 (1997).

Hernon, Jack. Column on Joe Black's struggles in the 1953 season. *Baseball Digest*, October 1953; orig. publ. *Pittsburgh Post-Gazette*.

Hoffman, John C. "Sour Grapes." *Baseball Digest*, February 1953.

Jet. "Fort Worth Holds Night for Dave Hoskins." September 11, 1952.

———. "Joe Black Says Dressen 'Ruined' His Pitching." January 28, 1954.

Lastner, Edward C. "I Remember . . . Bugle Field and the Label Man." *(Baltimore) Sun Magazine*, March 29, 1953.

Lewis, Allen. Column catching up with Joe Black when he first started working for Greyhound. *Baseball Digest*, March 1964; orig. publ. *Philadelphia Inquirer*.

Littwin, Mike. Column in which Joe Black recounts his years in baseball and career slide. *Baseball Digest*, March 1982; orig. publ. *Los Angeles Times*.

Maglie, Sal, with Robert H. Boyle. "The Great Giant-Dodger Days." *Sports Illustrated*, April 22, 1968.

Mariner, Sarah. "The Talmadge L. Hill Field House," *Morgan Magazine* 1 (2007).

Meany, Tom. "Baseball in 3 Languages." *Collier's*, August 20, 1954.

———. "Tom Meany's 1953 Baseball Preview." *Collier's*, February 28, 1953.

Newsweek. "Cliff Hanger." October 13, 1952.

Olsen, Jack. "In the Back of the Bus." *Sports Illustrated*, July 22, 1968.

Posnanski, Joe. "Stan Musial." *Sports Illustrated*, August 2, 2010.

Reese, Pee Wee, with Tom Cohane. "Reese's Own Story: 14 Years a Bum!" *Look*, March 9, 1954.

Smith, Shelley. "Baseball's Forgotten Pioneers." *Sports Illustrated*, March 30, 1992.

Stump, Al. "He's Never Out of Trouble." *Saturday Evening Post*, August 18, 1956.

Time. "And Still Champions." October 12, 1953.

———. "Old Potato Face." September 11, 1964.

Turkin, Hy. "Those Daffy Dodgers." *Coronet*, August 1952.

Tygiel, Jules. "The Negro Leagues." *OAH Magazine of History*, Summer 1992.

Other Printed Sources

Black, Joe. Commentaries in *The Best of By the Way*.

———. Funeral service eulogy for Jesse Owens, April 4, 1980.

Memorial service for Joe Black. Conducted by the Reverend Mark Anderson, May 25, 2002.

Videos

Black, Joe. Interview for Fay Vincent Oral History Collection, Baseball Hall of Fame.

"Integration of Baseball, The." Forum at Kenyon College, April 25, 2001.

1952 World Series. Chicago Film Studios. DVD.

Internet Sources

Baseball Almanac. www.baseball-almanac.com.

Baseball-Reference.com. www.baseball-reference.com.

Brown, Milbert O., Jr. "Lunch with a Gentleman: Brother Joe Black." Q Report. http://qreport.weebly.com/profileblack.html.

Encyclopedia of Arkansas History & Culture. www.encyclopediaofarkansas.net.

Harding, Thomas. "Mendez Dominated as Pitcher, Manager." Major League Baseball official website, February 9, 2006. www.mlb.com/news/article.jsp?ymd=20060208&content_id=1308711.

Gilbert, Steve. "Black's Influence Lives On." Major League Baseball official website, February 22, 2005. www.mlb.com/news/article.jsp?ymd=20050222&content_id=947826.

———. "Harvey MVP of Arizona Fall League." Major League Baseball official website, November 23, 2002. www.mlb.com/news/article.jsp?ymd=20021123&content_id=180445&vkey=news_mlb&fext=.jsp.

Historic Baseball. www.historicbaseball.com.

Major League Baseball official website. www.mlb.com.

Morgan State University official website. www.morgan.edu.

myCentralJersey.com.

Negro Leagues Baseball Museum's eMuseum. www.coe.ksu.edu/nlbemuseum.

Retrosheet. www.retrosheet.org.

Interviews

Anderson, Mark. November 11, 2008.

Black, Joseph Frank. June 7, 2009.

Bridges, Rocky. October 14, 2008.

Cobb, Steve. October 20, 2009.

Colangelo, Jerry. October 15, 2009.

Coleman, Len. October 23, 2008.

Dozer, Rich. October 22, 2009.

Erskine, Carl. October 21, 2008.

Garagiola, Joe. October 10, 2008.

Gonzalez, Luis. October 7, 2009.

Greer, Phyllis. December 30, 2008.

Hemond, Roland. October 12, 2009.

Irvin, Monte. December 5, 2008.

Koufax, Sandy. October 22, 2008.

Lester, Larry. November 18, 2008.

McCormack, Peter. October 24, 2008.

Pafko, Andy. November 6, 2008.

Parrish, Doris. January 20, 2009.

Phoenix, Angela. October 15, 2008.

Price, Clement. January 11, 2010.

Reinsdorf, Jerry. October 16, 2008; May 4, 2012.

Rhodes, Dusty. October 27, 2008.

Robinson, Frank. December 17, 2008.

Skowron, Bill "Moose." October 19, 2008.

Teets, John. October 15, 2008.

Thomson, Bobby. October 17, 2008.

Vincent, Fay. November 5, 2008.

Wilcox, Casey. July 14, 2009.

INDEX